THE SHORT
PROSE READER

THE SHORT PROSE READER

FIFTH EDITION

Gilbert H. Muller
*The City University of New York,
LaGuardia*

Harvey S. Wiener
The City University of New York

McGRAW-HILL BOOK COMPANY
New York   St. Louis   San Francisco   Aukland   Bogotá   Caracas
Colorado Springs   Hamburg   Lisbon   London   Madrid   Mexico   Milan
Montreal   New Delhi   Oklahoma City   Panama   Paris   San Juan
São Paulo   Singapore   Sidney   Tokyo   Toronto

This book was set in Goudy Oldstyle by the
College Composition Unit in cooperation with Black Dot, Inc.
The editors were Susan D. Hurtt and David Dunham;
the production supervisor was Janelle S. Travers.
The cover was designed by Amy Becker.
R. R. Donnelly & Sons Company was printer and binder.
Cover painting: *Girl Reading* by Jean Auguste Renior (Three Lions).

See Acknowledgments on page 481.
Copyrights included on this page by reference.

THE SHORT PROSE READER

1 2 3 4 5 6 7 8 9 0   DOC DOC   8 9 3 2 1 0 9 8

ISBN   0-07-044023-9

Library of Congress Cataloging-in-Publication Data

The Short prose reader.

1. College readers. 2. English language–Rhetoric.
I. Muller, Gilbert H., (date).   II. Wiener,
Harvey S.
PE1417.S446 1989   808'.0427   88-8337
ISBN 0-07-044023-9

ABOUT THE AUTHORS

Gilbert H. Muller, who received a Ph.D. in English and American Literature from Stanford University, is currently professor of English at LaGuardia Community College of the City University of New York. He has also taught at Stanford, Vassar, and several universities overseas. Dr. Muller is the author of the award-winning study *Nightmares and Visions: Flannery O'Connor and the Catholic Grotesque* and other critical texts. His essays and reviews have appeared in *The New York Times, The New Republic, The Nation, The Sewanee Review,* the *Georgia Review,* and elsewhere. He is also a noted author and editor of textbooks in English and composition, including *The McGraw-Hill Reader* and, with John Williams, *The McGraw-Hill Introduction to Literature.* Among Dr. Muller's awards are a National Endowment for the Humanities Fellowship, a Fulbright Fellowship, and a Mellon Fellowship.

Harvey S. Wiener, University Associate Dean for Academic Affairs of the City University of New York, codirects the National Testing Network in Writing (NTNW). He was founding president of the Council of Writing Program Administrators. Dr. Wiener is the author of many books on reading and writing for college students and their teachers, including *The Writing Room* (Oxford, 1981). He is coauthor with Richard Marius of *The McGraw-Hill College Handbook,* a reference grammar and rhetoric text. Dr. Wiener is a member of the Standing

Committee on Assessment for the National Council of Teachers of English, and he is chair of the Teaching of Writing Division of the Modern Language Association (1987). He has taught writing at every level of education from elementary school to graduate school. A Phi Beta Kappa graduate of Brooklyn College, he holds a Ph.D. in Renaissance literature from Fordham University. Dr. Wiener has won grants from the National Endowment for the Humanities, the Fund for the Improvement of Postsecondary Education, and the Exxon Education Foundation.

CONTENTS

ALTERNATE THEMATIC CONTENTS   **xvii**
PREFACE   **xxiii**

CHAPTER 1

On Writing   1

William Saroyan   *Why I Write*   5
A Pulitzer Prize–winning author explains how his determination "to understand the meaning of his own life" led him to live "in a special way" since the age of 9.

Dan Greenburg   *How I Overhauled My Mechanic's Novel*   14
According to author Dan Greenburg, writers can be just as unscrupulous as car mechanics—if they set their minds to it.

William Zinsser   *Simplicity*   22
According to this writer-teacher, "clutter is the disease of American writing." We must simplify. In this essay, Zinsser connects clear writing to clear thinking, which, he declares, doesn't appear nearly enough these days.

Joan Didion   *On Keeping a Notebook*   34
"Our notebooks give us away," claims Joan Didion, who shares with us the intimacies of her own notebooks over the years.

CHAPTER 2

On Reading   50

Eudora Welty   *Moon on a Silver Spoon*   52
One of America's best fiction writers reveals a long-standing

love affair—with books! "Long before I wrote stories, I listened to stories," she tells us.

Malcolm X   **Prison Studies**   62
"Reading had changed the course of my life forever," writes Malcolm X, who explains movingly how reading is both an activity of love and a tool of power.

Margaret Atwood   **Survival**   72
Canadian author Margaret Atwood relates how, almost against the odds, she came to delight in reading the stories of her own country.

George Steiner   **The Future of Reading**   82
George Steiner worries that in America, where nearly a quarter of the population is illiterate or semi-literate, and where microchips and video images may soon become more recognizable than the printed page, "the renewed miracle that is the encounter with a book" may soon become ancient history.

CHAPTER 3

Description   94

Margaret Laurence   **The Shack**   94
A small cabin on the Otonabee River in southern Ontario, Canada, is the focal point for one writer's environmentally lush workplace where she's entirely "content to be alone."

Maxine Hong Kingston   **Catfish in the Bathtub**   104
Do ducks' tongues, monkeys' brains, or camels' humps sound like good food to you? This essay might make you prefer to "live on plastic."

William Least Heat Moon   **Arizona 87**   111
Drive with this writer through the Arizona desert and into its mountains. The landscape is sometimes "reminiscent of old Chinese woodblock prints," but the towns have "no center, no focus for the eye and soul."

Richard Selzer   **The Discus Thrower**   119
A surgeon and an author offers a chilling, yet moving and dignified, description of a patient's last day.

CHAPTER 4

Narration   127

Elizabeth Wong   *The Struggle to Be an All-American Girl*   129
In a narrative of her youth, a writer remembers her efforts to obtain "a cultural divorce" from the heritage into which she was born.

Langston Hughes   *Salvation*   137
One of America's foremost poets tells of his childhood disillusionment as he struggles desperately to see Jesus.

Roger Wilkins   *I Became Her Target*   144
"Dead-Eye" Bean was the first teacher to make this present-day scholar aware that thinking was educational and that his opinions were valuable.

George Orwell   *A Hanging*   152
The renowned author of 1984 discovers how precious human life is as he tells of witnessing an execution in Burma. "It is curious," he recalls, "but 'til that moment, I had never realized what it meant to destroy a healthy, conscious man."

CHAPTER 5

Illustration   164

Randall Williams   *Daddy Tucked the Blanket*   166
A contemporary journalist shows what it means to be poor and how the environment of poverty can destroy families.

Ray Bradbury   *Tricks! Treats! Gangway!*   175
Here from the noted science fiction writer is the wonder of Halloween, 1928, with all its gorilla fangs, pumpkin pies, creaking stairs, black confetti, banshee trains, and much more.

Louis L'Amour   *How Wild Was the Old West?*   186
America's best-known writer of western fiction illustrates that the Old West was truly a wild place—at least more wild than the modern west.

Lewis Thomas *Death in the Open* 194
This biologist and popular writer says that death "is a natural marvel" throughout the universe of animals and plants; and that humans, sharing a kinship with other life forms, will have to stop seeing death as a catastrophe.

CHAPTER **6**

Comparison and Contrast 204

Rachel Carson *A Fable for Tomorrow* 206
One of America's most celebrated naturalists warns us of the future in a grim contrast between a flourishing environment and a destroyed landscape plagued by a mysterious curse.

Russell Baker *The Two Ismo's* 213
The ammunition in this columnist's "urban war zone" includes quiche, kiwi fruit, zippered plastic briefcases, and gourmet Swedish toothpaste as he explores two social doctrines: machismo *and* quichismo.

Ellen Goodman *The Tapestry of Friendships* 221
This piece, in which columnist Ellen Goodman talks about the difference between "buddies" and "friends," may heat up the battle between the sexes, but it certainly raises some important questions about the ways in which people relate to one another.

Bruno Bettelheim *Fairy Tales and Modern Stories* 230
One of the world's foremost child psychologists explains that traditional fairy tales give solace to children, but that modern tales "fail to provide the escape and consolation that children need."

CHAPTER **7**

Definition 238
Suzanne Britt Jordan *Fun, Oh Boy. Fun. You Could Die from It.* 240
If you've ever felt that you should have been having fun but

that somehow you weren't, this essay proves that you're not alone.

Gregg Easterbrook   *Escape Valve*   248
One of the results of modern living, according to this writer, is the "automatic-out," a means for avoiding long-term commitments. Here, he explains this trend toward escaping responsibilities, a trend that produces serious results in the way we develop relationships.

Elizabeth Janeway   **Soaps, Cynicism, and Mind Control**   256
Randomness as a way of life may work out just fine on television, but real life isn't the same as TV. Are we, a nation of video addicts, in danger of mind control by the Media Establishment?

Rita Mae Brown   **To the Victor Belongs the Language**   266
Revolution! Rebellion! Strong words, which form the basis for an essay that proves that "whoever wins the war redefines the language."

CHAPTER 8

Classification   275

Judith Viorst   *Friends, Good Friends—and Such Good Friends*   277
This popular writer believes that friendships "are conducted at many levels of intensity" and "meet different needs." Here she categorizes eight types of friends, including Convenience friends, Historical friends, and Crossroads friends.

E. B. White   **The Three New Yorks**   286
Natives, commuters, and those who come searching: These are the inhabitants of E. B. White's three cities in one in this fascinating look at the world's most talked about city.

James T. Baker   **How Do We Find the Student in a World of Academic Gymnasts and Worker Ants?**   294
This gently cynical essay introduces twelve types of students everyone knows and loves—including among others, the Performer, the Jock, the Lost Soul, the Worker Ant, and finally, the Student.

Aaron Copland   *What to Listen For in Music*   303
One of America's foremost composers appeals to the average
music listener to become more active—*not just to listen, but*
to listen "for something."

CHAPTER 9

Process Analysis   316

Sam Negri   *Loafing Made Easy*   318
Here are all the do's and don'ts of "America's most treasured
art form": the art of simply doing nothing.

Bruce Jay Friedman   *Eating Alone in Restaurants*   325
The author explains to us how to perform one of the most
dreaded activities on earth—and live through it.

Grace Lichtenstein   *Coors Beer*   335
Investigating the most famous beer in the West, this reporter
unlocks the secret to "the Coors mystique."

Ernest Hemingway   *Camping Out*   342
Avoiding insects. Getting a good rest. Cooking trout just
right. This essay can make anyone's next camping trip a suc-
cess.

CHAPTER 10

Cause-and-Effect Analysis   350

Anne Roiphe   *Why Marriages Fail*   353
In the United States, new marriages have a 50 percent chance
of succeeding—or failing, depending on your outlook. A con-
temporary novelist explains in this essay why "happily ever
after" may become an extinct phrase.

Arthur Miller   *Rite of Spring*   364
This famous playwright claims that a small garden plot with
rows of hot dogs and pastrami vines sounds good to him. Yet,

yearly he goes through the "back-breaking make-believe" of planting a vegetable garden. Why? "I garden," he writes, "because I must."

Linda Bird Francke   **The Ambivalence of Abortion**   372
Political convictions and personal experience make an unforgettable mix in this haunting essay about abortion.

Susan Jacoby   **When Bright Girls Decide That Math Is "A Waste of Time"**   383
A one-time straight-A algebra student explains why math and science are a no-woman's-land for promising young scholars.

CHAPTER 11

Argumentation and Persuasion   393

Stephen Leacock   **Softening the Stories for Children**   396
When the author tells an 8-year-old girl the real ending of "Little Red Riding Hood," she responds, "Oh, isn't that splendid!" Can kids really live with the horror and violence that adults often find in children's stories?

Joseph Wood Krutch   **The Vandal and the Sportsman**   407
Sports hunters are evil and their joy lies in the destruction of God's creatures. So argues a lifelong naturalist in this emotionally charged essay.

Judy Syfers   **I Want a Wife**   415
Author, wife, and mother, Judy Syfers ironically argues that men often take wives for granted. "My God," she concludes, "who wouldn't want a wife?"

James Baldwin   **If Black English Isn't a Language, Then Tell Me, What Is?**   421
"A language comes into existence by means of brutal necessity, and the rules of the language are dictated by what the language must convey." So saying, James Baldwin argues that black English isn't a dialect, but a language.

CHAPTER 12

Prose for Further Reading   432

Maxine Kumin   *In Deep*   433
*Kumin shares with us an idyll of early winter, in the forest,
moving in deep in a quest of the perfect trail—the other side.*

Akira Kurosawa   *Babyhood*   435
*Babyhood memories are "a form resembling out-of-focus bits
of film footage," says a modern cinematographer in this essay about his own infancy.*

Farley Mowat   *The Grey Seas Under*   438
*"He who would survive must learn to be a part of wind and
water, rock and soil," writes Ontarian Farley Mowat of the
sailors who simultaneously battle and love the raw nature of
the North Atlantic's "unquiet seaboard."*

Maya Angelou   *The Fight*   440
*When Joe Louis defeated Max Schmeling for the heavyweight
championship in 1936, more than just a boxing title was at
stake.*

Garrison Keillor   *A Return to Basics: Mealtime without Guilt*   443
*Do you prefer a meal to be "a joyous, life-affirming experi-
ence" or "a truly unique dining experience"? This writer-
radio commentator longs for unsophisticated meals and offers
guidelines for getting "back to basics in the food line."*

Tama Janowitz   *He Rocked, I Reeled*   447
*Which of your teachers have spoken to their classes "with the
honesty of one adult talking to others." Which were really "in
love" with their subjects? Fiction writer Janowitz tells us how
a few of her teachers have sparked an excitement about subjects that she thought would put her to sleep.*

Stephen King   *'Ever Et Raw Meat?' and Other Weird
Questions*   450
*"Do you ever write in the nude?" Strange question? Stephen
King, master of horror and suspense, has heard stranger, yet
at least he feels comfortable giving that one an honest
answer.*

Nora Ephron   *Living with My VCR*   455
*Confessions of "a compulsive videotaper"! Simultaneously
addicted to and hateful of her VCR, Ephron nevertheless goes
on taping, hoping she'll live long enough to be able to watch
everything she's recorded.*

Mordecai Richler   *My Grandmother's Illness*   459
*For a young Jewish boy in Montreal fifty years ago, life turns
sad and mysterious when his grandmother dies. But, he finds,
it doesn't end!*

Richard Rodriguez   *Complexion*   464
A man labeled feo *as a child (*feo *means "ugly" in Spanish)
remembers how his dark skin set him apart from those around
him.*

GLOSSARY   **468**

ACKNOWLEDGMENTS   **481**

ALTERNATE THEMATIC CONTENTS

Childhood and Family

William Saroyan   *Why I Write*   5

Eudora Welty   *Moon on a Silver Spoon*   52

Margaret Atwood   *Survival*   72

Maxine Hong Kingston   *Catfish in the Bathtub*   104

Elizabeth Wong   *The Struggle to Be an All-American Girl*   129

Langston Hughes   *Salvation*   137

Roger Wilkins   *I Became Her Target*   144

Randall Williams   *Daddy Tucked the Blanket*   166

Ray Bradbury   *Tricks! Treats! Gangway!*   175

Bruno Bettelheim   *Fairy Tales and Modern Stories*   230

Stephen Leacock   *Softening the Stories for the Children*   396

Akira Kurosawa   *Babyhood*   435

Maya Angelou   *The Fight*   440

Mordecai Richler   *My Grandmother's Illness*   459

Richard Rodriguez   *Complexion*   464

Social Problems and Issues

Malcolm X   *Prison Studies*   62

George Steiner   *The Future of Reading*   82

Richard Selzer   *The Discus Thrower*   119

Elizabeth Wong   *The Struggle to Be an All-American Girl*   129

Roger Wilkins   *I Became Her Target*   144

George Orwell   *A Hanging*   152

Randall Williams   *Daddy Tucked the Blanket*   166

Rachel Carson   *A Fable for Tomorrow*   206

Gregg Easterbrook   *Escape Valve*   248

Elizabeth Janeway   *Soaps, Cynicism, and Mind Control*   256

Anne Roiphe   *Why Marriages Fail*   353

Linda Bird Francke   *The Ambivalence of Abortion*   372

Judy Syfers   *I Want a Wife*   415

James Baldwin   *If Black English Isn't a Language, Then Tell Me, What Is?*   421

Richard Rodriguez   *Complexion*   464

Men and Women Today

Ellen Goodman   *The Tapestry of Friendships*   213

Elizabeth Janeway   *Soaps, Cynicism, and Mind Control*   256

Judith Viorst   *Friends, Good Friends—and Such Good Friends*   277

Anne Roiphe   *Why Marriages Fail*   353

Linda Bird Francke   *The Ambivalence of Abortion*   372

Susan Jacoby   *When Bright Girls Decide that Math Is "A Waste of Time"*   383

Judy Syfers   *I Want a Wife*   415

The Minority Experience

Malcolm X   *Prison Studies*   62

Maxine Hong Kingston   *Catfish in the Bathtub*   104

Elizabeth Wong   *The Struggle to Be an All-American Girl*   129

Roger Wilkins   *I Became Her Target*   144

George Orwell   *A Hanging*   152

James Baldwin   *If Black English Isn't a Language, Then Tell Me, What Is?*   421

Maya Angelou   *The Fight*   440

Richard Rodriguez   *Complexion*   464

City and Country

Margaret Laurence   *The Shack*   94

William Least Heat Moon   *Arizona 87*   111

Lewis Thomas   *Death in the Open*   194

Rachel Carson   *A Fable for Tomorrow*   206

Russell Baker   *The Two Ismo's*   222

E. B. White   *The Three New Yorks*   286

Ernest Hemingway   *Camping Out*   342

Arthur Miller   *Rite of Spring*   364

Maxine Kumin   *In Deep*   433

Garrison Keillor   *A Return to Basics: Mealtime without Guilt*   443

Sports, Travel, and Leisure

William Least Heat Moon   *Arizona 87*   111

Aaron Copland   *What to Listen for in Music*   303

Sam Negri   *Loafing Made Easy*   318

Bruce Jay Friedman   *Eating Alone in Restaurants*   325

Grace Lichtenstein   *Coors Beer*   335

Ernest Hemingway   *Camping Out*   342

Arthur Miller   *Rite of Spring*   364

Joseph Wood Krutch   *The Vandal and the Sportsman*   407

Farley Mowat   *The Grey Seas Under*   438

Garrison Keillor   *A Return to Basics: Mealtime without Guilt*   443

Nora Ephron   *Living with My VCR*   455

Psychology And Behavior

Joan Didion   *On Keeping a Notebook*   34

Dan Greenburg   *How I Overhauled My Mechanic's Novel*   14

Lewis Thomas   *Death in the Open*   194

Ellen Goodman   *Tapestry of Friendships*   213

Russell Baker   *The Two Ismo's*   222

Bruno Bettelheim   *Fairy Tales and Modern Stories*   230

Suzanne Britt Jordan   *Fun, Oh Boy. Fun. You Could Die from It.*   240

Gregg Easterbrook   *Escape Valve*   248

Elizabeth Janeway   *Soaps, Cynicism, and Mind Control*   256

Judith Viorst   *Friends, Good Friends—and Such Good Friends*   277

Sam Negri   *Loafing Made Easy*   318

Bruce Jay Friedman   *Eating Alone in Restaurants*   325

Stephen King   *'Ever Et Raw Meat?' and Other Weird Questions*   450

Nora Ephron   *Living with My VCR*   455

Science, Technology, and Medicine

Richard Selzer   *The Discus Thrower*   119

Lewis Thomas   *Death in the Open*   194

Rachel Carson   *A Fable for Tomorrow*   206

Grace Lichtenstein   *Coors Beer*   335

Language and Thought

Joan Didion   *On Keeping a Notebook*   34

William Saroyan   *Why I Write*   5

Dan Greenburg   *How I Overhauled My Mechanic's Novel*   14

William Zinsser   *Simplicity*   22

Eudora Welty   *Moon on a Silver Spoon*   52

Malcolm X   *Prison Studies*   62

Margaret Atwood   *Survival*   72

Bruno Bettelheim   *Fairy Tales and Modern Stories*   230

George Steiner   *The Future of Reading*   82

Rita Mae Brown   *To the Victor Belongs the Language*   266

Stephen Leacock   *Softening the Stories for Children*   396

James Baldwin   *If Black English Isn't a Language, Then Tell Me, What Is?*   421

Humor and Satire

Dan Greenburg   *How I Overhauled My Mechanic's Novel*   14

Langston Hughes   *Salvation*   137

Ellen Goodman   *The Tapestry of Friendships*   213

Russell Baker   *The Two Ismo's*   222

Suzanne Britt Jordan   *Fun, Oh Boy. Fun. You Could Die from It.*   240

James T. Baker   *How Do We Find the Student in a World of Academic Gymnasts and Worker Ants?*   294

Sam Negri   *Loafing Made Easy*   318

Bruce Jay Friedman   *Eating Alone in Restaurants*   325

Arthur Miller   *Rite of Spring*   364

Judy Syfers   *I Want a Wife*   415

Garrison Keillor   *A Return to Basics: Mealtime without Guilt*   443

Tama Janowitz   *He Rocked, I Reeled*   447

PREFACE

Now in its fifth edition, *The Short Prose Reader* continues to offer lively reading selections for college composition courses. Its twelve chapters cover all-important patterns of writing, offering students concise and lively prose models for analysis, discussion, and imitation. Designed as a practical text, it addresses the challenge that faces today's college students in reading and writing short essays.

The organization of *The Short Prose Reader* is one of its major strengths. In this edition we offer a new chapter to focus attention on the importance of reading in our culture. Chapter 1, "On Writing," is followed by a chapter offering four unique views of the craft of reading by well-known authors. Each of the following nine chapters contains four short essays that illustrate clearly a specific pattern or technique—description, narration, illustration, comparison and contrast, definition, classification, process analysis, causal analysis, or argumentation. For this edition we offer new selections in every chapter. We organize the text by starting with the forms of prose mastered most readily by college students, and by then moving carefully to more difficult types of analytical and argumentative writing. Students learn to build upon earlier techniques and patterns as they progress through the book.

The last chapter, consisting of ten essays, offers students the opportunity to read and to discuss short prose pieces that reflect the various rhetorical strategies.

Teachers and students will discover that the essays appeal to a broad audience. Readers will be excited by William Least Heat Moon's "Arizona 87," Langston Hughes's "Salvation," Ernest Hemingway's "Camping Out," Judy Syfer's "I Want a Wife," and the many other timely or controversial pieces included in the text. This is a readable text, and one that has ample representation by many different types of writers. Moreover, the essays, which range typically between 300 to 1,200 words, achieve their goals succinctly and clearly and are easy to read and to understand. The essays will alert students both to the *types* of college writing expected of them and to the *length* of an essay required frequently by teachers.

Finally, the exercises we have included for each essay are comprehensive and integrated—designed to develop and reinforce the key skills required in college writing. We have included two vocabulary exercises for each selection; the Words to Watch exercise alerts students to words they will read in context, and the Building Vocabulary exercise uses other effective methods (prefix/suffix, context clues, synonym/antonym, abstract/concrete) of teaching vocabulary. A section called Understanding the Writer's Ideas reinforces reading comprehension. Sections entitled Understanding the Writer's Techniques and Exploring the Writer's Ideas provide an excellent basis for class discussion and independent reading and analysis. The last exercise for each essay involves a dynamic approach to writing projects. Guided writing activities—a novel feature of *The Short Prose Reader* —tie the writing projects to the reading selections. Instead of simply being told to write an essay on a certain topic, students through Guided Writing will be able to move from step to step in the process of composition.

The Short Prose Reader can be used flexibly and effectively by students and teachers alike. The text is simple yet sophisticated, presenting essays and exercises that are easy to follow but never condescending. Weighing the needs and expectations of today's college freshmen, we have designed a rhetoric reader that can serve as the major text for the composition course.

We wish to thank our friend and aide, Don Linder, for the invaluable assistance he gave us in developing the text. Next, we wish to thank our colleagues over the country for their support and are especially grateful to those who read the manuscript for this and previous editions and offered helpful suggestions: Mary Bisney, California State Polytechnic University, Pomona; Harry Crosby, Boston University; Mary Daly, College of DuPage; Robert Esch, University of Texas, El Paso; Rowena Flanagan, Kansas City Kansas Community College; Doug Fossek, Santa Barbara City College; Albert Geritz, Ft. Hays State College; Owen W. Gilman, Jr., St. Joseph's University; Marc H. Goldsmith, Mitchell College; Sister Madonna Giesilman, Donnelley College; Wallace Goldstein, Westfield State College; Wilma H. Hasse, Mitchell College; Roland Holmes, University of Illinois, Champaign-Urbana; Sharon Katz, Iona College; Isabel Kidder, Holyoke Community College; Elizabeth Latosi-Sawin, Missouri Western State College: Robert Reising, Pembroke State University; Michael H. Riley, West Virginia Northern Community College; J. C. Searles, Pennsylvania State University; and Ann N. Weisner, New York Institute of Technology.

Gilbert H. Muller

Harvey S. Wiener

CHAPTER 1

On Writing

Writing is not an isolated act. It is a definitive and integral part of daily human communication.

Writing is historic. Whether we try to imagine the "meanings" of prehistoric cave drawings or we plow through a satellite-transmitted newspaper each Sunday morning, we are participating in the same human impulse to communicate ideas to other people.

Writing is a product—whether that product is Thoreau's *Walden* or a student's essay calling for a ban on smoking in the college cafeteria.

And, perhaps most crucially, writing is a process—a process of transferring ideas from head to hand. Certainly that process is not absolute; the steps in producing a written piece vary from writer to writer and follow no exact order. Still, considering some of the common elements in this process is instructive for anyone embarking on a study of writing.

Few writers begin without some warmup activity. Generally called prewriting, the steps they take before producing a draft almost always start with thinking about their topic. They talk to friends and colleagues; they browse in libraries and rifle through reference books; they read newspaper and magazine articles. Sometimes they jot down notes and lists in order to put on paper some of their thoughts in very rough form. Some writers use free-association: they record as thoroughly as possible their random, unedited ideas about the topic. Using the raw, often disorganized materials produced in this preliminary stage, many writers try to group related thoughts with a scratch outline or some other effort to bring order to their written notes.

In these early stages serious writers consider their *purpose* and their *audience*. Purpose means "intent," and all writers must know clearly what they intend to accomplish in a particular piece. Often the purpose evolves as the writer continues to think and write about the topic. The issue of audience is important too. Whom does the writer want to read the work? A clear sense of what readers may know and what they may expect helps a writer identify essential issues and choose appropriate language that can win the audience's support.

Prewriting efforts lead to a first draft. Like all works in progress, drafts are generally messy affairs—words crossed out or erased, loops and arrows drawn from one phrase to another, sentences scrawled in the margin.

As they read over their drafts, writers check for clarity of ideas and expression. Are thoughts *unified:* do they relate to an obvious main point? Are thoughts *coherent:* do they follow a logical plan, one idea flowing smoothly into the next? Which ideas require expansion with details? Which ideas should be eliminated? Which thoughts and words are vague or imprecise? In attempting to answer these questions, writers often try to find a friendly reader to look over the draft and to give advice. Whatever else they may look for at this stage, they do not pay much attention to spelling or other matters of correctness. Scissors and paste help in the transfer of one part of the text to another. A good word-processing program that can move blocks of sentences around on a computer screen saves time and simplifies revision.

One draft invariably leads to another. Of course, no one can predict how many drafts a piece of writing will require, but not many writers get by with fewer than two or three attempts. It's always necessary to produce a final copy—the manuscript that a writer will allow others to read and perhaps evaluate. At this point careful attention to sentence structure, grammar, and spelling is very important. The final copy is the writer's best, cleanest effort.

This brief overview sketches in some of the important

elements in the writing process. But you don't want to lose the idea that writing is both a process of inspiration and of craft. Many writers have tried to explain how the two connect in their own particular efforts to create. The novelist and short story writer Katherine Anne Porter, for example, tells how inspiration becomes communication in her writing: "Now and again thousands of memories converge, harmonize, and arrange themselves around a central idea in a coherent form, and I write...." Jean Cocteau, the playwright, asserts the need to shape inspiration into language for a page of writing: "To write, to conquer ink and paper, accumulate letters and paragraphs, divide them with periods and commas, is a different matter from carrying around the dream of a play or a book." The point made by Porter and Cocteau is that writing emerges from both creativity and skill, instruction and technique, talent and effort. As we said, writing is a process of inspiration *and* craft.

Why do people write?

We all (and we *all* can consider ourselves writers) attempt to explain things—what we see, what we feel, what we understand, what we experience, what we dream—so that we and others may better know the world and each other. We all—whether we are writing essays, poems, or stories, whether we are second graders attempting to describe a snowfall or philosophers attempting to explain the meaning of life—have an impulse, as James Baldwin states, "to examine attitudes, to go beneath the surface, to tap the source."

Because communication involves an audience, we need to be aware of a certain communal responsibility as writers. This is a responsibility to both form and content. As for content, we must be accurate—truthful, faithful to facts and details. As for form, we must carefully shape our words and sentences so that they represent what we perceive in our unique, exact, and precise way of viewing things.

It is no wonder that the four writers included in this chapter—four writers who represent a broad spectrum of personal histories, stylistic methods, and intellectual concerns— are all dedicated to exactitude and precision. Whether it's Joan Didion's desire to have "an accurate factual record of what I have been doing or thinking'' or William Zinsser's pleas for the preciseness that comes only with simplicity, all are minutely concerned with the nuts and bolts of the process of shaping what Baldwin terms the "explicit medium of language."

The four writers represented here also run the gamut of expository techniques discussed in subsequent chapters. None of their essays is simply a "set piece." For example, William Saroyan combines personal reminiscence with theories of art, while Dan Greenburg blends satire with comparison and narration. It can even be suggested that for some of the most successful writers, the process of writing may be even more important than the product.

Finally, although later on in this book you will find George Steiner lamenting a society where illiteracy is on a frightening upsurge and a floppy disk may become more easily recognizable than a printed page, the basic medium of communication is still words. And, in order for these words to survive from generation to generation, there must be writing. It will always be true, in the words of Henry Miller, that "Writing, like life itself, is a voyage of discovery."

Why I Write

William Saroyan

William Saroyan (1908–1981) won the 1939 Pulitzer Prize for his play *The Time of Your Life.* His novel *The Human Comedy* (1942) is both an ironic and optimistic look at the human condition. In this essay, Saroyan writes of how tragedy, memory, and art have combined to bring meaning to his life.

Words to Watch

vineyards (par. 4)   fields for growing wine grapes
sorrow (par. 5)   sadness
impelled (par. 6)   driven to do something
decline (par. 12)   gradual wasting away
seize (par. 12)   grab hold of
halt (par. 12)   stop
invariably (par. 13)   constantly
inevitably (par. 13)   unavoidably
impermanence (par. 15)   quality of not being permanent

1   It is a quarter of a century, almost, since my first book was published, but as I began to write when I was nine, I have been writing for forty years: that is to say, I have lived in a special way for forty years—the way that takes hold of a man who is determined to understand the meaning of his own life, and to be prepared to write about it.

2   But I think it goes even farther back than forty years. I think I began to live in my own special way when I became aware that I had memory. That happened before I was three. I also had a memory that went back to a time before I was *two,* but it was an isolated one. At that age I wasn't given to remembering *everything,* or rather I hadn't yet noticed that it had come to pass that I remembered.

3   In the past were some of the best things I had, several of

5

them gone: my father, for instance, who had died before I was three.

My first memory, the one that went back to a time when 4
I was not yet two, was of my father getting up onto a wagon, sitting beside my mother, and making a sound that told the horse to go. My two sisters and my brother and I sat in the back of the wagon as it moved slowly down a dusty road between vineyards on a hot afternoon in the summertime. I remembered sensing sorrow and feeling *with*—with mine, my people—a father, a mother, two sisters, a brother, our horse, our wagon, our pots and pans and books. The rest is lost in the sleep that soon carried me away. The next thing I knew my father was gone, which I didn't understand.

I was fascinated by having memory, and troubled by the 5
sorrow of it. I refused to accept the theory that things end, including people, including my father. I refused to believe that my father was dead. (In the sense that every man *is* his father, I wasn't much mistaken.)

All the same, I felt impelled from the time I knew I had 6
memory to do something about the past, about endings, about human death.

My first impulse was simple. I wanted to cause the im- 7
possible to happen, because if I was able to do that, I knew I would be able to cause *anything* to happen. Thus, death would not be death, if anybody wanted it not to be.

I found two large empty cans. One I filled with water. 8
The empty can I placed two feet from the full can. I asked myself to cause the water in the full can to pass into the empty can, by itself, because I wanted it to.

The experiment failed. I had begun with the maximum, I 9
had failed, and so I began to consider what might be the next best.

For a long time there didn't appear to be *any* next best at 10
all. It was a matter of all or nothing, or at any rate the equivalent of nothing: continuous *gradual* loss, and finally total loss, or death.

What could a man do about this? Wait? That didn't seem 11
to be enough.

Why should I be troubled by memory at all if all memory 12
told me was that things change, fail, decline, end, and die? I
didn't want good things to do that, and I didn't think they
should. How could I seize a good thing when I saw it and halt
its decline and death? As far as people were concerned, there
just didn't seem to be *any* way.

And so I came to accept the theory that as far as I knew, 13
as far as *anybody* knew, as far as there appeared to be any
order to the action of things at all, the end of the order was
invariably and inevitably decline, disappearance, and death.

And yet the world was full of people all the time. And 14
the earth, the sea, and the sky were full of all manner of other
living things: plants, animals, fish, birds.

Thus, something *did* stay, something *was* constant, or 15
appeared to be. It was the *kind* that stayed. *One* of a kind
couldn't stay, and couldn't apparently be made to. I myself
was one of a kind, and everybody I knew and loved was one
of a kind, and so what about us? What could I do about our
impermanence?

How could I halt this action? How had other men halted it? 16

I learned that they never had halted it. They had only 17
pretended to.

They had done this by means of art, or the putting of lim- 18
its upon the limitless, and thereby holding something fast and
making it seem constant, indestructible, unstoppable, unkillable, deathless.

A great painter painted his wife, his son, his daughter, 19
and himself, and then one by one they all moved along and
died. But the painting remained. A sculptor did the same thing
with stone, a composer with musical sounds, and a writer with
words.

Therefore, as the next best thing, art in one form or another 20
would have to be the way of my life, but which form of art?

Before I was eight I didn't think it could possibly be writ- 21
ing, for the simple reason that I couldn't read, let alone write,
and everybody else I knew could do both. At last, though, I
got the hang of reading and writing, and I felt (if I didn't
think), "This is for me."

It had taken me so long to learn to write that I consid- 22
ered being able to write the greatest thing that could happen to
anybody.

If I wrote something, it *was* written, it was itself, and it 23
might continue to be itself forever, or for what passes as forever.

Thus, I could halt the action of things, after all, and at 24
the same time be prepared to learn new things, to achieve new
forms of halting, or art.

That is roughly how and why I became a writer.   25

In short, I began to write in order to get even on death. 26

I have continued to write for many reasons.   27

A long time ago I said I write because it is the only way 28
I am willing to survive.

Mainly, though, I write because I want to.   29

BUILDING VOCABULARY

1. Although simple and direct on the surface, much of Saroyan's writing in this essay is quite beautifully crafted and full
   of meaning. Rewrite each of the following sentences and
   excerpts in your own words. With others in your class,
   compare the meaning and effect of the originals with the re-
   writes.

   a. My first impulse was simple. I wanted to cause the im-
      possible to happen, because if I was able to do that, I
      knew I would be able to cause *anything* to happen.
      Thus, death would not be death, if anybody wanted it
      not to be. (par. 7)
   b. The experiment failed. I had begun with the maximum,
      I had failed, and so I began to consider what might be
      the next best. (par. 9)
   c. It was a matter of all or nothing, or at any rate the equiv-
      alent of nothing: continuous *gradual* loss, and finally to-
      tal loss, or death. (par. 10)
   d. It was the *kind* that stayed. *One* of a kind couldn't stay,
      and couldn't apparently be made to. (par. 15)

e. They had done this by means of art, or the putting of limits upon the limitless, and thereby holding something fast and making it seem constant, indestructible, unstoppable, unkillable, deathless. (par. 18)

2. Write the *antonyms* (opposite meanings) for five of the Words to Watch. Then, use each antonym in an original sentence.

UNDERSTANDING THE WRITER'S IDEAS

1. How old is Saroyan at the time of writing this essay? How do you know?

2. In your own words, describe the "special way" in which Saroyan has lived? When did this "special way" of living begin for the author?

3. From what age does Saroyan remember his first memory? Summarize the memory in your own words. What is the importance of memory for this writer?

4. In what sort of environment did Saroyan live as a child?

5. How was Saroyan affected by his father's death? Explain the meaning of the parenthetical sentence: "(In the sense that every man *is* his father, I wasn't much mistaken.)" (par. 5)

6. In paragraph 7, Saroyan writes, "I wanted to cause the impossible to happen." Why? How did this desire relate to his father's death? How did he go about trying to cause the impossible? Did he succeed?

7. What *definition* does Saroyan offer of "art"? Why did he choose art as a way of life? What relationship did this choice have to memory? To his father's death? How did he come to choose writing among all the arts?

8. The title may be read in two ways: (a) Why Saroyan *started* to write, and (b) why he *continues* to write. Which seems predominant? Why? Cite the author's own reasons for both (a) and (b).

UNDERSTANDING THE WRITER'S TECHNIQUES

1. Is there a *thesis statement* (see Glossary) in this essay? Explain. Describe Saroyan's *purpose* for writing this essay. Who is his intended *audience?* Explain.

2. *Tone* refers to the writer's attitude or stance toward his or her subject (see Glossary) and is expressed in the word choices, rhythms, and overall "voice" of a piece of writing. How would you describe the *tone* of this essay? Point to three places in the essay that are particularly expressive of the tone.

3. What was your emotional response to reading the first paragraph of this essay? Explain what it was about Saroyan's writing that made you feel that way.

4. What idea is repeated in paragraphs 1 and 2? Why? For what effect?

5. A *process analysis* (see Chapter 9) tells the reader step-by-step how to do something. Trace the steps whereby Saroyan dealt with his father's death.

6. In the essay that closes this chapter, William Zinsser's "Simplicity," the author tells writers to work hard to simplify their writing. (Take a quick look at Zinsser's examples of how he worked to simplify that essay.) Do you get the sense that Saroyan "worked" at simplifying his essay? Do you think this is an early or late draft of the essay? Explain your answers.

7. Throughout this essay, Saroyan makes liberal use of *italics*. For what reason does he use them? Which uses are most effective? Are there any which you feel are unnecessary? Why?

8. This essay is composed of a series of relatively short paragraphs, some only one or two sentences long. What is the effect of this type of writing? Do you feel any choppiness or incompleteness? Why or why not?

9. Throughout the essay, the author asks a number of questions, especially in paragraphs 15 and 16. What is his purpose in asking these questions? To whom are they addressed? What effect do they create?

10. On first reading, it is possible that the words "the *kind*" in the second sentence of paragraph 15 might be read as having a double meaning. What are those two possible meanings? Which do you think Saroyan meant? Do you think he made a mistake in creating this ambiguity, or did he have a special purpose? Explain.

11. Do you think the title is meant as a question or as a statement? Explain your answer in the context of the essay.

12. The last eight paragraphs of the essay are only one sentence each, and the last five are especially short and simple. What effect does this cause?

EXPLORING THE WRITER'S IDEAS

1. What is your earliest memory? How old were you? What lasting effect has the memory had on you?

2. Compare the environment in which Saroyan lived with your own childhood surroundings.

3. Was Saroyan's reaction to his father's death typical? How does it compare with the way in which you have had to handle the loss of a loved one?

4. Have any of the arts given you the sort of consolation or life direction that they have provided for Saroyan? For example, at a time of stress or sadness, has anything in music, literature, or the visual arts ever changed your mood?

Do you practice any art form, either professionally or as a hobby? If so, explain why you do it and how it makes you feel.

IDEAS FOR WRITING

Guided Writing

Write an essay entitled "Why I _____ ." Fill in the blank with an activity that is very important to you, that you believe will remain so throughout your life, and that reflects your creative talents. For example, you might want to write about "Why I Paint," "Why I Play the Piano," or "Why I Cook"—or, if you prefer, "Why I Write."

1. Begin with a statement of why and for how long this activity has been important to you.

2. Dig deeply into your memory to relate an early memory that is tied to your choice to pursue this activity.

3. Tell about a particular incident or person that especially affected your choice of this activity.

4. Relate the process whereby you chose this "special way of living."

5. Throughout your essay use questions to help your reader understand your thought processes as you developed this way of life.

6. Write in a simple, direct way using mainly very short paragraphs.

7. Try to maintain an emotionally charged, serious tone.

8. End your essay with a series of quick, direct statements, the last of which should relate positively to your future in this activity.

More Writing Projects

1. Write an essay about how the loss of a close friend or relative significantly altered your life. (This loss doesn't have to be a death; it can be someone moving away or the breakup of a friendship, or some other loss.)

2. Write an essay entitled "Why I Would *Never* _____ ." Fill in the blank with an appropriate activity.

How I Overhauled My Mechanic's Novel

Dan Greenburg

In Dan Greenburg's take-off on repair service ethics, notice how humor can help carry a discussion of what ultimately can be a serious problem. Also note how Greenburg tells a story which, while relating to all our experiences, includes a great deal of information about the craft and skills of writing.

Words to Watch

handy (par. 5)   clever in doing things, especially with the hands

defective (par. 18)   not in proper working order

queasy (par. 29)   ill-at-ease; causing nausea

superficial (par. 29)   shallow in thought; concerned only with obvious meanings

customizing (par. 33)   making over specially for a particular purpose

cannibalize (par. 35)   to take apart something for parts to be used for something else

My mechanic was having trouble with his novel. Knowing I am an author, he asked if I could help. I told him I'd have a look. He told me he needed it back pretty soon. I told him it was my busy season, but I'd see what I could do. A couple days later my mechanic came by to see what I had found. "Well," I said, "I opened her up and took a look, and I'm afraid you've got a little trouble there." 1

"Serious trouble?" he asked. 2

"Probably not too serious. The timing's off on four of your six characters, and two of the others ought to be replaced." 3

"Do you think I might be able to do the work myself?" he asked. 4

I shrugged. "Don't know how handy you are," I said, "or what tools you got. You own a thesaurus?" 5

"A what?" he asked. 6

14

"That's what I thought," I said. "No, I don't think you 7
ought to do the work yourself. You get it all apart, you might
not be able to put the pieces back together again."

"Maybe you could help me," he said. "I'd pay you, of 8
course."

"I'm not cheap—$37.50 an hour. Plus parts." 9

"Parts?" 10

"You know—typing bond, carbon paper, typewriter rib- 11
bon, correction fluid, transparent tape—that kind of thing." I
scribbled an estimate on an index card. He looked at it and
whistled.

"Remember, that doesn't include syntax either," I said. 12

"Don't you think this is a little high?" he asked. I gave 13
him the names of a couple of my novelist friends and suggested he get competitive bids. He said he didn't really know
their work and guessed he'd stick with me.

"When do you think I could pick the manuscript up?" 14
he asked. I told him to check with me in about a week.

One week later to the day, he dropped by. "Is it ready?" 15
he asked.

"Afraid not," I said. "Once I opened her up and really 16
took a hard look, I discovered a few more problems."

"Like what?" he asked. 17

"Well, for one thing," I said, "there's a lot of cheap im- 18
agery in there that ought to come out—similes, metaphors,
personifications—they're just clogging up the action. You also
have some defective aphorisms. Then there's a hole in your
plot about a mile wide that needs to be filled up. Plus which
your superstructure is rusty and falling apart."

He seemed really upset. "What about those two charac- 19
ters you said ought to be replaced?"

"I'm afraid it's worse than that," I said. "If it was me, 20
I'd replace all six of them. They're really shot. It's not just
their timing that's off, it's their motivations—you left out their
motivations when you hooked them up, and now I can't even
get them to turn over, much less speak."

"I can't afford to replace all six of them." 21

"Well, then, maybe they can be rebuilt," I said. "But 22
you definitely need to replace your protagonist."

"My protagonist?" he asked.   23

"I'm afraid so."   24

He smiled sheepishly. "Look," he said. "I'm not even   25
sure I know what a protagonist *is*."

I pointed. "It's this guy right here, see?"   26

"But why does he need to be replaced?"   27

"He's weak. He's not going to be able to go the dis-   28
tance. He's going to give out in mid-plot, and when he does
he's going to tear the hell out of the whole thing—it'll be a real
mess."

My mechanic looked a little queasy. I almost felt sorry   29
for him. "Listen," I said, "I hate to have to be the bearer of
such bad news, but I figured you'd want to know the truth.
Another novelist might give you a different story, tell you all
you needed was a superficial tune-up—wider margins, a re-
type job, stuff like that—and just forget about your protagonist. But that's not the way I operate."

He nodded miserably. "How long before my protagonist   30
gives out?" he asked.

I shrugged. "Hard to say. Could be he'd last you all the   31
way up to the climax in the twelfth chapter. Could be he'd
give out in the first thirty pages. You just can't tell with a
weak protagonist. If it was me, I'd pick up a new one, slap it
in there and be done with it."

"How hard would it be to find one?" he asked. "A used   32
one, I mean. I don't know if I can afford a new one."

"Well," I said, "a novelist I know has just scrapped a   33
trilogy he's been working on. You could maybe make a deal
with him on *his* protagonist. In a piece that long, even a *minor*
character could work as a protagonist for you—after a little
customizing."

"Could you give this guy a call and see if he'd be willing   34
to sell me a minor character? A protagonist from a work that
size has got to be out of my price range."

"I'll call him," I said. "Of course, I don't know how ea-   35
ger he's going to be to cannibalize a whole trilogy to sell you
just one minor character."

"Look," he said, a pasty smile on his face, "maybe you   36
could ask for a special favor."

"I could," I said. "Unless..."   37

"Unless what?"   38
"Well," I said, "unless you've ever done any work on   39
his car."

BUILDING VOCABULARY

1. In this essay, Greenburg uses a number of words connected with the skills and processes of writing—both for
fiction and nonfiction. Look up and write definitions for the
following words:

syntax (par. 12)
manuscript (par. 14)
imagery (par. 18)
similes (par. 18)
metaphors (par. 18)
personifications (par. 18)
aphorisms (par. 18)
plot (par. 18)
characters (par. 19)
motivations (par. 20)
protagonist (par. 23)
climax (par. 31)
trilogy (par. 33)

2. In relating the dialogue with his mechanic, Greenburg uses
descriptions of actions to indicate each man's attitudes.
For each of the following phrases, explain what attitude the
italicized words express:

a. I *shrugged* (pars. 5 and 31)
b. I *scribbled* an estimate (par. 11)
c. He looked at it and *whistled* (par. 11)
d. He *smiled sheepishly* (par. 25)
e. He *nodded miserably* (par. 30)

UNDERSTANDING THE WRITER'S IDEAS

1. What is the mechanic's problem in this essay? Why does he approach Greenburg for assistance? How does Greenburg propose to solve the problem?

2. Briefly outline the story of this essay. Do the events seem as if they actually could have happened in this way? Why? What really *is* Greenburg's purpose in writing this essay? At what is he poking fun? What ideas is he really trying to convey to the reader?

3. What is a *thesaurus?* Why does Greenburg ask the mechanic if he owns one? Why, when the mechanic indicates that he doesn't know what a thesaurus is, does Greenburg say, "That's what I thought"?

4. In general, what is Greenburg's attitude towards his mechanic's literary skills? What does he think of the novel on first reading? How does that opinion change with a closer second reading? Cite a few examples to support your responses.

5. What is wrong with the mechanic's protagonist? What does Greenburg suggest he do to rectify his problems?

6. What does Greenburg suggest that another novelist might do if the mechanic took the novel elsewhere? Do you feel he is being completely honest on this point? Why?

7. What general part of the writing process is Greenburg actually describing in this essay? What specific writing skills does he mention?

UNDERSTANDING THE WRITER'S TECHNIQUES

1. How does Greenburg use *humor* in this essay? How does humor affect your reaction to the essay? Give examples of what you consider the most humorous sections.

2. Throughout the essay, Greenburg is actually comparing one professional relationship to another. What are they? How does Greenburg present a "new twist" on the old re-

lationship? Identify examples of how the author sustains the comparison.

3. Greenburg relies heavily upon dialogue to record the events in this essay. Why doesn't he simply tell us what happened? How does his technique make the essay more effective?

4. What is Greenburg's underlying attitude toward his mechanic as a professional and as a person (not just as a novelist)? Explain your answers with specific examples from the essay. How does the last line of the essay especially indicate that attitude? Explain the underlying meaning of the last line.

5. Greenburg uses quite a bit of informal language in this essay. For example, in paragraph 13 he writes, "He said he didn't really know their work and *guessed* he'd *stick* with me." Why is the author so informal throughout the essay? Find other examples of such informality and explain their meanings.

6. What kinds of readers do you think would be most interested in Greenburg's essay? Why? How does Greenburg's style reflect the tastes and interests of such readers? Support your answer with specific references to the essay.

EXPLORING THE WRITER'S IDEAS

1. We have all had "interesting" experiences with auto mechanics (or know of someone who has) in which we've felt helplessly at the mechanic's mercy and whim. Describe such an experience and its results.

2. Have you, or has anyone you have known, ever had the feeling of being cheated or "conned" by someone? How did you feel about it at the time? Did you try to get even? If so, how successful were you? If not, why not? How do you deal with feeling cheated? Is your technique effective? Is there any technique that you admire more than your own? Why?

3. Discuss how Greenburg takes a serious subject and deals with it in a funny way. How does humor help us deal with difficult situations?

IDEAS FOR WRITING

Guided Writing

Write an essay about how you once helped someone even though you felt that person hadn't previously been kind or fair to you.

1. Begin with a direct statement of what the person's problem was and why he or she chose to come to you for assistance.

2. Make sure you specify your relation to the other person.

3. Describe what you did at first and what your initial reaction was. How did the other person respond in turn?

4. Early in the essay, begin to report what you and the other person actually said to each other, and try to use the dialogue as a technique for developing the essay.

5. Indicate what you felt you could do for the other person's problem; also, indicate the other person's reactions.

6. Don't be too serious in your essay. Make it somewhat funny for your readers, even though you may be dealing with a fairly serious situation.

7. Where possible, use descriptions of how the two of you behaved around each other.

8. Close your essay by saying something to the other person, which subtly indicates your real feeling about that person's previous treatment of you.

More Writing Projects

1. Write about a time that you turned to someone for help with your own writing. Why did you need help? Did you

get what you wanted? Or, perhaps you can write about a time someone turned to you for help in writing. Were you able to provide assistance? How?

2. Tell about a time you needed to ask a favor from someone to whom you really didn't want to be obligated, but had no choice.

3. Write a conversation between two people in which the first is trying to convince the second to do something which he or she really doesn't want to do.

Simplicity

William Zinsser

In this chapter from *On Writing Well,* William Zinsser begins with a fairly pessimistic analysis of the clutter that pervades and degrades American writing, and he offers many examples to prove his point. Zinsser deals with almost all major aspects of the writing process—thinking, composing, awareness of the reader, self-discipline, rewriting, and editing—and concludes that simplicity is the key to them all.

Words to Watch

decipher (par. 2)   to make out the meaning of something obscure

adulterants (par. 3)   added substances which make something impure or inferior

mollify (par. 4)   to appease; to soothe

spell (par. 4)   a short period of time

assailed (par. 8)   attacked with words or physical violence

spruce (par. 8)   neat or smart in appearance

rune (par. 11)   character in an ancient alphabet

surfeit (par. 14)   an overabundant supply

superfluous (par. 15)   extra; more than is needed; wasteful

enumerate (par. 16)   to count or list in order

Clutter is the disease of American writing. We are a so- 1
ciety strangling in unnecessary words, circular constructions, pompous frills and meaningless jargon.

Who really knows what the average businessman is 2
trying to say in the average business letter? What member of an insurance or medical plan can decipher the brochure that tells him what his costs and benefits are? What father or mother can put together a child's toy—on Christmas Eve or any other eve—from the instructions on the box? Our national tendency is to inflate and thereby sound important. The airline pilot who wakes us to announce that he is presently anticipating experiencing considerable weather

wouldn't dream of saying that there's a storm ahead and it may get bumpy. The sentence is too simple—there must be something wrong with it.

But the secret of good writing is to strip every sentence 3 to its cleanest components. Every word that serves no function, every long word that could be a short word, every adverb which carries the same meaning that is already in the verb, every passive construction that leaves the reader unsure of who is doing what—these are the thousand and one adulterants that weaken the strength of a sentence. And they usually occur, ironically, in proportion to education and rank.

During the late 1960's the president of Princeton Univer- 4 sity wrote a letter to mollify the alumni after a spell of campus unrest. "You are probably aware," he began, "that we have been experiencing very considerable potentially explosive expressions of dissatisfaction on issues only partially related." He meant that the students had been hassling them about different things. As an alumnus I was far more upset by the president's syntax than by the students' potentially explosive expressions of dissatisfaction. I would have preferred the presidential approach taken by Franklin D. Roosevelt when he tried to convert into English his own government's memos, such as this blackout order of 1942:

> Such preparations shall be made as will completely obscure all Federal buildings and non-Federal buildings occupied by the Federal government during an air raid for any period of time from visibility by reason of internal or external illumination.

"Tell them," Roosevelt said, "that in buildings where 5 they have to keep the work going to put something across the windows."

Simplify, simplify. Thoreau said it, as we are so often re- 6 minded, and no American writer more consistently practiced what he preached. Open *Walden* to any page and you will find a man saying in a plain and orderly way what is on his mind:

> I love to be alone. I never found the companion that was so companionable as solitude. We are for the most part more lonely when we go abroad among men than when we stay in

our chambers. A man thinking or working is always alone, let him be where he will. Solitude is not measured by the miles of space that intervene between a man and his fellows. The really diligent student in one of the crowded hives of Cambridge College is as solitary as a dervish in the desert.

How can the rest of us achieve such enviable freedom 7 from clutter? The answer is to clear our heads of clutter. Clear thinking becomes clear writing: one can't exist without the other. It is impossible for a muddy thinker to write good English. He may get away with it for a paragraph or two, but soon the reader will be lost, and there is no sin so grave, for he will not easily be lured back.

Who is this elusive creature, the reader? He is a person 8 with an attention span of about twenty seconds. He is assailed on every side by forces competing for his time: by newspapers and magazines, by television and radio and stereo, by his wife and children and pets, by his house and his yard and all the gadgets that he has bought to keep them spruce, and by that most potent of competitors, sleep. The man snoozing in his chair with an unfinished magazine open on his lap is a man who is being given too much unnecessary trouble by the writer.

It won't do to say that the snoozing reader is too dumb or 9 too lazy to keep pace with the train of thought. My sympathies are with him. If a reader is lost, it is generally because the writer has not been careful enough to keep him on the path.

This carelessness can take any number of forms. Per- 10 haps a sentence is so excessively cluttered that the reader, hacking his way through the verbiage, simply doesn't know what it means. Perhaps a sentence has been so shoddily constructed that the reader could read it in any of several ways. Perhaps the writer has switched pronouns in mid-sentence, or has switched tenses, so the reader loses track of who is talking or when the action took place. Perhaps Sentence B is not a logical sequel to Sentence A—the writer, in whose head the connection is clear, has not bothered to provide the missing link. Perhaps the writer has used an important word incorrectly by not taking the trouble to look it up. He may think that ''sanguine'' and ''sanguinary'' mean the same thing, but the difference is a bloody big one. The reader can only infer (speaking of big differences) what the writer is trying to imply.

Faced with these obstacles, the reader is at first a remarkably tenacious bird. He blames himself—he obviously missed something, and he goes back over the mystifying sentence, or over the whole paragraph, piecing it out like an ancient rune, making guesses and moving on. But he won't do this for long. The writer is making him work too hard, and the reader will look for one who is better at his craft. **11**

The writer must therefore constantly ask himself: What am I trying to say? Surprisingly often, he doesn't know. Then he must look at what he has written and ask: Have I said it? Is it clear to someone encountering the subject for the first time? If it's not, it is because some fuzz has worked its way into the machinery. The clear writer is a person clear-headed enough to see this stuff for what it is: fuzz. **12**

I don't mean that some people are born clear-headed and are therefore natural writers, whereas others are naturally fuzzy and will never write well. Thinking clearly is a conscious act that the writer must force upon himself, just as if he were embarking on any other project that requires logic: adding up a laundry list or doing an algebra problem. Good writing doesn't come naturally, though most people obviously think it does. The professional writer is forever being bearded by strangers who say that they'd like to "try a little writing some time" when they retire from their real profession. Good writing takes self-discipline and, very often, self-knowledge. **13**

Many writers, for instance, can't stand to throw anything away. Their sentences are littered with words that mean essentially the same thing and with phrases which make a point that is implicit in what they have already said. When students give me these littered sentences I beg them to select from the surfeit of words the few that most precisely fit what they want to say. Choose one, I plead, from among the three almost identical adjectives. Get rid of the unnecessary adverbs. Eliminate "in a funny sort of way" and other such qualifiers—they do no useful work. **14**

The students look stricken—I am taking all their wonder- **15**

ful words away. I am only taking their superfluous words
away, leaving what is organic and strong.

"But," one of my worst offenders confessed, "I never 16
can get rid of anything—you should see my room." (I didn't
take him up on the offer.) "I have two lamps where I only
need one, but I can't decide which one I like better, so I keep
them both." He went on to enumerate his duplicated or unnecessary objects, and over the weeks ahead I went on throwing away his duplicated and unnecessary words. By the end of
the term—a term that he found acutely painful—his sentences
were clean.

"I've had to change my whole approach to writing," he 17
told me. "Now I have to *think* before I start every sentence
and I have to *think* about every word." The very idea amazed
him. Whether his room also looked better I never found out. I
suspect that it did.

Two pages of the final manuscript of this chapter. Although they look like a first draft, they have already been rewritten and retyped—like almost every other page—four or five times. With each rewrite I try to make what I have written tighter, stronger and more precise, eliminating every element that is not doing useful work, until at last I have a clean copy for the printer. Then I go over it once more, reading it aloud, and am always amazed at how much clutter can still be profitably cut.

---

is too dumb or too lazy to keep pace with the ~~writer's~~ train
of thought. My sympathies are ~~entirely~~ with him.) ~~He's not
so dumb~~. (If the reader is lost, it is generally because the
writer ~~of the article~~ has not been careful enough to keep
him on the ~~proper~~ path.

(This carelessness can take any number of ~~different~~ forms.
Perhaps a sentence is so excessively ~~long and~~ cluttered that
the reader, hacking his way through ~~all~~ the verbiage, simply
doesn't know what ⟨it⟩ ~~the writer~~ means. Perhaps a sentence has
been so shoddily constructed that the reader could read it in
any of ⟨several⟩ ~~two or three different~~ ways. ~~He thinks he knows what
the writer is trying to say, but he's not sure.~~ Perhaps the
writer has switched pronouns in mid-sentence, or ~~perhaps he~~
has switched tenses, so the reader loses track of who is
talking ~~to whom~~, or ~~exactly~~ when the action took place. Perhaps Sentence B is not a logical sequel to Sentence A -- the
writer, in whose head the connection is ~~perfectly~~ clear, has
not ⟨bothered to provide⟩ ~~given enough thought to providing~~ the missing link. Perhaps the writer has used an important word incorrectly by not
taking the trouble to look it up ~~and make sure~~. He may think
that "sanguine" and "sanguinary" mean the same thing, but)
~~I can assure you that~~ (the difference is a bloody big one ~~to the~~

~~reader.~~ *The reader* ~~He~~ can only ~~try to~~ infer **what** (speaking of big differences) what the writer is trying to imply.

/Faced with *these* ~~such a variety of~~ obstacles, the reader is at first a remarkably tenacious bird. He ~~tends to~~ blame(s) himself⸮ *He* ~~He~~ obviously missed something, ~~he thinks,~~ and he goes back over the mystifying sentence, or over the whole paragraph, piecing it out like an ancient rune, making guesses and moving on. But he won't do this for long. ~~He will soon run out of patience.~~ (The writer is making him work too hard, ~~) harder than he should have to work~~ — (and the reader will look for ~~a writer~~ *one* who is better at his craft.

(The writer must therefore constantly ask himself: What am I trying to say? ~~in this sentence?~~ Surprisingly often, he doesn't know. ~~And~~ Then he must look at what he has ~~just~~ written and ask: Have I said it? Is it clear to someone *encountering* ~~who is coming upon~~ the subject for the first time? If it's not, ~~clear,~~ it is because some fuzz has worked its way into the machinery. The clear writer is a person ~~who is~~ clear-headed enough to see this stuff for what it is: fuzz.

(I don't mean ~~to suggest~~ that some people are born clear-headed and are therefore natural writers, whereas *others* ~~other people~~ are naturally fuzzy and will ~~therefore~~ never write well. Thinking clearly is *a* ~~an entirely~~ conscious act that the writer must *force* ~~keep forcing~~ upon himself, just as if he were *embarking* ~~starting out~~ on any other ~~kind of~~ project that *requires* ~~calls for~~ logic: adding up a laundry list or doing an algebra problem ~~or playing chess~~. Good writing doeesn't ~~just~~ come naturally, though most people obviously think *it does*. ~~it's as easy as walking~~. The professional

BUILDING VOCABULARY

1. Zinsser uses a number of words and expressions drawn from areas other than writing; he uses them to make interesting combinations or comparisons in such expressions as *elusive creature* (par. 8), *hacking his way through the verbiage* (par. 10), and *a remarkably tenacious bird* (par. 11). Find other such expressions in this essay. Write simple explanations for the three above and the others that you find.

2. List all words or phrases in this essay that pertain to writing—the process, the results, the faults, the successes. Explain any with which you were unfamiliar.

3. Identify any other words in this essay that were new to you. Write their dictionary definitions.

UNDERSTANDING THE WRITER'S IDEAS

1. State simply Zinsser's meaning in the opening paragraph. What faults of "bad writing" does he mention in this paragraph?

2. To what is Zinsser objecting in paragraph 2?

3. What, according to the author, is the "secret of good writing"? Explain this "secret" in a few simple words of your own. What does Zinsser say detracts from good writing? What is the meaning of the word *ironically?* Why does Zinsser write that the incidence of these writing faults "occur, *ironically,* in proportion to education and rank"?

4. What was the "message" in the letter from the president of Princeton to the alumni? Why does Zinsser object to it? Was it more objectionable in form or content?

5. Who was Thoreau? What is *Walden?* Why are references to the two especially appropriate to Zinsser's essay?

6. What, according to Zinsser, is the relation between clear thinking and good writing? Can you have one without the

other? What is meant by a "muddy thinker" (par. 7)? Why is it "impossible for a muddy thinker to write good English"?

7. Why does the author think most people fall asleep while reading? What is his attitude towards such people?

8. Look up and explain the "big differences" between the words *sanguine* and *sanguinary; infer* and *imply.* What is Zinsser's point in calling attention to these differences?

9. In paragraph 12, Zinsser writes about a writer's necessary awareness of the composing process. What elements of the *process* of writing are included in that paragraph? In that discussion, Zinsser speaks of *fuzz* in writing. What does he mean by that word as it relates to the writing process? To what does Zinsser compare the writer's thinking process? Why does he use such simple comparisons?

10. Explain the meaning of the last sentence. What does it indicate about Zinsser's attitude towards his work?

UNDERSTANDING THE WRITER'S TECHNIQUES

1. Explain the use of the words *disease* and *strangling* in par. 1. Why does Zinsser use these words in an essay about writing?

2. For what purpose does Zinsser use a series of questions in paragraph 2?

3. Throughout this essay, Zinsser makes extensive use of examples to support general opinions and attitudes. What attitude or opinion is he supporting in paragraphs 2, 3, 4, 5, and 10? How does he use examples in each of those paragraphs?

4. Analyze the specific structure and organization of paragraph 3:

    a. What general idea about writing does he propose?
    b. Where does he place that idea in the paragraph?
    c. What examples does he offer to support his general idea?
    d. With what new idea does he conclude the paragraph? How is it related to the beginning idea?

5. Why does Zinsser reproduce exactly portions of the writings of a past president of Princeton University, President Franklin D. Roosevelt, and Henry David Thoreau? How do these sections makes Zinsser's writing clearer, more understandable, or more important?

6. What is the effect on the reader of the words, "Simplify. Simplify," which begin paragraph 6? Why does Zinsser use them at that particular point in the essay? What do they indicate about his attitude towards his subject? Explain.

7. Why does the author begin so many sentences in paragraph 10 with the word *Perhaps?* How does that technique help to *unify* (see page 24) the paragraph?

8. For what reasons does Zinsser include the two pages of "rough" manuscript as a part of the finished essay? What is he trying to show the reader in this way? How does seeing these pages help you to understand better what he is writing about in the completed essay?

9. Overall, how would you describe Zinsser's attitude toward the process and craft of writing? What would you say is his overall attitude toward the future of American writing? Is he generally optimistic or pessimistic? On what does his attitude depend? Refer to specifics in the essay to support your answer.

10. Do you think Zinsser expected other writers, or budding writers, to be the main readers of this essay? Why or why not? If so, with what main idea do you think he would like them to come away from the essay? Do you think readers who were not somehow involved in the writing process would benefit equally from this essay? Why?

EXPLORING THE WRITER'S IDEAS

1. Do you think that Zinsser is ever guilty in this essay of the very "sins" against writing about which he is upset? Could he have simplified any of his points? Select one of Zinsser's paragraphs in the finished essay and explain how you might rewrite it more simply.

2. In the reading that you do most often, have you noticed overly cluttered writing? Or, do you feel that the writing is at its clearest level of presentation and understanding for its audience? Bring to class some examples of this writing and be prepared to discuss it. In general, what do you consider the relation between the simplicity or complexity of a piece of writing and its intended readership?

3. In the note to the two rough manuscript pages included with this essay, Zinsser implies that the process of rewriting and simplifying may be endless. How do you know when to stop trying to rewrite an essay, story, or poem? Do you ever really feel satisfied that you've reached the end of the rewriting process?

4. Choose one of the rough manuscript paragraphs and compare it to the finished essay. Which do you feel is better? Why? Is there anything Zinsser deleted from the rough copy that you feel he should have retained? Why?

5. Comment on Zinsser's assertion that "Thinking clearly is a conscious act that the writer must force upon himself" (par. 13). How does this opinion compare with the opinions of the three other writers in this chapter?

IDEAS FOR WRITING

Guided Writing

In a 500- to 750-word essay, write about what you feel are some of the problems that you face as a writer.

1. In the first paragraph, identify the problems that you plan to discuss.

2. In the course of your essay, relate your problems more generally to the society-at-large.

3. Identify what, in your opinion, is the "secret" of good writing. Give specific examples of what measures to take to achieve that secret process and thereby to eliminate some of your problem.

4. Try to include one or two accurate reproductions of your writing to illustrate your composing techniques.

5. Point out what you believe were the major causes of your difficulties as a writer.

6. Toward the end of your essay, explain the type of writer that you would like to be in order to succeed in college.

More Writing Projects

1. Reread an essay that you wrote recently. Even if you've already received it back with a grade and comments from your instructor, rewrite the essay, simplifying where appropriate.

2. Compare the need to "simplify" in writing to the desirability of simplifying some other process or activity, such as making an omelet, buying an automobile, or learning to play tennis, for example.

3. Over a course of a few days, listen to the same news reporter or talk-show host on television or radio and make a list of at least ten examples that indicate the use of "unnecessary words, circular constructions, pompous frills, and meaningless jargon." Or, compile such a list from an article in a newspaper or magazine you read regularly. Then write an essay presenting and commenting on these examples.

On Keeping a Notebook

Joan Didion

Joan Didion is an American novelist and essayist whose works include the novel *Play It As It Lays* (1970) and the essay collection *The White Album* (1979). Much of her writing deals with what she considers an inherent lack of fulfillment in contemporary American life. In the essay that follows, Didion discusses the meanings and processes of keeping a notebook—what she describes as a "compulsive" and "inexplicable" impulse—which, nevertheless, is a valuable and often crucial prewriting activity. As you read this essay, consider what might prompt you to make notes on your experiences, thoughts, and feelings.

Words to Watch

crepe-de-Chine (par. 1)   a fine, soft, crinkly cloth

presentiment (par. 4)   a feeling that something is about to happen

verisimilitude (par. 7)   the appearance of truth; realism

delude (par. 8)   mislead

aperçus (par. 8)   insights

diffident (par. 10)   timid; unassertive

self-effacing (par. 10)   shy; expressing a negative self-image

affect (par. 10)   to put on a pretense

absorption (par. 10)   intense interest

patently (par. 11)   openly

indiscriminate (par. 11)   without plan or pattern

marginal (par. 12)   at the outer fringes of importance

ambergris (par. 13)   a waxy substance used in perfumery

magpie (par. 14)   a person who chatters noisily

" 'That woman Estelle,' " the note reads, " 'is partly the reason why George Sharp and I are separated today.' *Dirty crepe-de-Chine wrapper, hotel bar, Wilmington RR, 9:45 A.M. August Monday morning.*"

Since the note is in my notebook, it presumably has

some meaning to me. I study it for a long while. At first I have
only the most general notion of what I was doing on an August
Monday morning in the bar of the hotel across from the Pennsylvania Railroad station in Wilmington, Delaware (waiting for
a train? missing one? 1960? 1961? why Wilmington?), but I do
remember being there. The woman in the dirty crepe-de-Chine
wrapper had come down from her room for a beer, and the
bartender had heard before the reason why George Sharp and
she were separated today. "Sure," he said, and went on mopping the floor. "You told me." At the other end of the bar is a
girl. She is talking, pointedly, not to the man beside her but to
a cat lying in the triangle of sunlight cast through the open
door. She is wearing a plaid silk dress from Peck & Peck, and
the hem is coming down.

   Here is what it is: the girl has been on the Eastern Shore,   3
and now she is going back to the city, leaving the man beside
her, and all she can see ahead are the viscous summer sidewalks and the 3 A.M. long-distance calls that will make her lie
awake and then sleep drugged through all the steaming mornings left in August (1960? 1961?). Because she must go directly
from the train to lunch in New York, she wishes that she had
a safety pin for the hem of the plaid silk dress, and she also
wishes that she could forget about the hem and the lunch and
stay in the cool bar that smells of disinfectant and malt and
make friends with the woman in the crepe-de-Chine wrapper.
She is afflicted by a little self-pity, and she wants to compare
Estelles. That is what that was all about.

   Why did I write it down? In order to remember, of   4
course, but exactly what was it I wanted to remember? How
much of it actually happened? Did any of it? Why do I keep a
notebook at all? It is easy to deceive oneself on all those
scores. The impulse to write things down is a peculiarly compulsive one, inexplicable to those who do not share it, useful
only accidentally, only secondarily, in the way that any com-
pulsion tries to justify itself. I suppose that it begins or does
not begin in the cradle. Although I have felt compelled to
write things down since I was five years old, I doubt that my
daughter ever will, for she is a singularly blessed and accept-
ing child, delighted with life exactly as life presents itself to

her, unafraid to go to sleep and unafraid to wake up. Keepers
of private notebooks are a different breed altogether, lonely
and resistant rearrangers of things, anxious malcontents, children afflicted apparently at birth with some presentiment of
loss.

My first notebook was a Big Five tablet, given to me by   5
my mother with the sensible suggestion that I stop whining
and learn to amuse myself by writing down my thoughts. She
returned the tablet to me a few years ago; the first entry is an
account of a woman who believed herself to be freezing to
death in the Arctic night, only to find, when day broke, that
she had stumbled onto the Sahara Desert, where she would
die of the heat before lunch. I have no idea what turn of a five-
year-old's mind could have prompted so insistently "ironic"
and exotic a story, but it does reveal a certain predilection for
the extreme which has dogged me into adult life; perhaps if I
were analytically inclined I would find it a truer story than any
I might have told about Donald Johnson's birthday party or
the day my cousin Brenda put Kitty Litter in the aquarium.

So the point of my keeping a notebook has never been,   6
nor is it now, to have an accurate factual record of what I have
been doing or thinking. That would be a different impulse entirely, an instinct for reality which I sometimes envy but do
not possess. At no point have I ever been able successfully to
keep a diary; my approach to daily life ranges from the grossly
negligent to the merely absent, and on those few occasions
when I have tried dutifully to record a day's events, boredom
has so overcome me that the results are mysterious at best.
What is this business about "shopping, typing piece, dinner
with E, depressed"? Shopping for what? Typing what piece?
Who is E? Was this "E" depressed, or was I depressed? Who
cares?

In fact I have abandoned altogether that kind of pointless   7
entry; instead I tell what some would call lies. "That's simply
not true," the members of my family frequently tell me when
they come up against my memory of a shared event. "The
party was *not* for you, the spider was *not* a black widow, *it
wasn't that way at all.*" Very likely they are right, for not only
have I always had trouble distinguishing between what hap-

pened and what merely might have happened, but I remain unconvinced that the distinction, for my purposes, matters. The cracked crab that I recall having for lunch the day my father came home from Detroit in 1945 must certainly be embroidery, worked into the day's pattern to lend verisimilitude; I was ten years old and would not now remember the cracked crab. The day's events did not turn on cracked crab. And yet it is precisely that fictitious crab that makes me see the afternoon all over again, a home movie run all too often, the father bearing gifts, the child weeping, an exercise in family love and guilt. Or that is what it was to me. Similarly, perhaps it never did snow that August in Vermont; perhaps there never were flurries in the night wind, and maybe no one else felt the ground hardening and summer already dead even as we pretended to bask in it, but that was how it felt to me, and it might as well have snowed, could have snowed, did snow.

How it felt to me: that is getting closer to the truth about   8 a notebook. I sometimes delude myself about why I keep a notebook, imagine that some thrifty virtue derives from preserving everything observed. See enough and write it down, I tell myself, and then some morning when the world seems drained of wonder, some day when I am only going through the motions of doing what I am supposed to do, which is write—on that bankrupt morning I will simply open my notebook and there it will all be, a forgotten account with accumulated interest, paid passage back to the world out there: dialogue overheard in hotels and elevators and at the hatcheck counter in Pavillon (one middle-aged man shows his hat check to another and says, "That's my old football number"); impressions of Bettina Aptheker and Benjamin Sonnenberg and Teddy ("Mr. Acapulco") Stauffer; careful *aperçus* about tennis bums and failed fashion models and Greek shipping heiresses, one of whom taught me a significant lesson (a lesson I could have learned from F. Scott Fitzgerald, but perhaps we all must meet the very rich for ourselves) by asking, when I arrived to interview her in her orchid-filled sitting room on the second day of a paralyzing New York blizzard, whether it was snowing outside.

I imagine, in other words, that the notebook is about   9

other people. But of course it is not. I have no real business
with what one stranger said to another at the hatcheck counter
in Pavillon; in fact I suspect that the line "That's my old football number" touched not my own imagination at all, but
merely some memory of something once read, probably "The
Eighty-Yard Run." Nor is my concern with a woman in a
dirty crepe-de-Chine wrapper in a Wilmington bar. My stake
is always, of course, in the unmentioned girl in the plaid silk
dress. *Remember what it was to be me:* that is always the
point.

It is a difficult point to admit. We are brought up in the 10
ethic that others, any others, all others, are by definition more
interesting than ourselves; taught to be diffident, just this side
of self-effacing. ("You're the least important person in the
room and don't forget it," Jessica Mitford's governess would
hiss in her ear on the advent of any social occasion; I copied
that into my notebook because it is only recently that I have
been able to enter a room without hearing some such phrase in
my inner ear.) Only the very young and the very old may re-
count their dreams at breakfast, dwell upon self, interrupt
with memories of beach picnics and favorite Liberty lawn
dresses and the rainbow trout in a creek near Colorado
Springs. The rest of us are expected, rightly, to affect absorption in other people's favorite dresses, other people's trout.

And so we do. But our notebooks give us away, for how- 11
ever dutifully we record what we see around us, the common
denominator of all we see is always, transparently, shame-
lessly, the implacable "I." We are not talking here about the
kind of notebook that is patently for public consumption, a
structural conceit for binding together a series of graceful
pensées; we are talking about something private, about bits of
the mind's string too short to use, an indiscriminate and er-
ratic assemblage with meaning only for its maker.

And sometimes even the maker has difficulty with the 12
meaning. There does not seem to be, for example, any point in
my knowing for the rest of my life that, during 1964, 720 tons
of soot fell on every square mile of New York City, yet there
it is in my notebook, labeled "FACT." Nor do I really need to

remember that Ambrose Bierce liked to spell Leland Stanford's name "£eland $tanford" or that "smart women almost always wear black in Cuba," a fashion hint without much potential for practical application. And does not the relevance of these notes seem marginal at best?:

> In the basement museum of the Inyo County Courthouse in Independence, California, sign pinned to a mandarin coat: "This MANDARIN COAT was often worn by Mrs. Minnie S. Brooks when giving lectures on her TEAPOT COLLECTION."

> Redhead getting out of car in front of Beverly Wilshire Hotel, chinchilla stole, Vuitton bags with tags reading:

> MRS LOU FOX
> HOTEL SAHARA
> VEGAS

Well, perhaps not entirely marginal. As a matter of fact, 13 Mrs. Minnie S. Brooks and her MANDARIN COAT pull me back into my own childhood, for although I never knew Mrs. Brooks and did not visit Inyo County until I was thirty, I grew up in just such a world, in houses cluttered with Indian relics and bits of gold ore and ambergris and the souvenirs my Aunt Mercy Farnsworth brought back from the Orient. It is a long way from that world to Mrs. Lou Fox's world, where we all live now, and is it not just as well to remember that? Might not Mrs. Minnie S. Brooks help me to remember what I am? Might not Mrs. Lou Fox help me to remember what I am not?

But sometimes the point is harder to discern. What ex- 14 actly did I have in mind when I noted down that it cost the father of someone I know $650 a month to light the place on the Hudson in which he lived before the Crash? What use was I planning to make of this line by Jimmy Hoffa: "I may have my faults, but being wrong ain't one of them"? And although I think it interesting to know where the girls who travel with the Syndicate have their hair done when they find themselves on the West Coast, will I ever make suitable use of it? Might I not be better off just passing it on to John O'Hara? What is a recipe for sauerkraut doing in my notebook? What kind of

magpie keeps this notebook? *"He was born the night the Titanic went down."* That seems a nice enough line, and I even
recall who said it, but is it not really a better line in life than it
could ever be in fiction?

But of course that is exactly it: not that I should ever use 15
the line, but that I should remember the woman who said it
and the afternoon I heard it. We were on her terrace by the
sea, and we were finishing the wine left from lunch, trying to
get what sun there was, a California winter sun. The woman
whose husband was born the night the *Titanic* went down
wanted to rent her house, wanted to go back to her children in
Paris. I remember wishing that I could afford the house, which
cost $1,000 a month. "Someday you will," she said lazily.
"Someday it all comes." There in the sun on her terrace it
seemed easy to believe in someday, but later I had a low-grade
afternoon hangover and ran over a black snake on the way to
the supermarket and was flooded with inexplicable fear when
I heard the checkout clerk explaining to the man ahead of me
why she was finally divorcing her husband. "He left me no
choice," she said over and over as she punched the register.
"He has a little seven-month-old baby by her, he left me no
choice." I would like to believe that my dread then was for
the human condition, but of course it was for me, because I
wanted a baby and did not then have one and because I
wanted to own the house that cost $1,000 a month to rent and
because I had a hangover.

It all comes back. Perhaps it is difficult to see the value 16
in having one's self back in that kind of mood, but I do see it;
I think we are well advised to keep on nodding terms with the
people we used to be, whether we find them attractive company or not. Otherwise they turn up unannounced and surprise us, come hammering on the mind's door at 4 A.M. of a
bad night and demand to know who deserted them, who be-
trayed them, who is going to make amends. We forget all too
soon the things we thought we could never forget. We forget
the loves and the betrayals alike, forget what we whispered
and what we screamed, forget who we were. I have already
lost touch with a couple of people I used to be; one of them, a
seventeen-year-old, presents little threat, although it would be

of some interest to me to know again what it feels like to sit on
a river levee drinking vodka-and-orange-juice and listening to
Les Paul and Mary Ford and their echoes sing "How High the
Moon" on the car radio. (You see I still have the scenes, but
I no longer perceive myself among those present, no longer
could even improvise the dialogue.) The other one, a twenty-
three-year-old, bothers me more. She was always a good deal
of trouble, and I suspect she will reappear when I least want
to see her, skirts too long, shy to the point of aggravation, always the injured party, full of recriminations and little hurts
and stories I do not want to hear again, at once saddening me
and angering me with her vulnerability and ignorance, an ap-
parition all the more insistent for being so long banished.

It is a good idea, then, to keep in touch, and I suppose   17
that keeping in touch is what notebooks are all about. And we
are all on our own when it comes to keeping those lines open
to ourselves: your notebook will never help me, nor mine you.
"So what's new in the whiskey business?" What could that
possibly mean to you? To me it means a blonde in a Pucci
bathing suit sitting with a couple of fat men by the pool at the
Beverly Hills Hotel. Another man approaches, and they all regard one another in silence for a while. "So what's new in the
whiskey business?" one of the fat men finally says by way of
welcome, and the blonde stands up, arches one foot and dips
it in the pool, looking all the while at the cabana where Baby
Pignatari is talking on the telephone. That is all there is to
that, except that several years later I saw the blonde coming
out of Saks Fifth Avenue in New York with her California
complexion and a voluminous mink coat. In the harsh wind
that day she looked old and irrevocably tired to me, and even
the skins in the mink coat were not worked the way they were
doing them that year, not the way she would have wanted
them done, and there is the point of the story. For a while after that I did not like to look in the mirror, and my eyes would
skim the newspapers and pick out only the deaths, the cancer
victims, the premature coronaries, the suicides, and I stopped
riding the Lexington Avenue IRT because I noticed for the
first time that all the strangers I had seen for years—the man
with the seeing-eye dog, the spinster who read the classified

pages every day, the fat girl who always got off with me at Grand Central—looked older than they once had.

It all comes back. Even that recipe for sauerkraut: even 18 that brings it back. I was on Fire Island when I first made that sauerkraut, and it was raining, and we drank a lot of bourbon and ate the sauerkraut and went to bed at ten, and I listened to the rain and the Atlantic and felt safe. I made the sauerkraut again last night and it did not make me feel any safer, but that is, as they say, another story.

BUILDING VOCABULARY

1. Throughout this essay, Didion makes references to numerous people, places, events, books, and groups. The following is a list of twenty such references. From this list, select ten to research and write explanations for. Then, discuss the others with classmates so that you will understand the significance of all. (*Note:* The number of the paragraph in which the reference appears follows in parentheses.)

Peck & Peck (par. 2)
the Arctic (par. 5)
Sahara Desert (par. 5)
F. Scott Fitzgerald (par. 8)
the Pavillon (par. 8)
"The Eighty-Yard Run" (par. 8)
Colorado Springs (par. 9)
Ambrose Bierce (par. 12)
Leland Stanford (par. 12)
the Crash (par. 14)
Jimmy Hoffa (par. 14)
John O'Hara (par. 14)
the Syndicate (par. 14)
Les Paul (par. 16)
Mary Ford (par. 16)
Pucci (par. 17)
Beverly Hills Hotel (par. 17)
Lexington Avenue IRT (par. 17)

Grand Central (par. 17)
Fire Island (par. 18)

2. *Figurative language* derives from imaginative, creative comparisons and descriptions that are not strictly logical; sometimes it relies entirely on imaginative connections in the writer's mind, which require creative thinking on the reader's part to understand.

The following are but *a few* examples of the often startling figurative language that Didion uses throughout this essay. For each, look back to the point in the essay where it occurs and do your best to explain it in more *literal* (or realistic) terms. Then, find and list five more examples of figurative language in the essay.

   a. triangle of sunlight (par. 2)
   b. steamy mornings (par. 3)
   c. the vicious summer sidewalks (par. 3)
   d. a certain predilection for the extreme (par. 5)
   e. an instinct for reality (par. 6)
   f. some morning when the world seems drained of wonder (par. 8)
   g. that bankrupt morning (par. 8)
   h. a structural conceit for binding together a series of graceful *pensées* (par. 11)
   i. bits of the mind's string too short to use (par. 11)
   j. come hammering on the mind's door at 4 A.M. of a bad night (par. 16)

UNDERSTANDING THE WRITER'S IDEAS

1. What is the meaning of the first paragraph? If you hadn't read the second paragraph, would the first have had the same meaning? Any meaning? Explain.

2. Who is the woman "wearing a plaid silk dress from Peck & Peck" mentioned in paragraph 2? How do you know? Summarize the woman's situation. What does the author mean when she writes, "She wants to compare Estelles"?

3. What is Didion's opinion about "the impulse to write things down"? When did it begin for her? Does she feel that her daughter will do the same? Why? Does this please or displease Didion? Why? For what reason did Didion's mother first encourage her to write things down? What was her first story?

4. Summarize as clearly as possible Joan Didion's *reasons* for keeping a notebook. Then, summarize her *attitude* about keeping a notebook. Draw your answers from the essay and quote at least three specific statements in support of each summary.

5. What does the author specifically mention as *not* a good reason to keep a notebook? Why? What is Didion's distinction between keeping a notebook and keeping a diary? What is her attitude toward diaries? What have been the results of her attempts to keep diaries?

6. According to the author, how important is the distinction between what happened in the past and what might have happened? Why?

7. In paragraph 8, what lesson does the author learn from a "Greek shipping heiress" and how does she learn it? Do you know to whom she is referring? What does she mean when she writes parenthetically: "(a lesson I could have learned from F. Scott Fitzgerald, but perhaps we all must meet the very rich for ourselves)"?

8. According to Didion, what is the relation between the way we see others and the way we see ourselves? What does she mean by "*Remember what it was to be me:* that is always the point" (par. 9)? What does that process say about the process of writing? Why is it "a difficult point to admit" (par. 10)?

9. Throughout the essay, Didion stresses the critical necessity for a writer to know herself, "the implacable 'I' " (par. 11), very well. Why is this so important? Does Didion always seem comfortable with this emphasis on the

self? Explain your answers with specific references to the essay.

10. In her memory, does she prefer herself at age seventeen or at age twenty-three? Explain. Why is it so important to "keep in touch" with past eras in one's life?

11. What is the "It" of the sentence that begins paragraph 16: "It all comes back"? Why does Didion repeat this statement at the beginning of the final paragraph? Does "It" have a different meaning there?

UNDERSTANDING THE WRITER'S TECHNIQUES

1. What is Didion's main point here? Why is she writing this essay?

2. Throughout the essay, Didion is extremely thorough in her use of *details*. What is the effect of such thoroughness? Which descriptions do you find especially well-detailed?

3. For what reasons does Didion begin the essay with a short entry from one of her notebooks? On first reading, did the opening paragraph make sense to you? Why? In your own words, explain the relationship between paragraphs 1 and 2.

4. What is the significance of the five questions and one answer which begin paragraph 4?

5. *Hyperbole* (see Glossary) in writing is exaggeration used figuratively to make a point. Does Didion use hyperbole in this essay? Why? List five examples of hyperbolic writing from this essay and explain the point they are used to make.

6. Why does the author put quotation marks around the word "ironic" in paragraph 5?

7. In paragraph 7, Didion discusses *lies*. What is her meaning for that word as it is used in this paragraph? How is the

technique useful to her as a fiction writer? Support your answer with an example.

8. A *metaphor* is a figure of speech that imaginatively compares items from different categories (see Glossary). An *extended metaphor* carries the figure of speech past the initial comparison. How is the following citation from the essay an example of an extended metaphor: "...—on that bankrupt morning I will simply open my notebook and there it will all be, a forgotten account with accumulated interest"? Explain the meaning of the full extended metaphor.

9. How does Didion use short, introductory phrases as transitional devices between paragraphs and sections of this essay? Give examples. How does she use *repetition* as a transitional device between paragraphs 9 and 10? Where else in the essay does repetition play a significant role?

10. *Dialogue* is the written reproduction of speech or conversation (see Glossary). Where does Didion use dialogue in this essay? For what reason and to gain what effect?

11. *Narration* (see Chapter 4) is the telling of a story or series of events. *Anecdotes* are very short narrations, usually of an amusing or autobiographical nature. How does the author use an anecdote in paragraph 15? List at least three other uses of anecdotes and narration in the essay.

12. Based on Didion's essay, in what ways would keeping a notebook be a very valuable prewriting tool (see pages 34–42)?

13. What purpose of keeping a notebook answers the two questions at the end of paragraph 13: "Might not Mrs. Minnie S. Brooks help me to remember what I am? Might not Mrs. Lou Fox help me to remember what I am not?"

14. Describe what you think is the intended *audience* for this essay.

15. *Conclusions* (see Glossary) for essays should ideally make the reader feel that he or she has reached some logical endpoint of the discussion and that nothing important has

been omitted. Do you feel that Didion's conclusion is a good one? Does she have in mind any other purpose than simply "closing" the essay? Explain.

EXPLORING THE WRITER'S IDEAS

1. In the beginning of this essay, and at various points throughout, Didion relates one perception of people and events as recorded in her notebook and another perception as the initial entry is "fleshed out" as a piece of writing. She states: "I tell what some would call lies. . . . I always had trouble distinguishing between what happened and what merely might have happened, but I remain unconvinced that the distinction, for my purposes, matters.

   Similarly, Raymond Carver, another leading American fiction writer, says: "None of my stories really *happened,* of course—I'm not writing autobiography—but most of them bear a resemblance, however faint, to certain life occurrences or situations. But when I try to recall the physical surroundings or furnishings bearing on a story situation (what kind of flowers, if any, were present? Did they give off any odor? etc.), I'm often at a total loss. So I have to make it up as I go along—what the people in the story say to each other, as well as what they do then, after thus and so was said, and what happens to them next."

   In addition, a collection of short stories by the renowned Argentine writer Jorge Luis Borges is entitled *Ficciones,* which literally translates as "Fictions," but has the nuance of "Lies."

   Why do you think these writers see a connection between lies and fiction? Is it possible to view fiction as lies used in the service of telling the truth? Explain. (*Note:* You might want to read ahead to the essays by Langston Hughes, pages 137–139, and Roger Wilkins, pages 144–146, both of which deal with the changing perceptions of events as a person ages and how those changed perceptions can be used creatively.)

2. Reread this essay and pay special attention to the notebook

entries that Didion quotes. Do you find any particular pattern in what she chooses to note? Do the entries represent a particular *point of view* (see Glossary) or outlook on life? Explain.

3. Do you keep a diary, journal, or notebook? If so, how do you choose what to include as entries? What is most valuable to you about keeping a notebook? When did you begin? Why? Would you ever share your notebooks with others? Why or why not? Do you agree with Didion's statement that "our notebooks give us away"? What would someone learn about you from your notebooks?

IDEAS FOR WRITING

Guided Writing

Write an essay entitled "On Writing an Essay." Base your essay on the writing of the essay that you plan to write for this Guided Writing assignment.

1. Begin with some notes or a section of a rough draft for a paragraph of this essay.

2. Follow with an example from the finished paragraph. Briefly elaborate on how you transformed your prewriting notes into a final draft.

3. Discuss the first essay you remember writing. Tell about the process you used then.

4. Use narration to explain by what means you got from the rough to the finished draft of this essay. Include plenty of details, even if they don't seem directly related to writing: fixing a snack; watching the clock; watering the plants; blasting out some Springsteen; desperately searching for your lucky hat.

5. Try to use imaginative, original figurative language and

metaphors. Use at least one extended metaphor (see Glossary).

6. Tell about the personal effects of writing this essay (*besides* fulfilling the assignment!). How did you feel while writing it? When finishing it?

7. Write a conclusion that is purposefully somewhat open-ended.

More Writing Projects

1. Keep a notebook of your dreams for one week. Attempt to wake yourself at the end of a dream and write it down before you experience any interruptions. At the end of the week, reread your entries and try to discover a pattern in your dreams. Use one as the basis for a short story or essay.

2. Pair up with a classmate and keep a notebook *for each other* for one week. That is, each of you should write entries as though you were experiencing the other person's life. At the same time, keep a notebook for yourself. At the end of the week, compare your own notebook with the one kept for you by your partner.

CHAPTER 2

On Reading

The educator Mortimer J. Adler once observed in a celebrated essay, "How to Make a Book Your Own," that reading is like a conversation between you and the author. This "conversation" opens new universes, challenges your opinions, enhances your understanding of yourself and of others, of your past, present, and future. Knowledge of books—your ability to engage actively the minds of many writers who have much to tell you—is the mark of a literate person.

Just as you cannot be literate in today's complex world with weak writing skills, you cannot be literate with mediocre reading abilities. One of the writers in this section, George Steiner, laments the decline of reading, arguing that it is rapidly becoming a lost art. Admittedly, today we are surrounded by 150-channel cablevision, remote-control VCRs, and other high-tech video forms that tempt our eyes and compete for our attention. Yet precisely because we are in a challenging and potentially dangerous high-tech era, the ability to understand and learn from what others have written over time is an indispensable resource. After all, not everyone communicates by electronic media alone.

Of course, when we first learn to read as children we are not exclusively interested in practical knowledge that will help us prosper in today's society, but more perhaps in the mystery, magic, and enchantment of words that Eudora Welty describes in her essay in this section. As youngsters, many of us learned to read in much the same way as Scout Finch, the main character in Harper Lee's *To Kill a Mockingbird*. Sitting on her father's lap, she would follow the words on the page as he read aloud to her. Gradually, she came to know many words, and from the sounds or "phonics" that she internalized, she reached a point at which she had enough knowledge and information to figure out new words for herself.

As adults, we must strive for the same active, inquiring, critical intelligence that young people seem naturally blessed with during the act of reading. We must constantly engage ourselves with the text at hand. Of course, not everything we read demands equally careful thought, but with important reading material we should ask ourselves certain key questions:

- What is the writer's primary purpose?
- What is the precise issue or problem that the writer treats?
- Who is the writer? For whom is he or she writing?
- What information, conclusions, and recommendations does the writer present?
- What substantiating evidence does the writer provide to "prove" his or her case?
- Is the total message successful, objective, valid, or persuasive?

These are the minimal expectations that we should have of ourselves as we engage any writer in an active dialogue or debate over ideas.

In this chapter, each of the authors tells us something about his or her own relation to reading. For Eudora Welty, words came to her "as though fed...out of a silver spoon." Malcolm X tells us how reading was so powerful for him that it allowed him to tear down prison walls. Margaret Atwood writes of her bittersweet discovery of literature in her native Canada. And George Steiner openly shares with us his fears of the demise of literate and reading-centered society.

Moon on a Silver Spoon
Eudora Welty

Eudora Welty, born in 1909, is among America's foremost writers, often focusing on the strange ways of life in rural Mississippi. Her novel *The Optimist's Daughter* won the 1972 Pulitzer Prize, and her *Collected Stories* (1980) has been widely acclaimed. In this selection from her autobiography, *One Writer's Beginnings* (1984), Welty uses delightful descriptions and narrations of her childhood to tell how she developed her love for reading.

Words to Watch

sap (par. 4)   to drain away

gratitude (par. 10)   thankfulness

essential (par. 10)   absolutely necessary

keystone (par. 10)   something on which associated things depend for support

wizardry (par. 11)   magic

acute (par. 13)   very specific or serious

elders (par. 13)   older people

ailment (par. 14)   illness

insatiability (par. 16)   inability to be satisfied

lingers (par. 18)   stays with

On a visit to my grandmother's in West Virginia, I stood 1
inside the house where my mother had been born and where
she grew up.

"Here's where I first began to read my Dickens," 2
Mother said, pointing. "Under that very bed. Hiding my candle. To keep them from knowing I was up all night."

"But where did it all *come* from?" I asked her at last. 3
"All that Dickens?"

"Why, Papa gave me that set of Dickens for agreeing to 4
let them cut off my hair," she said. "In those days, they
thought very long, thick hair like mine would sap a child's

strength. I said *No!* I wanted my hair left the very way it was. They offered me gold earrings first. I said *No!* I'd rather keep my hair. Then Papa said, 'What about books? I'll have them send a whole set of Charles Dickens to you, right up the river from Baltimore, in a barrel.' I agreed.''

My mother had brought that set of Dickens to our house   5 in Jackson, Miss.; those books had been through fire and water before I was born, she told me, and there they were, lined up—as I later realized, waiting for *me*.

I learned from the age of two or three that any room in   6 our house, at any time of day, was there to read in, or to be read to. My mother read to me. She'd read to me in the big bedroom in the mornings, when we were in her rocker together, which ticked in rhythm as we rocked, as though we had a cricket accompanying the story. She'd read to me in the dining room on winter afternoons in front of the coal fire, with our cuckoo clock ending the story with "Cuckoo," and at night when I'd got in my own bed. I must have given her no peace.

It had been startling and disappointing to me to find out   7 that storybooks had been written by *people,* that books were not natural wonders, coming up of themselves like grass. Yet regardless of where they came from, I cannot remember a time when I was not in love with them—with the books themselves, cover and binding and the paper they were printed on, with their smell and their weight and with their possession in my arms, captured and carried off to myself.

Neither of my parents had come from homes that could   8 afford to buy many books, but though it must have been something of a strain on his salary, my father was all the while carefully selecting and ordering away for what he and Mother thought we children should grow up with.

Besides the bookcase in the living room, which was al-   9 ways called the library, there were the encyclopedia tables and dictionary stand under windows in our dining room. There was a full set of Mark Twain and a short set of Ring Lardner in

our bookcase, and those were the volumes that in time united
us as parents and children.

I live in gratitude to my parents for initiating me—and as   **10**
early as I begged for it, without keeping me waiting—into
knowledge of the word, into reading and spelling, by way of
the alphabet. They taught it to me at home in time for me to
begin to read before starting school. I believe the alphabet is
no longer considered an essential piece of equipment for traveling through life. In my day it was the keystone to knowledge. You learned the alphabet as you learned "Now I lay
me" and the Lord's Prayer, and your father's and mother's
name and address and telephone number, all in case you were
lost.

My love for the alphabet, which endures, grew out of re-   **11**
citing it, but before that, out of seeing the letters on the page.
In my own storybooks, before I could read them for myself, I
fell in love with various winding, enchanted-looking initials at
the heads of fairy tales. In "Once upon a time," an "O" had
a rabbit running it as a treadmill, his feet upon flowers. When
the day came, years later, for me to see the Book of Kells,
Gospels from the ninth century, all the wizardry of letter, initial and word swept over me, a thousand times over, and the
illustration, the gold, seemed a part of the word's beauty and
holiness that had been there from the start.

In my sensory education I include my physical aware-   **12**
ness of the word. Of a certain word, that is; the connection it
has with what it stands for. Around age six, perhaps, I was
standing by myself in our front yard waiting for supper, just at
that hour in a late summer day when the sun is already below
the horizon and the risen full moon in the visible sky stops being chalky and begins to take on light. There comes the moment, and I saw it then, when the moon goes from flat to
round. For the first time it met my eyes as a globe. The word
"moon" came into my mouth as though fed to me out of a silver spoon. Held in my mouth the moon became a word. It had
the roundness of a Concord grape that Grandpa took off his
vine and gave me to suck out of its skin and swallow whole, in
Ohio.

Long before I wrote stories, I listened for stories. Lis-   **13** tening *for* them is something more acute than listening *to* them. I supposed it's an early form of participation in what goes on. Listening children know stories are *there*. When their elders sit and begin, children are just waiting and hoping for one to come out, like a mouse from its hole.

When I was six or seven, I was taken out of school and 14 put to bed for several months for an ailment the doctor described as "fast-beating heart." I never dreamed I could learn away from the schoolroom, and that bits of enlightenment far-reaching in my life went on as ever in their own good time.

An opulence of storybooks covered my bed. As I read 15 away, I was Rapunzel, or the Goose Girl, or the princess in one of the *Thousand and One Nights* who mounted the roof of her palace every night and of her own radiance faithfully lighted the whole city just by reposing there.

My mother was very sharing of this feeling of insatiabil- 16 ity. Now, I think of her as reading so much of the time while doing something else. In my mind's eye *The Origin of Species* is lying on the shelf in the pantry under a light dusting of flour—my mother was a bread maker; she'd pick it up, sit by the kitchen window and find her place, with one eye on the oven.

I'm grateful, too, that from my mother's example, I 17 found the base for worship—that I found a love of sitting and reading the Bible for myself and looking up things in it.

How many of us, the Southern writers-to-be of my gen- 18 eration, were blessed in one way or another if not blessed alike, in not having gone deprived of the King James Version of the Bible. Its cadence entered into our ears and our memories for good. The evidence, or the ghost of it, lingers in all our books.

"In the beginning was the Word." 19

BUILDING VOCABULARY

1. Identify the following references to authors, books, and stories from Welty's essay:

    a. Charles Dickens
    b. Mark Twain
    c. Ring Lardner
    d. the Book of Kells
    e. Gospels
    f. Rapunzel
    g. the Goose Girl
    h. the *Thousand and One Nights*
    i. *The Origin of Species*
    j. the King James version of the Bible

2. Write definitions and your own sentences for the following words:

initiating (par. 10)
enchanted-looking (par. 11)
treadmill (par. 11)
holiness (par. 11)
enlightenment (par. 14)
opulence (par. 15)
radiance (par. 15)
reposing (par. 15)
deprived (par. 18)
cadence (par. 18)

UNDERSTANDING THE WRITER'S IDEAS

1. Where did Welty's grandmother come from? Where was Welty herself brought up? Why did Welty's grandparents want to cut off their daughter's hair?

2. For what reason did Welty's mother receive a set of Charles Dickens's works? What does this tell you about the attitude toward reading in Welty's family? Whathappened to the set of Dickens? Although Welty doesn't say so, what do you think she did with the books? Why?

3. How did the way Welty's mother felt toward books affect her child's attitude toward reading? In what ways did the

conditions in Welty's home contribute to her attitude toward books?

4. Why does the author write of her mother, "I must have given her no peace" (par. 6)?

5. Why was it "startling and disappointing" for Welty to find out that story books were written *by people?* Where did she think they came from? Aside from the stories themselves, what is it that the author loves so much about books?

6. For what reasons does Welty feel that learning the alphabet is so important? To what other learning processes does she compare it? Before she learned to recite her alphabet, why was it so important to her?

7. Explain in your own words what Welty considers to be the relation between physical sensations and learning words. According to the author, why is it important for parents to read to their children?

8. For what reason was the young Welty taken out of school? How did this affect her attitude toward reading? How did her mother influence her at this time?

9. At the time of writing this piece, Welty was in her mid-seventies. Explain what she sees as the relation between the Bible and southern writers of her generation. By what descriptions and references in the essay does she indicate her feelings for the Bible?

10. Identify the source of the final sentence. Why is it especially significant to this essay?

UNDERSTANDING THE WRITER'S TECHNIQUES

1. Why does Welty use an image (see Glossary) for her title instead of choosing a more straightforward one, such as Joan Didion's "On Keeping a Notebook" (pages 34–42),

Aaron Copland's "What to Listen for in Music" (pages 303–309), or Bruno Bettelheim's "Fairy Tales and Modern Stories" (pages 230–233)? What effect does she achieve with the title? What does the title mean?

2. A *reminiscence* is a narrative account of a special memory. How does Welty use reminiscence in this essay?

3. What is the main idea of Welty's essay? Is there any point at which she directly states that main idea? Explain.

4. The *tone* of an essay is the expression of the writer's attitude toward the topic (see Glossary). Describe the tone of this essay. What specifically about the writing contributes to that tone?

5. *Description* helps the reader to "see" objects and scenes, and to feel their importance through the author's eyes. *Narration*—the telling of a story—helps the reader follow a sequence of events. (See Chapters 3 and 4.) Both techniques rely on the writer's skill in choosing and presenting *details*. In what way does Welty make use of description and narration in this essay? How would you evaluate her use of details?

6. Placing words in *italics* emphasizes them. Where does the author use italics in this essay? Why does she use them?

7. What does Welty mean by the italicized phrase in the statement "Those books had been *through fire and water* before I was born" (par. 5)? How does the image contribute to the point she's making?

8. The writing of *dialogue,* often used as part of a narration, is the technique whereby a writer either reproduces words actually spoken or invents speech that logically fits into the essay or story. How does Welty use dialogue here? In what ways does it affect your understanding or enjoyment of the writing?

9. *Similes* are imaginative comparisons using the words "like" or "as" (see Glossary). Use of similes often enlivens the writing and makes it memorable.

In your own words explain what is being compared in the following similes drawn from Welty's essay, and tell how they contribute to the essay:

a. ...we were in her rocker together, which ticked in rhythm as we rocked, *as though we had a cricket accompanying the story.* (par. 6)

b. The word "moon" came into my mouth *as though fed to me out of a silver spoon.* (par. 12)

c. Listening children know stories are *there.* When their elders sit and begin, children are just waiting for one to come out, *like a mouse from its hole.* (par. 13)

10. Throughout this essay, Welty refers to "the word." Is she referring to a specific word or to a more abstract concept? Explain. Reread the essay and find and list all references to "the word." What is the relation between them all? How do they work to keep the essay *coherent* and *unified* (see Glossary)? How do they build to the reference in the final sentence? Why is "the Word" capitalized there?

EXPLORING THE WRITER'S IDEAS

1. Welty believes that it is very important for parents to read to their children. Some specialists in child development even advocate reading to infants still in the womb and to babies before they've spoken their first words. For what reasons might such activities be important? Do you personally feel they are important or useful? Would you read to an unborn infant? Why or why not? If you would, *what* would you read?

2. Welty was born in 1909 and obviously belongs to a different generation from the vast majority of college students today. Do you feel that her type of love and advocacy of reading are as valid for the current generation, raised on television, video, cassettes, VCRs, CDs, satellite dishes, and MTV? Explain.

3. Welty describes her love of books as going beyond the words and stories they contain to their physical and visual attributes. What objects—not other people—do you love or respect with that intensity? Tell a little about why and how you have developed this feeling.

IDEAS FOR WRITING

Guided Writing

Write an essay that describes your own attitude toward reading.

1. In order to set the stage for the discussion of your attitude, begin by recalling details about a moment with a parent or other adult.

2. Use dialogue as part of this scene.

3. Go as far back in your childhood as you can possibly remember and narrate two or three incidents that help explain the formation of your current attitude toward reading.

4. Use sensory language (color, sound, smell, touch, and taste) to show how the environment of the home where you grew up helped shape your attitude.

5. Tell about a particular, special childhood fascination with something you *saw*—not read—in a book.

6. Try to describe the first time you were conscious of the *meaning* of a particular word.

7. Use at least one *simile* in your essay.

8. Create and keep a consistent *tone* throughout the essay.

9. End your essay with an explanation of how a particular book has been continually influential to you, as well as to others of your generation.

10. Give your essay an unusual title that derives from some description in your essay.

More Writing Projects

1. Write an essay in which you explain why a parent should read regularly to a child.

2. In what way was one of your relatives—mother, father, brother or sister, aunt or uncle—an example to you during your childhood? Write an essay that explains your response.

Prison Studies

Malcolm X

Born Malcolm Little in Omaha, Nebraska, Malcolm X (1925–1965) was a charismatic leader of the black power movement and founded the Organization of Afro-American Unity. In prison, he became a Black Muslim. (He split with this faith in 1963 to convert to orthodox Islam.) "Prison Studies" is excerpted from the popular and fascinating *Autobiography of Malcolm X*, which he cowrote with *Roots* author Alex Haley. The essay describes the writer's struggle to learn to read, as well as the joy and power he felt when he won that struggle.

Words to Watch

emulate (par. 2)   imitate, especially from respect

motivation (par. 2)   reason to do something

tablets (par. 3)   writing notebooks

bunk (par. 9)   small bed

rehabilitation (par. 10)   the process of restoring to a state of usefulness or constructiveness

inmate (par. 10)   prisoner

corridor (par. 13)   hallway; walkway

vistas (par. 15)   mental overviews

confers (par. 15)   bestows; gives ceremoniously

alma mater (par. 15)   the college that one has attended

Many who today hear me somewhere in person, or on television, or those who read something I've said, will think I went to school far beyond the eighth grade. This impression is due entirely to my prison studies. 1

It had really begun back in the Charlestown Prison, when Bimbi first made me feel envy of his stock of knowledge. Bimbi had always taken charge of any conversation he was in, and I had tried to emulate him. But every book I picked up had few sentences which didn't contain anywhere from one to nearly all of the words that might as well have 2 been in Chinese. When I just skipped those words, of course, I really ended up with little idea of what the book said. So I had come to the Norfolk Prison Colony still going through only book-reading motions. Pretty soon, I would have quit even these motions, unless I had received the motivation that I did.

I saw that the best thing I could do was get hold of a dictionary—to study, to learn some words. I was lucky enough to reason also that I should try to improve my penmanship. It was sad. I couldn't even write in a straight line. It was both ideas together that moved me to request a dictionary along with some tablets and pencils from the Norfolk Prison Colony school.   3

I spent two days just riffling uncertainly through the dictionary's pages. I'd never realized so many words existed! I didn't know which words I needed to learn. Finally, to start some kind of action, I began copying.   4

In my slow, painstaking, ragged handwriting, I copied into my tablet everything printed on that first page, down to the punctuation marks.   5

I believe it took me a day. Then, aloud, I read back, to myself, everything I'd written on the tablet. Over and over, aloud, to myself, I read my own handwriting.   6

I woke up the next morning, thinking about those words—immensely proud to realize that not only had I written so much at one time, but I'd written words that I never knew were in the world. Moreover, with a little effort, I also could remember what many of these words meant. I reviewed the words whose meanings I didn't remember. Funny thing, from the dictionary first page right now, that "aardvark" springs to my mind. The dictionary had a picture of it, a long-tailed, long-eared, burrowing African mammal, which lives off termites caught by sticking out its tongue as an anteater does for ants.   7

I was so fascinated that I went on—I copied the dictionary's next page. And the same experience came when I studied that. With every succeeding page, I also learned of people and places and events from history. Actually the dictionary is like a miniature encyclopedia. Finally the dictionary's A section had filled a whole tablet—and I went on into the B's. That   8 was the way I started copying what eventually became the entire dictionary. It went a lot faster after so much practice helped me to pick up handwriting speed. Between what I wrote in my tablet, and writing letters, during the rest of my time in prison I would guess I wrote a million words.

I suppose it was inevitable that as my word-base broad- 9 ened, I could for the first time pick up a book and read and now begin to understand what the book was saying. Anyone who has read a great deal can imagine the new world that opened. Let me tell you something; from then until I left that prison, in every free moment I had, if I was not reading in the library, I was reading on my bunk. You couldn't have gotten me out of books with a wedge. Between Mr. Muhammad's teachings, my correspondence, my visitors—usually Ella and Reginald—and my reading of books, months passed without my even thinking about being imprisoned. In fact, up to then, I never had been so truly free in my life. . . .

As you can imagine, especially in a prison where there 10 was heavy emphasis on rehabilitation, an inmate was smiled upon if he demonstrated an unusually intense interest in books. There was a sizable number of well-read inmates, especially the popular debaters. Some were said by many to be practically walking encyclopedias. They were almost celebrities. No university would ask any student to devour literature as I did when this new world opened to me, of being able to read and *understand*.

I read more in my room than in the library itself. An in- 11 mate who was known to read a lot could check out more than the permitted maximum number of books. I preferred reading in the total isolation of my own room.

When I had progressed to really serious reading, every 12 night at about ten P.M. I would be outraged with the "lights out." It always seemed to catch me right in the middle of something engrossing.

Fortunately, right outside my door was a corridor light 13 that cast a glow into my room. The glow was enough to read by, once my eyes adjusted to it. So when "lights out" came, I would sit on the floor where I could continue reading in that glow.

At one-hour intervals the night guards paced past every- 14

room. Each time I heard the approaching footsteps, I jumped
into bed and feigned sleep. And as soon as the guard passed, I
got back out of bed onto the floor area of that light-glow,
where I would read for another fifty-eight minutes—until the
guard approached again. That went on until three or four every morning. Three or four hours of sleep a night was enough
for me. Often in the years in the streets I had slept less than
that.

    I have often reflected upon the new vistas that reading   15
opened to me. I knew right there in prison that reading had
changed forever the course of my life. As I see it today, the
ability to read awoke inside me some long dormant craving to
be mentally alive. I certainly wasn't seeking any degree, the
way a college confers a status symbol upon its students. My
homemade education gave me, with every additional book
that I read, a little bit more sensitivity to the deafness, dumbness, and blindness that was afflicting the black race in America. Not long ago, an English writer telephoned me from London, asking questions. One was, "What's your alma mater?"
I told him, "Books." You will never catch me with a free fifteen minutes in which I'm not studying something I feel might
be able to help the black man....

    Every time I catch a plane, I have with me a book that I   16
want to read—and that's a lot of books these days. If I weren't
out here every day battling the white man, I could spend the
rest of my life reading, just satisfying my curiosity—because
you can hardly mention anything I'm not curious about. I
don't think anybody ever got more out of going to prison than
I did. In fact, prison enabled me to study far more intensively
than I would have if my life had gone differently and I had attended some college. I imagine that one of the biggest troubles
with colleges is there are too many distractions, too much
panty-raiding, fraternities, and boola-boola and all of that.
Where else but in prison could I have attacked my ignorance
by being able to study intensely sometimes as much as fifteen
hours a day?

BUILDING VOCABULARY

1. Throughout the selection, Malcolm X uses *figurative* and *colloquial language* (see Glossary). *Figurative language* involves imaginative comparisons, which go beyond plain or ordinary statements. *Colloquial language* involves informal or conversational phrases and expressions.

   The following are examples of some of the figurative and colloquial usages in this essay. Explain each italicized word group in your own words.

   a. *going through* only *book-reading motions* (par. 2)
   b. I was *lucky enough* (par. 3)
   c. *Funny thing* (par. 7)
   d. can imagine *the new world that opened* (par. 9)
   e. *You couldn't have gotten me out of books with a wedge* (par. 9)
   f. an inmate was *smiled upon* (par. 10)
   g. to be practically *walking encyclopedias* (par. 10)
   h. ask any student *to devour literature* (par. 10)
   i. changed forever *the course of my life* (par. 15)
   j. *some long dormant craving* to be *mentally alive* (par. 15)
   k. *the deafness, dumbness, and blindness that was afflicting* the black race in America (par. 15)
   l. Every time I *catch a plane* (par. 16)
   m. every day *battling the white man* (par. 16)
   n. just *satisfying my curiosity* (par. 16)
   o. *boola-boola and all of that* (par. 16)
   p. I have *attacked my ignorance* (par. 16)

2. Find the following words in the essay. Write brief definitions for them *without using a dictionary*. If they are unfamiliar to you, try to guess their meaning based on the context in which they appear.

   a. riffling (par. 4)
   b. painstaking (par. 5)
   c. ragged (par. 5)
   d. emphasis (par. 10)
   e. distractions (par. 16)
   f. burrowing (par. 7)
   g. inevitable (par. 9)

UNDERSTANDING THE WRITER'S IDEAS

1. What was the highest level of formal education that the writer achieved? How is this different from the impression most people got from him? Why?

2. Who was Bimbi? Where did Malcolm X meet him? How was Bimbi important to the writer?

3. What does the author mean by writing that when he tried to read, most of the words "might as well have been in Chinese"? What happened when he skipped over such words? What motivated him to change his way of reading?

4. Why did Malcolm X start trying to improve his handwriting? How was it connected to his desire to improve his reading ability? Briefly describe how he went about this dual process. How did he feel after the first day of this process? Why?

5. How is the dictionary "like a miniature encyclopedia"?

6. Judging from this essay and his description of his "homemade education," how much time did Malcolm X spend in prison? Does the fact that he was in prison affect your appreciation of his learning process? How?

7. What is a "word-base" (par. 9)? What happened once the author's word-base expanded? How did this give him a sense of freedom?

8. Who is "Mr. Muhammad"?

9. Why did the prison officials like Malcolm X? What special privileges came to him as a result of this favorable opinion?

10. Why was Malcolm X angered with the "lights out" procedure? How did he overcome it?

11. What does the following sentence tell you about Malcolm X's life: "Often in the years in the streets I had slept less than that" (par. 14)?

12. Characterize the writer's opinion of a college education.

How does he compare his education to a college degree?
How did his education influence his understanding of his
place and role in American society?

13. In your own words, describe the writer's attitude toward
American blacks. Toward the relation between blacks and
whites?

14. To what main purpose in life does the writer refer? What
was the relation between this purpose and his feelings
about reading? Use one word to describe Malcolm X's attitude toward reading.

15. What is the meaning of the conclusion?

UNDERSTANDING THE WRITER'S TECHNIQUES

1. Later in the book, you will learn about the techniques of
Process Analysis (Chapter 9) and *Cause-and-Effect Analysis* (Chapter 10). Briefly, process analysis tells the reader
how something is done, while cause-and-effect analysis explains *why* one thing leads to or affects another.

   For this essay, outline step-by-step the process whereby
Malcolm X developed his ability to read and enthusiasm for
reading. Next, for each step in your outline, explain why
one step led to the next.

2. *Narration* (Chapter 4) is the telling of a story or the orderly
relating of a series of events. How does Malcolm X use
narration in this essay? How does he order the events of
his narration?

3. What is the effect of the author writing "Let me tell you
something" in paragraph 9?

4. How is the author's memory of the first page of the dictionary like a dictionary entry itself? What does this say about
the importance of this memory to the author?

5. *Tone* is a writer's attitude toward his or her subject (see

Glossary). Characterize the *tone* of this essay. What elements of the writing contribute to that tone? Be specific.

6. Which paragraphs make up the conclusion of this essay? How does the author develop his conclusion? How does he relate it to the main body of the essay? Do you feel that there is a change in *tone* (see Question 5) in the conclusion? Explain, using specific examples.

7. What is Malcolm X's main purpose in writing this essay? For whom is it intended? How do you know?

EXPLORING THE WRITER'S IDEAS

1. Malcolm X writes about his newly found love of reading and ability to read: "In fact, up to then, I never had been so truly free in my life." Has learning any particular skill or activity ever given you such a feeling of freedom or joy? Explain.

2. In paragraphs 15 and 16 Malcolm X is rather uncharitable toward a college education. What do you feel was the source of this attitude? Do you think any of his points here are valid? Why? What are your opinions about the quality of the college education you are receiving?

3. The writer also implies that, in some ways, the educational opportunities of prison were superior to those he would have had at college. What is his basis for this attitude? Have you ever experienced a circumstance in which being restricted actually benefited you? Explain.

4. Malcolm X held very strong opinions about the relations between blacks and whites in America. Do some library research on him to try to understand his opinions. You might begin by reading *The Autobiography of Malcolm X*, from which this essay was excerpted. Do you strongly agree or disagree with his feelings? Why?

5. Following Malcolm X's example, handwrite a page from a

dictionary (a pocket dictionary will be fine), copying everything—including punctuation—*exactly!*

How long did it take you? How did it make you feel? Did
you learn anything from the experience?

IDEAS FOR WRITING

Guided Writing

Write an essay in which you tell about an activity that you can
now perform but that once seemed impossible to you.

1. Open your essay with an example in which you compare
   what most people assume about your skill or background in
   the activity to what the reality is.

2. Mention someone who especially influenced you in your
   desire to master this activity.

3. Tell what kept you from giving up on learning this activity.

4. Explain step-by-step the *process* by which you learned
   more and more about the activity. Explain how and why
   one step led to the next.

5. Use *figurative* and *colloquial* language where you think it
   appropriate in your essay.

6. Describe in some detail how you overcame an obstacle, im-
   posed by others, which could have impeded your learning
   process.

7. Use your conclusion to express a deeply felt personal opinion and to generalize your learning of this skill to the population at large.

More Writing Projects

1. Describe a skill or activity that you have always wanted to
   learn, but have not learned yet. Explain why it interests
   you and why you have not learned it yet.

2. Tell about a time when you had to do something that was
against your will, but not physically or emotionally harmful. Did you derive any benefits from doing this thing? How
did you feel afterward? Would you do it again? Why?

Survival

Margaret Atwood

Margaret Atwood is a Canadian poet and novelist whose works, such as *The Edible Woman* (1969) and *Bodily Harm* (1981), often deal with alienation and people's insensitivities toward one another and the environment. In this selection from her 1972 book, *Survival: A Thematic Guide to Canadian Literature,* Atwood explains how, even as a budding Canadian writer, she was almost ignorant of Canadian literature. However, through her richly detailed descriptions, she also communicates the delight she came to experience—and still experiences—in reading Canadian authors.

Words to Watch

enhanced (par. 1)   made more valuable

sniveled (par. 2)   acted in a whining or emotionally weak manner

artifacts (par. 3)   simple, usually hand-made objects such as tools or ornaments (often refers to ancient objects)

stress (par. 4)   emphasis

snares (par. 4)   animal traps

posthaste (par. 4)   immediately

domestic (par. 5)   family- or home-related

menace (par. 5)   threat; danger

curricula (par. 6)   sets of academic courses

I started reading Canadian literature when I was young, 1 though I didn't know it was that; in fact I wasn't aware that I lived in a country with any distinct existence of its own. At school we were being taught to sing "Rule, Britannia" and to draw the Union Jack; after hours we read stacks of Captain Marvel, Plastic Man and Batman comic books, an activity delightfully enhanced by the disapproval of our elders. However, someone had given us Charles G. D. Roberts' *Kings in Exile* for Christmas, and I sniveled my way quickly through these heart-wrenching stories of animals caged, trapped and tormented. That was followed by Ernest Thompson Seton's *Wild Animals I Have Known,* if anything more upsetting because the animals were more actual—they lived in forests, not circuses—and their deaths more mundane: the deaths, not of tigers, but of rabbits.

No one called these stories Canadian literature, and I   2
wouldn't have paid any attention if they had; as far as I was concerned they were just something else to read, along with Walter Scott, Edgar Allan Poe and Donald Duck. I wasn't discriminating in my reading, and I'm still not. I read then primarily to be entertained, as I do now. And I'm not saying that apologetically: I feel that if you remove the initial gut response from reading—the delight or excitement or simply the enjoyment of being told a story—and try to concentrate on the meaning or the shape or the "message" first, you might as well give up, it's too much like all work and no play.

But then as now there were different levels of entertain-   3
ment. I read the backs of Shredded Wheat boxes as an idle pastime, Captain Marvel and Walter Scott as fantasy escape—I knew, even then, that wherever I lived it wasn't *there,* since I'd never seen a castle and the Popsicle Pete prizes advertised on the comic book covers either weren't available in Canada, or cost more—and Seton and Roberts as, believe it or not, something closer to real life. I *had* seen animals, quite a few of them; a dying porcupine was more real to me than a knight in armor or Clark Kent's Metropolis. Old mossy dungeons and Kryptonite were hard to come by where I lived, though I was quite willing to believe they existed somewhere else; but the materials for Seton's stick-and-stone artifacts and live-off-the-land recipes in *Wildwood Wisdom* were readily available, and we could make them quite easily, which we did. Most of the recipes were somewhat inedible, as you'll see if you try Cattail Root Stew or Pollen Pancakes, but the raw ingredients can be collected around any Canadian summer cottage.

However, it wasn't just the content of these books that   4
felt more real to me; it was their shapes, their patterns. The animal stories were about the struggle to survive, and Seton's practical handbook was in fact a survival manual: it laid much stress on the dangers of getting lost, eating the wrong root or berry, or angering a moose in season. Though it was full of helpful hints, the world it depicted was one riddled with pit-

falls, just as the animal stories were thickly strewn with traps and snares. In this world, no Superman would come swooping out of the sky at the last minute to rescue you from the catastrophe; no rider would arrive posthaste with a pardon from the King. The main thing was to avoid dying, and only by a mixture of cunning, experience and narrow escapes could the animal—or the human relying on his own resources—manage that. And, in the animal stories at any rate, there were no final happy endings or ultimate solutions; if the animal happened to escape from the particular crisis in the story, you knew there would be another one later on from which it wouldn't escape.

I wasn't making these analytical judgments at the time, 5 of course. I was just learning what to expect: in comic books and things like *Alice in Wonderland* or Conan Doyle's *The Lost World,* you got rescued or you returned from the world of dangers to a cozy safe domestic one; in Seton and Roberts, because the world of dangers was *the same* as the real world, you didn't. But when in high school I encountered—again as a Christmas present—something labeled more explicitly as Canadian Literature, the Robert Weaver and Helen James anthology, *Canadian Short Stories,* I wasn't surprised. There they were again, those animals on the run, most of them in human clothing this time, and those humans up against it; here was the slight mistake that led to disaster, here was the fatal accident; this was a world of frozen corpses, dead gophers, snow, dead children, and the ever-present feeling of menace, not from an enemy set over against you but from everything surrounding you. The familiar peril lurked behind every bush, and *I knew the names of the bushes.* Again, I wasn't reading this as Canlit, I was just reading it; I remember being elated by some stories (notably James Reaney's "The Bully") and not very interested in others. But these stories felt real to me in a way that Charles Dickens, much as I enjoyed him, did not.

I've talked about these early experiences not because I 6 think that they were typical but because I think that—significantly—they weren't: I doubt that many people my age had even this much contact, minimal and accidental though it was, with their own literature. (Talking about this now makes me feel about 102, because quite a lot has changed since then. But though new curricula are being invented here and there across the country, I'm not convinced that the *average* Canadian child or high school student is likely to run across much more Canadian literature than I did. *Why* this is true is of course one of our problems.)

Still, although I didn't read much Canadian writing, what   7 I did read had a shape of its own that felt different from the shapes of the other things I was reading. What that shape turned out to be, and what I felt it meant in terms of this country, became clearer to me the more I read.

BUILDING VOCABULARY

1. A writer will often use *allusions* (see Glossary) and references to people, events, places, literature, and aspects of a particular culture or era. In order to better understand Atwood's essay, try to identify as many of the following allusions as you can:

    a. "Rule, Britannia," the Union Jack, Captain Marvel, Plastic Man, Batman, G. D. Roberts, Ernest Thompson Seton (par. 1)
    b. Walter Scott, Edgar Allan Poe, Donald Duck (par. 2)
    c. Shredded Wheat, Popsicle Pete, Clark Kent's Metropolis, Kryptonite (par. 3)
    d. *Alice in Wonderland,* Conan Doyle, Charles Dickens (par. 5)

2. Atwood uses numerous common two-word expressions such as "gut response" (par. 2) and "idle pastime" (par. 3). Define these two expressions, then list and define five others from the essay.

3. Select the letter of the word that best defines the italicized word.

    1. *distinct*
    a. wonderful   **b.** cloudy   **c.** well-defined   **d.** careful
    2. *mundane*
    a. common   **b.** tragic   **c.** horrible   **d.** timely

3. *initial*
   a. nervous b. warm c. first d. alphabetic
4. *readily*
   a. inexpensively b. speedily c. willingly d. really
5. *inedible*
   a. unfit for consumption b. delicious c. difficult
   d. different
6. *depicted*
   a. ridiculed b. represented c. longed for d. hated
7. *cunning*
   a. speed b. trickery c. cleverness d. cuteness
8. *cozy*
   a. comfortable b. limited c. familiar d. boring
9. *explicitly*
   a. precisely b. sexually c. unhappily d. hopelessly
10. *fatal*
   a. deadly b. fated c. tragic d. weary
11. *elated*
   a. sad b. gleeful c. confused d. welcome
12. *minimal*
   a. short-lived b. fortunate c. minor d. major

UNDERSTANDING THE WRITER'S IDEAS

1. What point about the sense of national identity for Canadians of her generation (she was born in 1939) does Atwood make in the opening sentence? How does the next sentence illustrate that point? With what nation are "Rule, Britannia" and the Union Jack associated?

2. How did Atwood's parents' attitude toward comic books affect her enjoyment of them?

3. What nationality were the writers Charles G. D. Roberts and Ernest Thompson Seton? What did Atwood feel when she read them for the first time? Why did she read them? What were their respective subject matters?

4. Did the young Atwood enjoy reading? Was she choosy about what she read? What was her main reason for reading? What is it as an adult?

5. According to the writer, what happens if you concentrate too much on the "meaning" of what you are reading?

6. For what purpose would Atwood read things like Walter Scott or Captain Marvel? To where does the italicized *there* in paragraph 3 refer? How did writers such as Seton and Roberts, and the environments they described, feel to Atwood when she first read them? Why? Explain how her references to "Cat-tail Root Stew" and "Pollen Pancakes" connect with this feeling.

7. Summarize in your own words why it was not just Seton's and Roberts's subject matter, but also the "shapes" and "patterns" of their writing that held special significance for Atwood. What was their overview of life? What does their appeal tell you about Atwood's outlook as a child?

8. Contrast the two different types of "worlds of danger" discussed in paragraph 5.

9. How did Atwood react upon reading the anthology *Canadian Short Stories* when in high school? Why? Who are "those animals" (par. 5)? What is "Canlit"?

10. Does Atwood think that the majority of Canadians have a good sense of their national literature? Explain. How has the situation changed since she was a child? How has it remained the same? What is her idea about the connection between reading and self-image? Based on your understanding of the entire essay, what would you assume Atwood sees as "the shape" of Canadian literature as she refers to it in her conclusion?

UNDERSTANDING THE WRITER'S TECHNIQUES

1. Is there a single statement of the main idea of this essay?

Explain. Which paragraphs comprise the introduction, body, and conclusion of this essay?

2. For whom did Atwood write this essay? Is it equally significant to both Canadian and non-Canadian readers? Why?

3. *Transitions* (see Glossary) enable writers to move from one idea to the next, or one paragraph to the next, while maintaining the *coherence* (logical connections) of their ideas. It is interesting to note that Atwood consistently uses grammatical negatives in the first sentences of the paragraphs of this selection.

   Go through the essay and list some of the grammatical negatives that appear in the opening sentence of selected paragraphs. How does this pattern serve as a transition device? For what other reasons might she be using these constructions?

4. At the end of paragraph 2, why does the writer place the word "message" in quotation marks?

5. In paragraph 5, Atwood italicizes a statement of seemingly not much importance on its own: "*I knew the names of the bushes.*" Why does she place it in italics? How is it so significant to the paragraph or the essay?

6. The techniques of *description* and *illustration* (see Glossary) go hand in hand to make a writer's abstract ideas clear and vivid for readers. Generally, how does Atwood use description and illustration in this essay? Choose a particular paragraph and explain in detail what ideas the author's descriptions and illustrations make clear for you.

7. In the Building Vocabulary section, you identified various *allusions* (see page 75) in this essay. For what purpose did the author include so many allusions? Which were the most important to your understanding of the essay? Why?

8. Atwood uses four adjectives composed of between two and four words linked by hyphens. (*Stick-and-stone* in

paragraph 3 is one example.) Find and list the other three. What single word adjectives could she have used instead? How would that have altered the tone of the sentences in which these adjectives appear?

9. Paragraph 6 is at least half composed of an explanation in *parentheses*. What is the main point of paragraph 6? What is Atwood's reason for the parenthetical explanation? How would it have affected the paragraph's meaning if she had written all the same sentences but had omitted the parentheses?

10. What is the significance of the title of this essay? Are there possible multiple meanings? Explain your answer with specific references to the essay.

EXPLORING THE WRITER'S IDEAS

1. Clearly, Atwood is proud of her heritage as a Canadian, as well as of her status as a Canadian writer. Look up and define the following words: *nationalist, patriot, chauvinist*. Which word most closely describes Atwood's attitude in this essay? Why?

2. Atwood makes the point that if you try too hard to understand the "message" of a story, you are likely to miss its "delight or excitement." What different responses do you experience when reading for an assignment versus reading for your own reasons? Describe the differences. Which do you enjoy more? From which do you learn more? Explain. How do you feel that school reading assignments can be made more pleasurable?

3. Do you believe that different countries produce significantly different types of literature? Explain. Discuss some of the best-known authors from countries other than your own. How many have you read? In general, do you more enjoy reading works by authors from your own country (or region) or from elsewhere? Why? How are the two reading experiences different for you?

IDEAS FOR WRITING

Guided Writing

Write an essay that explains how you came to appreciate a particular aspect of your own national culture or ethnic background.

1. Begin by telling when you first became aware of this aspect of your culture. Tell how circumstances or the environment around you did not necessarily encourage your appreciation.

2. Introduce specific examples of this cultural aspect that were important in shaping your appreciation.

3. Where appropriate, use allusions as examples of other things that were more available to you than your own culture.

4. Use specific examples to support your point.

5. Throughout the essay, keep as an unstated purpose to educate your readers to the value and joy of this aspect of your culture.

6. Use clear transitions between paragraphs.

7. Describe how your initial attraction blossomed into a deep appreciation.

8. Explain to your readers your main reason for relating these early experiences. In this overall explanation, include a long parenthetical explanation.

9. Give your essay a one-word title.

More Writing Projects

1. In general, do you prefer to read fiction or nonfiction? Write an essay to explain why. Include specific examples of each.

2. What nation or culture do you feel is especially underrated by the general public? Write an essay that explains why and suggests remedies for this condition.

The Future of Reading

George Steiner

This essay was originally part of the R. R. Bowker Memorial Lecture delivered by educator-writer Steiner in 1985. The piece was then published in *Publishers Weekly* under the title "Books in an Age of Post-Literacy." In it, Steiner laments what he considers the disappearance of the "arts of reading," which he divides into three distinct categories.

Words to Watch

cite (par. 1)   quote by way of example

literacy (par. 1)   the ability to read and write

attendant (par. 2)   accompanying; simultaneous

cortex (par. 2)   the outer layer, or "gray matter," of the brain

hunch (par. 2)   strong, intuitive feeling

breach (par. 2)   break or violation

notion (par. 2)   idea

renders (par. 2)   causes to become

vital (par. 2)   essential

facet (par. 3)   phase; aspect

incommensurable (par. 5)   lacking a common basis for comparison

avocation (par. 6)   occupation that one pursues in addition to what one does for a living; hobby

scriptoria (par. 6)   rooms in medieval monasteries in which scribes hand-copied manuscripts

elite (par. 6)   superior group; upper layer of society

aliterate (par. 7)   lacking the ability to read or write

exigent (par. 8)   demanding

It is hardly necessary for me to cite all the evidence of   1
the depressing state of literacy. These figures from the Department of Education are sufficient: 27 million Americans cannot read at all, and a further 35 million read at a level that is less than sufficient to survive in our society.

But my own worry today is less that of the overwhelm- 2
ing problem of elemental literacy than it is of the slightly more
luxurious problem of the decline in the skills even of the
middle-class reader, of his unwillingness to afford those
spaces of silence, those luxuries of domesticity and time and
concentration, that surround the image of the classic act of
reading. It has been suggested that almost 80 percent of America's *literate,* educated teenagers can no longer read without
an attendant noise (music) in the background or a television
screen flickering at the corner of their field of perception. We
know very little about the cortex and how it deals with simultaneous conflicting input, but every common-sense hunch suggests we should be profoundly alarmed. This breach of concentration, silence, solitude goes to the very heart of our
notion of literacy; this new form of part-reading, of part-
perception against background distraction, renders impossible certain essential acts of apprehension and concentration, let alone that most important tribute any human being
can pay to a poem or a piece of prose he or she really loves,
which is to *learn it by heart.* Not by brain, by heart; the expression is vital.

Under these circumstances, the question of what future 3
there is for the arts of reading is a real one. Ahead of us lie
technical, psychic, and social transformations probably much
more dramatic than those brought about by Gutenberg. The
Gutenberg revolution, as we now know it, took a long time; its
effects are still being debated. The information revolution will
touch every facet of composition, publication, distribution,
and reading. No one in the book industry can say with any
confidence what will happen to the book as we've known it.

It now looks as if the arts of reading will fall into three 4
distinct categories. The first will continue to be the vast,
amorphous mass of reading for distraction, for momentary entertainment—the airport book. I suspect that this kind of reading will more and more involve not cheap paperbacks but cable transmissions to home screens. You will select the book
you wish, the speed at which you wish it to be presented on
the screen, the speed at which you wish the pages to be
turned. Some texts will be read to the viewer by a professional

reader. Whether or not the text will appear on the screen as it is being read is an open question.

The second kind of reading will be for information— 5 what De Quincey called "the literature of knowledge," to distinguish it from fiction, poetry, and drama, which he called "the literature of power." The means to acquire the literature of knowledge—the micro circuit, the silicon chip, the laser disc—will alter our habits beyond anything we can now conceive. "The Library of Babel," the library of all possible libraries that Borges imagined in his fable, will be literally and concretely accessible for personal and institutional use. We will be able to summon it up on a screen, and here the possibility of a basic change in the structures of attention and understanding is almost incommensurable.

What about reading in the old, private, silent sense? This 6 may become as specialized a skill and avocation as it was in the scriptoria and libraries of monasteries during the so-called Dark Ages. We now know these were in fact key ages, radiant in their patience, radiant in their sense of what had to be copied and preserved. Private libraries may once again become as notable and rare as they were when Erasmus and Montaigne were famous for theirs. The habit of furnishing a room, a large room, possibly, with shelves and filling them with books, not paperbacks but bound books, the attempt to collect the complete editions of an author (itself a very special concept) as well as the first editions, not necessarily the rare books of the Morgan Library but the first editions of a modern author, with the hope of owning everything by a writer—good, bad, or indifferent—whom one loves; the ability—above all, the wish— to attend to a demanding text, to master the grammar, the arts of memory, the tactics of repose and concentration that great books demand—these may once more become the practices of an elite, of a mandarinate of silence.

Such a mandarinate, such an elite of book men and book 7 women, will not have the power, the political reach, or the prestige that it had during the Renaissance and the Enlightenment, and almost to the end of the Victorian age. That power almost inevitably will belong to the aliterate. It will belong to the numerate. It will belong increasingly to those who, while technically almost unable to read a serious book and mostly unwilling to do so, can in preadolescence produce software of great delicacy, logical power, and conceptual depth. The power relations are shifting to them, to men and women who, having freed themselves from the heavy burden of actual alphabetic literacy and its constant referential habits, from the fact that almost all great literature refers to other great literature, are *creators*—nonreaders, but creators of a new kind.

Returning home one night, Erasmus is said to have seen a torn piece of print besmirched in the mud. As he bent to pick it up, he uttered a cry of joy, overcome by the wonder of the book, by the sheer miracle of what lies behind picking up such a message. Today, in a vast traffic jam on a highway or in a Manhattan grid, we can insert a cassette of the *Missa Solemnis* into a tape deck. We can, via paperbacks and soon cable television, demand, command, and compel the world's greatest, most exigent, most tragic or delightful literature to be served up for us, packaged and cellophaned for immediacy. These are great luxuries. But it is not certain that they really help the constant, renewed miracle that is the encounter with a book.

BUILDING VOCABULARY

1. Determine the meanings of the following excerpts from this essay and explain them in your own words.

   a. unwillingness to afford those spaces of silence, those luxuries of domesticity (par. 2)
   b. simultaneous conflicting input (par. 2)
   c. renders impossible certain essential acts of apprehension and concentration (par. 2)
   d. The vast, amorphous mass of reading for distraction (par. 4)
   e. is an open question (par. 4)
   f. the tactics of repose and concentration that great books demand (par. 6)
   g. It will belong to the numerate. (par. 7)

h. men and women who, having freed themselves from
the heavy burden of actual alphabetic literacy and its
constant referential habits (par. 7)
i. besmirched in the mud (par. 8)
j. packaged and cellophaned for immediacy (par. 8)

2. Identify these literary references:

Gutenberg
(Thomas) de Quincey
Babel
(Jorge Luis) Borges
Erasmus
Montaigne
the Morgan Library

3. Locate and list at least ten unfamiliar words from the essay. Do not include words that appear in either the Words
to Watch section or Exercises 1 or 2 above. Check a dictionary for meanings and then use each word in an original
sentence.

UNDERSTANDING THE WRITER'S IDEAS

1. According to Steiner in his opening paragraph, how bad
are the problems of illiteracy and underliteracy in this
country? If the population of the United States is approximately 240 million, what percentage are illiterate? Under-
literate?

2. What is the author's meaning in describing a reading level
"that is less than sufficient to survive in our society"?
How would a person's lack of reading skills make basic
survival a problem?

3. What is "elemental literacy"? With what problem is
Steiner more concerned? Why? Does he consider it a
more or less important problem than elemental literacy?
How do you know?

4. To whom do you think Steiner is referring when he writes
of the "middle-class reader"?

5. According to Steiner, what is a major problem with most teenagers who *can* read? What makes this problem so serious?

6. What does the author claim is the best way a reader can show admiration for a piece of writing? What does he mean when he writes, "Not by brain, by heart; the expression is vital"? Why is it vital? How does he play on the expression "by heart"?

7. In paragraph 3, Steiner describes the "technical, psychic, and social transformations" that lie ahead. Briefly describe the meaning of each category and how each one differs from the others.

8. Who was Gutenberg? What was the "Gutenberg revolution"? What is the "information revolution"? According to Steiner, how do they compare?

9. The middle section of this essay, paragraphs 4 through 7, is devoted to what Steiner considers the future of the "arts of reading." He divides this future into "three distinct categories."

   a. Name the three categories.
   b. Briefly summarize each category.
   c. What examples does the author present for each? Do you feel they are valid examples? Explain.
   d. What examples can *you* provide to illustrate each category?

10. Whose terminology is "the literature of knowledge" and "the literature of power"? How do they differ? What types of writing constitute each?

11. Why does Steiner use the term "so-called" to describe the Dark Ages?

12. For what reasons would traditional fine libraries be filled with hardbound rather than paperback books? How are the two kinds of books different? (Other than the obvious reasons, of course.) Which do you prefer? Why?

13. What does Steiner mean by a "mandarinate"? Where

does the term derive from? In your own words, describe Steiner's "worst case scenario" for the future balance of power between intellectuals and "nonreaders."

14. Explain the *denotations* and *connotations* (see Glossary) of the following sentence: "Today, in a vast traffic jam on a highway or in a Manhattan grid, we can insert a cassette of the *Missa Solemnis* into a tape deck." How does Steiner feel about this option? Explain.

15. What does the conclusion tell you about Steiner's mixed feelings toward the future of reading and toward the technical, psychic, and social transformations which confront us?

UNDERSTANDING THE WRITER'S TECHNIQUES

1. What is the writer's main point in this essay? Does he ever state it exactly? Why do you think he does (doesn't) state it exactly?

2. What is the effect of the wording of the opening sentence? Why does the author write that "it is hardly necessary" to say what he clearly feels is *extremely necessary* to say? What assumption does this statement show that he is making about his reader? In your opinion, who is the intended audience for this essay?

3. In the opening paragraph, Steiner makes use of hard facts—statistics. What does he aim to achieve by citing these statistics? Can we trust the figures? Why or why not?

4. In the middle of paragraph 2, why is the word "music" in parentheses after the word "noise"? What attitude of the author does this indicate?

5. *Images* are verbal pictures based on the perceptions of the five senses. What are the images of sound and sight in paragraph 2?

6. *Tone* (see Glossary) refers to the attitude a writer wants to convey to readers about the subject. What tone does Steiner use here? Does this tone indicate a straightforward, analytical approach to the problems discussed? Explain. List three specific examples from the text to illustrate the tone that you perceive.

7. *Diction* (see Glossary) refers to a writer's choice and use of words. We classify *levels of diction*—"informal," "academic," "low-class," "snobbish," and so forth. How would you describe the general level of diction in this essay? Does the level suit the subject matter? Why?

8. In paragraph 3, Steiner refers to "the *arts* of reading." Why does he use the plural? Why not "the *art* of reading"? Which would you more expect? Why?

9. Why does Steiner divide the future of the reading arts into "three distinct categories"? Does he devote equal space and development to each? Which does he feel is the most important? Why?

10. At the beginning of paragraph 6, the writer refers to the "so-called Dark Ages." In the following sentence, he uses the word "radiant" twice. What is the *irony* (see Glossary) that results from using these terms so close together?

EXPLORING THE WRITER'S IDEAS

1. In this essay, Steiner presents a fairly bleak picture of the future of the reading arts as they have been traditionally defined. Do you agree with Steiner's "doom and gloom" forecast? Is there anything about the tone of his essay that makes you more or less inclined to agree?

2. People often ask, "Why is there such a low rate of literacy in the world's most-advanced nation?" (The United States ranks forty-ninth among nations in literacy.) What is your answer to this question?

3. Steiner seems most alarmed that most people no longer
   value silence or solitude. He claims that "background distraction" and "simultaneous conflicting input" all but wipe
   out clear or deep thinking. How important is silence to you
   when you want to be thoughtful or creative? How important is it for you to have background music or images?
   Why?

4. Steiner mentions the "information revolution." He pre-
   dicts that it will change the way we read and prepare texts.
   Along those lines, most serious writers now regard a word
   processor as writers of ten years ago regarded an electric
   typewriter, writers of fifty years ago regarded a pencil and
   good eraser, and writers of a few hundred years ago regarded the quill and inkwell. What are your composing materials and methods? How do different materials, methods,
   and environments affect your ability to write? What do you
   think is the technical future of books and reading?

IDEAS FOR WRITING

Guided Writing

Write an essay entitled "The Future of _____ ."
Fill in the blank with some aspect of American society that
you believe will change dramatically.

1. Begin with a statement expressing your opinion of the current state of this part of American life.

2. To support your opinion, give at least one statistical example from a solid authority.

3. Focus on your specific emotional concern about the current state of this aspect of life.

4. Explain how most people misuse or put down this part of
   life. Offer several sensory *images* (see Glossary) to illustrate your explanation.

5. Concerning this aspect of life, compare the most important trends of the past with those of the present.

6. If appropriate, create categories to support your point.

7. Maintain a significant tone of concern throughout.

8. Make allusions to people and works associated with the subject.

9. Explain how recent changes in society have shifted the balance of power for those seriously concerned with or affected by this subject.

10. End by stating your own attachment to and concern for this subject.

More Writing Projects

1. Write an essay in which you consider truthfully how important you think it is for you to be a topnotch reader in order to succeed in life.

2. List all the books you have read in the past six months. Which did you like best? Least? Why? Compare your list with those of your classmates.

3. It is said that on the national average, Americans read less than one book per person annually. Take a survey of several people who are not students and find out how they fit the national average. Analyze your results by discussing the types of people you interviewed and explaining why your results were either similar to or dissimilar from the national average.

CHAPTER 3

Description

Since a writer's main purpose is to explain things clearly, description is an important aid to good writing. To add liveliness to an essay, descriptive details are necessary to create a visual impression of an object or a scene. As a technique in writing, description matches the sort of details we see in vivid and effective photographs. Good descriptive writers help the reader to "see" objects, scenes, and even moods by means of language.

The essays in this section reflect key qualities in all good descriptive writing. First, description relies on a basic talent that we all have—the ability to see, touch, taste, hear, or smell various elements in the world. Talented descriptive writers refine the power of their five senses in order to recreate people, places, things, emotions, and ideas. Second, in descriptive writing, the author must select details carefully. There might be thousands of details in any given scene, but clearly a writer cannot present all of them. Instead, the writer must choose only those details most useful in painting a picture for the reader. Third, writers must organize their descriptions carefully. With description, the writer must decide on a perspective (for instance, top to bottom, left to right, front to back) and then move carefully from detail to detail. The descriptive writer has a "camera eye" that ranges over its subject in a careful, consistent way. Fourth, descriptive writing creates a "dominant impression" of its subject. This main impression arises from the author's focus on a single subject, and from the feelings that the writer brings to that subject. Finally, descriptive writing offers a thesis or main idea concerning its subject, as does all sound writing. In short, description makes a point.

Writing good descriptive papers is a challenge, because we (like the authors in this section) have to look at our world anew, to remember, to search for meaningful details, to recreate the images around us. As we write descriptive paragraphs and essays, we should keep a basic goal in mind—to permit the reader to see the world that we describe in a fresh, vivid, and concrete way. As descriptive writers, we have to be willing to look at the world, perhaps for the first time, close up.

The Shack

Margaret Laurence

In this selection from Laurence's *Heart of a Stranger* (1976), the Canadian novelist combines lush natural imagery with "portions of memory, presences in the mind" to convey to us her sense of a place to work as a writer. Notice especially how her organization of details and creation of many of her own mysterious and exciting descriptions help create a tone of solitudinous contentment. The Otonabee River described here also figures significantly in Laurence's novel, *The Diviners*.

Words to Watch

slither (par. 1)   to slide or slip along

peril (par. 1)   danger

attributes (par. 2)   characteristics

molten (par. 2)   melted; liquified by heat

drabber (par. 5)   more plain; less fancy

unwieldy (par. 6)   awkward; clumsy; not easily managed

harbinger (par. 6)   something that foreshadows what is to come

dawdle (par. 9)   to delay or spend time idly

saplings (par. 9)   young trees

homesteaded (par. 9)   claimed land by living on and cultivating it

staunch (par. 10)   substantial; steadfast

armorial (par. 10)   like military armor or protective covering

The most loved place, for me, in this country has in fact 1
been many places. It has changed throughout the years, as I
and my circumstances have changed. I haven't really lost any
of the best places from the past, though. I may no longer inhabit them, but they inhabit me, portions of memory, presences in the mind. One such place was my family's summer
cottage at Clear Lake in Riding Mountain National Park, Man-
itoba. It was known to us simply as The Lake. Before the government piers and the sturdy log staircases down to the shore

94

were put in, we used to slither with an exhilarating sense of
peril down the steep homemade branch and dirt shelf-steps,
through the stands of thin tall spruce and birch trees slender
and graceful as girls, passing moss-hairy fallen logs and the
white promise of wild strawberry blossoms, until we reached
the sand and the hard bright pebbles of the beach at the edge
of the cold spring-fed lake where at nights the loons still cried
eerily, before too much humanshriek made them move away
north.

My best place at the moment is very different, although I   2
guess it has some of the attributes of that long-ago place. It is
a small cedar cabin on the Otonabee river in southern Ontario.
I've lived three summers there, writing, birdwatching, river-
watching. I sometimes feel sorry for the people in speedboats
who spend their weekends zinging up and down the river at
about a million miles an hour. For all they're able to see, the
riverbanks might just as well be green concrete and the river
itself flowing with molten plastic.

Before sunup, I'm wakened by birdvoices and, I may   3
say, birdfeet clattering and thumping on the cabin roof. Curs-
ing only slightly, I get up *temporarily,* for the pre-dawn ritual
of lighting a small fire in the old black woodstove (mornings
are chilly here, even in summer) and looking out at the early
river. The waters have a lovely spooky quality at this hour,
entirely mist-covered, a secret meeting of river and sky.

By the time I get up to stay, the mist has vanished and   4
the river is a clear ale-brown, shining with sun. I drink my coffee and sit looking out to the opposite shore, where the giant
maples are splendidly green now and will be trees of flame in
the fall of the year. Oak and ash stand among the maples, and
the grey skeletons of the dead elms, gauntly beautiful even in
death. At the very edge of the river, the willows are everywhere, water-related trees, magic trees, pale green in early
summer, silvergreen in late summer, greengold in autumn.

I begin work, and everytime I lift my eyes from the page   5
and glance outside, it is to see some marvel or other. The joyous dance-like flight of the swallows. The orange-black flash
of the orioles who nest across the river. The amazing takeoff
of a red-winged blackbird, revealing like a swiftly unfolded fan

the hidden scarlet in those dark wings. The flittering of the goldfinches, who always travel in domestic pairs, he gorgeous in black-patterned yellow feathers, she (alas) drabber in greenish grey-yellow.

A pair of great blue herons have their huge unwieldy nest 6 about half a mile upriver, and although they are very shy, occasionally through the open door I hear a sudden approaching rush of air (yes, you can *hear* it) and look up quickly to see the magnificent unhurried sweep of those powerful wings. The only other birds which can move me so much are the Canada geese in their autumn migration flight, their far-off wilderness voices the harbinger of winter.

Many boats ply these waterways, and all of them are 7 given mental gradings of merit or lack of it, by me. Standing low in the estimation of all of us along this stretch of the river are some of the big yachts, whose ego-tripping skippers don't have the courtesy to slow down in cottage areas and whose violent wakes scour out our shorelines. Ranking highest in my good books are the silent unpolluting canoes and rowboats, and next to them, the small outboard motorboats put-putting along and carrying patient fishermen, and the homemade houseboats, unspeedy and somehow cosy-looking, decorated lovingly with painted birds or flowers or gaudy abstract splodges.

In the quiet of afternoon, if no boats are around, I look 8 out and see the half-moon leap of a fish, carp or muskie, so instantaneous that one has the impression of having seen not a fish but an arc of light.

The day moves on, and about four o'clock Linda and Su- 9 san from the nearby farm arrive. I call them the Girls of the Pony Express. Accompanied by dogs and laughter, they ride their horses into my yard, kindly bringing my mail from the rural route postbox up the road. For several summers it was Old Jack who used to drive his battered Volkswagen up to fetch the mail. He was one of the best neighbours and most remarkable men I've ever known. As a boy of eighteen, he had homesteaded a hundred miles north of Regina. Later, he'd been a skilled toolmaker with Ford. He'd travelled to South America and done many amazing things. He was a man whose life had taught him a lot of wisdom. After his much-loved wife died, he moved out here to the river, spending as short a winter as possible in Peterborough, and getting back into his cottage the first of anyone in the spring, when the river was still in flood and he could only get in and out, hazardously, by boat. I used to go out in his boat with him, late afternoons, and we would dawdle along the river, looking at the forest stretches and the open rolling farmlands and vast old barns, and at the smaller things closeby, the heavy luxuriance of ferns at the water's rim, the dozens of snapping turtles with unblinking eyes, all sizes and generations of the turtle tribe, sunning themselves on the fallen logs in the river. One summer, Old Jack's eighty-fourth, he spent some time planting maple saplings on his property. A year later, when I saw him dying, it seemed to me he'd meant those trees as a kind of legacy, a declaration of faith. Those of us along the river, here, won't forget him, nor what he stood for.

After work, I go out walking and weed-inspecting. 10 Weeds and wildflowers impress me as much as any cultivated plant. I've heard that in a year when the milkweed is plentiful, the Monarch butterflies will also be plentiful. This year the light pinkish milkweed flowers stand thick and tall, and sure enough, here are the dozens of Monarch butterflies, fluttering like dusky orange-gold angels all over the place. I can't identify as many plants as I'd like, but I'm learning. Chickweed, the ragged-leafed lambs' quarters, the purple-and-white wild phlox with its expensive-smelling free perfume, the pink and mauve wild asters, the two-toned yellow of the tiny butter-and-eggs flowers, the burnt orange of devil's paintbrush, the staunch nobility of the huge purple thistles, and, almost best of all, that long stalk covered with clusters of miniature creamy blossoms which I finally tracked down in my wild-flower book—this incomparable plant bears the armorial name of the Great Mullein of the Figwort Family. It may not be the absolute prettiest of our wildflowers, but it certainly has the most stunning pedigree.

It is night now, and there are no lights except those of 11 our few cottages. At sunset, an hour or so ago, I watched the sun's last flickers touching the rippling river, making it look as

though some underwater world had lighted all its candles
down there. Now it is dark. Dinner over, I turn out the electric lights in the cabin so I can see the stars. The black sky-
dome (or perhaps skydom, like kingdom) is alive and alight.

  Tomorrow the weekend will begin, and friends will ar-   12
rive. We'll talk all day and probably half the night, and that
will be good. But for now, I'm content to be alone, because
loneliness is something that doesn't exist here.

BUILDING VOCABULARY

1. In your own words, write the meaning of each italicized
   word or phrase taken from the selection.

   a. *exhilarating* sense of *peril* (par. 1)
   b. loons still cried *eerily* (par. 1)
   c. *predawn ritual* (par. 3)
   d. *spooky* quality (par. 3)
   e. *gauntly* beautiful (par. 4)
   f. huge *unwieldy* nest (par. 6)
   g. *unhurried* sweep of those powerful wings (par. 6)
   h. boats *ply* these *waterways* (par. 7)
   i. low in *estimation* (par. 7)
   j. *gaudy, abstract splodges* (par. 7)
   k. so *instantaneous* (par. 8)
   l. heavy *luxuriance* of ferns (par. 9)
   m. as a kind of *legacy* (par. 9)
   n. this *incomparable* plan (par. 10)
   o. most *stunning pedigree* (par. 10)

2. Throughout this essay, Laurence uses two-word combinations (some hyphenated, some not) to create descriptive
   adjectives and nouns. Some seem to be word combinations
   that are already familiar, while others appear to be the author's own creations. Reread the essay and select *ten* such
   adjectives and *five* such nouns. Indicate for each whether
   you think it is one of the author's originals. Then choose

ten of the words and use each in an original sentence of
your own.

UNDERSTANDING THE WRITER'S IDEAS

1. What is "this country" mentioned in the first sentence?
   How do you know? What specific clues tell you which
   country Laurence writes about?

2. What was the author's first "most loved place"? What
   happened to it?

3. Briefly describe in your own words the environment of
   the Otonabee River where Laurence has her cabin.

4. What is the author's attitude toward speedboats on the
   river? Where does she express this attitude?

5. What is Laurence's "predawn ritual"? Why does she
   curse slightly during this time? What clues does she give
   the reader about the climate of the place?

6. Explain the descriptions "a secret meeting of river and
   sky" (par. 3) and "trees of flame" (par. 4).

7. What is Laurence's "work" which she mentions in paragraph 5? Does she go into great detail about her work?
   Why or why not?

8. Describe the author's overall attitude toward nature. Give
   specific examples from the essay to support your answer.

9. Why does the author give the boats on the river "mental
   gradings"? Are her reactions based purely on the mechanical nature of the different boats, or are there other factors
   involved? Support your answer with examples.

10. What are the "gaudy abstract splodges" mentioned at the
    end of paragraph 7?

11. Why does Laurence call Linda and Susan "the Girls of
    the Pony Express"?

12. Who was Old Jack? Describe the author's feelings toward
    him. At the end of paragraph 9, Laurence states that no
    one will forget "what he stood for." What did he stand
    for? How are the maple saplings "a kind of legacy, a dec-
    laration of faith"?

13. What does the writer do "after work"?

14. Explain the meaning of the parenthetical expression "(or
    perhaps skydom, like kingdom)" in paragraph 11. How
    does it relate to the overall main idea of this essay?

15. In the last paragraph, Laurence writes "and that will be
    good" in relation to her friends visiting and talking all day
    and night. Does she really feel it "will be good"? Why or
    why not?

UNDERSTANDING THE WRITER'S TECHNIQUES

1. Do you find the first sentence self-contradictory? Why
   does Laurence begin with such a statement? How does it
   affect the rest of her description? Where else does she
   seem to be contradicting herself? Why?

2. By what principles does Laurence organize the descriptive details in this essay? How does she use *time* as an organizing factor? List three specific examples.

3. Laurence uses figurative language throughout the essay
   (see Glossary). Pick out what you think are the most vivid
   and original figurative expressions. Defend your choices.

4. Evaluate Laurence's use of *transitions* (see Glossary).
   Specifically, how does she accomplish transitions between paragraphs 1 and 2? Paragraphs 4 and 5? Paragraphs 8 and 9? 9 and 10? 10 and 11?

5. Explain the description, "the grey skeletons of the dead
   elms, *gauntly beautiful* even in death" (par. 4). Why
   would she use images of death and suffering to express

beauty? How does this description fit with her overall view of nature?

6. *Hyperbole* is the use of descriptive exaggeration to make a point. Find two instances of hyperbole in this essay. What is the purpose of these hyperbolic descriptions?

7. What is the main idea of this essay? Writers often provide a single *thesis sentence* (see Glossary) to express the main idea. Is there a specific thesis statement in this essay? Where?

8. Most of the writing in this essay consists of long, flowing sentences. How does the author change that pattern toward the end of the essay? Why?

9. Does this essay contain a clearly defined introduction, body, and conclusion? (See Glossary.) If so, state which paragraphs make up each section.

10. Does Laurence ever really describe the shack of the title? Why? What does that tell you about her view of the relation between the shack and its environment?

EXPLORING THE WRITER'S IDEAS

1. The final sentence of this essay is somewhat puzzling: "But for now, I'm content to be alone, because loneliness is something that doesn't exist here." What do you feel is the difference between *being alone* and *loneliness?* Most people dislike or even fear loneliness. Are there times when being alone can be a good thing? Draw on your own experience to illustrate your answer. How do you deal with loneliness?

2. Throughout the essay, Laurence refers to misuse or disregard of nature by others on the river. We get the feeling that she is very critical of and annoyed by people who violate nature. Do you think her attitude is fair? Why? What have been your experiences with seeing natural beauty abused by vacationers, developers, hunters, and so on?

3. In describing Old Jack, the author states that the maple saplings he planted were meant as "a kind of legacy, a declaration of faith." Is there anything that you or someone you know has done that you would want considered as a part of your own legacy? Explain.

IDEAS FOR WRITING

Guided Writing

Write an essay in which you describe a favorite place at which you've spent a good deal of time.

1. Give your essay a short, direct title.

2. Begin with a short description of a previous, but long gone, favorite place and use a transition to associate it with the place of your essay.

3. Tell something of your connection to the place. How long have you known the place? Why do you go there? What do you do there?

4. Begin ordering your description by describing the start of a typical day at the place.

5. Order the rest of your essay by focusing on features of the environment at the place. Use supporting sensory details.

6. Try to create original two-word combinations that serve as vivid adjectives.

7. In one of the body paragraphs, describe how another person has significantly affected you and the place.

8. Be sure to use clear transitions between the main paragraphs of your essay. You might want to use time as an organizing principle in your essay.

9. Make sure your essay expresses a *dominant impression* of the place.

10. End your essay at the end of a day. Indicate how you be-

lieve the next day's activities would affect your current feelings about the place.

More Writing Projects

1. Write a description of the same place you described in the Guided Writing essay, but from the point of view of someone who felt intense dislike or discomfort at the place.

2. In a brief essay, describe an ideal place to which you'd like to go whenever you feel nervous or upset. This place may be a room or an outdoor place, and it may be real or imaginary. Use your imagination to create a real "rest haven."

Catfish in the Bathtub
Maxine Hong Kingston

In this selection from her best-selling *The Woman Warrior* (1976), Chinese-American author Maxine Hong Kingston describes various strange eating habits of her childhood. The author skillfully blends techniques of personal narration and rich sensory detailing to create a fascinating impression of another culture's daily life-style.

Words to Watch

dromedaries (par. 1)   one-humped camels

sensibility (par. 1)   ability to receive sensations

perched (par. 1)   resting on a bird's roost

scowls (par. 1)   expressions of displeasure

dismembering (par. 1)   taking apart bodily limbs and innards

sprains (par. 2)   sudden twists of joints such as ankles or wrists

unsettle (par. 3)   make uneasy or uncomfortable

tufts (par. 4)   small patches of hair

awobble (par. 6)   unsteady, teetering

toadstools (par. 7)   mushrooms

revulsion (par. 8)   a strong reaction away from something

My mother has cooked for us: raccoons, skunks, hawks, 1 city pigeons, wild ducks, wild geese, black-skinned bantams, snakes, garden snails, turtles that crawled about the pantry floor and sometimes escaped under refrigerator or stove, catfish that swam in the bathtub. "The emperors used to eat the peaked hump of purple dromedaries," she would say. "They used chopsticks made from rhinoceros horn, and they ate ducks' tongues and monkeys' lips." She boiled the weeds we pulled up in the yard. There was a tender plant with flowers like white stars hiding under the leaves, which were like the flower petals but green. I've not been able to find it since growing up. It had no taste. When I was as tall as the washing machine, I stepped out on the back porch one night, and some heavy, ruffling, windy, clawed thing dived at me. Even after getting chanted back to sensibility, I shook when I recalled that perched everywhere there were owls with great hunched shoulders and yellow scowls. They were a surprise for my mother from my father. We children used to hide under the beds with our fingers in our ears to shut out the bird screams and the thud, thud of the turtles swimming in the boiling water, their shells hitting the sides of the pot. Once the third aunt who worked at the laundry ran out and bought us bags of candy to hold over our noses; my mother was dismembering skunk on the chopping block. I could smell the rubbery odor through the candy.

In a glass jar on a shelf my mother kept a big brown hand   2
with pointed claws stewing in alcohol and herbs. She must have brought it from China because I do not remember a time when I did not have the hand to look at. She said it was a bear's claw, and for many years I thought bears were hairless. My mother used the tobacco, leeks, and grasses swimming about the hand to rub our sprains and bruises.

Just as I would climb up to the shelf to take one look af-   3
ter another at the hand, I would hear my mother's monkey story. I'd take my fingers out of my ears and let her monkey words enter my brain. I did not always listen voluntarily, though. She would begin telling the story, perhaps repeating it to a homesick villager, and I'd overhear before I had a chance to protect myself. Then the monkey words would unsettle me; a curtain flapped loose inside my brain. I have wanted to say, "Stop it. Stop it," but not once did I say, "Stop it."

"Do you know what people in China eat when they have   4
the money?" my mother began. "They buy into a monkey feast. The eaters sit around a thick wood table with a hole in the middle. Boys bring in the monkey at the end of a pole. Its neck is in a collar at the end of the pole, and it is screaming. Its hands are tied behind it. They clamp the monkey into the table; the whole table fits like another collar around its neck. Using a surgeon's saw, the cooks cut a clean line in a circle at the top of its head. To loosen the bone, they tap with a tiny hammer and wedge here and there with a silver pick. Then an old woman reaches out her hand to the monkey's face and up

to its scalp, where she tufts some hairs and lifts off the lid of
the skull. The eaters spoon out the brains."

    Did she say, "You should have seen the faces the mon- 5
key made"? Did she say, "The people laughed at the monkey
screaming"? It was alive? The curtain flaps closed like merciful black wings.

    "Eat! Eat!" my mother would shout at our heads bent 6
over bowls, the blood pudding awobble in the middle of the
table.

    She had one rule to keep us safe from toadstools and 7
such: "If it tastes good, it's bad for you," she said. "If it
tastes bad, it's good for you."

    We'd have to face four- and five-day-old leftovers until 8
we ate it all. The squid eye would keep appearing at breakfast
and dinner until eaten. Sometimes brown masses sat on every
dish. I have seen revulsion on the faces of visitors who've
caught us at meals.

    "Have you eaten yet?" the Chinese greet one another. 9
    "Yes, I have," they answer whether they have or not. 10
"And you?"

    I would live on plastic. 11

BUILDING VOCABULARY

1. Go through this essay again and list every animal mentioned. Then, write a short description of each, using the
   dictionary or encyclopedia if necessary.

2. Use any five of the Words to Watch in sentences of your
   own.

UNDERSTANDING THE WRITER'S IDEAS

1. What is Kingston saying about her childhood? How does
   her opening catalogue of foods that her mother prepared,
   combined with further descriptions of foods, support this

point? What are some of the "strange" foods that she ate but that are not mentioned in this first paragraph?

2. Who are "the emperors" mentioned in paragraph 1? What were some of their more unusual dishes?

3. What attacks and frightens the young Kingston on her back porch? Where did they come from? How do we know that she was a young girl at the time? Explain the meaning of "even after getting chanted back to sensibility."

4. At the end of the first paragraph, the author mentions methods she and her siblings used to shut out unpleasant sensory input. What were they?

5. For what purpose did her mother keep a bear's claw in a glass jar? Where did Kingston think it came from? Why?

6. What are "the monkey words"? Summarize the "monkey words" in your own language. Kingston says that she wanted to say "Stop it" to the monkey words, but didn't. Why didn't she?

7. What was Kingston's mother's attitude toward the taste of things in relation to their healthfulness?

8. Why would there sometimes be "revulsion on the faces of visitors" who watched the author's family eating?

9. What is the traditional Chinese greeting?

10. What is the author's overall attitude toward her mother? Explain.

UNDERSTANDING THE WRITER'S TECHNIQUES

1. Does Kingston ever make a direct *thesis statement?* Why or why not?

   In this essay, Kingston seems to shift in and out of various tenses deliberately. For example, in paragraph 3, she writes: "...a curtain *flapped* loose inside my brain. I *have wanted* to say...." Why do you think that Kingston uses such a technique? List three other examples of such tense shifts.

2. Comment on Kingston's use of transitions here. How do they contribute to the overall *coherence* of the essay? (See Glossary.)

3. How does Kingston use the five senses to create descriptive imagery? Give examples of her use of sounds, tastes, smells, sights, and feelings. Which are the most effective?

4. Eliminating the specific references to China, how do we know that the author is of Chinese background? Which details or references contribute to this understanding?

5. Evaluate the use of *dialogue* (records of spoken words or conversations) in this essay. What effect does it have on the flow of the writing? On our understanding of Kingston's main point?

6. In paragraph 1, why does the author give so much attention to the white flower stars with no taste? Is she merely describing yet another thing she ate, or does she have some other purpose? Explain.

7. Although other incidents or ideas are described rather briefly, Kingston devotes a full, detailed paragraph to a description of the monkey feast. Why?

8. Throughout the essay, Kingston combines very realistic description (the bear's claw, the turtles thudding against the cook pot, the monkey feast) with various *similes* and *metaphors* (see Glossary). Explain the meaning of the following uses of *figurative language* (see Glossary):

   a. a curtain flapped loose inside my brain (par. 3)
   b. The curtain flaps closed like merciful black wings. (par. 5)
   c. Sometimes brown masses sat on every dish. (par. 8)

9. What is the effect of the series of questions in paragraph 5? Why are some in quotations and others not?

10. Explain the meaning of the last sentence. How does it relate to Kingston's *purpose* in this essay?

EXPLORING THE WRITER'S IDEAS

1. Kingston certainly describes some "strange" foods and eating habits in this essay. But, what makes particular foods "strange"? What are some of the strangest foods you have ever eaten? Where did they come from? Why did you eat them? How did you react to them? What foods or eating habits that are common to your everyday life might be considered strange by people from other cultures?

2. In this essay, Kingston concentrates on her mother, mentioning her father only once. Speculate on why she excludes her father in this way, but base your speculation on the material of the essay.

3. As we all know, different cultures have very different customs. In this essay, for example, the author describes the Chinese way of greeting one another as well as the monkey feast, both of which are quite foreign to American culture. Describe different cultural customs that you have observed in your school, among your friends, in places around your city or town. How do you feel when you observe customs different from the ones you are familiar with? Do you believe that any particular custom is "right" or "wrong"? Why? Which custom among your own culture's would you most like to see changed? Why?

4. Describe your reaction to the monkey feast description.

5. For what reason do you think the Chinese greet each other with the words, "Have you eaten yet?" Attempt to do further research into this custom. List as many different ways as you know of people greeting one another.

IDEAS FOR WRITING

Guided Writing

Write an essay in which you describe a family custom or activity that had a powerful effect on you in your childhood.

1. Begin with a list of important objects related to this custom.

2. Show the role of your parents or other relatives in relation to these objects.

3. Briefly tell about an incident that affected you deeply.

4. Create strong sensory imagery related to this custom. Attempt to use at least one image for each of the five senses.

5. If possible, relate this custom to your family's ethnic or cultural background.

6. Focus on one special object used as part of this custom or activity and describe it in detail. What was its purpose?

7. Use dialogue in your essay, including some of the dialogue of your "inner voice."

8. Use transitions to make the parts of your essay cohere.

9. Mention how outsiders experienced this custom.

10. End your essay with a direct statement to summarize your current attitude toward the custom and those times in your life.

More Writing Projects

1. Write a description of an interesting custom or activity that you witnessed, a custom coming from outside your own cultural or social background. Include vivid sensory details.

2. Research and write a short report about the dating customs of a culture other than your own.

3. Describe in detail the most wonderful meal you have ever eaten.

Arizona 87

William Least Heat Moon

In this chapter from his 1982 book, *Blue Highways,* William Least Heat Moon presents us with a bittersweet, richly detailed description of the landscape he sees while driving his truck called *Ghost Dancing* through the Southwestern United States. As he drives through central Arizona, his careful eye photographs both the natural and the human landscape around him. In converting these snapshots to language, Least Heat Moon relies upon rich sensory detail and especially vivid and original comparisons.

Words to Watch

friable (par. 1)   easily crushed or pulverized

persnickety (par. 1)   fussy about small details

pollinate (par. 3)   to carry pollen to fertilize plant seeds

kamikaze (par. 3)   a member of a corps of Japanese pilots assigned to make a suicidal crash at a target

aerial (par. 3)   occurring in the air

cache (par. 4)   something hidden

marauding (par. 6)   roaming about in search of plunder

Apaches (par. 6)   a tribe of Native Americans of the southwestern United States

rodeo (par. 4)   a performance featuring cowboy stunts

badger (par. 7)   a burrowing animal with long claws

diabolic (par. 7)   devilish

unobtrusively (par. 9)   not very obviously

escarpment (par. 9)   a long cliff

coalesced (par. 12)   came together

I don't suppose that saguaros mean to give comic relief 1
to the otherwise solemn face of the desert, but they do. Standing on the friable slopes they are quite persnickety about, saguaros mimic men as they salute, bow, dance, raise arms to wave, and grin with faces carved in by woodpeckers. Older

111

plants, having survived odds against their reaching maturity of sixty million to one, have every right to smile.

The saguaro is ninety percent water, and a big, two- ² hundred-year-old cactus may hold a ton of it—a two-year supply. With this weight, a plant that begins to lean is soon on the ground; one theory now says that the arms, which begin sprouting only after forty or fifty years when the cactus has some height, are counterweights to keep the plant erect.

The Monday I drove northeast out of Phoenix, saguaros ³ were in bloom—comparatively small, greenish-white blossoms perched on top of the trunks like undersized Easter bonnets; at night, long-nosed bats came to pollinate them. But by day, cactus wrens, birds of daring aerial skill, put on the show as they made kamikaze dives between toothpick-size thorns into nest cavities, where they were safe from everything except the incredible ascents over the spines by black racers in search of eggs the snakes would swallow whole.

It was hot. The only shade along Arizona 87 lay under ⁴ the bottomsides of rocks; the desert gives space then closes it up with heat. To the east, in profile, rose the Superstition Mountains, an evil place, Pima and Maricopa Indians say, which brings on diabolic possession to those who enter. Somewhere among the granite and greasewood was the Lost Dutchman gold mine, important not for whatever cache it might hide as for providing a white dream.

North of the Sycamore River, saguaro, ocotillo, pal- ⁵ overde, and cholla surrendered the hills to pads of prickly pear the size of a man's head. The road climbed and the temperature dropped. At Payson, a mile high on the northern slope of the Mazatzal Mountains, I had to pull on a jacket.

Settlers once ran into Payson for protection from ma- ⁶ rauding Apaches; after the Apache let things calm down, citizens tried to liven them up again by holding rodeos in the main street. Now, streets paved, Payson lay quiet but for the whine of sawmills releasing the sweet scent of cut timber.

I stopped at an old log hotel to quench a desert thirst. A ⁷ sign on the door: NO LIVE ANIMALS ALLOWED. I guess you could bring in all the dead ones you wanted. A woman shouted,

"Ain't servin' now." Her unmoving eyes, heavy as if cast from lead, watched suspiciously for a live badger under my jacket or a weasel up my pantleg. "This is a fine old hotel," I said. She ignored me. "Do 8 you mind if I look at your big map?" She shrugged and moved away, safe from any live animal attack. I was hunting a place to go next. Someone had marked the Hopi Reservation to the north in red. Why not? As I left, I asked where I could water my lizard. She ignored that too.

Highway 260, winding through the pine forests of central 9 Arizona, let the mountains be boss as it followed whatever avenues they left open, crossing ridges only when necessary, slipping unobtrusively on narrow spans over streams of rounded boulders. But when 260 reached the massive escarpment called the Mogollon Rim, it had to challenge geography and climb the face.

I shifted to low, and Ghost Dancing pulled hard. A man 10 with a dusty, leathery face creased like an old boot strained on a bicycle—the old style with fat tires. I called a hello, he said nothing. At the summit, I waited to see whether he would make the ascent. Far below lay two cars, crumpled wads. Through the clear air I could count nine ranges of mountains, each successively grayer in a way reminiscent of old Chinese woodblock prints. The Mogollon was a spectacular place; the more so because I had not been anesthetized to it by endless Kodachromes. When the cyclist passed, I called out, "Bravo!" but he acknowledged nothing. I would have liked to talk to a man who, while his contemporaries were consolidating their little empires, rides up the Mogollon Rim on a child's toy. Surely he knew something about desperate men.

The top of the great scarp, elevation sixty-five hundred 11 feet, lay flat and covered with big ponderosas standing between dirty snowdrifts and black pools of snowmelt. I began anticipating Heber, the next town. One of the best moments of any day on the road was, toward sunset, looking forward to the last stop. At Heber I hoped for an old hotel with a little bar off to the side where they would serve A-1 on draft under a stuffed moosehead; or maybe I'd find a grill dishing up steak and eggs on blue-rimmed platters. I hoped for people who had good stories, people who sometimes took you home to see their collection of carved peach pits.

That was the hope. But Heber was box houses and a 12 dingy sawmill, a couple of motels and filling stations, a glass-and-Formica cafe. Heber had no center, no focus for the eye and soul: neither a courthouse, nor high church steeple, nor hotel. Nothing has done more to take a sense of civic identity, a feeling of community, from small-town America than the loss of old hotels to the motel business. The hotel was once where things coalesced, where you could meet both towns-people and travelers. Not so in a motel. No matter how you build it, the motel remains a haunt of the quick and dirty, where the only locals are Chamber of Commerce boys every fourth Thursday. Who ever heard the returning traveler exclaim over one of the great motels of the world he stayed in? Motels can be big, but never grand.

BUILDING VOCABULARY

1. *Compound words* are made up of two separate words joined together. They help intensify description by focusing on the connection between two words. Some compounds are formed by joining two nouns (*photograph, chairperson*); others combine nouns with nonnoun prefixes, suffixes, or combining forms (*childlike, self-pity*). Some compounds use hyphens between the two words, although the general current trend is to omit the hyphens. For example, such words as *today* or *tomorrow* were regularly hyphenated just 100 years ago. However, many compound words are still acceptable in all three steps of development: two separate words, a single hyphenated word, a single nonhyphenated word (war monger, war-monger, warmonger).

   Locate at least ten compound words that in Least Heat Moon's essay are formed by joining two nouns. Use each in a sentence of your own.

2. *Denotation* refers to the dictionary definition of a word; *connotation* refers to the various shades of meaning and

feeling readers bring to a word or phrase. Look up and write dictionary definitions for each of the words in italics. Then, explain in your own words the connotative meaning of each sentence or phrase.

   a. the otherwise *solemn* face of the desert (par. 1)
   b. to *quench* a desert thirst (par. 7)
   c. it had to *challenge* geography (par. 9)
   d. I had not been *anesthetized* by endless *Kodachromes* (par. 10)
   e. glass-and-*Formica* cafe (par. 12)

3. Least Heat Moon is a careful observer of the plants, rocks, and wildlife of the Arizona landscape. List six of the words drawn from this landscape and write dictionary definitions of them.

UNDERSTANDING THE WRITER'S IDEAS

1. What are the saguaros? What are the odds of their reaching full growth? How old may saguaros become? At what age do they begin to sprout arms?

2. For what purpose do the cactus wrens use the saguaros? What is the major danger to these birds?

3. Explain the sentence: "The only shade along Arizona 87 lay under the bottom sides of rocks." (par. 4)

4. What is the American Indian legend about Superstition Mountains? Explain the "diabolic possession." What is supposedly hidden in these mountains and what is its importance? What is meant by "a white dream"?

5. How was the weather in Payson different from the weather when the writer started driving through the desert? What used to be the atmosphere in Payson? What is it like now?

6. Paragraph 9 describes the route of Highway 260. In your own words, how does the highway relate to the environment that surrounds it?

7. What is Moon's attitude toward the man on the bicycle? What do we learn about the man's appearance? How does the man react to Moon? What does Moon describe as "a child's toy"? Why?

8. How do we know that some cars fell off the Mogollon Rim?

UNDERSTANDING THE WRITER'S TECHNIQUES

1. Writers often sharpen descriptions by making unusual comparisons. In this essay Least Heat Moon makes many such comparisons. Locate and explain the meaning of what each of the following things is compared to:

   a. The shape and look of the saguaros
   b. The saguaro blossoms
   c. The dives of the cactus wrens
   d. The appearance of the nine mountain ranges

   Locate and explain other comparisons in the essay.

2. How does Moon use elements of space and time to order details in this description? Why is this method effective? Why does he introduce himself ("I drove") in paragraph 3? Why does he wait until then to introduce himself?

3. What is the effect of the short sentence "It was hot" (par. 4) coming as it does after a number of much longer sentences in preceding paragraphs?

4. *Imagery* refers to clear, vivid description rooted in sensory detail. List several images of vivid details that employ the senses: sight (color and action), sound, smell, touch, and taste.

5. In describing the old log hotel in paragraphs 7 and 8, Moon uses *dialogue,* or accurate recordings of actual conversations (see Glossary). What is the effect of dialogue on that descriptive scene?

6. Least Heat Moon makes use of humor to make biting observations about the hotel in Payson. Explain what he

means by "I guess you could bring in all the dead ones you wanted" (par. 7) and "As I left, I asked where I could water my lizard" (par. 8). Why does the woman ignore him? Why does he use biting humor in this way?

7. Least Heat Moon does not simply present factual details of the Arizona desert. Instead, his descriptions are highly subjective, colored with personal emotions. Locate five sentences of highly subjective description. Why is he so subjective? What impression does he give you of the scenes he describes? How does his subjectivity help create the *tone* of this essay? What is that tone?

8. Do you find the ending suitable? Is it too abrupt or is it consistent with the rest of the selection? Explain. Remember, this selection is a complete chapter of a book by the author.

EXPLORING THE WRITER'S IDEAS

1. In the final paragraph Least Heat Moon writes about the disappearance of "civic identity" or "a feeling of community" from small-town America. He blames this loss on the replacement of once-bustling hotels with impersonal motels. Do you think the writer believes this is the only reason for the change? In your experience, how else have American small towns lost their unique flavors or identities?

2. In paragraph 10, in discussing the bicyclist, the author writes, "Surely he knew something about desperate men." Why do you think he feels this way about the cyclist?

IDEAS FOR WRITING

Guided Writing

Write a short essay describing a landscape you traveled through at one time. This can be a city, suburban, or countryside landscape.

1. Begin by concentrating on a particular or dominant element of the landscape.

2. Focus on the environmental conditions and the weather. Note any changes of the climate.

3. Arrange your description as you travel in time from place to place in the landscape.

4. Include at least one interaction with another person who helped you to formulate your feelings about the place.

5. Use concrete sensory detail as you write images of color, action, sound, smell, touch, and taste.

6. Use vivid and varied comparisons to describe what you saw.

7. Conclude your essay with a description and explanation of something that either greatly disappointed or excited you about your travels through this place.

More Writing Projects

1. Concentrating on both the setting and the person, write a short description of a chance encounter with someone, as Least Heat Moon does with the bicyclist on the Mongollon Rim. End by coming to a conclusion about this person's personality.

2. Describe a particular place that you feel has been changed very much by modernization. Include descriptions of both the old and the new ways the place looks and feels. Also include your reactions to both the old and the new.

The Discus Thrower

Richard Selzer

Richard Selzer, a surgeon, gives his readers vivid insights into the excitement as well as the pathos of the world of medicine. His books include *Rituals of Surgery* (1974) and *Mortal Lesions* (1977). His essays are widely published in magazines, including *Esquire, Harper's,* and *Redbook.* In this essay, Selzer dramatically describes a patient's final day.

Words to Watch

furtive (par. 1)   sly
pruned (par. 2)   cut back; trimmed
facsimile (par. 2)   an exact copy
shard (par. 20)   a broken piece; fragment
forceps (par. 20)   an instrument used in operations for holding or pulling
athwart (par. 21)   leaning across
probes (par. 33)   investigates thoroughly
hefts (par. 33)   tosses; heaves

I spy on my patients. Ought not a doctor to observe his 1
patients by any means and from any stance, that he might the
more fully assemble evidence? So I stand in the doorways of
hospital rooms and gaze. Oh, it is not all that furtive an act.
Those in bed need only look up to discover me. But they
never do.

From the doorway of Room 542 the man in the bed 2
seems deeply tanned. Blue eyes and close-cropped white
hair give him the appearance of vigor and good health. But
I know that his skin is not brown from the sun. It is rusted,
rather, in the last stage of containing the vile repose within.
And the blue eyes are frosted, looking inward like the windows of a snowbound cottage. This man is blind. This man
is also legless—the right leg missing from midthigh down,

the left from just below the knee. It gives him the look of a bonsai, roots and branches pruned into the dwarfed facsimile of a great tree.

Propped on pillows, he cups his right thigh in both hands. Now and then he shakes his head as though acknowledging the intensity of his suffering. In all of this he makes no sound. Is he mute as well as blind?   3

The room in which he dwells is empty of all possessions—no get-well cards, small, private caches of food, day-old flowers, slippers, all the usual kick-shaws of the sickroom. There is only the bed, a chair, a nightstand, and a tray on wheels that can be swung across his lap for meals.   4

"What time is it?" he asks.   5

"Three o'clock."   6

"Morning or afternoon?"   7

"Afternoon."   8

He is silent. There is nothing else he wants to know.   9

"How are you?" I say.   10

"Who is it?" he asks.   11

"It's the doctor. How do you feel?"   12

He does not answer right away.   13

"Feel?" he says.   14

"I hope you feel better," I say.   15

I press the button at the side of the bed.   16

"Down you go," I say.   17

"Yes, down," he says.   18

He falls back upon the bed awkwardly. His stumps, unweighted by legs and feet, rise in the air, presenting themselves. I unwrap the bandages from the stumps, and begin to cut away the black scabs and the dead, glazed fat with scissors and forceps. A shard of white bone comes loose. I pick it away. I wash the wounds with disinfectant and redress the stumps. All this while, he does not speak. What is he thinking behind those lids that do not blink? Is he remembering a time when he was whole? Does he dream of feet? Of when his body was not a rotting log?   19

He lies solid and inert. In spite of everything, he remains impressive, as though he were a sailor standing athwart a slanting deck.   20

"Anything more I can do for you?" I ask.   21
For a long moment he is silent.   22
"Yes," he says at last and without the least irony. "You   23
can bring me a pair of shoes."
In the corridor, the head nurse is waiting for me.   24
"We have to do something about him," she says.   25
"Every morning he orders scrambled eggs for breakfast, and,
instead of eating them, he picks up the plate and throws it
against the wall."
"Throws his plate?"   26
"Nasty. That's what he is. No wonder his family doesn't   27
come to visit. They probably can't stand him any more than
we can."
She is waiting for me to do something.   28
"Well?"   29
"We'll see," I say.   30
The next morning I am waiting in the corridor when the   31
kitchen delivers his breakfast. I watch the aide place the tray
on the stand and swing it across his lap. She presses the button to raise the head of the bed. Then she leaves.
In time the man reaches to find the rim of the tray, then   32
on to find the dome of the covered dish. He lifts off the cover
and places it on the stand. He fingers across the plate until he
probes the eggs. He lifts the plate in both hands, sets it on the
palm of his right hand, centers it, balances it. He hefts it up
and down slightly, getting the feel of it. Abruptly, he draws
back his right arm as far as he can.
There is the crack of the plate breaking against the wall   33
at the foot of his bed and the small wet sound of the scrambled
eggs dropping to the floor.
And then he laughs. It is a sound you have never heard.   34
It is something new under the sun. It could cure cancer.
Out in the corridor, the eyes of the head nurse narrow.   35
"Laughed, did he?"   36
She writes something down on her clipboard.   37
A second aide arrives, brings a second breakfast tray,   38
puts it on the nightstand, out of his reach. She looks over at
me shaking her head and making her mouth go. I see that we
are to be accomplices.

"I've got to feed you," she says to the man.   39
"Oh, no you don't," the man says.   40
"Oh, yes I do," the aide says, "after the way you just   41
did. Nurse says so."
"Get me my shoes," the man says.   42
"Here's oatmeal," the aide says. "Open." And she   43
touches the spoon to his lower lip.
"I ordered scrambled eggs," says the man.   44
"That's right," the aide says.   45
I step forward.   46
"Is there anything I can do?" I say.   47
"Who are you?" the man asks.   48
In the evening I go once more to that ward to make my   49
rounds. The head nurse reports to me that Room 542 is deceased. She has discovered this quite by accident, she says.
No, there had been no sound. Nothing. It's a blessing, she
says.
I go into his room, a spy looking for secrets. He is still   50
there in his bed. His face is relaxed, grave, dignified. After a
while, I turn to leave. My gaze sweeps the wall at the foot of
the bed, and I see the place where it has been repeatedly
washed, where the wall looks very clean and very white.

BUILDING VOCABULARY

1. In this essay, Selzer uses a few words that derive from languages other than English. Look up the following words
   and tell what language they come from. Then, write a definition for each:

   a. *bonsai*
   b. *kick-shaws*
   c. *caches*

2. Use these words from the essay in complete sentences of
   your own: *vile, repose, dwarfed, glazed, inert, accomplices.*

UNDERSTANDING THE WRITER'S IDEAS

1. What reason does Selzer give for a doctor's spying on his patients?

2. What does the man in Room 542 look like? Why is his skin brown? How does Selzer know he is blind? Why does Selzer think the patient may be mute? When do we know that he is not mute?

3. What is the author's meaning of the phrase "vile repose"?

4. How do we know that this patient does not receive many visitors?

5. Aside from wanting to know the time of day, what is the patient's one request? Do you think he is serious about his request? Why?

6. Why does the patient hurl his food tray against the wall?

7. For what reason does the head nurse complain about the patient?

8. What does Selzer feel and think about the patient? How do you know?

UNDERSTANDING THE WRITER'S TECHNIQUES

1. Throughout the essay, Selzer asks a number of questions. Locate at least three of these questions that are not a part of the dialogue. To whom do you think they are addressed? What is their effect on the reader?

2. Like William Least Heat Moon, Selzer heightens the description by making vivid and unusual comparisons. Locate and explain in your own words three comparisons that you feel are especially descriptive and intriguing.

3. Selzer uses some very short sentences interspersed among longer ones. Locate at least four very short sen-

tences. How do they draw your attention to the description?

4. Locate in Selzer's essay at least five examples of vivid description (imagery) relating to illness. What is their emotional effect on the reader?

5. How does Selzer use *dialogue* to reveal the personality of the patient? of the doctor? of the head nurse?

6. In paragraph 24, Selzer states that the patient delivers his request "without the least irony." *Irony* (see Glossary) is saying what is opposite to what one means. Why might Selzer have expected irony from the patient? Why might someone in the sick man's condition use irony? What do you think the man means by his request "You can bring me a pair of shoes"—if, in fact, the remark is not an ironical one?

7. What does the title of the essay mean? What is a discus thrower? Why has Selzer chosen an ancient image of an athlete as the title of this essay? In what way is the title ironic?

8. Why does Selzer use such an unusual word as *kick-shaws* (par. 4)?

9. *Double entendre* is a French expression that indicates that something has a double meaning, each equally valid. What might be the two meanings of the nurse's words "It's a blessing"?

10. In this essay, the author uses a *framing* device: that is, he opens and closes the essay with a similar image or idea. What is that idea? Why is it effective? What are the differences in the use of this idea in the opening and closing paragraphs?

11. The heart of this essay is the patient's insistence upon throwing his breakfast plate at the wall, and yet Selzer does not attempt to explain the man's reasons for such an act. Why do you think the man hurls his breakfast across the room each morning—and why does he laugh? Why

does Selzer not provide an analysis of the action? How does the title help us see Selzer's attitude toward the man's act?

EXPLORING THE WRITER'S IDEAS

1. In the beginning of the essay Selzer asks, "Ought not a doctor to observe his patients by any means from any stance, that he might more fully assemble evidence?" Do you feel that a doctor should have this right? Why? What rights do you believe patients should have in a hospital?

2. The head nurse in Selzer's description seems fed up with the patient in Room 542. Why do you think she feels this way? Do you think that a person in her position has the right to express this feeling on his or her job? Why or why not?

3. The patient's attitude is influenced by his physical state and his nearness to death. How have physical ailments or handicaps changed the attitudes of people you have known? How has an illness influenced your thoughts at any time?

IDEAS FOR WRITING

Guided Writing

Describe a person you have observed who was seriously ill, in danger, or under great stress.

1. Base your description upon close observation of the person during a short but concentrated span of time: a morning or afternoon, an hour or two, even a few minutes.

2. Begin with a short, direct paragraph in which you introduce the person and the critical situation he or she faces.

3. Include yourself ("I") in the description.

4. Describe the vantage point from which you are "spying" or observing, and focus on the particular subject of the scene.

5. Throughout your essay, ask key questions.

6. Use imagery and original comparisons to highlight the description of your subject.

7. Include some dialogue with either the subject or another person.

8. Describe at least one very intense action performed by your subject.

9. Tell how the subject and scene had changed when you next saw them.

More Writing Projects

1. Describe a hospital room in which you stayed or visited some other person. Focus on your sensory perceptions of the place.

2. Describe an interaction you had with a person who was blind or deaf or was disabled in some other way. In your description, focus closely on the person's features. Write about your reactions during and after the interaction.

CHAPTER 4

Narration

Narration is the telling of a story. As a technique in essay writing, it normally involves a discussion of events that are "true" or real, events that take place over a period of time. Narration helps a writer explain things and, as such, it is an important skill for the kind of writing often required of you.

Writers who use narration usually rely on descriptive details to advance their stories. Moreover, in the narrative essay, there always must be some purpose in the telling, a purpose that goes beyond mere enjoyment of the story itself. Consequently, narration in an essay advances a thesis, or main idea. For example, if you had to write an essay on the happiest event in your life, you might choose to narrate the day your team won the state championship. You would establish your thesis—your main point—quickly, and then go on to tell about the event itself. In short, you would use narration as a means to an end—to make a significant statement about an important moment in your life.

The manner in which you relate this event depends on the simplicity or complexity of the story that you want to tell. If the season before the winning game was itself filled with excitement, you certainly would want to explain that and to trace the exciting events over a period of time. If the championship itself provided most of the thrills, you would want to concentrate on a much shorter period of time, breaking your narration down to days, hours, even minutes, instead of months. Learning to present time—whether in a single personal event, a series of related events, a historical occurrence, or an aging process—is one of the key elements in narrative prose.

Normally in a narrative essay you would start at the beginning and move to the end, or from past to present, or from old to new, but there are many other ways to relate events in the narrative essay. For instance, you could begin an essay on the death of someone important to you by detailing the day of the funeral, and then moving backward in time to flesh out the events leading up to the funeral. For beginners this "flashback" technique often causes very confused writing; but skilled writers know how to "jump around" in time without confusing the reader, blurring the thesis, or destroying the progression of the essay.

As with descriptive writing, the narrative essay requires a careful selection of details. Certain moments within any time order are more important than others, and these crucial moments will be emphasized and developed fully by a good writer. Other moments, significant but less important than the main moments, will take up less space, while unimportant items will be eliminated entirely. However, the writer must connect each event in the time span to other events that come before or after. Here, transitions of time—words like "afterwards," "soon," "a day later," "suddenly"—serve as bridges to connect the various moments in the narrative pattern.

There are other aspects of narration that appear in this chapter. For example, you must select a point of view for your story—whether presenting events through your own eyes or from a more objective or detached position. You must also decide on the value of dialogue (recording of conversations). Finally, you must be aware that other techniques of prose writing (like description) can reinforce your narrative pattern. Fortunately, most individuals have a basic storytelling ability and know how to develop stories that make a point. Once you master narration as a writing pattern, you will be able to use it in a variety of situations.

The Struggle to Be an All-American Girl

Elizabeth Wong

In this poignant remembrance, Elizabeth Wong tells of the hurts and sorrows of her bicultural upbringing. Wong effectively blends concrete description and imaginative comparisons to give a vivid look into the life of a child who felt she had a Chinese exterior but an American interior.

Words to Watch

stoically (par. 1)   without showing emotion
dissuade (par. 2)   to talk out of doing something
ideographs (par. 7)   Chinese picture symbols used to form words
disassociate (par. 8)   to detach from association
vendors (par. 8)   sellers of goods
gibberish (par. 9)   confused, unintelligible speech or language
pidgin (par. 10)   simplified speech that is usually a mixture of two or more languages

It's still there, the Chinese school on Yale Street where 1 my brother and I used to go. Despite the new coat of paint and the high wire fence, the school I knew 10 years ago remains remarkably, stoically the same.

Every day at 5 P.M., instead of playing with our fourth- 2 and fifth-grade friends or sneaking out to the empty lot to hunt ghosts and animal bones, my brother and I had to go to Chinese school. No amount of kicking, screaming, or pleading could dissuade my mother, who was solidly determined to have us learn the language of our heritage.

Forcibly, she walked us the seven long, hilly blocks from 3 our home to school, depositing our defiant tearful faces before the stern principal. My only memory of him is that he swayed on his heels like a palm tree, and he always clasped his impatient twitching hands behind his back. I recognized him as a

repressed maniacal child killer, and knew that if we ever saw
his hands we'd be in big trouble.

We all sat in little chairs in an empty auditorium. The   4
room smelled like Chinese medicine, an imported faraway
mustiness. Like ancient mothballs or dirty closets. I hated that
smell. I favored crisp new scents. Like the soft French perfume that my American teacher wore in public school.

There was a stage far to the right, flanked by an Ameri-   5
can flag and the flag of the Nationalist Republic of China,
which was also red, white and blue but not as pretty.

Although the emphasis at the school was mainly lan-   6
guage—speaking, reading, writing—the lessons always began
with an exercise in politeness. With the entrance of the
teacher, the best student would tap a bell and everyone would
get up, kowtow, and chant, "Sing san ho," the phonetic for
"How are you, teacher?"

Being ten years old, I had better things to learn than   7
ideographs copied painstakingly in lines that ran right to left
from the tip of a *moc but,* a real ink pen that had to be held in
an awkward way if blotches were to be avoided. After all, I
could do the multiplication tables, name the satellites of Mars,
and write reports on "Little Women" and "Black Beauty."
Nancy Drew, my favorite book heroine, never spoke Chinese.

The language was a source of embarrassment. More   8
times than not, I had tried to disassociate myself from the nag-
ging loud voice that followed me wherever I wandered in the
nearby American supermarket outside Chinatown. The voice
belonged to my grandmother, a fragile woman in her seventies
who could outshout the best of the street vendors. Her humor
was raunchy, her Chinese rhythmless, patternless. It was
quick, it was loud, it was unbeautiful. It was not like the quiet,
lilting romance of French or the gentle refinement of the
American South. Chinese sounded pedestrian. Public.

In Chinatown, the comings and goings of hundreds of   9
Chinese on their daily tasks sounded chaotic and frenzied. I
did not want to be thought of as mad, as talking gibberish.
When I spoke English, people nodded at me, smiled sweetly,
said encouraging words. Even the people in my culture would
cluck and say that I'd do well in life. "My, doesn't she move

her lips fast,'' they would say, meaning that I'd be able to keep up with the world outside Chinatown.

My brother was even more fanatical than I about speak- 10 ing English. He was especially hard on my mother, criticizing her, often cruelly, for her pidgin speech—smatterings of Chinese scattered like chop suey in her conversation. "It's not 'What it is,' Mom,'' he'd say in exasperation. "It's 'What *is* it, what *is* it, what *is* it!'' Sometimes Mom might leave out an occasional "the'' or "a,'' or perhaps a verb of being. He would stop her in mid-sentence: "Say it again, Mom. Say it right.'' When he tripped over his own tongue, he'd blame it on her: "See, Mom, it's all your fault. You set a bad example.''

What infuriated my mother most was when my brother 11 cornered her on her consonants, especially "r.'' My father had played a cruel joke on Mom by assigning her an American name that her tongue wouldn't allow her to say. No matter how hard she tried, "Ruth'' always ended up "Luth'' or "Roof.''

After two years of writing with a *moc but* and reciting 12 words with multiples of meanings, I finally was granted a cultural divorce. I was permitted to stop Chinese school.

I thought of myself as multicultural. I preferred tacos to 13 egg rolls; I enjoyed Cinco de Mayo more than Chinese New Year.

At last, I was one of you; I wasn't one of them. 14

Sadly, I still am. 15

BUILDING VOCABULARY

For each of the words in italics, choose the letter of the word or expression that most closely matches its meaning.

1. the *stern* principal (par. 3)
   a. military **b.** very old **c.** immoral **d.** strict
2. *repressed* maniacal child killer (par. 3)
   a. quiet **b.** ugly **c.** held back **d.** retired
3. an imported faraway *mustiness* (par. 4)
   a. country **b.** moth balls **c.** chair **d.** staleness

4. a *fragile* woman (par. 8)
   a. elderly **b.** frail **c.** tall **d.** inconsistent
5. her humor was *raunchy* (par. 8)
   a. obscene **b.** unclear **c.** childish **d.** very funny
6. thought of as *mad* (par. 9)
   a. foreign **b.** angry **c.** stupid **d.** crazy
7. quiet *lilting* romance of French (par. 8)
   a. musical **b.** tilting **c.** loving **d.** complicated
8. what *infuriated* my mother most (par. 11)
   a. angered **b.** humiliated **c.** made laugh **d.** typified

UNDERSTANDING THE WRITER'S IDEAS

1. What did Elizabeth Wong and her brother do every day after school? How did that make them different from their friends? What was their attitude toward what they did? How do you know?

2. What does Wong mean when she says of the principal "I recognized him as a repressed child killer"? Why were she and her brother afraid to see his hands?

3. What was the main purpose of going to Chinese school? What did Wong feel she had learned at "regular" American school? Which did she feel was more important? What are *Little Women, Black Beauty,* and *Nancy Drew?*

4. In the first sentence of paragraph 8, what language is "the language"?

5. What was Wong's grandmother like? What was Wong's attitude toward her? Why?

6. When Wong spoke English in Chinatown, why did the others think it was good that she moved her lips quickly?

7. What was her brother's attitude toward speaking English? How did he treat their mother when she tried to speak English? Why was it unfortunate that the mother had the American name *Ruth?* Who gave her that name? Why?

8. Explain the expression "he tripped over his own tongue" (par. 10)

9. In paragraph 13, Wong states, "I thought of myself as multicultural." What does that mean? What are tacos, egg rolls, and Cinco de Mayo? Why is it surprising that Wong includes those items as examples of her multiculturalism?

10. Who are the "you" and "them" of paragraph 14? Explain the significance of the last sentence. What does it indicate about Wong's attitude toward Chinese school from the vantage point of being an adult?

UNDERSTANDING THE WRITER'S TECHNIQUES

1. What is Wong's purpose in writing this narrative? Is the technique of narration an appropriate one to her purpose? Why or why not?

2. Wong does not state a thesis directly in a thesis sentence. How does her title imply a thesis? If you were writing a thesis sentence of your own for this essay, what would it be?

3. This narrative contains several stories. The first one ends after paragraph 7 and tells about Wong's routine after 5:00 P.M. on school days. Paragraphs 8 and 9, 10 and 11, and 12 and 13 offer other related narratives. Summarize each of these briefly. How does Wong help the reader shift from story to story?

4. The writer of narration will present *time* in a way that best fulfills the purpose of the narration. This presentation may take many forms: a single, personal event; a series of related events; a historical occurrence; an aging process. Obviously Wong chose a series of related events. Why does she use such a narrative structure to make her point? Could she have chosen an alternative plan, do you think? Why or why not?

5. Writers of narration often rely upon descriptive details to flesh out their stories. Find examples of sensory language here that makes the scene come alive for the reader.

6. Writers often use figurative comparisons to enliven their writing and to make it more distinctive. A *simile* is an imaginative form of figurative comparison using "like" or "as" to connect two items. One thing is similar to another in this figure. A *metaphor* is a figure of speech in which the writer compares two items not normally thought of as similar, but unlike in a simile, the comparison is direct— that is, it does not use "like" or "as." In other words, one thing is said to be the other thing, not merely to be like it. For example, if you wanted to compare love to a rose, you might use these two comparisons:

   Simile: My love is *like* a red, red rose.
   Metaphor: My love *is* a red, red rose.

   In Wong's essay, find the similes and metaphors in paragraphs 2, 3, 4, 10, and 12. For each, name the two items compared and explain the comparison in your own words.

7. Narratives often include lines of spoken language, that is, one person in the narrative talking alone or to another. Wong uses quoted detail sparsely here. Why did she choose to limit the dialogue? How effective is the dialogue that appears here? Where do you think she might have used more dialogue to advance the narrative?

8. The last two paragraphs are only one sentence each. Why do you think the author chose this technique?

9. What is the irony in the last sentence of the essay? (See Glossary). How would the meaning of the last sentence change if you eliminated the word *sadly?* What is the irony in the title of the essay?

10. What is the tone (see Glossary) of this essay? How does the tone here compare with Maxine Hong Kingston's description of her family's eating habits (see pages 104–106)?

EXPLORING THE WRITER'S IDEAS

1. Wong and her brother deeply resented being forced to attend Chinese school. When children very clearly express displeasure or unhappiness, should parents force them to do things anyway? Why or why not?

2. On one level this essay is about a clash of cultures, here the ancient Chinese culture of Wong's ancestry and the culture of the twentieth-century United States. Is it possible for someone to maintain connections to his or her ethnic or cultural backgrounds and at the same time to become an all-American girl or boy? What do people of foreign backgrounds gain when they become completely Americanized? What do they lose?

3. Because of their foreign ways, the mother and grandmother clearly embarrassed the Wong children. Under what other conditions that you can think of do parents embarrass children? Children, parents?

IDEAS FOR WRITING

Guided Writing

Write a narration in which you tell about some difficult moment that took place in grade school or high school, a moment that taught you something about yourself, your needs, or your cultural background.

1. Provide a concrete description of the school.

2. Tell in correct sequence about the event.

3. Identify people who play a part in this moment.

4. Use concrete, sensory description throughout your essay.

5. Use original similes and metaphors to make your narrative clearer and more dramatic.

6. Use dialogue (or spoken conversation) appropriately in order to advance the narrative.

7. In your conclusion, indicate what your attitude toward this moment is now that you are an adult.

8. Write a title that implies your thesis.

More Writing Projects

1. In an essay, tell about your happiest childhood memory and explain why it made you happy.

2. Write a short narration about an experience you had with a person of another culture.

Salvation

Langston Hughes

For more than forty years, Langston Hughes (1902–1967) was a major figure in American literature. In poetry, essays, drama, and fiction he attempted, as he said himself, "to explain and illuminate the Negro condition in America." This selection from his autobiography, *The Big Sea* (1940), tells the story of his "conversion" to Christ. Salvation was a key event in the life of his community, but Hughes tells comically how he bowed to pressure by permitting himself to be "saved from sin."

Words to Watch

dire (par. 3)   terrible; disastrous

gnarled (par. 4)   knotty; twisted

rounder (par. 6)   watchman; policeman

deacons (par. 6)   members of the clergy or laypersons who are appointed to help the minister

serenely (par. 7)   calmly; tranquilly

knickerbockered (par. 11)   dressed in short, loose trousers that are gathered below the knees

I was saved from sin when I was going on thirteen. But 1 not really saved. It happened like this. There was a big revival at my Auntie Reed's church. Every night for weeks there had been much preaching, singing, praying, and shouting, and some very hardened sinners had been brought to Christ, and the membership of the church had grown by leaps and bounds. Then just before the revival ended, they held a special meeting for children, "to bring the young lambs to the fold." My aunt spoke of it for days ahead. That night I was escorted to the front row and placed on the mourners' bench with all the other young sinners, who had not yet been brought to Jesus.

My aunt told me that when you were saved you saw a 2 light, and something happened to you inside! And Jesus came

into your life! And God was with you from then on! She said
you could see and hear and feel Jesus in your soul. I believed
her. I had heard a great many old people say the same thing
and it seemed to me they ought to know. So I sat there calmly
in the hot, crowded church, waiting for Jesus to come to me.

The preacher preached a wonderful rhythmical sermon,   3
all moans and shouts and lonely cries and dire pictures of hell,
and then he sang a song about the ninety and nine safe in the
fold, but one little lamb was left out in the cold. Then he said:
"Won't you come? Won't you come to Jesus? Young lambs,
won't you come?" And he held out his arms to all us young
sinners there on the mourners' bench. And the little girls
cried. And some of them jumped up and went to Jesus right
away. But most of us just sat there.

A great many old people came and knelt around us and   4
prayed, old women with jet-black faces and braided hair, old
men with work-gnarled hands. And the church sang a song
about the lower lights are burning, some poor sinners to be
saved. And the whole building rocked with prayer and song.

Still I kept waiting to *see* Jesus.   5

Finally all the young people had gone to the altar and   6
were saved, but one boy and me. He was a rounder's son
named Westley. Westley and I were surrounded by sisters and
deacons praying. It was very hot in the church, and getting
late now. Finally Westley said to me in a whisper: "God
damn! I'm tired o' sitting here. Let's get up and be saved." So
he got up and was saved.

Then I was left all alone on the mourners' bench. My   7
aunt came and knelt at my knees and cried, while prayers and
songs swirled all around me in the little church. The whole
congregation prayed for me alone, in a mighty wail of moans
and voices. And I kept waiting serenely for Jesus, waiting,
waiting—but he didn't come. I wanted to see him, but nothing
happened to me. Nothing! I wanted something to happen to
me, but nothing happened.

I heard the songs and the minister saying: "Why don't   8
you come? My dear child, why don't you come to Jesus?
Jesus is waiting for you. He wants you. Why don't you come?
Sister Reed, what is this child's name?"

"Langston," my aunt sobbed.   9

"Langston, why don't you come? Why don't you come 10
and be saved? Oh, Lamb of God! Why don't you come?"

Now it was really getting late. I began to be ashamed of 11
myself, holding everything up so long. I began to wonder what
God thought about Westley, who certainly hadn't seen Jesus
either, but who was now sitting proudly on the platform,
swinging his knickerbockered legs and grinning down at me,
surrounded by deacons and old women on their knees praying. God had not struck Westley dead for taking his name in
vain or for lying in the temple. So I decided that maybe to
save further trouble, I'd better lie, too, and say that Jesus had
come, and get up and be saved.

So I got up.   12

Suddenly the whole room broke into a sea of shouting, 13
as they saw me rise. Waves of rejoicing swept the place.
Women leaped in the air. My aunt threw her arms around me.
The minister took me by the hand and led me to the platform.

When things quieted down, in a hushed silence, punctuated 14
by a few ecstatic "Amens," all the new young lambs were
blessed in the name of God. Then joyous singing filled the room.

That night, for the last time in my life but one—for I was a 15
big boy twelve years old—I cried. I cried, in bed alone, and
couldn't stop. I buried my head under the quilts, but my aunt
heard me. She woke up and told my uncle I was crying because
the Holy Ghost had come into my life, and because I had seen
Jesus. But I was really crying because I couldn't bear to tell her
that I had lied, that I had deceived everybody in the church, that
I hadn't seen Jesus, and that now I didn't believe there was a
Jesus any more, since he didn't come to help me.

BUILDING VOCABULARY

1. Throughout this essay, Hughes selects words dealing with
   religion to emphasize his ideas. Look these words up in a
   dictionary. Then tell what *connotations* the following
   words have for you. (See Glossary).

   a. sin (par. 1)
   b. mourner (par. 1)

    c. lamb (par. 3)
    d. salvation (title)

2. Locate additional words that deal with religion.

3. When Hughes talks about lambs in the fold—and lambs in general—he is using a figure of speech, a comparison. What is being compared? How does religion enter into the comparison? Why is it useful as a figure of speech?

UNDERSTANDING THE WRITER'S IDEAS

1. According to Hughes's description, what is a revival meeting like? What is the effect of the "preaching, singing, praying, and shouting" on the "sinners" and the "young lambs"?

2. Why does Westley "see" Jesus? Why does Langston Hughes come to Jesus?

3. How does the author feel after his salvation? Does Hughes finally believe in Christ after his experience? How do you know?

UNDERSTANDING THE WRITER'S TECHNIQUES

1. Is there a thesis statement in the essay? Where is it located?

2. How does the first paragraph serve as an introduction to the narrative?

3. What is the value of description in this essay? List several instances of vivid description that contribute to the narrative.

4. Where does the main narration begin? How much time passes in the course of the action?

5. In narration, it is especially important to have effective *transitions*—or word bridges—from stage to stage in the action. Transitions help the reader shift easily from idea to idea, event to event. List several transition words that Hughes uses.

6. A piece of writing has *coherence* if all its parts relate clearly and logically to each other. Each sentence grows naturally from the sentence before it; each paragraph grows naturally from the paragraph before it. Is Hughes's essay coherent? Which transitions help advance the action and relate the parts of a single paragraph to each other? Which transitions help connect paragraphs together? How does the way Hughes organized this essay help establish coherence?

7. A story (whether it is true or fiction) has to be told from the first-person ("I, we"), second-person ("you"), or third-person ("he, she, it, they") *point of view*. Point of view in narration sets up the author's position in regard to the action, making him either a part of the action or an observer of it.

   a. What is the point of view in "Salvation"—is it first, second, or third person?
   b. Why has Hughes chosen this point of view instead of any other? Can you think of any advantages to this point of view?

8. What is your opinion about the last paragraph, the conclusion of this selection? What does it suggest about the mind of a twelve-year-old boy? What does it say about adults' misunderstanding of the activities of children?

9. What does the word "conversion" mean? What conversion really takes place in this piece? How does that compare to what people usually mean when they use "conversion" in a religious sense?

EXPLORING THE WRITER'S IDEAS

1. Hughes seems to suggest that we are forced to do things because of social pressures. Do you agree with his sugges-

tion? Do people do things because their friends or families expect them to? To what extent are we part of the "herd"? Is it possible for a person to retain individuality under pressure from a group? When did you bow to group pressures? When did you resist?

2. Do you find the religious experience in Hughes's essay unusual or extreme? Why or why not? How do *you* define religion?

3. Under what circumstances might a person lie in order to satisfy others? Try to recall a specific episode in which you or someone you know was forced to lie in order to please others.

IDEAS FOR WRITING

Guided Writing

Narrate an event in your life where you (or someone you know) gave in to group pressure or were forced to lie in order to please those around you.

1. Start with a thesis statement.

2. Set the stage for your narrative in the opening paragraph by telling where and when the incident took place. Use specific names for places.

3. Try to keep the action within as brief a time period as possible. If you can write about an event that took no more than a few minutes, so much the better.

4. Use description to sketch in the characters around you. Use colors, actions, sounds, smells, sensations of touch to fill in details of the scene.

5. Use effective transitions of time to link sentences and paragraphs.

6. Use the last paragraph to explain how you felt immediately after the incident.

More Writing Projects

1. Explain an abstract word like "salvation," "sin," "love," or "hatred" by narrating an event that reveals the meaning of the word to you.

2. Narrate an important event that affected your relationship to family, friends, or your community during your childhood.

3. Tell about an important religious experience you remember. You might want to narrate an event about your own "conversion."

I Became Her Target

Roger Wilkins

Roger Wilkins, who is a senior fellow at the Institute for Policy Studies in Washington, D.C., and chairperson of the Pulitzer Prize Board, here tells the story of how an understanding teacher may well have changed the course of his life. Wilkins's narration explores questions of racism as he talks about how a series of positive classroom incidents helped him renew his self-esteem. Note how the writer shifts between his childhood and adult perceptions to help weave his narrative.

Words to Watch

decade (par. 1) a ten-year period

pristine (par. 2) uncorrupted; fresh and clean

deplored (par. 5) regretted strongly on a moral level

incipient (par. 8) in the beginning stages

derivative (par. 9) taken or received from another source

groused (par. 13) complained; grumbled

ventured (par. 13) undertook a risk

mortified (par. 14) subjected to humiliation

My favorite teacher's name was "Dead-Eye" Bean. Her 1
real name was Dorothy. She taught American history to eighth
graders in the junior high section of Creston, the high school
that served the north end of Grand Rapids, Mich. It was the
fall of 1944. Franklin D. Roosevelt was president; American
troops were battling their way across France; Joe DiMaggio
was still in the service; the Montgomery bus boycott was
more than a decade away, and I was a 12-year-old black new-
comer in a school that was otherwise all white.

My mother, who had been a widow in New York, had 2
married my stepfather, a Grand Rapids physician, the year before, and he had bought the best house he could afford for his
new family. The problem for our new neighbors was that their
neighborhood had previously been pristine (in their terms) and

they were ignorant about black people. The prevailing wisdom
in the neighborhood was that we were spoiling it and that we
ought to go back where we belonged (or alternatively, ought
not intrude where we were not wanted). There was a lot of angry talk among the adults, but nothing much came of it.

But some of the kids, those first few weeks, were quite   3
nasty. They threw stones at me, chased me home when I was
on foot and spat on my bike seat when I was in class. For a
time, I was a pretty lonely, friendless and sometimes frightened kid. I was just transplanted from Harlem, and here in
Grand Rapids, the dominant culture was speaking to me insistently.

I can see now that those youngsters were bullying and   4
culturally disadvantaged. I knew then that they were bigoted,
but the culture spoke to me more powerfully than my mind
and I felt ashamed for being different—a nonstandard person.

I now know that Dorothy Bean understood most of that   5
and deplored it. So things began to change when I walked into
her classroom. She was a pleasant-looking single woman, who
looked old and wrinkled to me at the time, but who was probably about 40.

Whereas my other teachers approached the problem of   6
easing in their new black pupil by ignoring him for the first few
weeks, Miss Bean went right at me. On the morning after having read our first assignment, she asked me the first question.
I later came to know that in Grand Rapids, she was viewed as
a very liberal person who believed, among other things, that
Negroes were equal.

I gulped and answered her question and the follow-up.   7
They weren't brilliant answers, but they did establish the facts
that I had read the assignment and that I could speak English.
Later in the hour, when one of my classmates had bungled an
answer, Miss Bean came back to me with a question that required me to clean up the girl's mess and established me as a
smart person.

Thus, the teacher began to give me human dimensions,   8
though not perfect ones for an eighth grader. It was somewhat
better to be an incipient teachers' pet than merely a dark pres-

ence in the back of the room onto whose silent form my classmates could fit all the stereotypes they carried in their heads.

A few days later, Miss Bean became the first teacher   9
ever to require me to think. She asked my opinion about
something Jefferson had done. In those days, all my opinions
were derivative. I was for Roosevelt because my parents were
and I was for the Yankees because my older buddy from
Harlem was a Yankee fan. Besides, we didn't have opinions
about historical figures like Jefferson. Like our high school
building or old Mayor Welch, he just was.

After I had stared at her for a few seconds, she said: 10
"Well, should he have bought Louisiana or not?"

"I guess so," I replied tentatively.   11

"Why?" she shot back.   12

Why! What kind of question was that, I groused silently.   13
But I ventured an answer. Day after day, she kept doing that
to me, and my answers became stronger and more confident.
She was the first teacher to give me the sense that thinking
was part of education and that I could form opinions that had
some value.

Her final service to me came on a day when my mind   14
was wandering and I was idly digging my pencil into the writing surface on the arm of my chair. Miss Bean impulsively
threw a hunk of gum eraser at me. By amazing chance, it hit
my hand and sent the pencil flying. She gasped, and I crept
mortified after my pencil as the class roared. That was the ice
breaker.

Afterward, kids came up to me to laugh about "Old   15
Dead-Eye Bean." The incident became a legend, and I, a part
of that story, became a person to talk to.

So that's how I became just another kid in school and   16
Dorothy Bean became "Old Dead-Eye."

BUILDING VOCABULARY

1. While not technically *figures of speech* or *idiomatic expressions* (see Glossary), the following word groups from the

essay have *connotative* value in their contexts. (*Denotation* is a word's literal, or dictionary, meaning; *connotation* conveys its subjective "shades" of meaning.) For each of the following word groups, explain in your own words the denotative meaning. Then, going back to the essay, explain their connotative value in the *specific context* of the essay.

    a. The prevailing wisdom (par. 2)
    b. the dominant culture (par. 3)
    c. a nonstandard person (par. 4)
    d. culturally disadvantaged (par. 4)
    e. human dimensions (par. 8)

2. Use any of five of the Words to Watch in original sentences.

UNDERSTANDING THE WRITER'S IDEAS

1. What subject, at what level, when, and where did "Dead-Eye" Bean teach? What was her real name? Why was she called "Dead-Eye"? How old was Wilkins when he was in her class?

2. Briefly explain in your own words how the author got from Harlem, New York, to Grand Rapids, Michigan.

3. What was the racial makeup of his new school? What can you assume about the racial makeup of his old school? Why?

4. Into what social class do you think Wilkins's family fit after they moved to Grand Rapids? Identify clues from the essay that support your opinion.

5. What was the attitude towards the Wilkinses in their new neighborhood? Why? How did the reactions to the Wilkinses differ among the neighborhood adults and the kids? What specific actions did each group take? Why does Wilkins say the youngsters were "culturally disadvantaged''? What was the effect of the neighbors' reactions on the young Wilkins?

6. Explain the metaphor in paragraph 3: ''the dominant culture was speaking to me insistently.''

7. Describe Dorothy ''Dead-Eye'' Bean as a person. What was her attitude on the racism that the young Wilkins was experiencing?

8. What was the result of Bean's first question to Wilkins? Why did she later ask him to answer another question? What was the result that time? How did Dorothy Bean's actions *immediately* change the young Wilkins's life?

9. How did Dorothy Bean require Wilkins *to think?* Ultimately, how did she change his life?

10. Why did Bean throw the eraser at Wilkins? Although it seems a rather hostile act, why did it turn out for the good? Explain the meaning of ''That was the ice-breaker.''

11. What is the main point of Wilkins's tale about Dead-Eye Bean?

UNDERSTANDING THE WRITER'S TECHNIQUES

1. What is the thesis of Wilkins's essay?

2. A *memoir* is a narrative composed from personal experience. On what personal experience is this memoir based? Is using the memoir form an effective technique to communicate the author's ideas? Why?

3. *Chronological order* in narration refers to the arrangement of events in the order they occurred in time, beginning with the one in the most distant past. How does Wilkins use chronological order in this essay? Outline the chronology. What transitions does he use to tie together that chronology?

4. A writer will use *allusions* (see Glossary) to help place the events in an essay at a particular time in history. Identify the following allusions from this essay and tell how they help set the historical moment: Joe DiMaggio; Franklin D. Roosevelt; the Montgomery bus boycott.

5. Wilkins helps to structure the essay by contrasting his "then" and "now" views of certain incidents. Compare his "then" and "now" views of (a) the kids in the Grand Rapids neighborhood and (b) Dorothy Bean. How do these contrasts help structure the essay?

6. Why does Wilkins use the term "Negroes" rather than "Blacks" in paragraph 6? How would the impact of the sentence have changed if he had used "Blacks"?

7. Usually parenthetical expressions are used to add or further clarify information. Reread paragraph 2. For what other reasons might Wilkins have added the parenthetical expressions?

8. How many narratives do you identify here? How does Wilkins weave them together?

9. At two points, the author uses expressions that might have *double meanings* within the context of this essay. Explain the possible double meanings of "a dark presence" (par. 8) and "her final service" (par. 14). Could the title be construed as having a double meaning as well? How so?

10. How did you react to the final sentence? Does it adequately conclude this essay? Does it fit in tone with the rest of the essay? Explain your answers.

EXPLORING THE WRITER'S IDEAS

1. Langston Hughes writes in "Salvation" (pages 137–139) of a childhood moment that occurred when he was about the same age as Wilkins in this essay. Although they come from different eras (Hughes about thirty years earlier),

both boys faced important changes in their lives as reflected in the essays. What do you think was most similar
about their experiences? Most different?

2. Throughout the essay, Wilkins compares his perceptions of
incidents from his point of view when a child with his perceptions of them as an adult. How has the distance of years
affected your views of various childhood incidents? Which
viewpoint do you feel is more accurate? Which is more
helpful to you in understanding your present life situation?

3. Comparing the adults' and children's responses to his family moving into an all-white neighborhood, Wilkins indicates that in many ways the children were much nastier. It
is often said that children can be very cruel to an outsider
or to someone "different." Why do children react so forcefully? From where do most youngsters learn their tactics?
How is it possible to bring up children who are less aggressive or nasty?

IDEAS FOR WRITING

Guided Writing

Write a narrative essay that focuses on a childhood incident
with a teacher, an incident that had lasting effects on you because it helped you solve a problem, face an unpleasant truth,
or understand yourself better.

1. Begin by identifying the teacher, the place, and the level of
your class.

2. State the year of the incident and include *allusions* to set
the time period.

3. Tell what the incident was and how it also involved others
(for example, your parents, your brothers and sisters).

4. Describe the teacher in more subjective terms than in your
first paragraph. Use rich sensory detail. State particular

qualities of the teacher that helped that teacher affect you as strongly as he or she did.

5. Use chronological order in your narration of the incident.

6. Throughout the essay, contrast your perceptions of this problem when you were a child with your perceptions in retrospect as an adult.

7. Include some dialogue between you and your teacher.

8. In your conclusion explain how this teacher changed your life.

More Writing Projects

1. Narrate an incident during which you felt you were the victim of bigotry, racism, sexism, or other form of prejudice.

2. Write an essay about something you did that significantly changed another person's life.

A Hanging

George Orwell

One of the masters of English prose, George Orwell (1903–1950) often used narration of personal events to explore important social issues. Notice here how he involves the reader in a simple yet fascinating and tragic story, almost as if he were writing fiction. Orwell takes a brief time span and expands that moment with specific language. At one point, as you will see, the purpose of the narrative comes into sharp focus.

Words to Watch

sodden (par. 1)   heavy with water

absurdly (par. 2)   ridiculously

desolately (par. 3)   gloomily; lifelessly; cheerlessly

prodding (par. 3)   poking or thrusting at something

Dravidian (par. 4)   any member of a group of intermixed races of southern India and Burma

pariah (par. 6)   outcast; a member of a low caste of southern India and Burma

servile (par. 11)   slave-like; lacking spirit or independence

reiterated (par. 12)   repeated

abominable (par. 13)   hateful; disagreeable; unpleasant

timorously (par. 15)   fearfully

oscillated (par. 16)   moved back and forth between two points

garrulously (par. 20)   in a talkative manner

refractory (par. 22)   stubborn

amicably (par. 24)   in a friendly way; peaceably

It was in Burma, a sodden morning of the rains. A sickly 1 light, like yellow tinfoil, was slanting over the high walls into the jail yard. We were waiting outside the condemned cells, a row of sheds fronted with double bars, like small animal cages. Each cell measured about ten feet by ten and was quite bare within except for a plank bed and a pot of drinking water.

In some of them brown silent men were squatting at the inner bars, with their blankets draped round them. These were the condemned men, due to be hanged within the next week or two.

One prisoner had been brought out of his cell. He was a   2 Hindu, a puny wisp of a man, with a shaven head and vague liquid eyes. He had a thick, sprouting moustache, absurdly too big for his body, rather like the moustache of a comic man on the films. Six tall Indian warders were guarding him and getting him ready for the gallows. Two of them stood by with rifles with fixed bayonets, while the others handcuffed him, passed a chain through his handcuffs and fixed it to their belts, and lashed his arms tight to his sides. They crowded very close about him, with their hands always on him in a careful, caressing grip, as though all the while feeling him to make sure he was there. It was like men handling a fish which is still alive and may jump back into the water. But he stood quite unresisting, yielding his arms limply to the ropes, as though he hardly noticed what was happening.

Eight o'clock struck and a bugle call, desolately thin in   3 the wet air, floated from the distant barracks. The superintendent of the jail, who was standing apart from the rest of us, moodily prodding the gravel with his stick, raised his head at the sound. He was an army doctor, with a grey toothbrush moustache and a gruff voice. "For God's sake hurry up, Francis," he said irritably. "The man ought to have been dead by this time. Aren't you ready yet?"

Francis, the head jailer, a fat Dravidian in a white drill   4 suit and gold spectacles, waved his black hand. "Yes sir, yes sir," he bubbled. "All iss satisfactorily prepared. The hangman iss waiting. We shall proceed."

"Well, quick march, then. The prisoners can't get their   5 breakfast till this job's over."

We set out for the gallows. Two warders marched on ei-   6 ther side of the prisoner, with their files at the slope; two others marched close against him, gripping him by arm and shoulder, as though at once pushing and supporting him. The rest of us, magistrates and the like, followed behind. Suddenly, when we had gone ten yards, the procession stopped short without any order or warning. A dreadful thing had happened—a dog, come goodness knows whence, had appeared in the yard. It came bounding among us with a loud volley of barks, and leapt round us wagging its whole body, wild with glee at finding so many human beings together. It was a large woolly dog, half Airedale, half pariah. For a moment it pranced round us, and then, before anyone could stop it, it had made a dash for the prisoner, and jumping up tried to lick his face. Everyone stood aghast, too taken aback even to grab at the dog.

"Who let that bloody brute in here?" said the superin- 7 tendent angrily. "Catch it, someone!"

A warder, detached from the escort, charged clumsily af- 8 ter the dog, but it danced and gambolled just out of his reach, taking everything as part of the game. A young Eurasian jailer picked up a handful of gravel and tried to stone the dog away, but it dodged the stones and came after us again. Its yaps echoed from the jail walls. The prisoner, in the grasp of the two warders, looked on incuriously, as though this was another formality of the hanging. It was several minutes before someone managed to catch the dog. Then we put my handkerchief through its collar and moved off once more, with the dog still straining and whimpering.

It was about forty yards to the gallows. I watched the 9 bare brown back of the prisoner marching in front of me. He walked clumsily with his bound arms, but quite steadily, with that bobbing gait of the Indian who never straightens his knees. At each step his muscles slid neatly into place, the lock of hair on his scalp danced up and down, his feet printed themselves on the wet gravel. And once, in spite of the men who gripped him by each shoulder, he stepped slightly aside to avoid a puddle on the path.

It is curious, but till that moment I had never realised 10 what it means to destroy a healthy, conscious man. When I saw the prisoner step aside to avoid the puddle, I saw the mystery, the unspeakable wrongness, of cutting a life short when it is in full tide. This man was not dying, he was alive just as we were alive. All the organs of his body were working—bowels digesting food, skin renewing itself, nails growing, tissues forming—all toiling away in solemn foolery. His nails would still be growing when he stood on the drop, when he was falling through the air with a tenth of a second to live. His eyes saw the yellow gravel and the grey walls, and his brain still remembered, foresaw, reasoned—reasoned even about puddles. He and we were a party of men walking together, seeing, hearing, feeling, understanding the same world; and in two minutes, with a sudden snap, one of us would be gone—one mind less, one world less.

The gallows stood in a small yard, separate from the main grounds of the prison, and overgrown with tall prickly weeds. It was a brick erection like three sides of a shed, with planking on top, and above that two beams and a crossbar with the rope dangling. The hangman, a grey-haired convict in the white uniform of the prison, was waiting beside his machine. He greeted us with a servile crouch as we entered. At a word from Francis the two warders, gripping the prisoner more closely than ever, half led, half pushed him to the gallows and helped him clumsily up the ladder. Then the hangman climbed up and fixed the rope round the prisoner's neck. 11

We stood waiting, five yards away. The warders had formed in a rough circle round the gallows. And then, when the noose was fixed, the prisoner began crying out on his god. It was a high, reiterated cry of "Ram! Ram! Ram! Ram!", not urgent and fearful like a prayer or a cry for help, but steady, rhythmical, almost like the tolling of a bell. The dog answered the sound with a whine. The hangman, still standing on the gallows, produced a small cotton bag like a flour bag and drew it down over the prisoner's face. But the sound, muffled by the cloth, still persisted, over and over again: "Ram! Ram! Ram! Ram! Ram!" 12

The hangman climbed down and stood ready, holding the lever. Minutes seemed to pass. The steady, muffled crying from the prisoner went on and on, "Ram! Ram! Ram!" never faltering for an instant. The superintendent, his head on his chest, was slowly poking the ground with his stick; perhaps he was counting the cries, allowing the prisoner a fixed number—fifty, perhaps, or a hundred. Everyone had changed colour. The Indians had gone grey like bad coffee, and one or two of the bayonets were wavering. We looked at the lashed, hooded 13 man on the drop, and listened to his cries—each cry another second of life; the same thought was in all our minds: oh, kill him quickly, get it over, stop that abominable noise!

Suddenly the superintendent made up his mind. Throw- 14 ing up his head he made a swift motion with his stick. "Chalo!" he shouted almost fiercely.

There was a clanking noise, and then dead silence. The 15 prisoner had vanished, and the rope was twisting on itself. I let go of the dog, and it galloped immediately to the back of the gallows; but when it got there it stopped short, barked, and then retreated into a corner of the yard, where it stood among the weeds, looking timorously out at us. We went round the gallows to inspect the prisoner's body. He was dangling with his toes pointed straight downwards, very slowly revolving, as dead as a stone.

The superintendent reached out with his stick and poked 16 the bare body; it oscillated, slightly. "*He's* all right," said the superintendent. He backed out from under the gallows, and blew out a deep breath. The moody look had gone out of his face quite suddenly. He glanced at his wristwatch. "Eight minutes past eight. Well, that's all for this morning, thank God."

The warders unfixed bayonets and marched away. The 17 dog, sobered and conscious of having misbehaved itself, slipped after them. We walked out of the gallows yard, past the condemned cells with their waiting prisoners, into the big central yard of the prison. The convicts, under the command of warders armed with lathis, were already receiving their breakfast. They squatted in long rows, each man holding a tin pannikin, while two warders with buckets marched round ladling out rice; it seemed quite a homely, jolly scene, after the hanging. An enormous relief had come upon us now that the job was done. One felt an impulse to sing, to break into a run, to snigger. All at once everyone began chattering gaily.

The Eurasian boy walking beside me nodded towards the 18 way we had come, with a knowing smile: "Do you know, sir, our friend (he meant the dead man), when he heard his appeal had been dismissed, he pissed on the floor of his cell. From

fright—Kindly take one of my cigarettes, sir. Do you not admire my new silver case, sir? From the boxwallah, two rupees
eight annas. Classy European style.''

Several people laughed—at what, nobody seemed certain. 19

Francis was walking by the superintendent, talking gar- 20
rulously: "Well, sir, all hass passed off with the utmost satis-
factoriness. It wass all finished—flick! like that. It iss not always so—oah, no! I have known cases where the doctor wass
obliged to go beneath the gallows and pull the prisoner's legs
to ensure decease. Most disagreeable!''

"Wriggling about, eh? That's bad,'' said the superinten- 21
dent.

"Ach, sir, it iss worse when they become refractory! 22
One man, I recall, clung to the bars of hiss cage when we went
to take him out. You will scarcely credit, sir, that it took six
warders to dislodge him, three pulling at each leg. We reasoned with him. 'My dear fellow,' we said, 'think of all the
pain and trouble you are causing to us!' But no, he would not
listen! Ach, he wass very troublesome!''

I found that I was laughing quite loudly. Everyone was 23
laughing. Even the superintendent grinned in a tolerant way.
"You'd better all come out and have a drink,'' he said quite
genially. "I've got a bottle of whisky in the car. We could do
with it.''

We went through the big double gates of the prison, into 24
the road. "Pulling at his legs!'' exclaimed a Burmese magis-
trate suddenly, and burst into a loud chuckling. We all began
laughing again. At that moment Francis's anecdote seemed
extraordinarily funny. We all had a drink together, native and
European alike, quite amicably. The dead man was a hundred
yards away.

BUILDING VOCABULARY

1. It is often possible to figure out the meaning of a difficult
word by using context clues—clues in surrounding words
and sentences. Without a dictionary, make an "educated

guess" on the definitions of the words in italics below. Before you guess, look back to the paragraph for clues. Afterward, check your guess in a dictionary.

   a. *condemned* men (par. 1)
   b. puny *wisp* of a man (par. 2)
   c. Indian *warders* (par. 2)
   d. careful *caressing* grip (par. 2)
   e. stood *aghast* (par. 6)
   f. it danced and *gambolled* (par. 7)
   g. *solemn* foolery (par. 10)
   h. armed with *lathis* (par. 17)
   i. a tin *pannikin* (par. 17)
   j. quite *genially* (par. 23)

2. What are definitions for the words below? Look at words within them, which you may be able to recognize.

   a. moodily
   b. dreadful
   c. Eurasian
   d. incuriously
   e. formality

3. Complete the following vocabulary exercises:

   a. Select any five words from the Words to Watch section on page 152 and write a sentence of your own for each.
   b. Select any five words from Exercises 1 and 2 above and write a sentence of your own for each.

UNDERSTANDING THE WRITER'S IDEAS

1. What is the main point that the writer wishes to make in this essay? Which paragraph tells the author's purpose most clearly? Which sentence in that paragraph best states the main idea of the essay?

2. The events in the essay occur in Burma, a country in Asia. Describe in your own words the specific details of the action.

3. Who are the major characters in this essay? Why might you include the dog as a major character?

4. In a narrative essay the writer often tells the events in chronological order. Examine the following events from "A Hanging." Arrange them in the order in which they occurred.

    a. A large wooly dog tries to lick the prisoner's face.
    b. A Eurasian boy talks about his silver case.
    c. The superintendent signals "Chalo!" to the hangman.
    d. One prisoner, a Hindu, is brought from his cell.
    e. Francis discusses with the superintendent a prisoner who had to be pulled off the bars of his cage.
    f. The prisoner steps aside to avoid a puddle as he marches to the gallows.

5. What is the author's opinion of *capital punishment* (legally killing someone who has disobeyed the laws of society)? How does the incident with the puddle suggest that opinion, even indirectly?

UNDERSTANDING THE WRITER'S TECHNIQUES

1. In the first paragraph of the essay, we see clear images such as "brown silent men were squatting at the inner bars, with their blankets draped around them." The use of color and action make an instant appeal to our sense of sight.

    a. What images in the rest of the essay do you find most vivid?
    b. Which sentence gives the best details of sound?
    c. What word pictures suggest action and color?
    d. Where do you find words that describe a sensation of touch?

2. In order to make their images clearer, writers use *figurative language* (see Glossary). "A Hanging" is especially rich in *similes,* which are comparisons using the word *like* or *as.*

   a. What simile does Orwell use in the first paragraph in order to let us see how the light slants over the jail yard
   walls? How does the simile make the scene clearer?

   b. What other simile does Orwell use in the first paragraph?

   c. Discuss the similes in the paragraphs listed below. What
   are the things being compared? Are the similes, in your
   opinion, original? How do they contribute to the image
   the author intends to create?

   (1) It was like man handling a fish....(par. 2)

   (2) A thick sprouting moustache...rather like the moustache of a comic man in the films. (par. 2)

   (3) It was a high, reiterated cry...like the tolling of a
   bell. (par. 12)

   (4) The Indians had gone grey like bad coffee....''
   (par. 13)

   (5) He was dangling with his toes pointed straight downwards, slowly revolving, as dead as a stone. (par. 15)

3. You know that an important feature of narration is the writer's ability to look at a brief span of time and to expand that
moment with specific language.

   a. How has Orwell limited the events in ''A Hanging'' to a
   specific moment in time and place?

   b. How does the image ''a sodden morning of the rains''
   in paragraph 1 set the mood for the main event portrayed in the essay? What is the effect of the image
   ''brown silent men''? Why does Orwell describe the
   prisoner as ''a puny wisp of a man, with a shaven head
   and vague liquid eyes''? (par. 2) Why does the author
   present him in almost a comic way?

   c. What is the effect of the image about the bugle call in
   paragraph 3? Why does Orwell create the image of the
   dog trying to lick the prisoner's face (par. 6)? How does
   it contribute to his main point? In paragraph 12, Orwell
   tells us that the dog whines. Why does he give that detail? Discuss the value of the images about the dog in
   paragraphs 15 and 17.

   d. Why does Orwell offer the image of the prisoner step-
   ping aside ''to avoid a puddle on the path''? How does it

advance the point of the essay? What is the effect of the image of the superintendent poking the ground with his stick (par. 13)?

  e. What is the importance of the superintendent's words in paragraph 3? What is the value of the Eurasian boy's conversation in paragraph 18? How does the dialogue in paragraphs 20 to 24 contribute to Orwell's main point?

  f. Why has Orwell left out information about the crime the prisoner committed? How would you feel about the prisoner if you knew he were, say, a rapist, a murderer, a molester of children, or a heroin supplier?

4. Analyze the point of view in the essay. Is the ''I'' narrator an observer, a participant, or both? Is he neutral or involved? Support your opinion.

5. In ''A Hanging,'' Orwell skillfully uses several forms of *irony* to support his main ideas. Irony, in general, is the use of language to suggest the opposite of what is said. First, there is *verbal irony,* which involves a contrast between what is said and what is actually meant. Second, there is *irony of situation,* where there is a contrast between what is expected or thought appropriate and what actually happens. Then, there is *dramatic irony,* in which there is a contrast between what a character says and what the reader (or the audience) actually knows or understands.

  a. In paragraph 2, why does Orwell describe the prisoner as a *comic* type? Why does he emphasize the prisoner's *smallness?* Why does Orwell write that the prisoner ''hardly noticed what was happening''? Why might this be called ironic?

  b. When the dog appears in paragraph 6, how is its behavior described? How do the dog's actions contrast with the situation?

  c. What is the major irony that Orwell analyzes in paragraph 10?

  d. In paragraph 11, how does the fact that one prisoner is being used to execute another prisoner strike you?

  e. Why is the Superintendent's remark in paragraph 11— ''*He's* all right''—a good example of verbal irony?

    f. After the hanging, the men engage in seemingly normal actions. However, Orwell undercuts these actions through the use of irony. Find at least three examples of irony in paragraphs 17 to 24.

EXPLORING THE WRITER'S IDEAS

1. Orwell is clearly against capital punishment. Why might you agree or disagree with him? Are there any crimes for which capital punishment is acceptable to you? If not, what should society do with those convicted of serious crimes?

2. Do you think the method used to perform capital punishment has anything to do with the way we view it? Is death by hanging or firing squad worse than death by gas or by the electric chair? Or are they all the same? Socrates—a Greek philosopher convicted of conspiracy—was forced to drink *hemlock,* a fast acting poison. Can you accept that?

3. Orwell shows a variety of reactions people have to an act of execution. Can you believe the way the people behave here? Why? How do you explain the large crowds that gathered to watch public executions in Europe in the sixteenth and seventeenth centuries?

IDEAS FOR WRITING

Guided Writing

Write a narrative theme of four or five paragraphs in which you tell about a punishment you either saw or received. Use sensory language, selecting your details carefully. At one point in your paper—as Orwell does in paragraph 10—state your opinion or interpretation of the punishment clearly.

1. Use a number of images that name colors, sounds, smells, and actions.

2. Try to write at least three original similes. Think through your comparisons carefully. Make sure they are logical. Avoid overused comparisons like "He was white as a ghost."

3. Set your narrative in time and place. Tell the season of the year and the place in which the event occurred.

4. Fill in details of the setting. Show what the surroundings look like.

5. Name people by name. Show details of their actions. Quote some of their spoken dialogue.

6. Use the first-person point of view.

More Writing Projects

1. Write a narrative essay in which you tell the story of an execution from the point of view of either the executioner or the person condemned to die. Focus on the last moments before the execution.

2. Write an essay in which you narrate an event that turned out differently from what you expected—a blind date, a picnic, a holiday. Try to stress the irony of the situation.

3. Write a narrative that describes a vivid event in which you hid your true feelings about the event, such as a postelection party, the wedding of someone you disliked, a job interview, a visit to the doctor.

CHAPTER 5

Illustration

One convenient way for writers to present and to support a point is through *illustration*—that is, by means of several examples to back up an idea. Illustration helps a writer put general or abstract thoughts into specific examples. It also holds a reader's interest: We all respond to concrete instances when we are trying to understand a point. Certainly, you are no stranger to illustration as a way to present information. Every time you try to explain why you believe or feel something to be true, and you give more than one case to back it up, you are using this technique.

Suppose you want to share with a friend your belief that the Los Angeles Dodgers are a great baseball team. First you might point out the pitching staff; then you might bring up the quality hitters; then the fielders; then the management. Your friend would, no doubt, expect you to explain each of those illustrations by giving some details. And so you would name a couple of first-rate pitchers, perhaps describe them and state their won-lost record; you would tell which of the hitters you thought outstanding and point out their runs-batted-in and their hitting averages; you would describe a good fielder or two in action, even telling a story, perhaps, of one really first-rate play you saw when the Dodgers pounded the Reds.

When you present illustrations, it is best to have *several* reasons that lead you to a certain conclusion. A single, isolated example might not convince anyone easily, unless it is a strong, extended example. You have to make decisions, of course, about the number and kinds of details to offer for each example. Sometimes each illustration will itself require a few different examples to make the point. And you have to decide which illustration to give first: No doubt you would save the most important for last.

As you have probably guessed, when you write an essay of illustration you will be using much of what you have already learned so far. Techniques of description and narration will help you support and organize your examples clearly and strongly. In fact, a number of ways to develop essays discussed later on—comparison, cause and effect, process analysis, definition, and classification—lend themselves to development by illustration. The selections you will read in this section show how four writers use illustration to advance their ideas.

Daddy Tucked the Blanket

Randall Williams

Randall Williams was a reporter for *The Alabama Journal* when he wrote this autobiographical essay. He is trying here to show how the social conditions of the poor have an ugly effect upon personal relationships. A number of examples point out how his family reacted to each other and to the environment created by poverty.

Words to Watch

humiliating (par. 5)   lowering the pride or dignity of someone
shiftless (par. 7)   incapable; inefficient; lazy
articulate (par. 7)   able to express oneself clearly
teetering (par. 8)   wavering; moving unsteadily
deteriorating (par. 12)   becoming worse
futility (par. 13)   the quality of being useless
abuse (par. 16)   mistreatment
psyche (par. 20)   the soul; the self; the mind
affluent (par. 21)   wealthy
grandeur (par. 23)   magnificence

About the time I turned 16, my folks began to wonder 1 why I didn't stay home any more. I always had an excuse for them, but what I didn't say was that I had found my freedom and I was getting out.

I went through four years of high school in semirural Al- 2 abama and became active in clubs and sports; I made a lot of friends and became a regular guy, if you know what I mean. But one thing was irregular about me: I managed those four years without ever having a friend visit at my house.

I was ashamed of where I lived. I had been ashamed for 3 as long as I had been conscious of class.

We had a big family. There were several of us sleeping in 4 one room, but that's not so bad if you get along, and we always did. As you get older, though, it gets worse.

Being poor is a humiliating experience for a young per- 5
son trying hard to be accepted. Even now—several years removed—it is hard to talk about. And I resent the weakness of
these words to make you feel what it was really like.

We lived in a lot of old houses. We moved a lot because 6
we were always looking for something just a little better than
what we had. You have to understand that my folks worked
harder than most people. My mother was always at home, but
for her that was a full-time job—and no fun, either. But my
father worked his head off from the time I can remember in
construction and shops. It was hard, physical work.

I tell you this to show that we weren't shiftless. No mat- 7
ter how much money Daddy made, we never made much
progress up the social ladder. I got out thanks to a college
scholarship and because I was a little more articulate than the
average.

I have seen my Daddy wrap copper wire through the 8
soles of his boots to keep them together in the wintertime. He
couldn't buy new boots because he had used the money for
food and shoes for us. We lived like hell, but we went to
school well-clothed and with a full stomach.

It really is hell to live in a house that was in bad shape 10 9
years before you moved in. And a big family puts a lot of wear
and tear on a new house, too, so you can imagine how one
goes downhill if it is teetering when you move in. But we lived
in houses that were sweltering in summer and freezing in winter. I woke up every morning for a year and a half with plaster
on my face where it had fallen out of the ceiling during the
night.

This wasn't during the Depression; this was in the late 10
60's and early 70's.

When we boys got old enough to learn trades in school, 11
we would try to fix up the old houses we lived in. But have
you ever tried to paint a wall that crumbled when the roller
went across it? And bright paint emphasized the holes in the
wall. You end up more frustrated than when you began, especially when you know that at best you might come up with
only enough money to improve one of the six rooms in the
house. And we might move out soon after, anyway.

The same goes for keeping a house like that clean. If you 12
have a house full of kids and the house is deteriorating, you'll
never keep it clean. Daddy used to yell at Mama about that, but
she couldn't do anything. I think Daddy knew it inside, but he
had to have an outlet for his rage somewhere, and at least yelling
isn't as bad as hitting, which they never did to each other.

But you have a kitchen which has no counter space and 13
no hot water, and you will have dirty dishes stacked up. That
sounds like an excuse, but try it. You'll go mad from the sheer
sense of futility. It's the same thing in a house with no closets.
You can't keep clothes clean and rooms in order if they have
to be stacked up with things.

Living in a bad house is generally worse on girls. For one 14
thing, they traditionally help their mother with the housework.
We boys could get outside and work in the field or cut wood
or even play ball and forget about living conditions. The sky
was still pretty.

But the girls got the pressure, and as they got older it be- 15
came worse. Would they accept dates knowing they had to
"receive" the young man in a dirty hallway with broken windows, peeling wallpaper and a cracked ceiling? You have to
live it to understand it, but it creates a shame which drives the
soul of a young person inward.

I'm thankful none of us ever blamed our parents for this, 16
because it would have crippled our relationships. As it worked
out, only the relationship between our parents was damaged.
And I think the harshness which they expressed to each other
was just an outlet to get rid of their anger at the trap their lives
were in. It ruined their marriage because they had no one to
yell at but each other. I knew other families where the kids got
the abuse, but we were too much loved for that.

Once I was about 16 and Mama and Daddy had had a 17
particularly violent argument about the washing machine,
which had broken down. Daddy was on the back porch—
that's where the only water faucet was—trying to fix it and
Mamma had a washtub out there washing school clothes for
the next day and they were screaming at each other.

Later that night everyone was in bed and I heard Daddy 18
get up from the couch where he was reading. I looked out

from my bed across the hall into their room. He was standing
right over Mama and she was already asleep. He pulled the
blanket up and tucked it around her shoulders and just stood
there and tears were dropping off his cheeks and I thought I
could faintly hear them splashing against the linoleum rug.

Now they're divorced.   19

I had courses in college where housing was discussed,   20
but the sociologists never put enough emphasis on the impact
living in substandard housing has on a person's psyche. Especially children's.

Small children have a hard time understanding poverty.   21
They want the same things children from more affluent families
have. They want the same things they see advertised on television, and they don't understand why they can't have them.

Other children can be incredibly cruel. I was in elemen-   22
tary school in Georgia—and this is interesting because it is the
only thing I remember about that particular school—when I
was about eight or nine.

After Christmas vacation had ended, my teacher made   23
each student describe all his or her Christmas presents. I became more and more uncomfortable as the privilege passed
around the room toward me. Other children were reciting the
names of the dolls they had been given, the kinds of bicycles
and the grandeur of their games and toys. Some had lists
which seemed to go on and on for hours.

It took me only a few seconds to tell the class that I had   24
gotten for Christmas a belt and a pair of gloves. And then I
was laughed at—because I cried—by a roomful of children
and a teacher. I never forgave them, and that night I made my
mother cry when I told her about it.

In retrospect, I am grateful for that moment, but I re-   25
member wanting to die at the time.

BUILDING VOCABULARY

1. For each expression in italics in Column A select from Column B the best definition. On a separate sheet of paper,
   write the correct letter after each number.

Column A	*Column B*
1 one thing was *irregular* about me	**a** absolute
2 *conscious* of class	**b** object to
3 I *resent* the weakness	**c** way to express anger
4 houses that were *sweltering*	**d** are expected to
5 an *outlet for his rage*	**e** force
6 the *sheer* sense of futility	**f** not correct
7 they *traditionally* help mother	**g** very hot
8 the *impact* living in substandard housing has	**h** unbelievably
9 *incredibly* cruel	**i** aware
10 in *retrospect*	**j** looking back

UNDERSTANDING THE WRITER'S IDEAS

1. Why did the author never have a friend visit his house? How did he explain to his parents the fact that, at sixteen, he did not stay home any more?

2. Describe some of the situations Williams remembers about the houses in which he lived as a child. Why was it hard to keep the houses clean? Why was living in such a house so bad for the author's sisters? Why did the family keep moving around?

3. Why did the Williams family never "progress up the social ladder"? Why does he stress the idea that the family was not shiftless?

4. Why, according to the author, was his parent's relationship damaged? Why were they frequently having violent arguments? How does Williams show the love his father had for his mother?

5. Why does the author believe that children can be incredibly cruel?

6. What is the meaning of the last paragraph? For which moment do you think the author is grateful, the moment in school or the moment in which his mother cried? Why would he be grateful for either of those moments?

UNDERSTANDING THE WRITER'S TECHNIQUES

1. What is Williams's main point in this essay? Which sentence expresses the writer's *thesis?*

2. What details does Williams offer to illustrate the fact that he lived in bad houses? Which details are clearest to you?

3. How does Williams illustrate how little money his father had for himself?

4. How does Williams illustrate the way his parents argued? What elements of narration do you find in that example? Where else does the author use narrative as part of an illustration?

5. In which illustrations does the writer use description? Where do you find good descriptive details in this essay? On the whole, though, the author has not used descriptive language very much. Why? Where would you have liked to see more concrete detail?

6. One way that the writer has for tying together his ideas is by frequently reminding the reader of his thesis. Review your response to question 1 above; then, find words or word groups later on in the essay that repeat the main point, either through the same words or through words that mean the same or similar things.

7. This essay is written in a very simple style. How does the writer achieve this simplicity? Is it the vocabulary? How would you describe it? Is it the sentence structure? What kinds of sentences does Williams write most of the time? What is the effect of the numerous short paragraphs? What

is your reaction to the two paragraphs that have only one sentence in each of them?

8. Do the writer's illustrations support his main point successfully? Why do you think he chose illustration as a way to develop his idea? Which illustration do you find most effective? Why does he tell the story about his experience in school after Christmas one year at the *end* of the essay?

9. When a writer exaggerates emotions, he is often accused of *sentimentality*. In sentimental writing the author plays with the reader's emotions simply for their own sake. Would you call Williams sentimental? Why? Which images deliberately convey an emotional stance? Do you feel as if he is exaggerating emotions here? Where has he *avoided* sentimentality when he might have played up the scene for its emotional content?

EXPLORING THE WRITER'S IDEAS

1. Williams says that it is hard to talk about his humiliating past experiences, and then he says, "I resent the weakness of these words to make you feel what it was really like." Do you agree that words are weak in conveying feeling to someone who might not have experienced that feeling? Williams is talking about *humiliation* and how words are not strong enough to make people feel it. What other feeling have you had that might be hard to convey in words? Despite the fact that the author complains about words, he writes, nonetheless, about his experiences. How do you explain that?

2. Has Williams fairly presented the condition of poverty in America? How does his own situation show some ways that a family or an individual may overcome certain features of poverty? Would you say that poverty in a rural area is the same as poverty in a large city like Atlanta, or Chicago, or New York?

3. Do you agree with Williams's analysis that his father and mother yelled at each other because they needed an outlet

for their anger? Do you think the need for such an outlet
can force apart two people who love each other? Is it possible for people to fight constantly and still to love each
other? What instances from your own experience can you
quote to demonstrate these points? How do you account
for the fact that despite poverty and frequent fights, some
parents stay together without divorcing?

4. The author suggests that housing plays an important part in
the development of a person's psyche. Do you agree?
Why? What ingredients would you list for perfect home
conditions? Would you include anything other than simple
physical conditions like walls that do not crumble or washing machines that work?

5. Williams's father and mother obviously sacrificed many of
their own needs and comforts for their children. Do you believe that parents should make such sacrifices? Why or
why not?

6. Do you agree that living in a bad house is more difficult for
girls than boys? Why?

IDEAS FOR WRITING

Guided Writing

On a separate sheet of paper, fill in the blanks in this sentence
and then write an essay of 350 to 500 words in which you use
illustration to present your ideas:

Being _____ is a _____
experience for a young person.

1. For the blank spaces select words which reflect important
aspects of your own experiences. You do not have to pick
negative qualities: You might say, "Being *free* is an *essential* experience for a young person." Or, you might follow
one of these other suggestions if you cannot think of one of
your own. But be sure to avoid overused words like *good,
bad, nice, fantastic,* or *interesting.*

a. Being *lonely* is a *terrible* experience for a young person.
b. Being *frightened* is an *unforgettable* experience for a young person.
c. Being *loved* is a *vital* experience for a young person.
d. Being *"different"* is a *sad* experience for a young person.

2. Use the sentence you have written as the thesis sentence of your paragraph. Build an introduction around it.

3. Illustrate your thesis with examples drawn from your own experience. Provide at least three illustrations.

4. If your illustrations require narrative, follow the techniques you learned in Chapter 2 about good narration.

5. If you have to use description, make sure you follow the suggestions in Chapter 1 about good description. Use concrete, sensory language to help your reader see your points clearly.

6. Connect the different illustrations in your essay by referring to the main point in your thesis sentence.

More Writing Projects

1. Write an essay of illustration in which you show how certain conditions affected your parents' relationship. You might show the effect of *poverty* on their lives; or you might show the effect of a *city, love, religion, education, superstition, fear, children* on their lives. Feel free to name any condition you choose.

2. Write an essay in which you provide illustrations to show the nature of poverty in your neighborhood, city, or state. You may want to select illustrations from your own experience or observation. Or, you might want to use other sources, like newspaper articles, books, magazines, presentations on radio or television.

Tricks! Treats! Gangway!

Ray Bradbury

Ray Bradbury (1920–) is noted for his science fiction writing—you may have read *Farenheit 451* or have seen the movie—but in this piece he is recalling a special time of year for a boy who grew up in the midwest in the 1920s and 1930s. Illustrations drawn from his childhood show what a grand time Halloween really was in Illinois.

Words to Watch

corrupted (par. 2)   spoiled; ruined

induce (par. 2)   cause; bring about

climax (par. 6)   the highest point of interest or excitement

corn shocks (par. 7)   bunches of corn sheaves drawn together to dry

grisly renderings (par. 8)   terrifying examples

crump-backed (par. 8)   creased; humpbacked

caldron (par. 10)   a large kettle

banshee (par. 10)   a female spirit that warns of death

bereavements (par. 10)   losses of people through death

serpentines (par. 10)   coils

papier-mâché (par. 10)   a material made of paper pulp that can be molded into objects when moist

vulnerable (par. 15)   open to attack

disemboweled (par. 17)   with the bowels or entrails removed

Halloweens I have always considered wilder and richer 1 and more important than even Christmas morn. The dark and lovely memories leap back at me as I see once again my ghostly relatives, and the lurks and things that creaked stairs or sang softly in the hinges when you opened a door.

For, you see, I have been most fortunate in the selection 2 of my aunts and uncles and midnight-minded cousins. My grandma gave me her old black-velvet opera cape to cut into batwings and fold about myself when I was eight. My aunt

175

gave me some white candy fangs to stick in my mouth and
make delicious and most terrible smiles. A great-aunt encouraged me in my witchcrafts by painting my face into a skull and
stashing me in closets to induce cardiac arrest in passing cousins or upstairs boarders. My mother corrupted me completely
by introducing me to Lon Chaney in *The Hunchback of Notre
Dame* when I was three.

In sum, Halloween has always been *the* celebration for   3
me and mine. And those Halloweens in the late 1920s and
early '30s come back to me now at the least scent of candle-
wax or aroma of pumpkin pies.

Autumns were a combination of that dread moment   4
when you see whole windows of dime stores full of nickel
pads and yellow pencils meaning School is Here—and also the
bright promise of October, that stirring stuff which lurks in the
blood and makes boys break out in joyful sweats, planning
ahead.

For we *did* plan ahead in the Bradbury houses. We were   5
three families on one single block in Waukegan, Ill. My
grandma and, until he died in 1926, grandpa, lived in the corner house; my mom and dad, and my brother Skip and I, in
the house next south of that; and around the block my Uncle
Bion, whose library was wise with Edgar Rice Burroughs and
ancient with H. Rider Haggard.

1928 was one of the prime Halloween years. Everything   6
that was grandest came to a special climax that autumn.

My Aunt Neva was 17 and just out of high school, and   7
she had a Model-A Ford. "Okay, kiddo," she said around
about October 20. "It's coming fast. Let's make plans. How
do we use the attics? Where do we put the witches? How
many corn shocks do we bring in from the farms? Who gets
bricked up in the cellar with the Amontillado?"

"Wait, wait, wait!" I yelled—and we made a list. Neva   8
drew pictures and made paintings of the costumes we would
all wear to make the holiday truly fascinating and horrible.
That was Costume Painting Night. When Neva finished, there
were sketches of Grandma as the nice mother in "The Monkey's Paw," paintings of my dad as Edgar Allan Poe, some
fine grisly renderings of my brother as crump-backed Quasi-

modo, and myself playing my own xylophone skeleton as Dr. Death.

After that came, in one flying downpour, Costume Cut- 9 ting Night, Mask Painting Night, Cider Making Night, Candle Dippling and Taffy Pulling Night, and Phonograph Playing Night, when we picked the spookiest music. Halloween, you see, didn't just stroll into our yards. It had to be seized and shaped and *made* to happen!

My grandparents' home, then, was a caldron to which 10 we might bring hickory sticks that looked like witches' broken arms and leaves from the family graveyard out where the banshee trains ran by at night souling the air with bereavements. To their house, upstairs and down, must be fetched corn shocks from fields just beyond the burying tombs, and pumpkins. And from Woolworth's, orange-black crepe serpentines, and bags of black confetti which you tossed on the wind, yelling, "A witch just sneezed!" and papier-mâché masks that smelled like a sour dog's fur after you had snuffed in and out while running. All of it had to be fetched, carried, touched, held, sniffed, crunched along the way.

October 29 and 30 were almost as great as October 31, 11 for those were the late afternoons, the cool, spicy dusks when Neva and Skip and I went out for the Slaughter and final Gathering.

"Watch out, pumpkins!" 12

I stood by the Model A as the sun furnaced the western 13 sky and vanished, leaving spilled-blood and burnt-pumpkin colors behind. "Pumpkins, if they had any brains, would hide tonight!" said I.

"Yeah," said Skip. "Here comes the Smiler with the 14 Knife!" I beamed, feeling my Boy Scout knife in my pocket.

We reached our uncles' farms and went out to dance 15 around the corn shocks and grab great armfuls and wrestle them like dry Indian ghosts back to the rumble seat. Then we went back to get the harvest-moon pumpkins. They burrowed in the cereal grass, but they could not escape the Smiler and his friends. Then home, with the cornstalks waving their arms wildly in the wind behind us, and the pumpkins thudding and running around the floorboards trying to escape. Home to-

ward a town that looked vulnerable under burning clouds,
home past real graveyards with real cold people in them, your
brother and sister, and you thinking of them suddenly and
knowing the true, deep sense of Halloween.

The whole house had to be done over in a few short,   16
wildly laughing hours. All staircases must be eliminated by
grabbing leaves out of dining-room tables and covering the
steps so you could only scrabble and slip up and then slide,
shrieking, down, down, down into night. The cellar must be
mystified with sheets hung on lines in a ghostly maze through
which giggling and screaming banshees must blunder and flee,
children suddenly searching for mothers, and finding spiders.
The icebox must be stashed with chicken viscera, beef hearts,
ox tongues, tripe, chicken legs and gizzards, so that at the
height of the party the participants, trapped in the coal cellar,
might pass around the "parts" of the dead witch: "Here's her
heart!...Here's her finger!...Here's her eyeball!"

Then, everything set and placed and ready, you run out   17
late from house to house to make certain-sure that each boy-
ghost remembers, that each girl-become-witch will be there
tomorrow night. Your gorilla fangs in your mouth, your
winged cape flapping, you come home and stand in front of
your grandparents' house and look at how great and spooky it
has become, because your sappy aunt and your loony brother
and you yourself have magicked it over, doused the lights, lit
all the disemboweled pumpkins and got it ready like a dark
beast to devour the children as they arrive through its open-
mouth door tomorrow night.

You sneak up on the porch, tiptoe down the hall, peer   18
into the dim pumpkin-lit parlor and whisper: "Boo."

And that's *it*.   19

Oh, sure, Halloween arrived. Sure, the next night was   20
wild and lovely and fine. Apples swung in doorways to be nib-
bled by two dozen hungry mice-children. Apples and gargling
kids almost drowned in water tubs while ducking for bites.

But the party was almost unimportant, wasn't it? Prepa-   21
ration was 70 percent of the lovely, mad game. As with most
holidays, the getting set, the gathering sulfur for the explosion, was sweeter, sadder, lovelier than the stampede itself.

That Halloween of 1928 came like the rusted moon up in   22 the sky—sailing, and then down like that same moon. And it was over. I stood in the middle of my grandma's living room and wept.

On the way home across the lawn to my house, I saw the pile of leaves I had made just that afternoon. I ran and dived in, and vanished. I lay there under the leaves, thinking. This is what it's like to be dead. Under grass, under dirt, under leaves. The wind blew and stirred the grand pile. Way out in farm country, a train ran past, wailing its whistle. The sound cut my soul. I felt the tears start up again. I knew if I stayed I would never get out of the grass and leaves; I would truly be dead. I jumped up, yelling, and ran in the house. 23

Later, I went to bed. "Darn," I said in the middle of the night. 24

"Darn what?" asked my brother, awake in bed beside me. 25

"365 darn days until Halloween again. What if I die, waiting?" 26

"Why, then," said my brother, after a long silence, "you'll *be* Halloween. Dead people *are* Halloween." 27

"Hey," said I, "I never *thought* of that." 28

"Think," said my brother. 29

I thought: 365 days from now... 30

Gimme a pad, some paper. Neva, rev up that Model A! Skip, hunch your back! Farmyards, grow pumpkins! Graveyards, shiver your stones! Moon, rise! Wind, hit the trees, blow up the leaves! Up, now, run! Tricks! Treats! Gangway! 31

And a small boy in midnight Illinois, suddenly glad to be alive, felt something on his face. Between the snail-tracks of his tears...a smile. 32

And then he slept. 33

BUILDING VOCABULARY

1. Bradbury has often used informal expressions in this essay. First, explain the meaning of the words in italics in each group below. Then suggest a word or phrase that an author who wished to be more formal might have used instead.

   a. *"Okay, kiddo"* (par. 7)

  b. When we picked the *spookiest* music (par. 9)
  c. Your *sappy* aunt and your *loony* brother and yourself
    have *magicked* it over (par. 17)
  d. *Gangway!* (par. 31)

2. A number of figurative expressions (see Glossary) spark
   this essay. In the list of examples of simile, metaphor, and
   personification below, explain each figure. (Personification
   is giving an object, thing, or idea lifelike or human qualities.) What is being compared to what? What other figures
   can you find in the essay?

  a. Halloween, you see, didn't just stroll into our yards. It
    had to be seized and shaped and *made* to happen! (*per-
    sonification*) (par. 9)
  b. My grandparents' home was a caldron (*metaphor*) to
    which we might bring hickory sticks that looked like
    witches' broken arms....(*simile*) (par. 10)
  c. where the *banshee* trains *ran* by at night (*metaphor*)
    (par. 10)
  d. papier mâché masks that smelled *like* a *sour dog's fur*
    (*simile*) (par. 10)
  e. the sun *furnaced* the Western sky (*personification*) and
    vanished, leaving *spilled blood* and *burnt pumpkin col-
    ors* behind (*metaphor*) (par. 13)

UNDERSTANDING THE WRITER'S IDEAS

1. What part of the essay most clearly states the author's
   purpose?

2. What two things did autumn signify to Bradbury?

3. What were some of the various activities for the Bradburys before October 29?

4. Why were October 29 and 30 almost as great as October
   31? What did Bradbury and Neva and Skip do?

5. What is the "true, deep sense of Halloween"?

6. How did the young Bradburys change the house into a Halloween place?

7. How do the activities before Halloween compare with the activities after it? Which activities did the narrator prefer?

8. Why does the author say "Darn" in the middle of the night after Halloween? Why is he unhappy?

9. How does his brother ease Bradbury's unhappiness?

10. Why does the author smile just before he goes to sleep?

UNDERSTANDING THE WRITER'S TECHNIQUES

1. How is this essay an example of *illustration?* What examples does Bradbury give to show he has been lucky to have Halloween-minded relatives? How does he illustrate that "1928 was one of the prime Halloween years"?

2. The examples Bradbury offers to show the quality of the 1928 Halloween vary in their length and degree of development. Which examples are developed most fully?

3. In any essay of illustration the writer will often provide a simple listing of examples to demonstrate a point he is trying to make. Paragraph 15 offers a listing of details, but none of the examples is fully developed. Why does Bradbury use this technique here? What other paragraphs offer a listing of details to illustrate a point?

4. Check your responses to the question in Building Vocabulary 2. How do all the figurative expressions contribute to Bradbury's topic? How are most of the metaphors and similes related to the topic and to each other?

5. Underline some sentences that you think have the best sensory details. Where does the author use color? action? sound? smell?

6. Look at the last sentence in paragraph 9: "All of it had to

be fetched, curried, touched, held, sniffed, crunched along the way.'' Why has Bradbury used so many verbs? What is the effect upon the reader?

7. It is clear that the style here is simple, direct, and informal. Why has the writer chosen such a style? How is it related to the topic of the essay? to the character represented in it?

8. What is the meaning of the title? Why do you think Bradbury selected it? How does it reflect the personality of a young boy?

9. To enrich the meaning of an essay, a writer will often use *allusion,* a reference to some other work in literature (see Glossary). The statement made by Aunt Neva, ''Who gets bricked up in the cellar with the Amontillado?'' is an allusion to a short story by Edgar Allan Poe, ''The Cask of Amontillado.'' What is that brief story about? Why would Bradbury want to allude to Poe in this essay about Halloween? What other references to literature does the writer make (see paragraphs 2 and 8)? Explain them, or ask your instructor to if you are not familiar with them.

10. In what sequence has Bradbury presented the events in this essay? How has he used the order he selects to create a kind of suspense, a building up from minor events to major ones?

11. Before he states his purpose in this essay, Bradbury offers a couple of paragraphs of introduction. What information does he deal with in his introduction? How does that information set the stage for the real point of the essay?

EXPLORING THE WRITER'S IDEAS

1. It is a strong statement to make that Halloween is ''wilder and richer and more important than Christmas morn.'' Does Bradbury support his point well? In your experience,

is Halloween so wild, so rich, and so important a holiday? Why? In your family, is there a special holiday for which everyone makes grand preparations? Describe it.

2. Bradbury's wild view of Halloween was, to a large degree, encouraged by his relatives' reaction to the holiday, too. How do your views about some holiday—like the Fourth of July, Thanksgiving, even Halloween—compare with or differ from the views of your relatives? In what cases do your relatives enrich your appreciation? detract from it?

3. What is the real significance of Halloween (check the dictionary or encyclopedia)? Why does that holiday still have a hold on the imagination of children today? Bradbury says that passing by a graveyard, he knew from the dead the "true deep sense of Halloween." Do you agree? Is *that* the true sense of Halloween?

4. Bradbury says in paragraph 20 that the party was less important than the preparation for it. Would you agree, in general, that the *preparation* for an event—such as a holiday, a wedding, a party—is often more important than the event itself? Explain your answer by giving a specific example from your own life.

5. How are Bradbury's feelings after Halloween is over typical of feelings any young child would have? How is he able to overcome these feelings? Are children generally able to cope with disappointment in the way young Bradbury has?

IDEAS FOR WRITING

Guided Writing

Write an essay of 500 words in which you *illustrate* the value to you of some holiday you celebrate.

1. Write an introduction that builds up to your thesis, as Bradbury has. State in your thesis sentence just how you

feel about the holiday. Is it a wild time, like Bradbury's Halloween, or deeply religious, or just a time of nonstop fun with marvelous meals and parties?

2. Decide on an effective order for the illustrations you present. If you offer examples to support an idea about one particular holiday (the Christmas of 1986, for example) you might want to use chronology. If you present several examples (drawn over a number of years) to show why one holiday is important to you, you might again use chronology. But you might also want to tell the events according to their importance, saving the most important for last.

3. Depending upon how many examples you offer, develop your illustrations with enough details. Some of your illustrations will require expanded treatment, others will not. In any case, offer at least three examples to support your point.

4. Since you are drawing from your own experience, you will want to use sensory language—colors, smells, actions, sounds, images of touch. Try to use figurative expressions as effectively as Bradbury has.

5. After you present and develop your illustrations, discuss in your conclusion how you feel after the holiday is over.

More Writing Projects

1. In recent years, Halloween has become a rather dangerous holiday where innocent children often come to harm by thoughtless, mean adults. Write an essay of 350 to 500 words illustrating the dangers of Halloween. Or, write an essay in which you show by means of illustration what steps your town or community takes to prevent Halloween accidents.

2. Write an essay in which you show how one relative shared in the joys or pains of your childhood experiences. Select as illustration important moments that you can narrate clearly and in concrete, sensory language.

3. Do some research about a local festival, the preparations for it, and the activities involved in its celebration. Or, you might choose to investigate a more remote festival in another part of the country, such as the chili contest in Texas, sausage festivals in Wisconsin, pie-eating contests associated with State Fairs. After you collect your research, write a four- or five-paragraph essay illustrating different features of this festival.

How Wild *Was* the Old West?

Louis L'Amour

Louis L'Amour is considered the best-selling and most prolific writer of Westerns. His devotion to authenticity and accuracy in his novels has earned him respect for a kind of writing that is sometimes thought of as not so serious, and in 1984, he was awarded the Medal of Freedom by President Reagan. In this selection, L'Amour uses numerous illustrations from others' research and from daily life, as well as many comparisons between the present and the past, to show us that the Old West was indeed a place and era of violence, uncertainty, and turbulence.

Words to Watch

hostile (par. 2) antagonistic; malicious

skirmishes (par. 2) small, brief battles

civilians (par. 2) persons not in military or other service

desperadoes (par. 4) bandits, criminals of the Old West

drought (par. 8) prolonged period of dryness

saloon (par. 10) barroom

brothels (par. 10) houses of prostitution

veteran (par. 12) former member of the armed forces

firearms (par. 12) weapons such as pistols and rifles

fanfare (par. 15) a showy display

notoriety (par. 15) fame, particularly unfavorable

Was the West really wild? Let's look at some *facts*. 1

Between 1865 and 1892, the U.S. Army fought 823 bat- 2
tles with hostile Indians, and 149 battles in one year—1867.
This says nothing about the many skirmishes fought by Indians and civilians.

Judge Isaac Parker, the so-called Hanging Judge, who was 3
appointed to clean up the outlaws in the Indian Territory, had at
one time or another 200 marshals serving his court. These were
such men as portrayed by John Wayne in "True Grit" and its

sequel. In the period from 1865 to 1891, 65 of those marshals were killed in the line of duty. Considering the fact that these marshals were selected because of their skill at tracking as well as with guns, that is an extremely high casualty rate.

Historian Peter Hertzog listed 539 known desperadoes 4 operating in New Mexico in the years 1865 to 1890. This was an incomplete list, and of course these desperadoes did not confine themselves to New Mexico. Many of them were also known in Texas and Arizona.

Passengers traveling west from St. Louis in the earliest 5 days of stage travel paid $200 for the trip to California, a 24-day journey, and were advised to provide themselves with a Sharps rifle and 100 rounds of ammunition.

Author Neill Wilson reports that in one stretch of 14 years 6 there were 347 robberies or attempted robberies of Wells Fargo stages, and two guards were killed as well as four drivers. The would-be stage robbers did not fare so well and crime along the stage routes certainly did not pay, for in that same period, 16 robbers were killed and seven more hanged by citizens in favor of immediate justice. To add to the general unhappiness of the outlaws, 240 of them were convicted and sent to prison.

The express and banking-company detectives were 7 among the most able officers in the West, and very few stage robbers escaped unpunished.

Western pioneers had heard many stories of warlike In- 8 dians, of outlaws, drought, storm and hunger. They expected it to be tough but it was usually worse than they had been told.

Despite that, there were many who never saw a gun bat- 9 tle or a warlike Indian. Many of the Indians were peace-loving citizens, and Judge Parker was only sent to Fort Smith to establish his court because of Indian objections to the white outlaws hiding out in their territory.

The pioneers brought civilization with them, and al- 10 though a saloon or a store was usually built first, a church and a school were not far behind. In the wild mining boom camps of Tombstone and Deadwood there were also sewing circles, box socials, camp meetings, theaters and dances. The shootings usually took place in the so-called red-light district among the brothels and saloons.

The men and women who came West were usually 11
strong individualists, perfectly capable of handling their own
affairs. It was not the custom to ask for help, although the
spirit of cooperation was everywhere. There was no telephone
with which to call the law or warn of an Indian attack. The
settler had to handle such things himself and on the spot.

One never knew whom he was facing when trouble 12
came. The farmer plowing his field or the cowboy driving cattle might be a veteran of several wars. Chris Madsen, who became a deputy United States marshal, had been born in Den-
mark, served seven years in the French Foreign Legion, then
came to America and served as a sergeant with the Fifth Cav-
alry in the Indian Wars. There were men on the Western fron-
tier who had served in armies everywhere. Five of those who
died with Custer had once served on the Vatican Guard. The
point is, they were accustomed to the use of firearms.

Guns were an accepted way of settling disputes. This 13
was held over from the old Code Duello, which grew out of
trial by combat and the belief that if two men fought to settle
a problem, God would ensure a victory for the right man.

It is often said the weapons of the time were not accu- 14
rate. I could list a lot of dead men who wish that had been
true. Great accuracy was possible, as demonstrated by such
men as Maj. Frank North, leader of the Pawnee Battalion Indian scouts and one of the finest pistol shots in the West. Major North never engaged in a gun battle with any one man, but
he did lead his scouts in many a skirmish, and in a gunfight he
would have been one of the best.

Most gunfighters went about their business without fanfare 15
or notoriety. Often they were gamblers who followed the boom
towns and were to be found where the action was, be it Abilene,
Dodge City, Fort Worth, El Paso, Deadwood or Tombstone.

There were range wars in a dozen states, for the men 16
who settle a wild country are inclined to administer justice
over the sights of a Winchester. John Slaughter was a cattle-
man, Doc Holliday a dentist, Temple Houston a lawyer; and
Wild Bill Hickok's family had once been tenant farmers for
William Shakespeare.

Yes, the West was wild, wilder than most are able to be- 17

lieve, but those who came first opened a wide land for those who would follow, and over the grasslands where the buffalo roamed there are universities now, and hospitals and jet trails in the sky.

BUILDING VOCABULARY

1. Identify the following *allusions* (see Glossary) in this essay: the Indian Territory (par. 3); John Wayne in "True Grit" (par. 3); the French Foreign Legion (par. 12); Abilene, Dodge City, Forth Worth, El Paso, Deadwood, Tombstone (par. 15); Doc Holliday and Wild Bill Hickok (par. 16).

2. In your own words, explain the following phrases:
   a. casualty rate (par. 3)
   b. rounds of ammunition (par. 5)
   c. warlike Indians (par. 9)
   d. perfectly capable of handling their own affairs (par. 11)
   e. range wars (par. 16)

UNDERSTANDING THE WRITER'S IDEAS

1. What is the specific meaning of the phrase "the West" as it is used throughout the essay? Why is the word "west" capitalized?

2. In paragraph 2, the writer gives statistics concerning battles between the U.S. Army and "hostile Indians." What is his purpose in stating these statistics? What does he mean by the statement "This says nothing about the many skirmishes fought by Indians and civilians"?

3. Who was Judge Isaac Porter? What role did he play in the Old West? By what means did he accomplish his job?

4. How would you describe the early transportation between St. Louis and California? Explain your answer with specific illustrations from the essay.

5. What was the Wells Fargo? According to L'Amour, who

fared better in confrontations between the Wells Fargo
and would-be robbers? How do you know? Explain the
meaning of the italicized words in L'Amour's statement
that "16 robbers were killed and seven more *hanged by
citizens in favor of immediate justice*" (par. 6).

6. According to the writer, what was the quality of life for
   early western pioneers? What sentence best summarizes
   L'Amour's opinion? What examples does he offer to support this opinion?

7. Explain in your own words the statement in paragraph 10
   that "the pioneers brought civilization with them." What
   does L'Amour mean by "civilization" in this sentence?
   What examples does he offer? Identify the following expressions in paragraph 10: boom camps, sewing circles,
   box socials, camp meetings, red-light district.

8. Why does L'Amour state that "the men and women who
   came West were usually strong individualists?" How
   would you define an *individualist?*

9. What was the importance of guns in the Old West? Explain in your own words the "Code Duello" (par. 13).

10. According to L'Amour, what type of people were most gun-
    fighters? In what manner did they conduct their business?

11. Explain the meaning of the statement that "the men who
    settle a wild country are inclined to administer justice
    over the sights of a Winchester" (par. 16). What is a Win-
    chester?

12. Ultimately, what is L'Amour's answer to his opening
    question? Was the west wild or not? Explain.

UNDERSTANDING THE WRITER'S TECHNIQUES

1. Why does L'Amour begin the essay with a question? How
   does he indicate the method he plans to use to answer that
   question? Why does he use italics for the word "facts"?

2. List all the paragraphs in which the writer makes use of
   statistics as an illustration device. What is the effect of
   these statistics on the essay? On your understanding of
   L'Amour's main ideas?

3. Are transitions between paragraphs and ideas smooth and
   easy to follow? Explain your answer with specific examples from the essay.

4. How does the writer make use of the research done by others and of the opinions expressed by others? List and explain some examples of this technique.

5. L'Amour uses numerous illustrations in this essay. Which
   do you feel are the most effective? The least effective? Explain your opinions. State the main idea of each of the following paragraphs: 10, 11, 14, and 15. How do these ideas
   relate to the essay's overall thesis? Explain how the author
   uses illustration in each of those paragraphs.

6. Does L'Amour ever answer his opening question? If so,
   where in the essay does the answer appear most specifically? Why does he place the answer at that point? Do you
   find this technique effective or not? Explain.

7. What is the Vatican Guard? Who was Custer? Why might it
   be considered *ironic* (see Glossary) that five of Custer's
   soldiers were former Vatican Guards? Explain the *irony* in
   the sentence, "I could list a lot of dead men who wish that
   had been true" (par. 14).

8. In the final paragraph, how does L'Amour make his discussion of the past relevant to the present? Specifically, how
   does he use illustration to make this connection? In which
   other paragraphs does he compare or associate life in the
   Old West with contemporary life?

EXPLORING THE WRITER'S IDEAS

1. Many people, children and adults alike, have a real fascination with life in the Old West. How would you explain
   this fascination? What elements of that era or life-style

might be especially exciting or attractive to contemporary audiences? Tell about any interest you have in the Old West.

2. Although television programs about the Old West are not currently popular, they were immensely popular in the 1950s and 1960s. For many years before that, films about the Old West were big hits. What are some films or TV programs you've seen concerning the Old West? Which have been most interesting? Why? Compare different images of the west as portrayed in various of these films and programs. How do they compare with L'Amour's view of the west?

3. At the end of this essay, L'Amour suggests a certain loss of the "wildness" of the west. Do you feel this is true? If so, do you feel the trend is positive or negative? In general, do you believe there are any true frontiers or wilderness areas left in this country? In other parts of the world? If so, should they be "tamed"? Explain.

4. Some critics say that the history of the Old West as we have it is primarily a history of white males, and that women, blacks, and native Americans are given little attention in these histories. Do you agree with this criticism? What evidence can you find to support your opinion?

IDEAS FOR WRITING

Guided Writing

Write an essay entitled "How _____ *was (were)* the _____ ?" Fill in the first blank with a descriptive adjective; fill in the second with an era, place, person, event, or condition from the past. For example, "How Swinging *Were* the Sixties?" or "How Great *Was* the Great Depression?" or "How Good *Was* the Beatles' Music?"

1. Begin with a question that restates your title.

2. Suggest a way in which you will respond to that question.

3. In the first few paragraphs, use statistics or other hard facts to illustrate your answer to the opening question.

4. Refer to the ideas or conclusions of an expert or writer about your topic.

5. Establish three subtopics that relate to your thesis and use numerous examples from everyday life to illustrate these subtopics.

6. Try to use historical allusions to help establish the "tone" of the period about which you are writing.

7. End your essay with a clear answer to your opening question and make some association between the past era, place, or event and related current conditions.

More Writing Projects

1. Research a specific event that took place in the Old West (Custer's Last Stand, the gunfight at the O.K. Corral, the shooting of Jesse James, or some other event) and write an essay about how it was especially illustrative of the "wildness" of that era.

2. Bring to class books with authentic old photos or drawings of the Old West and write brief descriptions of what each illustrates about life during that period.

Death in the Open

Lewis Thomas

Dr. Lewis Thomas is president of the Memorial Sloan-Kettering Cancer Center in New York City. He has written numerous articles about science, medicine, and life structures and cycles geared for the lay reader. His observations often bring fascinating clarity to the cycles of life and death on our planet. The following essay, a brilliant inquiry into the "natural marvel" of death, appears in his book *Lives Of A Cell* (1974), which won the National Book Award for Arts and Letters in 1975.

Words to Watch

voles (par. 1)   the members of any one of several species of small rodents

impropriety (par. 2)   an improper action or remark

progeny (par. 4)   descendants or offspring

mutation (par. 4)   a sudden genetic change

amebocytes (par. 4)   one-celled organisms

stipulated (par. 6)   made a special condition for

incongruity (par. 6)   something which is not consistent with its environment

conspicuous (par. 7)   very obvious

inexplicably (par. 7)   unexplainably

anomalies (par. 10)   irregularities

notion (par. 11)   an idea

detestable (par. 11)   hateful

synchrony (par. 11)   simultaneous occurrence

Most of the dead animals you see on highways near the [1] cities are dogs, a few cats. Out in the countryside, the forms and coloring of the dead are strange; these are the wild creatures. Seen from a car window they appear as fragments, evoking memories of woodchucks, badgers, skunks, voles, snakes, sometimes the mysterious wreckage of a deer.

It is always a queer shock, part a sudden upwelling of 2
grief, part unaccountable amazement. It is simply astounding
to see an animal dead on a highway. The outrage is more than
just the location; it is the impropriety of such visible death,
anywhere. You do not expect to see dead animals in the open.
It is the nature of animals to die alone, off somewhere, hidden.
It is wrong to see them lying out on the highway; it is wrong to
see them anywhere.

Everything in the world dies, but we only know about it 3
as a kind of abstraction. If you stand in a meadow, at the edge
of a hillside, and look around carefully, almost everything you
can catch sight of is in the process of dying, and most things
will be dead long before you are. If it were not for the constant
renewal and replacement going on before your eyes, the whole
place would turn to stone and sand under your feet.

There are some creatures that do not seem to die at all; 4
they simply vanish totally into their own progeny. Single cells
do this. The cell becomes two, then four, and so on, and after
a while the last trace is gone. It cannot be seen as death; bar-
ring mutation, the descendants are simply the first cell, living
all over again. The cycles of the slime mold have episodes that
seem as conclusive as death, but the withered slug, with its
stalk and fruiting body, is plainly the transient tissue of a developing animal; the free-swimming amebocytes use this or-
gan collectively in order to produce more of themselves.

There are said to be a billion billion insects on the earth 5
at any moment, most of them with very short life expectancies
by our standards. Someone has estimated that there are 25
million assorted insects hanging in the air over every temper-
ate square mile, in a column extending upward for thousands
of feet, drifting through the layers of the atmosphere like
plankton. They are dying steadily, some by being eaten, some
just dropping in their tracks, tons of them around the earth,
disintegrating as they die, invisibly.

Who ever sees dead birds, in anything like the huge num- 6
bers stipulated by the certainty of the death of all birds? A
dead bird is an incongruity, more startling than an unexpected
live bird, sure evidence to the human mind that something has

gone wrong. Birds do their dying off somewhere, behind things, under things, never on the wing.

Animals seem to have an instinct for performing death   7 alone, hidden. Even the largest, most conspicuous ones find ways to conceal themselves in time. If an elephant missteps and dies in an open place, the herd will not leave him there; the others will pick him up and carry the body from place to place, finally putting it down in some inexplicably suitable location. When elephants encounter the skeleton of an elephant out in the open, they methodically take up each of the bones and distribute them, in a ponderous ceremony, over neighboring acres.

It is a natural marvel. All of the life of the earth dies, all   8 of the time, in the same volume as the new life that dazzles us each morning, each spring. All we see of this is the odd stump, the fly struggling on the porch floor of the summer house in October, the fragment on the highway. I have lived all my life with an embarrassment of squirrels in my backyard, they are all over the place, all year long, and I have never seen, anywhere, a dead squirrel.

I suppose it is just as well. If the earth were otherwise,   9 and all the dying were done in the open, with the dead there to be looked at, we would never have it out of our minds. We can forget about it much of the time, or think of it as an accident to be avoided, somehow. But it does make the process of dying seem more exceptional than it really is, and harder to engage in at the times when we must ourselves engage.

In our way, we conform as best we can to the rest of   10 nature. The obituary pages tell us of the news that we are dying away, while the birth announcements in finer print, off at the side of the page, inform us of our replacements, but we get no grasp from this of the enormity of scale. There are 3 billion of us on the earth, and all 3 billion must be dead, on a schedule, within this lifetime. The vast mortality, involving something over 50 million of us each year, takes place in relative secrecy. We can only really know of the deaths in our households, or among our friends. These, detached in our minds from all the rest, we take to be unnatural events, anomalies, outrages. We speak of our own dead in low voices; struck down, we say, as though visible death can only occur for cause, by disease or violence, avoidably. We send off for flowers, grieve, make ceremonies, scatter bones, unaware of the rest of the 3 billion on the same schedule. All of that immense mass of flesh and bone and consciousness will disappear by absorption into the earth, without recognition by the transient survivors.

Less than a half century from now, our replacements will 11 have more than doubled the numbers. It is hard to see how we can continue to keep the secret, with such multitudes doing the dying. We will have to give up the notion that death is catastrophe, or detestable, or avoidable, or even strange. We will need to learn more about the cycling of life in the rest of the system, and about our connection to the process. Everything that comes alive seems to be in trade for something that dies, cell for cell. There might be some comfort in the recognition of synchrony, in the information that we all go down together, in the best of company.

BUILDING VOCABULARY

1. Thomas uses *adjectives* freely throughout this essay to create vivid descriptions. Adjectives can be fairly obvious in their modification of nouns; for example: a *red* caboose, a *cold* winter, and a *slender* woman. However, Thomas makes imaginative and often unique use of adjectival expressions. Explain the meaning of each of the following:

   a. *queer* shock (par. 2)
   b. *unaccountable* amazement (par. 2)
   c. *visible* death (pars. 2 and 10)
   d. *transient* tissue (par. 4)
   e. *ponderous* ceremony (par. 7)
   f. *neighboring* acres (par. 7)
   g. *natural* marvel (par. 8)
   h. *vast* majority (par. 10)
   i. *relative* secrecy (par. 10)
   j. *transient* survivors (par. 11)

2. An *idiom* is an expression that has a special meaning only when taken as a whole; taken separately, the words may not make sense.

What are the meanings of the following idioms:

   a. upswelling of grief (par. 2)
   b. catch sight of (par. 3)
   c. on the wing (par. 6)
   d. in time (par. 7)
   e. no grasp on (par. 10)
   f. for cause (par. 10)

UNDERSTANDING THE WRITER'S IDEAS

1. Why does Thomas feel that it is strange to see dead animals in the countryside? How are dead animals more varied in the country than in the city? According to Thomas, for what reason is it a shock to see a dead animal on the road?

2. In paragraph 3, Thomas suggests that death is often an "abstraction." What does he mean by this statement? How does he suggest we can make death something more real? In your own words, for what reasons does he suggest we accept the life-death cycle as a more concrete idea?

3. Why, according to Thomas, do single cells seem not to die?

4. What is the meaning of the question at the beginning of paragraph 6? How does it relate to the theme of the essay? To what does the author compare seeing a dead bird? Why does he call it an "incongruity"? How is it "sure evidence...that something has gone wrong"?

5. Explain the process of death among elephants as Thomas describes it.

6. Explain the meaning of "the old stump" in paragraph 8. What two examples of "the old stump" does Thomas offer?

7. What example from personal experience does Thomas give to show that dead animals seem "to disappear"?

8. Explain the meaning of the first sentence of paragraph 9. In your own words, tell why Thomas feels the way he does.

9. What is the "secret" in paragraph 11?

10. Thomas says, "In our own way, we conform as best we can to the rest of nature." What does he mean? What supporting examples does he offer? What is the result? What examples does Thomas give of our reactions to the death of other human beings?

11. Why does Thomas say we must change our attitude toward death? How does he suggest that we do so?

UNDERSTANDING THE WRITER'S TECHNIQUES

1. Study the introductory paragraphs. Why does the author offer several examples? Why is "the mysterious wreckage of a deer" an especially effective example?

2. Are there any clear illustrations in paragraph 2? Why or why not? What is the effect? Explain the connection between paragraphs 2 and 3.

3. Paragraphs 4 to 8 use illustrations to support a series of generalizations or topic sentences. Put a checkmark by the topic sentence in these paragraphs and identify the generalization. Then, analyze the illustrations used to support each one. Which examples are the most specific; the most visual; the most personal? Are there any extended examples?

4. How does paragraph 9 serve as a transition to the topic of paragraph 10? Why does Thomas use statistics in paragraph 10? How do they drive his point home?

5. What is Thomas's thesis in this essay? In what way is it reinforced by the concluding paragraph?

6. The author's use of pronouns in this essay is interesting. First, trace the use of first-person pronouns ("I," "we," "my," "our"). Why does Thomas use such pronouns? Why is their use in paragraph 8 especially effective? Next, consider Thomas's frequent use of the pronoun *it*. (Beginning writers are often instructed to minimize their use of such pronouns as *it, this,* and *that* because they are not specific and may leave the reader confused). Explain what the word *it* stands for in paragraphs 2, 4, 8, and 9. Why does Thomas use a word whose meaning may be confusing?

7. Thomas uses *figurative language* (see Glossary) in this essay, particularly *similes* and *metaphors* (see Glossary). Explain in your own words the meanings of the following similes and metaphors:

   a. *the mysterious wreckage* of a deer (par. 1)
   b. episodes that seem *as conclusive as death* (par. 4)
   c. drifting through the layers of the atmosphere *like plankton* (par. 5)

8. We may say that the expression "dropping in their tracks" in paragraph 5 is a kind of pun. (A *pun* is a humorous use of a word or an expression that suggests two meanings.) What is the popular expression using the words *dropping* and *flies* that Thomas' phrase puns on?

9. Thomas makes use of a technique called "repetition with a difference," that is, saying *almost* the same thing for added emphasis. Explain how repetition with a difference adds effectiveness to the sentences in which each of the following expressions is used:

   a. alone, hidden (par. 7)
   b. each morning, each spring (par. 8)
   c. unnatural events, anomalies, outrages (par. 10)
   d. catastrophe, or detestable, or avoidable, or even strange (par. 11)

10. *Parallelism* is a type of sentence structure within a paragraph that creates a balance in the presentation of ideas and adds emphasis. It often uses a repeating pattern of subjects and verbs, prepositional phrases, questions, and so on (see Glossary). How does Thomas use parallelism in paragraph 3? paragraph 10? paragraph 11?

EXPLORING THE WRITER'S IDEAS

1. We might say that Thomas's title, "Death in the Open," is a double entendre (that is, has a double meaning; see Glossary). In what two ways may we interpret the phrase "in the open" as it relates to the contents of the essay? How do the two meanings relate to the philosophical points Thomas makes, especially in the two opening paragraphs and in the conclusion? Do you feel it is important to be more "open" about death? Why?

2. In paragraph 10, Thomas writes, "We speak of our own dead in low voices; struck down, we..." "Struck down" is used here as a *euphemism* (a word or phrase used to replace others that are upsetting or distasteful; see Glossary). What other euphemisms do we have for death? Euphemisms for dying are often used to explain death to children. Do you think it is right, or necessary, to use such "guarded language" with youngsters? Why? For what other words or expressions do we commonly use euphemisms?

3. At the end of the essay, Thomas suggests that we might be less comfortable with death if we understood it more clearly as a natural, common occurrence. What are your feelings about this philosophy?

4. According to Thomas's views in paragraph 9, because we don't often see dead animals "in the open," we are less prepared when we do encounter death. Do you think this reasoning is correct? Why or why not?

5. In paragraph 7 Thomas explains the process of death among elephants. What is your impression of the elephant

herd's behavior at the death of one of its members? Why does Thomas call it "a natural marvel"? Have you ever heard the expression "the elephant dying grounds"? What does it mean?

IDEAS FOR WRITING

Guided Writing

Write an essay in which you illustrate "_____ in the open." Fill the blank with a word of your choice, a word that reflects some phenomenon, emotion, or idea that has features often hard to understand. You might write about birth in the open, concerts in the open, love in the open, fear in the open, war in the open, for example.

1. Develop an introduction with general examples that are relevant to your topic.

2. Add one or two paragraphs in which you speculate or philosophize on the phenomenon you are writing about.

3. Point out how the topic is most common throughout nature, society, or the world.

4. Give at least three extended examples that illustrate your topic.

5. Use the first-person pronouns "I" and "we" to add emphasis.

6. Illustrate ways in which we are generally unaware of certain features of the topic or tend to hide these features.

7. Try to include at least one statistic in your essay.

8. Use some idiomatic expression in your essay.

9. Conclude your essay with some examples of how and why we can become more "open" about the topic.

More Writing Projects

1. Write an essay in which you use examples to tell of your first experiences with death. You may want to write about the death of a relative, a friend, an acquaintance, a celebrity, or a pet.

2. Visit a place in the countryside (or a park) for one hour. Make a written record as you walk around detailing all evidence of natural death that you come across. Then write an illustrative essay on natural death as you observed it.

3. In your library, explore various burial practices among different races, religions, or ethnic groups and write an essay in which you illustrate several of these practices.

CHAPTER 6

Comparison and Contrast

Comparison and contrast is a method of analyzing likenesses and differences between two or more subjects. Writers use comparison and contrast simply because it is often the best way to explain something. An object or an idea is often better understood only when its features stand next to those of another object or idea. We appreciate soccer when we compare it with football; we understand communism when we see it in the light of capitalism.

In *comparison*, the likenesses or similarities appear in a carefully organized manner. In *contrast*, the approach centers on the differences between two items. Often you will employ only comparison or only contrast in an essay, but it is also possible to combine both methods in the same paper.

You frequently make comparisons and contrasts in the course of your daily life. If you have to select an accounting course during registration, you might find out about the instructors for the various sections before making a choice. If you want to buy a new car, you might locate comparative performance ratings for models that interest you most. If you are planning to buy ten packages of hot dogs for a barbecue, you might check prices, product quality, and other details before choosing one brand over another. In all cases, you employ a thought pattern that sorts out likenesses and differences and arrives at a decision based on a comparative analysis of items.

The pattern of comparison and contrast in writing is more carefully organized than the comparative pattern we employ in everyday situations. Yet both circumstances demand common sense. For one thing, any strong pattern of comparison and contrast treats items that are only in the same category or class. It makes little or no sense to compare an accounting teacher with a history teacher, a car with an ant, or a hot dog with a head of lettuce. Second, there always has to be a basis for your comparison; in other words, you compare or contrast two items in order to make a decision or choice about them. And third, you always try to deal with all-important aspects of the things being compared before arriving at a final determination. These common-sense characteristics of comparison and contrast apply to our pattern of thought as well as to our pattern of writing.

When you write a comparison and contrast essay, you should begin by identifying clearly the subjects of your comparison and by establishing the basis of your comparison. The thesis sentence performs this function for you (''Professor Smith is a better accounting teacher than Professor Williams because he is more experienced, more structured, and more intelligent''). There are three main ways to present your points of comparison (block, alternating, and combination); each will be dealt with in detail in this chapter. It is necessary to note here, however, that in presenting your material you should maintain a balance in the treatment of the two subjects in your comparison. In other words you do not want to devote most of your essay to subject A, and only a small fraction to subject B. Proper arrangement and balance of items in a comparative essay is a major consideration.

A Fable for Tomorrow

Rachel Carson

Rachel Carson wrote a number of books and articles in the 1950s and 1960s that alerted Americans to dangers facing our natural environment. In this section from *Silent Spring* (1962), look for the ways in which Carson establishes a series of contrasts for her imaginary American town.

Words to Watch

migrants (par. 2) people, animals, or birds that move from one place to another

blight (par. 3) a disease or condition that kills or checks growth

maladies (par. 3) illnesses

moribund (par. 4) dying

pollination (par. 5) the transfer of pollen (male sex cells) from one part of the flower to another

granular (par. 7) consisting of grains

specter (par. 9) a ghost; an object of fear or dread

stark (par. 9) bleak; barren; standing out in sharp outline

There was once a town in the heart of America where all 1 life seemed to live in harmony with its surroundings. The town lay in the midst of a checkerboard of prosperous farms, with fields of grain and hillsides of orchards where, in spring, white clouds of bloom drifted above the green fields. In autumn, oak and maple and birch set up a blaze of color that flamed and flickered across a backdrop of pines. Then foxes barked in the hills and deer silently crossed the fields, half hidden in the mists of the fall mornings.

Along the roads, laurel, viburnum and alder, great ferns 2 and wildflowers delighted the traveler's eye through much of the year. Even in winter the roadsides were places of beauty, where countless birds came to feed on the berries and on the seed heads of the dried weeds rising above the snow. The countryside was, in fact, famous for the abundance and variety of its bird life, and when the flood of migrants was pouring through in spring and fall people traveled from great distances to observe them. Others came to fish the streams, which flowed clear and cold out of the hills and contained shady pools where trout lay. So it had been from the days many years ago when the first settlers raised their houses, sank their wells, and built their barns.

Then a strange blight crept over the area and everything 3 began to change. Some evil spell had settled on the community: mysterious maladies swept the flocks of chickens; the cattle and sheep sickened and died. Everywhere was a shadow of death. The farmers spoke of much illness among their families. In the town the doctors had become more and more puzzled by new kinds of sickness appearing among their patients. There had been several sudden and unexplained deaths not only among adults but even among children, who would be stricken suddenly while at play and die within a few hours.

There was a strange stillness. The birds, for example— 4 where had they gone? Many people spoke of them, puzzled and disturbed. The feeding stations in the backyards were deserted. The few birds seen anywhere were moribund; they trembled violently and could not fly. It was a spring without voices. On the mornings that had once throbbed with the dawn chorus of robins, catbirds, doves, jays, wrens, and scores of other bird voices there was now no sound; only silence lay over the fields and woods and marsh.

On the farms the hens brooded, but no chicks hatched. 5 The farmers complained that they were unable to raise any pigs—the litters were small and the young survived only a few days. The apple trees were coming into bloom but no bees droned among the blossoms, so there was no pollination and there would be no fruit.

The roadsides, once so attractive, were now lined with 6 browned and withered vegetation as though swept by fire. These, too, were silent, deserted by all living things. Even the streams were now lifeless. Anglers no longer visited them, for all the fish had died.

In the gutters under the eaves and between the shingles 7 of the roofs, a white granular powder still showed a few patches; some weeks before it had fallen like snow upon the roofs and the lawns, the fields and streams.

No witchcraft, no enemy action had silenced the rebirth **8** of new life in this stricken world. The people had done it themselves.

This town does not actually exist, but it might easily **9** have a thousand counterparts in America or elsewhere in the world. I know of no community that has experienced all the misfortunes I describe. Yet every one of these disasters has actually happened somewhere, and many real communities have already suffered a substantial number of them. A grim specter has crept upon us almost unnoticed, and this imagined tragedy may easily become a stark reality we all shall know.

BUILDING VOCABULARY

1. In the second paragraph, find at least five concrete words that relate to trees, birds, and vegetation. How many of these objects could you identify? Look in a dictionary for the meanings of those words you do not know.

2. Try to identify the italicized words through the context clues (see Glossary) provided by the complete sentence.

   a. half-hidden in the *mists*. (par. 1)
   b. when the first settlers *raised* their houses. (par. 2)
   c. *stricken* suddenly at play. (par. 3)
   d. the hens *brooded,* but no chicks hatched. (par. 5)
   e. *Anglers* no longer visited them, for all the fish had died. (par. 6)

UNDERSTANDING THE WRITER'S IDEAS

1. What is the quality of the world that Carson describes in her opening paragraph? If you had to describe it in just one or two words, which would you use?

2. What are some of the natural objects that Carson describes in her first two paragraphs? Why does she not focus on simply one aspect of nature—like animals, trees, or flowers?

3. How does Carson describe the "evil spell" that settles over the countryside?

4. What does Carson mean when she declares, "It was a spring without voices" (par. 4)? Why does she show that the critical action takes place in the springtime?

5. What do you think is the "white granular powder" that Carson refers to in paragraph 7? Why does she not explain what it is or where it came from?

6. In paragraph 9, the author states her basic point. What is it? Does she offer a solution to the problem that she poses?

UNDERSTANDING THE WRITER'S TECHNIQUES

1. What is the purpose of the description in this essay? Why does the writer use such vivid and precise words?

2. A *fable* is a story with a moral; in other words, a fable is a form of teaching narrative. How does Carson structure her narrative in this essay?

3. Where in this essay does Carson begin to shift from an essentially optimistic tone to a negative one?

4. Does Carson rely on comparison or contrast in this essay?

5. In this selection Carson uses what we call the *block method* of comparison and contrast. The writer presents all information about one subject, and then all information about a second subject, as in the diagram below:

A

B

   a. How does Carson use this pattern in her essay?

   b. Are there actually two subjects in this essay, or two different aspects of one subject? How does chronology relate to the block structure?

   c. Are the two major parts of Carson's essay equally weighted? Why or why not?

   d. In the second part of the essay, does Carson ever lose sight of the objects introduced in the first part? What new terms does she introduce?

6. How can you explain paragraphs 8 and 9—which do not involve narration, description, or comparison and contrast—in relation to the rest of the essay? What is the nature of Carson's conclusion?

EXPLORING THE WRITER'S IDEAS

1. Today chemicals are used to destroy crop insects, to color and preserve food, and to purify our water, among other things. Would Carson term this "progress"? Would you? Do you think that there are inadequate safeguards and controls in the use of chemicals? What recent examples of chemical use have made the news?

2. Why would you agree or disagree that factories and corporations should protect the environment that they use? Should a company, for example, be forced to clean up an entire river that it polluted? What about oil spills?

3. Have there been any problems with the use of chemicals and the environment in your own area? Describe them. How do local citizens feel about these problems?

4. Do you think that it will be possible in the future for Americans "to live in harmony" with their natural surroundings? Why do you believe what you do?

IDEAS FOR WRITING

Guided Writing

Write a fable (an imaginary story with a moral) in which you contrast one aspect of the life of a person, community, or nation with another.

1. Begin with a phrase similar to Carson's "There was once...." so that the reader knows you are writing a narrative fable.

2. Relate your story to an American problem.

3. Use the block method in order to establish your contrast. Write first about one aspect of the topic and then about the other.

4. Use sensory detail in order to make your narrative clear and interesting.

5. Make certain that you establish an effective transition as you move into the contrast.

6. In the second part of your essay, be sure to refer to the same points you raised in the first part.

7. Use the conclusion to establish the "moral" of your fable.

More Writing Projects

1. Write an essay that contrasts the behavior of a person you knew sometime ago with his or her current behavior.

2. Develop a contrastive essay on a place you know well, one that has changed for better or worse. Explain the place as it

once was, and as it is now. Use concrete images that appeal to color, action, sound, smell, and touch.

3. Examine the two extremes of the ecology issue today.

4. Using the block method, compare and contrast Carson's fable with the fable you wrote in Guided Writing.

The Two Ismo's

Russell Baker

Russell Baker's witty column "The Sunday Observer" runs each week in *The New York Times* and provides readers with numerous insights into modern life. In this 1982 piece, he treats us to a tongue-in-cheek comparison between two kinds of social behavior in American cities.

Words to Watch

doctrines (par. 1)   beliefs that are taught as truths
adherents (par. 1)   believers in a particular doctrine
dogma (par. 1)   a tenet or code of beliefs
blitz (par. 2)   a fast, intensive raid or campaign
recourse (par. 5)   a source of aid or assistance
primp (par. 8)   to dress in a careful or finicky manner
Ou sont les neiges d'antan? (par. 11)   French for "Where are the snows of yesteryear?"

American city life is now torn by two violently opposed 1 doctrines of social conduct. One is machismo. Its adherents pride themselves on being "machos." The opposing dogma is quichismo (pronounced "key shizmo"), and its practitioners call themselves quiche-o's (pronounced "key shows").

A good study of a quichismo victory over machismo in 2 an urban war zone can be found in Philip Lopate's "Quiche Blitz on Columbus Avenue," included in his recent book, "Bachelorhood." Curiously, however, Mr. Lopate refers to the quichismo doctrine by its French name, *quichisme*.

In doing so he unwittingly reveals that he is himself a 3 quiche-o of the highest order, for no macho would dream of using a French word when discussing philosophy, and even the average quiche-o would avoid a word as difficult to pronounce as *quichisme* for fear of getting it wrong and being sneered at as unquiche-o.

For practitioners of quichismo there is no defense against 4

213

being sneered at, and they live in dread of it. The machismo adherent, on the other hand, positively enjoys being sneered at since it entitles him to punch the sneerer in the nose, a ritual act ceremonially confirming that he is truly macho.

When a quiche-o is sneered at, his only recourse is to jog 5 until he achieves a higher sense of total fulfillment. This is one reason behind the machismo slogan, "Machos have more fun."

Maybe so, quiche-o's say, but machos don't have 6 French dry cleaning or white bucks. Machos prefer no dry cleaning at all though they sometimes get their clothes pressed if they've slept in them all week and want to impress females during the weekend.

Machos impress females by taking them to bars after 7 opening the top four buttons on their shirts to show off the hair on their chests. Quiche-o women impress males by inviting them to dinner and serving salad from the carry-out gourmet shop, followed by a kiwi fruit. There are no macho women. If there were they would serve pigs' feet and beer because machos believe that real people don't eat salad, kiwi fruit or anything else that comes from gourmet shops.

Quiche-o people buy swedish toothpaste at gourmet drug- 8 stores, Italian loafers at gourmet shoe shops, newspapers at gourmet newsstands and dogs at gourmet pet centers. Afterwards they have them wormed by gourmet veterinarians. They also go to the islands for a month or two, especially Bermuda, St. Bart's, Barbados and Trinidad. Machos also go to the islands—Coney and Long—usually for a Sunday afternoon. To primp for these vacations, machos first go to the barber.

No quiche-o has set foot in a barber shop for the last 20 9 years. He goes to a gourmet hairdresser for a styling, then, before jetting off to the islands, goes to the gourmet luggage shop for suitcases covered with the initials of gourmet designers. The macho packs a change of underwear and a drip-dry shirt in a zippered plastic briefcase his uncle brought back from a 1977 convention of T-shirt salesmen.

Quiche-o's are always redecorating. Machos are always 10 repainting the room that has the TV set in it. When a macho's couch and chairs are finally ruined he goes to a department store and buys "a suit of furniture." Quiche-o furniture is never ruined, but it goes out of style every two years, and when it does the quiche-o goes to an environmental systems boutique and buys a new environment.

No quiche-o would ever take a walk in his undershirt un- 11 less it had something amusing printed on it, like *"Ou sont les neiges d'antan?"* No macho would ever appear on the beach in a male bikini. No quiche-o would ever wear black U.S. Keds with white soles and laces. No macho would ever walk into a hardware store and ask for a wok spatula.

Machos don't see anything funny about New Jersey. 12 Quiche-o's never laugh at people who drive Volvos, people who pay $5.50 for a hamburger or quiche jokes, unless they're told by another quiche-o. Quiche-o's like a lot of butcher block and stainless steel. Machos like a lot of children.

Machos never bake carrot cake and don't go out with 13 women who do. Quiche-o's are proud of their cholesterol levels and never belch in public and never go out with women who do since they recognize them instantly as unquiche-o and unlikely ever to serve them a salad dinner that concludes with a kiwi fruit.

BUILDING VOCABULARY

1. In this essay Baker uses a number of *geographical* references in paragraph 8. Identify the following locations:

   Bermuda
   St. Bart's (St. Bartholomew's Island)
   Barbados
   Trinidad
   Coney Island
   Long Island

2. Define the following foods or cooking utensils mentioned in the essay:

   quiche
   kiwi fruit
   pig's feet
   wok spatula

butcher block
carrot cake

3. Match the words in Column A (all from paragraph 4) with the correct meanings in Column B.

Column A
  1 practitioner
  2 sneered at
  3 ritual
  4 ceremonially
  5 confirming

Column B
  a supporting
  b showed contempt
  c one who engages in
     some technique
  d praying
  e system of rites
  f showed great pleasure
  g ritualistically

UNDERSTANDING THE WRITER'S IDEAS

1. What is quichisme? What is machismo?

2. What does Baker mean when he identifies Philip Lopate as "a quiche-o of the highest order"?

3. How do the two groups respond to sneering?

4. What is the attitude of each group toward clothing? How would you characterize the tasks of each group? Why are there no macho women?

5. For what reasons do both machos and quiche-o's avoid saying the word "quichisme"?

6. In what ways do macho men and quiche-o men try to impress women? How does each group prepare for vacations?

UNDERSTANDING THE WRITER'S TECHNIQUES

1. What is the thesis statement of this essay? What two things are identified as the subjects for treatment? Is the essay a

contrast or a *comparison?* What key words does Baker use to indicate that he is dealing primarily with similarities or differences?

2. Along with the block method (see page 209), comparison and contrast essays can also be organized according to the *alternating method.* When using the alternating method, the writer gives a point-by-point treatment of both subjects A and B. The effect looks like this:

A
B

A
B

A
B

In other words, some discussion of both subjects A and B is presented in each paragraph. Something is said about one and then about the other subject as the writer discusses some specific feature of his or her topic.

a. How does the author use the alternating method in paragraph 1? How does he achieve *balance* between subjects A and B in the opening paragraph?

b. How is the one-sentence paragraph 3 ("In doing so...") a good example of the alternating method?

c. Identify sentences in paragraphs 10 and 11 that reflect Baker's use of the alternating method.

d. For each of paragraphs 3 to 13, identify the primary focus for contrast between each of the subjects.

e. What advantages does the alternating method have over the block method? What disadvantages does the alternating method have?

3. How does Baker use definition (see pages 238 to 239) in the opening paragraph of this essay? How does he use *illustration* (see pages 164 to 165) in the essay?

4. With the alternating method it is very important to use smooth-flowing and interesting *transitions* within and between paragraphs. In this essay, one of Baker's main transition techniques is the use of *repetition with a difference* (see page 200). How does he use this method in paragraphs 7, 8, 10, 11, and 12? What key word does he repeat to make the transition between paragraphs 8 and 9?

5. A satire (see Glossary) is a humorous treatment of a subject in order to expose the subject's vices, follies, or stupidities. Why may this essay be considered a satire on city dwellers? What follies does Baker point up for each of the two groups he is dealing with?

6. As one technique for humor, Baker uses repetition of the word "gourmet" in paragraphs 7 through 9. What does the word mean? How does the repetition achieve the humorous effects Baker wants? What other repetitions do you find here?

7. Baker plays on words as another technique to achieve humor. How does he achieve humorous effects in paragraph 8 by playing on the word "islands"? What word is he playing on within the phrase "a suit of furniture" in paragraph 10? Why does he place the phrase in quotation marks? Why does he use a question in French in paragraph 11?

8. Why does Baker refer to Philip Lopate's book? Might Baker have eliminated paragraphs 2 and 3? Why did he choose to include those paragraphs in the essay?

9. Whom do you think is the intended audience for this essay? Why?

EXPLORING THE WRITER'S IDEAS

1. Baker is implying that people's social behavior reflects the kind of status they want to achieve in society. Often that

behavior makes them affected—that is, they pretend to certain tastes and preferences just because fashion dictates them. What affected people have you met? What kind of social behavior would you expect from someone who wanted to be thought of as an intellectual, as upper class, as radical, or as a great lover, for example?

2. In the last decade gourmet shops and boutiques have grown in numbers, and more and more people are interested in purchasing items there. How do you account for the popularity of such places? Why might you choose to purchase something at a gourmet shop or a boutique? Why is Baker poking fun at those people who buy at boutiques and gourmet shops?

3. A recent best-selling humor book was *Real Men Don't Eat Quiche* by Bruce Feirstein. The author's main premise was like Baker's but with a difference. Feirstein believes that not only are quiche-o's and machos at opposite ends of the social scale but also that machos are the much more desirable group to belong to. If you had to choose, would you choose to be macho or quiche-o? Why? Is it necessary to choose between the two, or is it possible to combine features from both groups?

4. Baker as a city dweller understandably focuses his essay on urban personalities. How could you expand the idea of quiche-o's and machos to suburban areas? Rural farm areas? Small towns?

IDEAS FOR WRITING

Guided Writing

Write an essay in which you contrast two types of people in the area where you live.

1. In your first paragraph, write a clear thesis statement that uses key words to indicate the contrast your essay will make.

2. Give the two types of people special names and define those names to help the reader understand your special use of them.

3. Use the alternating method of development in your essay.

4. Base your essay on personal observation of the two types of people.

5. Make sure each paragraph has a special point of contrast around which you organize your examples.

6. Use repetition with a difference as one device to accomplish smooth transitions between subjects in your discussions.

7. Give clear-cut examples of how each group would act in certain situations.

8. Try to cite at least one other writer who has discussed the same subject.

9. If possible, aim for some humorous effects by using satire, repetition, or plays on words.

More Writing Projects

1. Using the alternating method, write an essay in which your generation and your parents' generation did something such as dating, throwing a party, preparing for the future, or some such activity.

2. In one or two paragraphs, compare or contrast two teachers with distinctly different qualities.

The Tapestry of Friendships
Ellen Goodman

Syndicated columnist for the *Boston Globe, Washington Post,* and
other newspapers, Ellen Goodman presents a thought-provoking
comparison of two categories of human relations in this selection
from her book *Close to Home.* Notice especially how she blends personal experience with a clipped, direct journalistic style to examine
the ways in which "friends" and "buddies" relate to one another.

Words to Watch

slight (par. 1)   not having much substance

fragility (par. 2)   condition of being easily broken or harmed

resiliency (par. 2)   condition of being able to recover easily from mis-
fortune or change

binge (par. 4)   spree; indulgence

atavistic (par. 5)   manifesting a throwback to the past

culled (par. 5)   chosen from

palpably (par. 8)   in a way that can be touched or felt

loathsome (par. 10)   detestable; hateful

wretched (par. 13)   miserable; woeful

claustrophobic (par. 16)   uncomfortable at being confined in small
places

It was, in many ways, a slight movie. Nothing actually 1
happened. There was no big-budget chase scene, no bloody
shoot-out. The story ended without any cosmic conclusions.

Yet she found Claudia Weill's film *Girlfriends* gentle and 2
affecting. Slowly, it panned across the tapestry of friendship—
showing its fragility, its resiliency, its role as the connecting
tissue between the lives of two young women.

When it was over, she thought about the movies she'd 3
seen this year—*Julia, The Turning Point* and now *Girlfriends.*
It seemed that the peculiar eye, the social lens of the cinema,

221

had drastically shifted its focus. Suddenly the Male Buddy movies had been replaced by the Female Friendship flicks.

This wasn't just another binge of trendiness, but a kind 4
of *cinéma vérité*. For once the movies were reflecting a shift, not just from men to women but from one definition of friendship to another.

Across millions of miles of celluloid, the ideal of friend- 5
ship had always been male—a world of sidekicks and "pardners," of Butch Cassidys and Sundance Kids. There had been something almost atavistic about these visions of attachments—as if producers culled their plots from some pop anthropology book on male bonding. Movies portrayed the idea that only men, those direct descendants of hunters and Hemingways, inherited a primal capacity for friendship. In contrast, they portrayed women picking on each other, the way they once picked berries.

Well, that duality must have been mortally wounded in 6
some shootout at the You're OK, I'm OK Corral. Now, on the screen, they were at least aware of the subtle distinction between men and women as buddies and friends.

About 150 years ago, Coleridge had written, "A wom- 7
an's friendship borders more closely on love than man's. Men affect each other in the reflection of noble or friendly acts, whilst women ask fewer proofs and more signs and expressions of attachment."

Well, she thought, on the whole, men had buddies, while 8
women had friends. Buddies bonded, but friends loved. Buddies faced adversity together, but friends faced each other. There was something palpably different in the way they spent their time. Buddies seemed to "do" things together; friends simply "were" together.

Buddies came linked, like accessories, to one activity or 9
another. People have golf buddies and business buddies, college buddies and club buddies. Men often keep their buddies in these categories, while women keep a special category for friends.

A man once told her that men weren't real buddies until 10
they'd been "through the wars" together—corporate or athletic or military. They had to soldier together, he said.

Women, on the other hand, didn't count themselves as friends until they'd shared three loathsome confidences.

Buddies hang tough together; friends hang onto each 11 other.

It probably had something to do with pride. You don't 12 show off to a friend; you show need. Buddies try to keep the worst from each other; friends confess it.

A friend of hers once telephoned her lover, just to find 13 out if he were home. She hung up without a hello when he picked up the phone. Later, wretched with embarrassment, the friend moaned, "Can you believe me? A thirty-five-year-old lawyer, making a chicken call?" Together they laughed and made it better.

Buddies seek approval. But friends seek acceptance. 14

She knew so many men who had been trained in re- 15 straint, afraid of each other's judgment or awkward with each other's affection. She wasn't sure which. Like buddies in the movies, they would die for each other, but never hug each other.

She'd reread *Babbit* recently, that extraordinary cata- 16 logue of male grievances. The only relationship that gave meaning to the claustrophobic life of George Babbitt had been with Paul Riesling. But not once in the tragedy of their lives had one been able to say to the other: You make a difference.

Even now men shocked her at times with their descrip- 17 tion of friendship. Does this one have a best friend? "Why, of course, we see each other every February." Does that one call his most intimate pal long distance? "Why, certainly, whenever there's a real reason." Do those two old chums ever have dinner together? "You mean alone? Without our wives?"

Yet, things were changing. The ideal of intimacy wasn't 18 this parallel playmate, this teammate, this trenchmate. Not even in Hollywood. In the double standard of friendship, for once the female version was becoming accepted as the general ideal.

After all, a buddy is a fine life-companion. But one's 19 friends, as Santayana once wrote, "are that part of the race with which one can be human."

BUILDING VOCABULARY

1. The first six paragraphs of this essay use many words and expressions related to film. Explain the meaning or connotation of each of the following such words and expressions. Pay special attention to their context in Goodman's article.

   a. big-budget chase scene (par. 1)
   b. bloody shoot-out (par. 1)
   c. it panned (par. 2)
   d. the peculiar eye (par. 3)
   e. the social lens of the cinema (par. 3)
   f. shifted its focus (par. 3)
   g. flicks (par. 3)
   h. *cinéma vérité* (par. 4)
   i. millions of miles of celluloid (par. 5)
   j. plots (par. 5)
   k. on the screen (par. 6)

2. Write *antonyms* (words with opposite meanings) for the following words in the Words to Watch section. Then use each antonym in a sentence.

   slight
   fragility
   resiliency
   atavistic
   palpably
   loathsome
   wretched

UNDERSTANDING THE WRITER'S IDEAS

1. What is the main idea of this essay? Which sentence serves as the thesis statement? What two subjects form the basis for comparison in this essay?

2. What does the author mean when she writes that the movie "ended without any cosmic conclusions" (par. 1)? Is she being critical or descriptive in this statement? Explain.

3. Who is the "she" first mentioned at the beginning of paragraph 2 and referred to throughout the essay?

4. What pattern of change does the author note in the same-year releases of the films *Julia, The Turning Point,* and *Girlfriends?* Does she feel this is a superficial or real change? How do you know?

5. What is the author's main complaint about the ways in which movies have traditionally portrayed friendships? What example does she offer? Explain the meaning of the sentence, "Movies portrayed the idea that only men, those direct descendants of hunters and Hemingway, inherited a primal capacity for friendship" (par. 5). What is "male bonding"?

6. What two allusions does Goodman combine to produce the expression "The You're OK, I'm OK Corral"? Explain the full meaning of the sentence in which that expression appears.

7. According to Goodman, what is the main difference between male and female friendships? Which type do you think she prefers? Why?

8. What quality of friendships is suggested by the title?

9. What is meant by "the double standard of friendship"?

10. How does Goodman's conclusion support her preference for male or female types of friendships?

UNDERSTANDING THE WRITER'S TECHNIQUES

1. Like most well-constructed essays, this one has three clear sections: introduction; body; conclusion. Specify which paragraphs make up each section. Does this seem a good balance? Explain.

2. How would you describe the effect of the writing in the opening paragraph? Does it give you a clear idea of the subject of this essay? Is that important in this essay? Why?

3. In the beginning, Goodman uses a number of *metaphors* (see Glossary), including the title. Explain the following metaphors in your own words:

   a. The Tapestry of Friendships (title and par. 2)
   b. the connecting tissue between the lives of two young women (par. 2)

   In what ways do the two metaphors convey similar ideas? Which do you prefer? Why?

4. What is the effect of the use of the pronoun "she" throughout the essay? Why do you suppose Goodman chose to use "she" rather than "I"?

5. Among the main purposes of a comparison or contrast essay are (a) *to explain* something unfamiliar in terms of something already familiar; (b) *to understand* better two things already known by comparing them point for point; (c) *to evaluate* the relative value of two things. Which of these objectives most closely describes Goodman's purpose? Explain.

6. Which of the three methods of writing comparison essays—block, alternating, or combination—dominates in this essay? Explain.

7. Who is the intended audience for this essay? Why?

8. There are four literary *allusions* (see Glossary) in this essay: (a) Hemingway, (b) Coleridge, (c) *Babbitt,* and (d) Santayana. Identify each and explain why Goodman chose to include them.

9. Throughout the essay, Goodman uses short, direct sentences and relatively short paragraphs. What is her purpose for that? Does it allow for adequate development of this subject matter? Why or why not?

10. At what points does Goodman make use of relatively *extended illustrations*?

11. Goodman chooses to point out the contrasts between her

two subjects in short, directly contrasting sentences or clauses, beginning with paragraph 8: "...men had buddies, while women had friends. Buddies bonded, but friends loved."

Go through the essay and list all such opposing statements. How do these statements affect your reading of the essay?

12. How does Goodman use *repetition* as a transitional device in the essay?

13. What is the effect of the series of questions that comprise paragraph 17? How is it like a dialogue? Why are some of the questions in quotation marks and others not?

14. A good conclusion for an essay of comparison or contrast will either (a) restate the main idea, (b) offer a solution, or (c) set a new frame of reference by generalizing from the thesis. Which approach or combination of approaches does Goodman use? How effective is her conclusion? Why?

EXPLORING THE WRITER'S IDEAS

1. Do you agree with Goodman's basic distinction between female and male friendships? How closely does it relate to your own experiences? Do you have any friendships that don't fit into either of the two categories she describes?

2. In the beginning of this essay, Goodman refers to the "binge of trendiness" toward pop anthropology and psychology. Such books, periodicals, and syndicated columns as *Psychology Today, Women Who Love Too Much,* and Dr. Joyce Brothers—to name just a few—are widely read. What's more, radio call-in shows offering on-the-air advice (such as *The Dr. Ruth Show* and *The Toni Grant Show*) are nationally syndicated and immensely popular.

What are your feelings about such media presentations? Do you think they are useful? Are there instances when they might be harmful? Why do you think they are so popular?

3. Why does Goodman avoid any discussion of friendship between men and women? Do you feel this omission in any way affects the forcefulness or completeness of her essay? Explain.

IDEAS FOR WRITING

Guided Writing

Write an essay that contrasts the ways in which men and women perceive or approach some aspect of interpersonal relationships. You might choose, for example, dating, parenting, expressing affection, or divorce.

1. Begin with a description of some depiction of the subject in the contemporary media (for example, a film, TV program, book, video, commercial).

2. Staying with the same medium, give other examples that illustrate how the medium is shifting away from the old, established ways of viewing the subject. Use language specific to that medium.

3. In the rest of your introductory section, use a few metaphors.

4. As a transitional device, cite a statement from a well-known authority (not necessarily on the particular subject).

5. State the main idea of your essay at the beginning of the body section.

6. Develop your contrast using short, direct, opposing statements that summarize the different approaches of men and women.

7. Develop at least two of these opposing statements through extended personal examples.

8. Make your preference for either approach *implicit* (subtle) rather than *explicit* (obvious) throughout.

9. Make the last paragraph of the body of your essay a series of questions that form an internal dialogue.

10. Conclude with a statement that generalizes the main differences and your evaluation of the two approaches.

More Writing Projects

1. Write an essay about two films (or books, plays, or television programs) that portray contrasting views of friendship, love, or marriage.

2. Compare the ways you relate to two close friends.

3. Write an essay that compares and/or contrasts what was considered attractive in two different time periods in America. You may either focus your essay on one sex or attempt to discuss both.

Fairy Tales and Modern Stories

Bruno Bettelheim

Bruno Bettelheim was born in Austria in 1903 and came to the United States in 1939. For many years he has been one of the major child psychologists in the world. In this selection, taken from *The Uses of Enchantment* (1976), Bettelheim compares fairy tales and realistic stories, analyzing the effect that they have on both children and adults. As you read this essay, keep in mind the various stories he is comparing.

Words to Watch

realistic (par. 1)   having to do with real things

props (par. 1)   supports

elaboration (par. 1)   a thing worked out in detail

rankled (par. 1)   caused pain or resentment

idyllic (par. 2)   pleasing and simple

protracted (par. 2)   drawn out

gratifications (par. 2)   things that cause satisfaction

sustained (par. 3)   maintained; supported; comforted

effected (par. 4)   brought to pass; accomplished

consolation (par. 5)   comfort

vagaries (par. 5)   odd notions; unexpected actions

extricating (par. 5)   setting free; getting out of; releasing

prevail (par. 5)   to triumph; to gain the advantage

asocial (par. 5)   not social

The shortcomings of the realistic stories with which 1
many parents have replaced fairy tales is suggested by a comparison of two such stories—"The Little Engine That Could" and "The Swiss Family Robinson"—with the fairy tale of "Rapunzel." "The Little Engine That Could" encourages the child to believe that if he tries hard and does not give up, he will finally succeed. A young adult has recalled how much impressed she was at the age of seven when her mother read her

this story. She became convinced that one's attitude indeed affects one's achievements—that if she would now approach a task with the conviction that she could conquer it, she would succeed. A few days later, this child encountered in first grade a challenging situation: she was trying to make a house out of paper, gluing various sheets together. But her house continually collapsed. Frustrated, she began to seriously doubt whether her idea of building such a paper house could be realized. But then the story of "The Little Engine That Could" came to her mind; twenty years later, she recalled how at that moment she began to sing to herself the magic formula "I think I can, I think I can, I think I can..." So she continued to work on her paper house, and it continued to collapse. The project ended in complete defeat, with this little girl convinced that she had failed where anybody else could have succeeded, as the Little Engine had. Since "The Little Engine That Could" was a story set in the present, using such common props as engines that pulled trains, this girl had tried to apply its lesson directly in her daily life, without any fantasy elaboration, and had experienced a defeat that still rankled twenty years later.

Very different was the impact of "The Swiss Family   2 Robinson" on another little girl. The story tells how a shipwrecked family manages to live an adventurous, idyllic, constructive, and pleasurable life—a life very different from this child's own existence. Her father had to be away from home a great deal, and her mother was mentally ill and spent protracted periods in institutions. So the girl was shuttled from her home to that of an aunt, then to that of a grandmother, and back home again, as the need arose. During these years, the girl read over and over again the story of this happy family who lived on a desert island, where no member could be away from the rest of the family. Many years later, she recalled what a warm, cozy feeling she had when, propped up by a few large pillows, she forgot all about her present predicament as she read this story. As soon as she had finished it, she started to read it over again. The happy hours she spent with the Family Robinson in that fantasy land permitted her not to be defeated by the difficulties that reality presented to her. She was able to counteract the impact of harsh reality by imaginary gratifications. But since the story was not a fairy tale, it merely gave her a temporary escape from her problems; it did not hold out any promise to her that her life would take a turn for the better.

Consider the effect that "Rapunzel" had on a third girl.   3
This girl's mother had died in a car accident. The girl's father, deeply upset by what had happened to his wife (he had been driving the car), withdrew entirely into himself and handed the care of his daughter over to a nursemaid, who was little interested in the girl and gave her complete freedom to do as she liked. When the girl was seven, her father remarried, and, as she recalled it, it was around that time that "Rapunzel" became so important to her. Her stepmother was clearly the witch of the story, and she was the girl locked away in the tower. The girl recalled that she felt akin to Rapunzel because the witch had "forcibly" taken possession of her, as her stepmother had forcibly worked her way into the girl's life. The girl felt imprisoned in her new home, in contrast to her life of freedom with the nursemaid. She felt as victimized as Rapunzel, who, in her tower, had so little control over her life. Rapunzel's long hair was the key to the story. The girl wanted her hair to grow long, but her stepmother cut it short; long hair in itself became the symbol of freedom and happiness to her. The story convinced her that a prince (her father) would come someday and rescue her, and this conviction sustained her. If life became too difficult, all she needed was to imagine herself as Rapunzel, her hair grown long, and the prince loving and rescuing her.

"Rapunzel" suggests why fairy tales can offer more to   4
the child than even such a very nice children's story as "The Swiss Family Robinson." In "The Swiss Family Robinson," there is no witch against whom the child can discharge her anger in fantasy and on whom she can blame the father's lack of interest. "The Swiss Family Robinson" offers escape fantasies, and it did help the girl who read it over and over to forget temporarily how difficult life was for her. But it offered no specific hope for the future. "Rapunzel," on the other hand,

offered the girl a chance to see the witch of the story as so evil that by comparison even the "witch" stepmother at home was not really so bad. "Rapunzel" also promised the girl that her rescue would be effected by her own body, when her hair grew long. Most important of all, it promised that the "prince" was only temporarily blinded—that he would regain his sight and rescue his princess. This fantasy continued to sustain the girl, though to a less intense degree, until she fell in love and married, and then she no longer needed it. We can understand why at first glance the stepmother, if she had known the meaning of "Rapunzel" to her stepdaughter, would have felt that fairy tales are bad for children. What she would not have known was that unless the stepdaughter had been able to find that fantasy satisfaction through "Rapunzel," she would have tried to break up her father's marriage and that without the hope for the future which the story gave her she might have gone badly astray in life.

It seems quite understandable that when children are asked to name their favorite fairy tales, hardly any modern tales are among their choices. Many of the new tales have sad endings, which fail to provide the escape and consolation that the fearsome events in the fairy tale require if the child is to be strengthened for meeting the vagaries of his life. Without such encouraging conclusions, the child, after listening to the story, feels that there is indeed no hope for extricating himself from his despairs. In the traditional fairy tale, the hero is rewarded and the evil person meets his well-deserved fate, thus satisfying the child's deep need for justice to prevail. How else can a child hope that justice will be done to him, who so often feels unfairly treated? And how else can he convince himself that he must act correctly, when he is so sorely tempted to give in to the asocial proddings of his desires?

BUILDING VOCABULARY

1. *Jargon* is specialized vocabulary that appears in a certain profession or discipline. Bettelheim might be expected to

use a certain amount of jargon from psychology. (Fortunately, he keeps it to a minimum.) Try to figure out what Bettelheim means by the following terms:

   a. fantasy elaboration (par. 1)
   b. imaginary gratifications (par. 2)
   c. escape fantasies (par. 4)
   d. fantasy satisfaction (par. 4)
   e. asocial proddings (par. 5)

2. Write sentences in which you use the following words correctly:

   a. impressed (par. 1)
   b. conviction (par. 1)
   c. impact (par. 2)
   d. predicament (par. 2)
   e. victimized (par. 3)
   f. astray (par. 4)
   g. sorely (par. 5)

3. Would you say that the level of vocabulary in this essay is concrete or abstract? Why?

UNDERSTANDING THE WRITER'S IDEAS

1. Check in the children's book section of your library to summarize the stories and fairy tales Bettelheim discusses. How many stories is he examining in this essay?

2. What is the most important similarity between *The Little Engine That Could* and *The Swiss Family Robinson?*

3. What is the effect on children of *The Little Engine That Could?* How does it influence the adult whom Bettelheim introduces in paragraph 1?

4. How does Bettelheim summarize the story of *The Swiss Family Robinson?* Does this story, according to the author, have a beneficial effect on adults with problems?

5. Explain why "Rapunzel" was so important to the girl who had lost her mother in the car accident.

6. Why do fairy tales benefit readers more than modern fairy tales and realistic stories do? What do traditional fairy tales provide?

7. What does Bettelheim mean by his last sentence, "And how else can he convince himself that he must act correctly, when he is so sorely tempted to give in to the asocial proddings of his desires?"

UNDERSTANDING THE WRITER'S TECHNIQUES

1. Where does Bettelheim state his main point? How clear is his statement of it? Does he indicate in his thesis sentence his plan of development for the essay?

2. How does Bettelheim order his essay in terms of comparison and contrast? What is interesting about the pattern he chooses?

3. Where does the writer use narration? Why does he use it? How does it support the technique of comparison and contrast?

4. What is the function of paragraph 1? of paragraph 2? of paragraph 3?

5. How does the writer organize paragraph 4?

6. Is the same amount of emphasis given to "Rapunzel" as to the two "realistic" tales? Why or why not?

7. In concluding paragraphs of comparison and contrast papers, it is common to bring the two subjects together for a final observation. Does Bettelheim follow this strategy? How does he organize his subjects in the last paragraph?

8. How does Bettelheim achieve clear transitions from paragraph to paragraph? Discuss some of the words he uses so that his ideas are connected together clearly.

EXPLORING THE WRITER'S IDEAS

1. Bettelheim suggests that certain types of fairy tales help us to cope with problems. Do you agree or disagree? What particular fairy tale do you remember that might help a child deal with his or her problems?

2. Why do most children clearly take delight from traditional fairy tales?

3. Look again at Bettelheim's psychoanalysis of the three children whom he uses as examples in his essay. Do you accept his explanations of their behavior? How might his ideas be criticized by other psychologists?

4. Which fairy tales—traditional or modern—appealed to you as a child? Why were you so fond of them?

5. If exposure to certain types of fairy tales can affect us seriously, then what can we conclude about our exposure to stories on television, film, and other types of media? Is it fair to generalize about television from Bettelheim's argument?

IDEAS FOR WRITING

Guided Writing

Write an essay in which you compare and/or contrast two or three fairy tales or stories that you remember from early childhood. Or, do the same for two films, two television programs, two newspapers, or two subjects from another media form.

1. State the purpose of your comparison as soon as you can.

2. Decide on the best pattern of development (block, alternating, or a combination of both) for your purposes.

3. List the point of comparison or contrast that you plan to cover for each subject.

4. Be certain to support each point with substantial detail. Summarize parts of stories that bear out your point. Quote where you have to.

5. Make certain that, in the closing paragraph, you draw conclusions about all the subjects treated.

More Writing Projects

1. Write an essay in which you compare or contrast two newspapers or magazines. Be prepared to compare and contrast their contents, and also to indicate the type of audience at which they are aimed. Write a comparative paper on your findings.

2. Compare and contrast the style of writing of any two writers in this section.

3. Select two heroes or heroines from popular children's stories or fairy tales; compare and contrast the two characters in regard to personality and behavior.

CHAPTER 7

Definition

Definition is a way of explaining an important word so that the reader knows, as exactly as possible, what you mean by it. You probably have written essays requiring short "dictionary definitions" of words that were not clear to the reader. However, there are terms that require longer definitions because they may be central to the writer's thought. When an entire essay focuses on the meaning of a key word or group of related words, you will need to employ "extended definition" as a method of organization.

Words requiring extended definition tend to be abstract, controversial, or complex. Terms like "freedom," "pornography," and "communism" reflect the need for extended definition. Such words depend on extended definition because they are often confused with some other word or term; because they are easily misunderstood; or because they are of special importance to the writer, who chooses to redefine the term for his or her own purposes. We can, of course, simply offer an extended definition of a word for the sake of definition itself; this is valid. But we usually have strong opinions about complex and controversial words, and, consequently, we try to provide an extended definition for the purpose of illuminating a thesis. The word "abortion" could be defined objectively, with the writer tracing its history, explaining its techniques, and describing its effects on the patient. Yet many writers asked to provide an extended definition of "abortion" would have strong personal opinions about the term. They

238

would want to develop a thesis about it, perhaps covering much of the same ground as the objective account, but taking care that the reader understands the word as they do. It is normal for us to have our own opinions about any word, but in all instances we must make the reader understand fully what we mean by it.

Writers use several techniques to develop extended definitions. One common strategy is to define some general group to which the subject belongs (for instance, the mallard is a member of a larger group of ducks), and to show how the word differs from all other words in that general group. A second technique is to give the etymology of a word—its origin and history in the language—to help the reader. Yet another method of extended definition is to deal with what you do *not* mean by the term—a technique called "negation." Finally, many methods that you already learned can be used profitably in extended definition. You can define a word by narrating an event that reveals its meaning; you can provide specific examples, even a simple listing, to illustrate what you mean by a term; you can compare and contrast related terms; you can describe details that help to establish meaning.

Extended definition involves no single pattern of essay organization, but rather a group of available strategies that you use depending on your purpose and on the word itself. The word selected may be ordinary and relatively concrete, or it may be abstract and complex like "randomness." Often, as in the essays on "fun" and, later, on "mind control," the definition is never directly stated, but is understood or put together from the information a writer gives. Because so many methods can be applied effectively in an essay of extended definition, you should be able to organize and develop this type of composition easily.

Fun, Oh Boy. Fun. You Could Die from It.

Suzanne Britt Jordan

Most of us never really consider exactly what it means to have a good time. Suzanne Britt Jordan, a writer who claims she "tries to have fun, but often fails," offers an extended definition of the word "fun" by pointing out what it is *not*.

Words to Watch

puritan (par. 3)   one who practices or preaches a more strict moral code than that which most people now follow

selfless (par. 4)   unselfish; having no concern for oneself

fetish (par. 5)   something regarded with extravagant trust or respect

licentiousness (par. 9)   a lack of moral restraints

consumption (par. 9)   act of taking in or using up a substance; eating or drinking

epitome (par. 11)   an ideal; a typical representation

capacity (par. 12)   the ability to hold something

damper (par. 13)   something that regulates or that stops something from flowing

reverently (par. 13)   respectfully; worshipfully

blaspheme (par. 13)   to speak of without reverence

weary (par. 14)   tired; worn-out

horizon (par. 14)   the apparent line where the earth meets the sky

scan (par. 14)   to examine something carefully

Fun is hard to have.   1

Fun is a rare jewel.   2

Somewhere along the line people got the modern idea   3
that fun was there for the asking, that people deserved fun,
that if we didn't have a little fun every day we would turn into
(sakes alive!) puritans.

"Was it fun?" became the question that overshadowed   4
all other questions: good questions like: Was it moral? Was it

kind? Was it honest? Was it beneficial? Was it generous? Was it necessary? And (my favorite) was it selfless?

When the pleasure got to be the main thing, the fun fetish 5 was sure to follow. Everything was supposed to be fun. If it wasn't fun, then by Jove, we were going to make it fun, or else.

Think of all the things that got the reputation of being fun. 6 Family outings were supposed to be fun. Sex was supposed to be fun. Education was supposed to be fun. Work was supposed to be fun. Walt Disney was supposed to be fun. Church was supposed to be fun. Staying fit was supposed to be fun.

Just to make sure that everybody knew how much fun 7 we were having, we put happy faces on flunking test papers, dirty bumpers, sticky refrigerator doors, bathroom mirrors.

If a kid, looking at his very happy parents traipsing 8 through that very happy Disney World, said, "This ain't fun, ma," his ma's heart sank. She wondered where she had gone wrong. Everybody told her what fun family outings to Disney World would be. Golly gee, what was the matter?

Fun got to be such a big thing that everybody started to 9 look for more and more thrilling ways to supply it. One way was to step up the level of danger or licentiousness or alcohol or drug consumption so that you could be sure that, no matter what, you would manage to have a little fun.

Television commercials brought a lot of fun and fun- 10 loving folks into the picture. Everything that people in those commercials did looked like fun: taking Polaroid snapshots, swilling beer, buying insurance, mopping the floor, bowling, taking aspirin. We all wished, I'm sure, that we could have half as much fun as those rough-and-ready guys around the locker room, flicking each other with towels and pouring champagne. The more commercials people watched, the more they wondered when the fun would start in their own lives. It was pretty depressing.

Big occasions were supposed to be fun. Christmas, 11 Thanksgiving and Easter were obviously supposed to be fun. Your wedding day was supposed to be fun. Your wedding night was supposed to be a whole lot of fun. Your honeymoon was supposed to be the epitome of fundom. And so we ended

up going through every Big Event we ever celebrated, waiting
for the fun to start.

It occurred to me, while I was sitting around waiting for   12
the fun to start, that not much is, and that I should tell you just
in case you're worried about your fun capacity.

I don't mean to put a damper on things. I just mean we   13
ought to treat fun reverently. It is a mystery. It cannot be
caught like a virus. It cannot be trapped like an animal. The
god of mirth is paying us back for all those years of thinking
fun was everywhere by refusing to come to our party. I don't
want to blaspheme fun anymore. When fun comes in on little
dancing feet, you probably won't be expecting it. In fact, I bet
it comes when you're doing your duty, your job, or your
work. It may even come on a Tuesday.

I remember one day, long ago, on which I had an espe-   14
cially good time. Pam Davis and I walked to the College Village drug store one Saturday morning to buy some candy. We
were about 12 years old (fun ages). She got her Bit-O-Honey.
I got my malted milk balls, chocolate stars, Chunkys, and a
small bag of M & M's. We started back to her house. I was
going to spend the night. We had the whole day to look forward to. We had plenty of candy. It was a long way to Pam's
house but every time we got weary Pam would put her hand
over her eyes, scan the horizon like a sailor and say, "Oughta
reach home by nightfall," at which point the two of us would
laugh until we thought we couldn't stand it another minute.
Then after we got calm, she'd say it again. You should have
been there. It was the kind of day and friendship and occasion
that made me deeply regretful that I had to grow up.

It was fun.   15

BUILDING VOCABULARY

1. *Trite language* refers to words and expressions that have
   been overused and, consequently, have lost much of their
   effectiveness. People do rely on trite language in their conversations, but writers usually avoid overused expressions.

However, a good writer will be able to introduce such vocabulary at strategic points. Examples of trite language in
Jordan's essay appear below. Explain in your own words
what they mean:

   a. a rare jewel (par. 2)
   b. by Jove (par. 5)
   c. golly gee (par. 8)
   d. his ma's heart sank (par. 8)

2. For each of the following words drawn from Jordan's essay, write a denotative definition. Then list four connotations (see Glossary) each word has for you.

   a. overshadow (par. 4)
   b. flunking (par. 7)
   c. traipsing (par. 8)
   d. swilling (par. 10)
   e. mirth (par. 13)

3. Select five words from the Words to Watch section and use
them in sentences of your own.

UNDERSTANDING THE WRITER'S IDEAS

1. What are some of the things Jordan says fun is not?

2. What does Jordan suggest we did to something if it wasn't
already fun? Identify some of the things she says are "supposed" to be fun.

3. In paragraph 9, Jordan lists some common things that certainly aren't any fun. How does she say people made them
fun anyway?

4. What are some of the ways people make fun even more
thrilling?

5. What does Jordan list as looking like fun on television commercials?

6. Discuss the relationship between big occasions and the experience of fun. Explain the meaning of the statement, "It may even come on a Tuesday."

7. Describe Jordan's attitude concerning how much in life really is fun. According to Jordan, how should we treat fun? Why? Is it something she says can only be experienced at special times?

8. How old was Jordan at the time she remembers having an especially good time with her friend Pam? Describe in your own words why she had such a good time that day. What are some of the candies she remembers buying? Why was it especially funny when Pam would say, "Oughta reach home by nightfall"?

9. For what reason does Jordan feel regretful at the end of the essay? Although she is regretful, do you think she is actually sad? Why?

UNDERSTANDING THE WRITER'S TECHNIQUES

1. Does Jordan ever offer a single-sentence definition of "fun"? Where? Is that sentence sufficient to define the concept? Why?

2. Jordan employs the technique of *negation*—defining a term through showing what it is *not*—so strongly in this essay that the writing verges on *irony*. Irony is using language to suggest the opposite of what is said (see Glossary). Explain the irony in paragraphs 9, 10, and 11.

3. Why does the author continually point out things that are supposed to be fun? What is she trying to tell us about these things?

4. Writers usually avoid vague words such as "everything" or "everybody" in their writing, yet Jordan uses these words frequently in this essay. Explain her purpose in deliberately avoiding concrete terms.

5. What is the *tone* (see Glossary) of this essay? Is it fun? How does Jordan create this tone? Much of the writing in this essay has a very conversational quality to it, as though the author were speaking directly to the reader. Locate five words or phrases that have this quality.

6. Why does Jordan use so many examples and illustrations in this essay? Which paragraphs use multiple illustrations with special effectiveness?

7. There is a definite turning point in this essay where Jordan switches from an ironic to an affirmative point of view in which she begins to explain what fun *can be* rather than what it *is not*. One paragraph in particular serves as the transition between the two attitudes. Which one is it? Which is the first paragraph to be mostly affirmative? What is the result of this switch?

8. Jordan uses specific brand names in the essay. Locate at least four of them. Why do you think she uses these brand names instead of names that simply identify the object?

9. What is the function of narration in the development of this essay? Where does the author *narrate* an imagined incident? Where does she use a real incident? Why does Jordan use narration in this paper?

10. Compare the effects of the two simple, direct statements that begin and end the essay. Why does Jordan not develop a more elaborate introduction and conclusion?

EXPLORING THE WRITER'S IDEAS

1. Jordan begins her essay by stating, "Fun is hard to have." At one point she indicates that "Fun got to be such a big thing that everybody started looking for more and more thrilling ways to supply it" (par. 9). Do you think that fun is hard to have? Why or why not? What relationship does the epidemic use of drugs and alcohol have to our difficulties in having fun today?

2. The author raises the question of how at big events we are sometimes left "waiting for the fun to start" (par. 11). What functions do events or occasions such as holidays, weddings, or birthdays play in our society? Why is there an emphasis placed on having fun at those events? Do you think there should be such an emphasis? Why?

3. This essay appeared as a guest editorial in the *New York Times*. We do not usually think of the *New York Times* as a "fun" newspaper, but rather as one that deals with serious issues of international significance. Jordan's article might be considered popular writing or light reading. Do you feel there is a place in the media—newspapers, magazines, radio, television—for a mixture of "heavy" and "light" attitudes? What well-respected newspapers or magazines that you know include articles on popular topics? What subjects do you think would currently be most appealing to popular audiences?

4. At the end of the essay, Jordan seems to imply that it is easier for children to have fun than it is for grownups. Do you agree? Is the basic experience of fun any different for kids or for adults? Do you feel it was any easier for people to have fun in days past than it is now? Why?

IDEAS FOR WRITING

Guided Writing

Select one of the following highly connotative terms for various types of experiences and write an extended definition about it: love, creativity, alienation, prejudice, fidelity.

1. Prepare for your essay by consulting a good dictionary for the lexical definition of the term. However, instead of beginning with this definition, start with some catchy, interesting opening statements related to the definition.

2. Write a thesis sentence that names the word you will define

and that tells the special opinion, attitude, or point of view you have about the word.

3. Attempt to establish the importance of your subject by considering it in terms of our current understanding of fun.

4. Use the technique of negation (see page 239) by providing various examples and illustrations of what your topic *is not* in order to establish your own viewpoint of what it *is*.

5. Use other strategies—description, narration, comparison and contrast, and so forth—to aid in clearly establishing an extended definition of your topic.

6. At the end of your essay dramatize through narration at least one personal experience that relates the importance of the topic to your life.

More Writing Projects

1. From a book of popular quotations (*Bartlett's Familiar Quotations, The Oxford Dictionary of Quotations*) check under the heading "fun" and select a number of statements about fun by professional writers. Then write an essay in which you expand one of those definitions. Draw upon your own experiences or readings to support the definition you choose to expand.

2. Write an extended definition of "triumph," using the main techniques seen in the Jordan essay.

Escape Valve

Gregg Easterbrook

A contemporary journalist, Gregg Easterbrook tries here to define a phrase that he has coined to identify a phenomenon of modern life. Take note of the way he develops his definition by means of personal anecdote, history, and causal analysis. As you read, think about whether or not you know anyone guilty of "automatic-out."

Words to Watch

deep-rooted (par. 3)   firmly planted

foundations (par. 4)   underlying supports

stints (par. 5)   fixed shares of work to be performed within a given time period

truism (par. 5)   statement of a very obvious truth

hierarchies (par. 6)   bodies of people organized or classified according to rank

integrity (par. 7)   adherence to a code of behavior: honesty; uprightness

perpetuate (par. 9)   prolong the existence of

A man and woman I know moved in together recently. It 1 was, as such occasions are, a moment of sentiment and celebration. It was also a limited engagement. Before moving in, they had already set a fixed date when they would break up.

They explained their reasons to one and all. In a year, 2 the woman planned to change jobs and cities; the man did not plan to follow. An eventual split is unfortunate, they said, but also inevitable, so why not plan on it? Yet, far from being a sad twist of fate, my woman friend's scheduled departure, I fear, was a liberating force, making possible whatever short-term romance the couple will enjoy. Without the escape clause of a pre-set termination of their affair, they might never have lived together at all.

This situation is not unique. More and more, people are 3 ordering their lives along a principle I call the "automatic-

248

out." In love, friendship, work, and the community, people increasingly prefer arrangements that automatically end at some pre-set date. Automatic-out is not a phenomenon confined to my still-unsettled generation (the late 20's), with its flair for "flexible" styles of life. It is a force in society as a whole, as more of us hunger for lives that appear stable and deep-rooted but lack the complications of commitment.

Automatic-out may have its foundations in the pre-set **4** cycles of academic life. In recent decades, an ever-higher percentage of the population has been able to attend college and postgraduate schools. That's a good thing for the cause of education but perhaps not so good for society's spirit. Longtime students learn to view institutions as places where people briefly come to rest, and from which they will be automatically removed on a date known years in advance. They also tend to see institutions as a means by which to take things for themselves, instead of adding things for others.

So it may be no surprise that professionals—usually the **5** beneficiaries of advanced schooling—seem increasingly uninterested in staying put. Or, if they remain with one organization, lean toward fellowships, temporary assignments, and other stints with automatic-outs. For some time, this has been a troubling truism of Washington. A Brookings Institution study shows that Government-agency managers immediately below the rank of Presidential appointees turn over, on average, every 21 months. Now it is becoming true of private enterprise as well. According to the Conference Board, a business research organization, top corporate executives now switch jobs every 4.5 years on average—an all-time high.

The job-switching mania, it is sometimes suggested, **6** stems from a combination of boredom and expectations of promotion. But most switches among Government agencies and corporate hierarchies do not involve dramatic changes of life; they are changes from one job to another fairly similar to it, in a fairly similar organization. The number of top-level positions available doesn't increase just because the switching rate is increasing.

The switch mania is, I think, motivated by the desire for **7** automatic-outs. When you know in advance that you will soon be changing jobs, you are relieved of concern for the overall integrity of your institution—whether the quality of its products, the fairness of its service, the odds of its survival. You have a built-in excuse for selfishness ("I'll be leaving in a year anyway") and can concentrate on advancing yourself, secure in the knowledge that if you fail to improve your organization—or, as in the case of so many business and Government managers, actively damage it—you personally won't suffer. You'll be one step ahead of the crumbling walls.

It seems to be the same way in love. If a romance operates **8** under some pre-set restriction, neither partner feels obliged to sacrifice his interests for joint interests. Why sacrifice for something not expected to last anyway? Thus, the short-term benefits of marriage and living together (companionship, warmth, convenience) remain popular. But long-term obligation to the institution of marriage has fallen into disrepute among many young people. Children and family life are especially in disrepute today, for whenever children are present there is no easy out, emotionally or legally. The weekend romance is especially desirable today, not because "people move around more now" but because distance guarantees an automatic-out. Just step back on the plane Sunday night.

Many troublesome aspects of life perpetuate themselves **9** through downward-drawing spirals. As corporate and public institutions fall deeper into disrepair, as men and women become increasingly small-minded and cool to the touch, there seems all the more reason to opt for automatic-outs. Who wants to be committed to the kinds of people and organizations at loose in the world today? This, of course, helps only to accelerate the decay. Many people capable of helping right what's wrong with society seek instead mainly to exempt themselves from responsibility for its condition. Why should I care? I'll be leaving in a year anyway.

BUILDING VOCABULARY

Match each term in Column A below with an appropriate definition from Column B. There are two more definitions than you need.

Column A	Column B
1 inevitable (par. 2)	**a** disgrace
2 stable (par. 3)	**b** attractive
3 beneficiaries (par. 5)	**c** stimulated to action
4 mania (par. 6)	**d** speed up
5 motivated (par. 7)	**e** intense, abnormal
6 disrepute (par. 8)	desire for something
7 disrepair (par. 9)	**f** automatic
8 opt (par. 9)	**g** resistant to change
9 accelerate (par. 9)	**h** free from obligation
10 exempt (par. 9)	**i** choose
	j unavoidable
	k state of neglect
	l those who receive
	advantages

UNDERSTANDING THE WRITER'S IDEAS

1. What arrangement does the couple the author knows make? What reasons do they offer for this arrangement?

2. What is the "automatic-out" principle? Why does the author believe that it appeals to society as a whole and not just to his own generation of men and women in their late twenties?

3. What, according to Easterbrook, are the foundations for automatic-out?

4. What does the Brookings Institution study demonstrate? How does the Conference Board reinforce that study in a business setting?

5. What are the reasons generally offered for what Easterbrook calls "the job-switching mania"? Why are top-level positions not increasing in number? How does Easterbrook explain the switch mania?

6. For what reason does the desire to switch operate for love as well as for jobs? What are the short-term benefits of marriage and living together? Why, according to the au-

. thor, has the long-term obligation to marriage fallen into disrepute? Why is the weekend romance attractive?

7. How does the automatic-out serve to accelerate the decay of people and institutions today?

UNDERSTANDING THE WRITER'S TECHNIQUES

1. Which sentence of this essay is the thesis sentence? Why does Easterbrook not place it in the opening paragraph?

2. What is your opinion of the introduction in paragraphs 1 and 2? What is the value to the essay of the incident about the author's acquaintances? What rhetorical technique appears?

3. Where does the writer use negation (see page 239)?

4. In paragraph 4 why does he give backgrounds to the concept "automatic-out"?

5. Why does Easterbrook present findings of the Brookings Institution and the Conference Board? How do the findings enhance his point?

6. Where does the writer use causal analysis (see Glossary)? Why does he use it?

7. What transitions serve to connect one paragraph to the next? Look especially at the first sentence in paragraphs 3, 4, 5, 6, 7, and 8.

8. In paragraphs 3, 7, and 8 Easterbrook uses parenthetical expressions. Why does he choose to place information in parentheses?

9. The writer frames a number of questions in the essay. For example, in paragraph 8, he says, "Why sacrifice for something not expected to last anyway?" What is the value of the question? Why doesn't Easterbrook answer it? What other unanswered questions appear?

10. What is your opinion of the conclusion? How does East-
    erbrook establish a new, broader context for the term
    "automatic-out"? Why does he choose that context to
    close the essay?

11. Why do you think that the essay is called "Escape Valve"
    instead of "Automatic-Out"? What is an escape valve?
    Used here, of course, the title is metaphorical (see Glos-
    sary). What value is there in using the metaphorical title in
    this case?

12. What is your reaction to the conclusion? Why does Eas-
    terbrook end by condemning the automatic-out philoso-
    phy? Do you find the last two sentences effective?
    Why?

EXPLORING THE WRITER'S IDEAS

1. Has Easterbrook defined clearly a recognizable principle in
   today's society as you view it? Why do you feel as you do?
   What evidence of the automatic-out do you find among
   your family, friends, or acquaintances? Have you yourself
   ever entered into a relationship based upon automatic-out?

2. Easterbrook blames in part the academic institution—our
   public and private schools and colleges—for our acceptance of the value in short-term commitments. Why might
   you agree or disagree with him? What other forces or institutions may encourage short-term commitments?

3. Do you agree that the high level of job switching apparent
   today is related more to the desire for escaping commitments than to "boredom and expectations of promotion"?
   Defend your answer.

4. Why might you agree or disagree that "marriage has fallen
   into disrepute among many young people"? Is automatic-
   out a real threat to marriage as a basic institution of our
   culture? Why? (Look ahead to the essay "I Want a Wife"
   by Judy Syfers for another perspective on marriage.)

5. Answer the question in paragraph 9: "Who wants to be committed to the kinds of people and organizations at loose in the world today?"

6. The writer states that "many people capable of helping right what's wrong with society" try "to exempt themselves from responsibility for its condition." What are some of the things wrong with society today? How might people right those wrongs?

IDEAS FOR WRITING

Guided Writing

Choose a word or term that you think is opposite in meaning to "automatic-out" and write an essay of 500 to 750 words in which you define that term. You may choose a word or term like *commitment, staying in, holding on, hanging in,* or some such expression. You may even want to coin your own phrase.

1. Start with an anecdote about friends or acquaintances and explain it. Your anecdote should demonstrate the word or phrase that you are trying to define.

2. In your thesis statement name the term and give an expanded definition of it in a paragraph or two.

3. Explain the foundations or the history of the situation your term is naming as Easterbrook does in paragraph 4 of his essay.

4. If possible, present data to support your interpretation of the term.

5. Give examples to expand your meanings further. Draw your examples from people at work or from personal relationships with other people.

6. Use an occasional unanswered question to challenge the reader.

7. If you can, use negation to help you define the term.

8. Connect your paragraphs with transitions that relate one idea thoughtfully to the next.

9. In your conclusion, place the term in a broader perspective, one that goes beyond the specific conditions you are explaining.

10. Try to give your essay a metaphorical title.

More Writing Projects

1. Easterbrook uses the term "switch mania" when he writes about jobs. Think about the term and then write a definition of it as it pertains to our culture today.

2. An "escapist" is someone who looks to break loose from unpleasant realities through self-deceiving fantasy or entertainment. In an essay write an extended definition of the word "escapist." Draw upon your own experiences and (or) your readings to support your definition.

Soaps, Cynicism, and Mind Control

Elizabeth Janeway

Elizabeth Janeway is the author of *Man's World, Woman's Place*, and *Powers of the Weak;* these, and her forthcoming book, focus acutely on sociological uses of power and manipulation. "Soaps, Cynicism, and Mind Control" appeared in the January 1985 issue of *Ms.* magazine. It explains the dangers of allowing oneself to be too influenced by the media; in so doing, the essay establishes a definition for the abstract notion of *randomness*.

Words to Watch

heightened (par. 1)   made more exciting

catering (par. 1)   supplying what is required or desired

kin (par. 2)   relatives

fidelity (par. 3)   faithfulness to another person

amnesiac (par. 3)   a person who has temporarily lost his or her memory

differentiates (par. 4)   discerns separate characteristics of something

inevitability (par. 4)   the condition of not being able to be avoided or evaded

potentiality (par. 4)   the ability to develop

counsel (par. 6)   to give advice

passivity (par. 8)   attitude of submissiveness or inactivity

subordinates (par. 10)   makes less important

ideology (par. 10)   a system of belief about a subject, often social, political, or economic in nature

What does the powerful teaching tool of television have 1
to say to its viewers about desirable attitudes toward life and its problems? And what does the Media Establishment assume that *we* assume about the way this world functions? With these questions, I approached soap operas and evening series—programs that claimed to present ordinary existence,

though heightened for drama and catering to everyone's curiosity about how the other half lives.

In between commercial breaks, I noted a deeply disturbing factor in so many of the dramas: the lack of any sense of process, of the eternal truth that events have consequences, and that people can and do influence what happens to them and to others. What I saw instead was a consistent, insistent demonstration of *randomness,* a statement that life is unpredictable and out of control. With rare exceptions what happens on-screen suggests that no one can trust her or his own judgment and (other side of the same coin) that no one, friend, kin, or lover, is really trustworthy.   2

We may identify with the actors because we all face unpredictable events, but we get no clues to coping with them. No one seems talented at solving the puzzles of life: even J.R. Ewing was shot. Nobody shows us how to decide on the fidelity of kin or associates, no love is certain. Let a wedding date be set and you can be pretty sure the ceremony won't come off. Report a death and expect the corpse to show up in a future segment fleeing a crime, amnesiac, or as survivor of a "fatal" plane crash. Says one of a pair of embracing lovers, "I don't know anything about you." Par for the course. Later in the same segment (of "Another World") a young woman tells a young man she doesn't love him. But wait a minute! She has been hypnotized, it seems, in a program I missed, and here she is on tape declaring she *does* love him to the hypnotist. Not only don't we/they know anything about the others in their lives, they/we don't understand ourselves either. The Guiding Lights we seek are shrouded in fog.   3

Now drama, and indeed fiction as a whole, has always aimed at surprising its audiences. But those surprises end by showing us something we hadn't known, some truth, about existence. It may be a tragic truth, but tragedy can strengthen us to face the future because it explains and illustrates the processes that lead to defeat instead of victory. And knowledge is power. Even when it tells us some things can't be changed, it differentiates inevitability from potentiality; and moreover, it gives us a chance to plan our own responses: we can't change the weather, but we can take an umbrella when we go out.   4

Our intervention in ongoing existence is shown to be possible. Beginning with childhood fables and fairy tales, such stories bring us useful messages about the workings of the real world and what human beings can do to influence it.

That's not what the TV programs say. The people on the 5 screen are adrift in a world of happenstance, and the messages warn that no action will do any good.

Certainly there's a lot of randomness in the world. Stable 6 unchanging small-town life is fading from the American scene and close ties to extended families are rare. Most of us meet a lot of strangers from unfamiliar backgrounds. Women who have moved into formerly all-male preserves have had to learn or invent patterns of relationships as well as new processes of doing things. These women have begun to take risks and forget old lessons in helplessness. But daily there appears on the screen counsel that the world is unpredictable, that one can't hope to plan or gain control of events. Moreover when we see the rare realistic portrayal of work-life (where competence, daring, and imagination may be rewarded), attention is concentrated on the personal. Intimate relationships are chancy and dangerous, comes the word, but they're the only things that matter.

Randomness, like guilt, is a powerful tool for social con- 7 trol. Survivors of the Holocaust and refugees from Stalin's "Gulag Archipelago" record how personality was deliberately broken down by those in control disrupting their prisoners' normal expectations. Guards separated consequences from action and thus persuaded prisoners that it was hopeless for them to plan a particular behavior, hopeless for them to imagine a future. Survival became a matter of utter chance. Inmates of the camps were thus reduced to subhuman, mindless robots who moved as they were told to.

Today in El Salvador (and who can say how many other 8 places?), terror activates the randomness of danger. No one knows where the death squads will strike next, and therefore people can't take any reasonable action and expect to ensure greater safety. If safety exists at all, it lies in passivity and hiding. *Time* magazine quotes an expert on Central America in a recent issue: "Anybody can be killed with virtual impunity.

You do not want to investigate because you might find out, and finding out can itself be fatal.''

But it's not only in extreme situations that randomness 9 can be used to promote self-policing. If the powerful can divide the majority of ordinary folk into disconnected, self-protecting individuals, they need not fear organized resistance. And when television suggests to a woman that even her friends had better not be trusted, it is denying comradeship, sisterhood—and joint action.

I don't suggest that this is a conscious media conspiracy 10 intended to keep women and other groups in their subordinate places. *It doesn't need to be.* Standard practice and the mythic ideology that enforces it have always played up individual effort as a way of establishing one's value and one's deserts. For instance, the Supreme Court has underlined that message by limiting affirmative action remedies that can be awarded to a group or class. Legal recourse must now be sought by *individuals* rather than on a group basis. When the media repeats this message, it need only appeal to what we've often heard before: success means learning the rules and following them. Don't trust your colleagues. The big world of action is both dangerous and mysterious, you'll never really understand it. Stay out of it, sit still, don't try.

Will we follow that message more than two generations 11 after women won the ballot? Let us refuse the posture of the powerless. People who have begun to feel strong don't have to accept victimization.

BUILDING VOCABULARY

1. While Janeway never really uses *trite language* (see page 242), she does use a number of expressions in fairly common use in daily conversation and media talk or writing. Try to rewrite each of the following expressions in your own words, using less common language; try to create original, interesting expressions.

   a. teaching tool (par. 1)

    b. Media Establishment (par. 1)
    c. how the other half lives (par. 1)
    d. commercial breaks (par. 2)
    e. other side of the same coin (par. 2)
    f. Par for the course (par. 3)
    g. shrouded in fog (par. 3)
    h. a tragic truth (par. 4)
    i. knowledge is power (par. 4)
    j. adrift in a world of happenstance (par. 5)
    k. all-male preserves (par. 6)
    l. a matter of utter chance (par. 7)
    m. with virtual impunity (par. 8)
    n. ordinary folk (par. 9)
    o. a conscious media conspiracy (par. 10)

2. Identify these *allusions* (see Glossary) from Janeway's essay:

    a. J.R. Ewing (par. 3)
    b. "Another World" (par. 3)
    c. the Holocaust (par. 7)
    d. Stalin (par. 7)
    e. "Gulag Archipelago" (par. 7)
    f. El Salvador (par. 8)
    g. the death squads (in El Salvador) (par. 8)
    h. *Time* magazine (par. 8)
    i. the Supreme Court (par. 10)
    j. affirmative action (par. 10)

UNDERSTANDING THE WRITER'S IDEAS

1. What are *soap operas* and *evening series?* Give some current examples of each. What does the author say is the intended purpose of these types of programs? How does she say that purpose is altered? Why is it?

2. According to Janeway, how do television dramas present an unrealistic view of life? What attitude toward trust do they convey?

3. Based on your understanding of Janeway's article, who do you think she would say is more capable of dealing with "unpredictable events"—dramatic characters or their viewers? Explain your answer.

4. Explain in your own words the main idea of paragraph 4. What is Janeway's point about the purposes of drama and fiction? What is especially enlightening about tragedy? How do fairy tales and fables fit into this explanation? How do TV programs differ in purpose and effect from the types of drama and fiction that Janeway respects? How is their message significantly different from that of good fiction?

5. What recent changes in American society does Janeway mention in paragraph 6? What is her opinion of those changes? Why are they useful examples to advance the theme of this essay?

6. What does Janeway mean in paragraph 6 by the expression "old lessons in helplessness"? What attitude does she convey in the sentence in which it appears?

7. In the last sentence of paragraph 6, the author uses the expression, "comes the word." From *where* does *the word* come? What is *the word?* In light of her title and theme in this essay, how is that expression particularly appropriate?

8. What, according to the author, is the connection between "randomness" and "mind control"? What does she mean by randomness? What examples of that connection does she provide? For what reason does she choose such examples?

9. What does Janeway suggest is the relation between a powerful minority and a "majority of ordinary folks"? How do notions of individuality play a role in this relation?

10. What is the author's opinion about the ways in which the media affects the lives of women? Explain your answer with specific references to the article.

11. Ultimately, how do you understand Janeway to define the concept of randomness? Does she define predominantly through indicating its causes, effects, or manifestations?

UNDERSTANDING THE WRITER'S TECHNIQUES

1. How does Janeway use questions in the first paragraph to establish a context for her discussion? Does she ask these questions to search for specific answers or are they rhetorical questions (*rhetorical questions* are meant to stimulate thought rather than specific answers)? Explain.

2. What is defined in this essay? Does Janeway state that definition directly? In brief, what would you say is her thesis in this essay? Why does she use definition as her key organizing technique? How does she use minor definitions to build to her major definition?

3. What is *cynicism* (write a dictionary definition of the term)? How is the first sentence of paragraph 2 an example of cynicism? Find at least three other examples of cynicism in this essay.

4. Comment on Janeway's use of *illustration* (see pages 164–165) in this essay. From where does she draw most of her examples? Which are the most effective? Which least? Why?

5. Explain the author's use of double subject pronouns (*we/they; they/we*) in paragraph 3. What relation between viewer and character does this technique establish? Why does Janeway want to establish such a connection?

6. What is the *double entendre* (*Double entendre* is a French expression indicating that something has a double meaning, each equally valid.) of the phrase "The Guiding Lights" as it is used in paragraph 3?

7. Why is paragraph 5 so short in comparison to the others in this essay? How does it act as a key turning point in the essay?

8. What is the purpose of italicizing the sentence, *It doesn't need to be*, in paragraph 10? What is the effect?

9. For whom is Janeway writing this article? Why do you

think so? What "message" is she attempting to convey to that audience? In the last three paragraphs, how does Janeway gear her definition to a feminist perspective? Where does she forecast that perspective earlier in the essay? How do the examples that she chooses in paragraphs 9–11 help create this perspective?

10. Would you characterize the messages and tone of paragraph 10 as more *ironic* (see Glossary) or *cynical?* Why?

11. Janeway begins this article by concentrating on TV soaps and dramas, yet by the end, she is dealing with a much wider range of influences. How does she accomplish this broadening of her scope of ideas? Why does she do so? Do you feel she accomplished the transition smoothly and that she maintained *unity* and *coherence* (see Glossary) throughout the essay?

EXPLORING THE WRITER'S IDEAS

1. In this article, Elizabeth Janeway writes about such highly-charged issues as *mind control* and *conscious media conspiracy*. Do you think such things actually exist? If so, to what extent? Do you believe that any sort of media conspiracy currently exists? If so, explain its causes and give examples of its manifestations. What can be done about it? If you don't think it exists, why do you feel so many people are concerned about it these days?

2. Would you say Janeway believes in fate or predestination? Why or why not?

3. In paragraph 4, Janeway writes about the powerful effects of drama and fiction, and she gives us examples of what we can learn from them. She includes, also, childhood fables and fairy tales. Give examples of how reading, seeing, or hearing certain fiction, either as a child or as an adult, has influenced your present way of life. (Bruno Bettelheim, pages 230–233, has some interesting ideas on childhood stories.)

4. Look up the origin of the term *soap opera*. How did the phrase develop?

5. Janeway defines success as "learning the rules and following them." Do you agree with that definition? Why or why not? How might it be possible for someone to achieve success without following the rules?

IDEAS FOR WRITING

Guided Writing

Write a definition of *mind control*. Focus your essay on a medium other than television *or* on a specific aspect of television broadcasting. For example, you may want to focus on newspapers or magazines, *or* on TV news, or advertisements or music videos.

1. Begin your essay with a series of rhetorical questions to set the context for your investigation of the particular medium.

2. State clearly what you feel the underlying purpose of that medium is (as it affects mind control).

3. Give examples of how the medium presents a view of life other than that which is usual or realistic.

4. Give examples—both general and specific—of this unrealistic view of things.

5. Make some statement about what effect this unrealistic view has on us as media consumers.

6. Explain the potential positive uses of this medium.

7. About halfway through your essay, begin a pointed discussion of how the medium you've chosen tends to manipulate our perceptions of the world around us.

8. About two-thirds through the essay, narrow your point of perspective so that you focus more clearly on one segment of the medium's audience.

9. Include contemporary examples and historical allusions that illustrate both causes and effects of this mind control.

10. End your essay with a strong statement of how people can overcome the "control" of this medium.

More Writing Projects

1. Write an extended definition of any abstract term that is currently popular in the jargon of sociology or pop psychology. Develop your definition with illustrations of both causes and effects.

2. Write about a time when you were influenced by the media to do something you wouldn't have ordinarily considered doing: buying something, talking with others in a certain way, dressing differently, and so on.

To the Victor Belongs the Language
Rita Mae Brown

Rita Mae Brown is a novelist whose works include *High Hearts* and *Southern Discomfort*. This essay is taken from her *Starting from Scratch: A Writer's Manual* (1988), a fascinating look at language and the creative process that goes far beyond the usual cut-and-dried rules and references. Notice how she uses definition not only to inform and explain, but also to entertain the reader and to illustrate strong sociopolitical opinions.

Words to Watch

pendulum (par. 2) a mechanism that swings freely back and forth under the force of gravity

via (par. 3) by way of

yield (par. 4) give way to

lingers (par. 4) stays on

vibrant (par. 6) alive; healthy

tarot deck (par. 6) a deck of illustrated cards thought to be able to predict the future

dangle (par. 6) hang loosely and so as to be able to swing freely

potent (par. 7) strong; forceful

benign (par. 7) not harmful

subversion (par. 8) an attempt to undermine the established way

bloodbath (par. 8) massacre

tyrant (par. 8) absolute, oppressive ruler

indiscriminately (par. 9) without any plan or order

attendant (par. 9) accompanying; following as a consequence

Language is the road map of a culture. It tells you where its 1 people come from and where they are going. A study of the English language reveals a dramatic history and astonishing versatility. It is the language of survivors, of conquerors, of laughter.

A word is more like a pendulum than a fixed entity. It 2 can sweep by your ear and through its very sound suggest hidden meanings, preconscious associations. Listen to these words: "blood," "tranquil," "democracy." Besides their literal meanings, they carry associations that are cultural as well as personal.

One word can illustrate this idea of meaning in flux: 3 "revolution." The word enters English in the 14th century from the Latin via French. (At least that's when it was first written; it may have been spoken earlier.) "Revolution" means a turning around; that was how it was used. Most often "revolution" was applied to astronomy to describe a planet revolving in space. The word carried no political meaning.

"Rebellion" was the loaded political word. It too comes 4 from Latin (as does about 60 percent of our word pool), and it means a renewal of war. In the 14th century "rebellion" was used to indicate a resistance to lawful authority. This can yield amusing results. Whichever side won called the losers rebels—they, the winners, being the repositories of virtue and more gunpowder. This meaning lingers today. The Confederate fighters are called rebels. Since the North won that war, it can be dismissed as a rebellion and not called a revolution. Whoever wins the war redefines the language.

"Revolution" did not acquire a political meaning in En- 5 glish until at least the 16th century. Its meaning—a circular movement—was still tied to its origin but had spilled over into politics. It could now mean a turnaround in power. This is more complicated than you might think.

The 16th century, vibrant, cruel, progressive, held as a 6 persistent popular image the wheel of fortune—an image familiar to anyone who has played with a tarot deck. Human beings dangle on a giant wheel. Some are on the bottom turning upward, some are on the top, and some are hurtling toward the ground. It's as good an image as any for the sudden twists and turns of Fate, Life or the Human Condition. This idea was so dominant at the time that the word "revolution" absorbed its meaning. Instead of a card or a complicated explanation of the wheel of fortune, that one word captured the concept. It's a concept we would do well to remember.

Politically, "rebellion" was still the more potent word. 7 Cromwell's seizure of state power in the mid-17th century came to be called the Great Rebellion, because Charles II followed Cromwell in the restoration of monarchy. Cromwell didn't call his own actions rebellious. In 1689 when William and Mary took over the throne of England, the event was tagged the Glorious Revolution. "Revolution" is benign here and politically inferior in intensity to "rebellion."

By 1796 a shift occurred and "revolution" had come to mean the subversion or overthrow of tyrants. Rebellion, specifically, was a subversion of the laws. Revolution was personal. So we had the American Revolution, which dumped George III out of the Colonies, and the French Revolution, which gave us the murder of Louis XVI and the spectacle of a nation devouring itself. If you're a Marxist you can recast that to mean one class destroying another. At any rate, the French Revolution was a bloodbath and "revolution" began to get a bad name as far as monarchists were concerned and holy significance as far as Jacobins were concerned. By that time "revolution" was developing into the word we know today—not just the overthrow of a tyrant but action based on belief in a new principle. Revolution became a political idea, not just a political act.

The Russian Revolution, the Chinese Revolution, the Cuban Revolution—by now "revolution" is the powerful word, not "rebellion." In the late 1960's and early 1970's young Americans used the word "revolution" indiscriminately. True, they wanted political power, they were opposed to tyrants and believed in a new political principle (or an old one, depending on your outlook) called participatory democracy. However, that period of unrest, with its attendant creativity, did not produce a revolution. The word quickly became corrupted until by the 80's "revolution" was a word used to sell running shoes.

Whither goest thou, Revolution?

BUILDING VOCABULARY

1. Explain the meaning of the terms and phrases in italics. Look up any words you don't recognize.

   a. A study of the English language *reveals a dramatic history and astonishing versatility.* (par. 1)

   b. *a fixed entity* (par. 2)

   c. suggest hidden meanings, *preconscious associations* (par. 2)

   d. this idea of meaning *in flux* (par. 3)

   e. 60 percent of our *word pool* (par. 4)

   f. being *the repositories of virtue* and more gunpowder (par. 4)

   g. Its meaning—*a circular movement*—was still *tied to* its origin but had *spilled over* into politics. (par. 5)

   h. when William and Mary took over *the throne of England* (par. 7)

   i. *the spectacle of a nation devouring itself* (par. 8)

   j. "revolution" began *to get a bad name* as far as monarchists were concerned and *holy significance* as far as Jacobins were concerned (par. 8)

2. Throughout the essay, Brown makes extensive use of historical *allusions* (see Glossary) including allusions to historical figures and groups, sociopolitical movements, and places. There are fifteen allusions in all. See if you can find and list all fifteen, then choose ten to identify in depth.

3. In paragraph 4, the author states that about 60 percent of words used in English originate in Latin. From what other languages do English words derive? Select ten of the Words to Watch (or any others from this essay) and use a dictionary to list their derivations. (Try to find at least half that do not derive from Latin.)

UNDERSTANDING THE WRITER'S IDEAS

1. What is the meaning of the opening sentence?

2. According to the author, is English a language that has followed a fixed and steady course in its development? Explain.

3. Explain in your own words what the author means when

she writes of words such as "blood," "tranquil," or "democracy" that "besides their literal meanings, they carry associations that are cultural as well as personal" (par. 1). Write the literal meanings of those words, then write three cultural and personal associations for each.

4. From what language does the English word "revolution" come? When did it enter the English language? What was its earliest recorded meaning in English? From where did the word "rebellion" come? When? What was its original meaning?

5. Why does Brown write: "Whoever wins the war redefines the language" (par. 4)? How does she illustrate this statement?

6. With reference to this essay, outline the changes in cultural associations for the words "revolution" and "rebellion" over the centuries. How were they different? Similar? How did they help to define each other?

7. Briefly describe the sixteenth-century concept of the "wheel of fortune." How did its meaning change from a literal image to an abstract concept?

8. At what point in history did "revolution" become a more politically powerful word than "rebellion"? Why?

9. What is Brown's attitude toward the French Revolution? If one accepts her opinion, how did the French Revolution significantly alter the meaning of the word "revolution"?

10. According to Brown, what was the attitude of young Americans in the 1960s and 1970s? By what events was this attitude shaped? Does Brown feel this attitude was positive or negative? Explain.

11. What is Brown's opinion about the use of the word "revolution" in the 1980s?

12. Explain the meaning of the final sentence.

UNDERSTANDING THE WRITER'S TECHNIQUES

1. Writers can use one of several techniques to develop an extended definition. They include (a) showing how a particular term differs from others that belong to the same general category, (b) developing the etymology of a term (its origin and history in the language), and (c) using negation to show what the term does *not* mean.

   Which of these three techniques best describes Brown's predominant method in this essay? Does she also make use of the other two techniques? If so, where?

   Write a paragraph-by-paragraph outline that traces the development of the predominant technique throughout the essay.

2. How does Brown use the principle of *chronological order* (see Glossary) in this essay?

3. Is there a single thesis statement in the essay? If so, what is it?

4. How does Brown use a *metaphor* in paragraph 1 and a *simile* in paragraph 2 to increase the reader's understanding of language and words?

5. Where is *negation* used in this essay?

6. Who was Brown's intended audience for this essay? How does her choice of subject help you to understand her intended audience? Name three other factors that made you decide that this was Brown's audience.

7. Most essays of definition focus on a single term or concept. Why does Brown choose to define two terms in this essay? In what ways do the two definitions complement each other? Which is the primary term being defined? How do you know?

8. Describe the author's overall purpose in writing this essay. (Refer, if you like, to the introduction to this chapter.)

9. Describe the overall *tone* of this essay. Does the tone befit the subject? How does she use *irony* and *sarcasm* (see Glossary) in the essay? Give examples of each. How do the irony and sarcasm influence your reading of this piece?

10. One might say that the last line is written in such a way as to give it an almost biblical tone. Why would Brown choose this tone? What stylistic elements contribute to that tone?

11. Where does the author use *illustration* in this essay? Comparison and contrast?

12. Would you characterize this definition as primarily *objective* or *subjective* (see Glossary)? Why?

13. Brown clearly indicates the depth of her research and grasp of history through the many historical *allusions* (see Glossary and the Building Vocabulary section) included here. What is their value to the essay? Is it essential that the reader be able to identify each of the allusions? Why or why not?

14. Describe at least two methods by which Brown achieves smooth *transitions* and maintains *coherence* throughout the essay. Give examples.

EXPLORING THE WRITER'S IDEAS

1. The *Oxford English Dictionary,* which you can find in the reference section of the library, traces the etymology of nearly all words in the English language. It includes the historical development of words, with examples of recorded usage, and makes fascinating reading. Select five words from this essay and read their etymologies in the *OED.*

2. In paragraph 1, Brown writes of the "astonishing versatility" of the English language. Later in the book from which this selection is excerpted, she writes: "Fortunately for writers of English we possess the largest vocabulary in the

world.'' Do you feel English is a particularly versatile and expressive language? If so, in what areas of communication is it most versatile or expressive?

Do you speak or write a language other than English? If so, which do you feel is the best suited for your self-expression? Why? If you don't speak another language, are there any languages you enjoy listening to or looking at even if you can't understand? What makes you feel this way?

3. Americans are sometimes criticized for being essentially monolingual (able to speak only one language). By comparison, many other cultures are multilingual (able to speak more than one language), with the second language often being English. Do you feel people miss anything by being monolingual? For what reasons do you believe the majority of Americans do not learn languages other than English? For what reasons do you feel people all over the world are trying to learn English?

4. In paragraph 3, Brown alludes to the differences between the spoken and the written language—that most often words enter a language's oral communication before they become part of the written language. Give some examples of the differences between oral and written language usage today.

IDEAS FOR WRITING

Guided Writing

Write an extended definition of a term that you feel is critical to the understanding of a particular field of study or skilled activity. For example, if you choose the field-of-study approach, you might consider defining *dig* in archeology, *memory* in computer science, or *comic strip* in pop culture. If you choose a skilled activity, you might consider defining *pas de deux* in ballet, *space* in architecture, or *focal point* in painting.

1. Begin with an original metaphor.

2. Isolate the most important element of the study or activity. Introduce it in paragraph 2 with an original simile expressing the need for illustrating and defining a particular term.

3. Give examples of other terms that also need definition.

4. Write a clear thesis statement that categorizes two subtopics to help organize your definition.

5. Introduce a secondary, closely related term that can be compared or contrasted with the first in order to produce a clearer definition.

6. Chronologically discuss the etymology of the two terms, continually illustrating the way they relate to each other.

7. Try to include interesting historical allusions.

8. Make use of negation.

9. Don't shy away from making the essay subjective—that is, interjecting your opinions.

10. End your essay with an observation about recent developments in your field of study or activity.

More Writing Projects

1. Write an extended definition of a term that describes a current, serious social issue—for example, homelessness, financial uncertainty, unemployment, substance abuse.

2. Write an extended definition of the term "Yuppie."

CHAPTER 8

Classification

Classification is the arrangement of information into groups or categories in order to make clear the relationships among members of the group. Writers need to classify, because it helps them present a mass of material by means of some orderly system. Related bits of information seem clearer when presented together as parts of a group. We are always classifying things in our daily lives: We put all our text books on one shelf or in one corner of the desk; we count on similar items in the supermarket being grouped together so we can buy all our canned vegetables or snacks in a single area; we make categories in our minds of the teachers we like, of the relatives who annoy us, and of the cars that look sleekest on the road. In classifying, we show how things within a large body of information relate to each other; we organize those things into groups so that they make sense to us and to anybody else who is interested in what we are thinking, or saying, or doing.

Classification helps writers explain relationships to their readers. First, a writer will *analyze* a body of material in order to divide some large subject into categories. Called *division* or *analysis,* this first task helps split an idea or an object into parts. Then, some of the parts can serve as categories into which the writer can fit individual pieces that share some common qualities. So, if you wanted to write about sports, for example, you might first break the topic down—*divide* it—into *team sports* and *individual sports* (although there are many other ways you might have made the division). Then you

275

could group together (*classify*) baseball, soccer, and football in the first category; and, perhaps, boxing, wrestling and tennis in the second. Your purpose in dividing or analyzing is to determine the parts of a whole (team sports and individual sports *are* very different).

Division does not always require that classification follow it. Your purpose in classifying, however, is to show how things in a group are similar. (Baseball, soccer, and football have interesting similarities as team sports; boxing, wrestling, and tennis—stressing individual achievement—are related, too.) Yet division and classification do work together. If you emptied the contents of a pocketbook onto a table, you would begin to divide those contents into groups. Through division, you would identify objects relating to finances, objects relating to personal care, objects relating to school work. Once you had the divisions clear, you would place objects in each category: money, checks, and credit cards in the first; cosmetics, a comb, perfume in the second; pens, pencils, a notebook in the third.

When you divide and classify for writing, you have to keep several things in mind. You have to think carefully about the division of the topic so that you limit the overlap from group to group. That is best achieved by creating categories different enough from each other so there is no blending. Since you, the writer, have to establish the groups (and sometimes there are many different ways to set up groups for the same topic), you need to use a principle of classification that is sensible, accurate, and complete. Do not force categories just for the sake of making groups. You have to show how things in a group relate to each other, and this you must do without ignoring their differences and without making them stereotypes. If you stereotype objects in a group (whether the objects are people, things, or ideas), you will be oversimplifying them, taking away their individuality, and forcing them to fit your categories.

Classification resembles outlining. It provides the writer with a plan of organization. Whether the subject is personal, technical, simple, complex, or abstract, the writer can organize material about it into categories, and can move carefully from one category to another in developing an essay.

Friends, Good Friends—And Such Good Friends

Judith Viorst

In this essay Judith Viorst, who writes for numerous popular magazines, examines types of friends in her life. Her pattern of development is easy to follow, because she tends to stay on one level in the process of classification. As you read this essay, try to keep in mind the similarities and distinctions that Viorst makes among types of friends, as well as the principles of classification that she uses.

Words to Watch

nonchalant (par. 3)   showing an easy unconcern or disinterest

endodontist (par. 14)   a dentist specializing in diseases of dental pulp and root canals.

sibling (par. 16)   brother or sister

dormant (par. 19)   as if asleep; inactive

self-revelation (par. 22)   self-discovery; self-disclosure

calibrated (par. 29)   measured; fixed; checked carefully

Women are friends, I once would have said, when they 1 totally love and support and trust each other, and bare to each other the secrets of their souls, and run—no questions asked—to help each other, and tell harsh truths to each other (no, you can't wear that dress unless you lose ten pounds first) when harsh truths must be told.

Women are friends, I once would have said, when they 2 share the same affection for Ingmar Bergman, plus train rides, cats, warm rain, charades, Camus, and hate with equal ardor Newark and Brussels sprouts and Lawrence Welk and camping.

In other words, I once would have said that a friend is a 3 friend all the way, but now I believe that's a narrow point of view. For the friendships I have and the friendships I see are conducted at many levels of intensity, serve many different functions, meet different needs and range from those as all-

277

the-way as the friendship of the soul sisters mentioned above
to that of the most nonchalant and casual playmates.

Consider these varieties of friendship: 4

1. Convenience friends. These are the women with   5
whom, if our paths weren't crossing all the time, we'd have no
particular reason to be friends: a next-door neighbor, a woman
in our car pool, the mother of one of our children's closest
friends or maybe some mommy with whom we serve juice and
cookies each week at the Glenwood Co-op Nursery.

Convenience friends are convenient indeed. They'll lend   6
us their cups and silverware for a party. They'll drive our kids
to soccer when we're sick. They'll take us to pick up our car
when we need a lift to the garage. They'll even take our cats
when we go on vacation. As we will for them.

But we don't, with convenience friends, ever come too   7
close or tell too much; we maintain our public face and emotional distance. "Which means," says Elaine, "that I'll talk
about being overweight but not about being depressed. Which
means I'll admit being mad but not blind with rage. Which
means I might say that we're pinched this month but never
that I'm worried sick over money."

But which doesn't mean that there isn't sufficient value   8
to be found in these friendships of mutual aid, in convenience
friends.

2. Special-interest friends. These friendships aren't inti-   9
mate, and they needn't involve kids or silverware or cats.
Their value lies in some interest jointly shared. And so we
may have an office friend or a yoga friend or a tennis friend or
a friend from the Women's Democratic Club.

"I've got one woman friend," says Joyce, "who likes,   10
as I do, to take psychology courses. Which makes it nice for
me—and nice for her. It's fun to go with someone you know
and it's fun to discuss what you've learned, driving back from
the classes." And for the most part, she says, that's all they
discuss.

"I'd say that what we're doing is *doing* together, not be-   11
ing together," Suzanne says of her Tuesday-doubles friends.
"It's mainly a tennis relationship, but we play together well.
And I guess we all need to have a couple of playmates."

I agree.   12

My playmate is a shopping friend, a woman of marvelous 13
taste, a woman who knows exactly *where* to buy *what,* and
furthermore is a woman who always knows beyond a doubt
what one ought to be buying. I don't have the time to keep up
with what's new in eyeshadow, hemlines and shoes and
whether the smock look is in or finished already. But since
(oh, shame!) I care a lot about eyeshadow, hemlines and
shoes, and since I don't *want* to wear smocks if the smock
look is finished, I'm very glad to have a shopping friend.

3. Historical friends. We all have a friend who knew us 14
when...maybe way back in Miss Meltzer's second grade,
when our family lived in that three-room flat in Brooklyn,
when our dad was out of work for seven months, when our
brother Allie got in that fight where they had to call the police,
when our sister married the endodontist from Yonkers and
when, the morning after we lost our virginity, she was the
first, the only, friend we told.

The years have gone by and we've gone separate ways 15
and we've little in common now, but we're still an intimate
part of each other's past. And so whenever we go to Detroit
we always go to visit this friend of our girlhood. Who knows
how we looked before our teeth were straightened. Who
knows how we talked before our voice got unBrooklyned.
Who knows what we ate before we learned about artichokes.
And who, by her presence, puts us in touch with an earlier
part of ourself, a part of ourself it's important never to lose.

"What this friend means to me and what I mean to her," 16
says Grace, "is having a sister without sibling rivalry. We
know the texture of each other's lives. She remembers my
grandmother's cabbage soup. I remember the way her uncle
played the piano. There's simply no other friend who remembers those things."

4. Crossroads friends. Like historical friends, our cross- 17
roads friends are important for *what was*—for the friendship
we shared at a crucial, now past, time of life. A time, perhaps,
when we roomed in college together; or worked as eager
young singles in the Big City together; or went together, as my
friend Elizabeth and I did through pregnancy, birth and that
scary first year of new motherhood.

Crossroads friends forge powerful links, links strong 18

enough to endure with not much more contact than once-
a-year letters at Christmas. And out of respect for those crossroads years, for those dramas and dreams we once shared, we
will always be friends.

   5. Cross-generational friends. Historical friends and 19
crossroads friends seem to maintain a special kind of intimacy—dormant but always ready to be revived—and though
we may rarely meet, whenever we do connect, it's personal
and intense. Another kind of intimacy exists in the friendships
that form across generations in what one woman calls her
daughter-mother and her mother-daughter relationships.

   Evelyn's friend is her mother's age—"but I share so much 20
more than I ever could with my mother"—a woman she talks to
of music, of books and of life. "What I get from her is the benefit
of her experience. What she gets—and enjoys—from me is a
youthful perspective. It's a pleasure for both of us."

   I have in my own life a precious friend, a woman of 65 21
who has lived very hard, who is wise, who listens well; who
has been where I am and can help me understand it; and who
represents not only an ultimate ideal mother to me but also the
person I'd like to be when I grow up.

   In our daughter role we tend to do more than our share 22
of self-revelation; in our mother role we tend to receive what's
revealed. It's another kind of pleasure—playing wise mother
to a questing younger person. It's another very lovely kind of
friendship.

   6. Part-of-a-couple friends. Some of the women we call 23
our friends we never see alone—we see them as part of a couple at couples' parties. And though we share interests in many
things and respect each other's views, we aren't moved to
deepen the relationship. Whatever the reason, a lack of time
or—and this is more likely—a lack of chemistry, our friendship remains in the context of a group. But the fact that our
feeling on seeing each other is always, "I'm *so* glad she's
here" and the fact that we spend half the evening talking together says that this too, in its own way, counts as a friendship.

   (Other part-of-a-couple friends are the friends that came 24
with the marriage, and some of these are friends we could live

without. But sometimes, alas, she married our husband's best friend; and sometimes, alas, she *is* our husband's best friend. And so we find ourself dealing with her, somewhat against our will, in a spirit of what I'll call *reluctant* friendship.)

7. Men who are friends. I wanted to write just of women friends, but the women I've talked to won't let me—they say I must mention man-woman friendships too. For these friendships can be just as close and as dear as those that we form with women. Listen to Lucy's description of one such friendship:

"We've found we have things to talk about that are different from what he talks about with my husband and different from what I talk about with his wife. So sometimes we call on the phone or meet for lunch. There are similar intellectual interests—we always pass on to each other the books that we love—but there's also something tender and caring too."

In a couple of crises, Lucy says, "he offered himself, for talking and for helping. And when someone died in his family he wanted me there. The sexual, flirty part of our friendship is very small, but *some*—just enough to make it fun and different." She thinks—and I agree—that the sexual part, though small is always *some,* is always there when a man and a woman are friends.

It's only in the past few years that I've made friends with men, in the sense of a friendship that's *mine,* not just part of two couples. And achieving with them the ease and the trust I've found with women friends has value indeed. Under the dryer at home last week, putting on mascara and rouge, I comfortably sat and talked with a fellow named Peter. Peter, I finally decided, could handle the shock of me minus mascara under the dryer. Because we care for each other. Because we're friends.

8. There are medium friends, and pretty good friends, and very good friends indeed, and these friendships are defined by their level of intimacy. And what we'll reveal at each of these levels of intimacy is calibrated with care. We might tell a medium friend, for example, that yesterday we had a fight with our husband. And we might tell a pretty good friend that this fight with our husband made us so mad that we slept

on the couch. And we might tell a very good friend that the reason we got so mad in that fight that we slept on the couch had something to do with that girl who works in his office. But it's only to our very best friends that we're willing to tell all, to tell what's going on with that girl in his office.

The best of friends, I still believe, totally love and sup-   30 port and trust each other, and bare to each other the secrets of their souls, and run—no questions asked—to help each other, and tell harsh truths to each other when they must be told.

But we needn't agree about everything (only 12-year-old   31 girl friends agree about *everything*) to tolerate each other's point of view. To accept without judgment. To give and to take without ever keeping score. And to *be* there, as I am for them and as they are for me, to comfort our sorrows, to celebrate our joys.

BUILDING VOCABULARY

1. Find *antonyms* (words that mean the opposite of given words) for the following entries:

   a. harsh (par. 1)
   b. mutual (par. 8)
   c. crucial (par. 17)
   d. intimacy (par. 29)
   e. tolerate (par. 31)

2. The *derivation* of a word—how it originated and where it came from—can make you more aware of meanings. Your dictionary normally lists abbreviations (for instance, L. for Latin, Fr. for French) for word origins, and sometimes explains fully the way a word came into use. Look up the following words to determine their origins:

   a. psychology (par. 10)
   b. historical (par. 14)
   c. sibling (par. 16)
   d. Christmas (par. 18)
   e. sexual (par. 27)

UNDERSTANDING THE WRITER'S IDEAS

1. What is Viorst's definition of friendship in the first two paragraphs? Does she accept this definition? Why or why not?

2. Name and describe in your own words the types of friends that Viorst mentions in her essay.

3. In what way are "convenience friends" and "special interest friends" alike? How are "historical friends" and "crossroads friends" alike?

4. What does Viorst mean when she writes, "In our daughter role we tend to do more than our share of self-revelation; in our mother role we tend to receive what's revealed" (par. 22)?

5. How do part-of-a-couple friends who came with the marriage differ from primary part-of-a-couple friends?

6. Does Viorst think that men can be friends for women? Why or why not? What complicates such friendships?

7. For Viorst, who are the best friends?

UNDERSTANDING THE WRITER'S TECHNIQUES

1. Which paragraphs make up the introduction in this essay? How does Viorst organize these paragraphs? Where does she place her thesis sentence?

2. How does the thesis sentence reveal the principles of classification (the questions Viorst asks to produce the various categories) that the author employs in the essay?

3. Does Viorst seem to emphasize each of her categories equally? Is she effective in handling each category? Why or why not? Do you think that men belong in the article as a category? For what reasons?

4. Analyze the importance of illustration in this essay. From what sources does Viorst tend to draw her examples?

5. How do definition and comparison and contrast operate in the essay? Cite specific examples of these techniques.

6. The level of language in this essay tends to be informal at times, reflecting patterns that are as close to conversation as to formal writing. Identify some sentences that seem to resemble informal speech. Why does Viorst try to achieve a conversational style?

7. Which main group in the essay is further broken down into categories?

8. Analyze Viorst's conclusion. How many paragraphs are involved? What strategies does she use? How does she achieve balanced sentence structure (parallelism) in her last lines?

EXPLORING THE WRITER'S IDEAS

1. Do you accept all of Viorst's categories of friendship? Which categories seem the most meaningful to you?

2. Try to think of people you know who fit into the various categories established by Viorst. Can you think of people who might exist in more than one category? How do you explain this fact? What are the dangers in trying to stereotype people in terms of categories, roles, backgrounds, or functions?

3. Viorst maintains that you can define friends in terms of functions and needs (see paragraph 3 and paragraphs 29 to 31). Would you agree? Why or why not? What principle or principles do you use to classify friends? In fact, *do* you classify friends? For what reasons?

IDEAS FOR WRITING

Guided Writing

Using the classification method, write an essay on a specific group of individuals—for instance, *types of friends, types of enemies, types of students, types of teachers, types of politicians, types of dates*—and so forth.

1. Establish your subject in the first paragraph. Also indicate to the reader the principle(s) of classification that you plan to use. (For guidelines look again at the second sentence in paragraph 3 of Viorst's essay.)

2. Start the body of the essay with a single short sentence that introduces categories (see paragraph 4). In the body, use numbers and category headings ("Convenience friends"... "Special interest friends") to separate groups.

3. Try to achieve a balance in the presentation of information on each category. Define each type and provide appropriate examples.

4. If helpful, use comparison and contrast to indicate from time to time the similarities and differences among groups. Try to avoid too much overlapping of groups, since this is harmful to the classification process.

5. Employ the personal "I" and other conversational techniques to achieve an informal style.

6. Return to your principle(s) of classification and amplify this feature in your conclusion. If you want, make a value judgment, as Viorst does, about which type of person in your classification scheme is the most significant.

More Writing Projects

1. Write an essay classifying the varieties of love.

2. Classify varieties of show business comedians, singers, talk show hosts, star athletes, or the like.

3. Compare and contrast the views of friendships expressed in Viorst's essay and Ellen Goodman's "The Tapestry of Friendships" (pages 213–215).

The Three New Yorks

E. B. White

E. B. White, whose frequently used book *The Elements of Style* is well known to college composition students, here classifies "The Three New Yorks." Although the selection is an excerpt from his book *Here is New York* (1949), the descriptive illustrations remain remarkably fresh after more than thirty years. Look closely at the way White clearly defines his categories of classification, then skillfully blends them to create a vivid sense of the whole city.

Words to Watch

turbulence (par. 1)   wild commotion

locusts (par. 1)   migratory grasshoppers that travel in swarms, stripping vegetation as they pass over the land

quest (par. 1)   pursuit; search

disposition (par. 1)   temperament; way of acting

deportment (par. 1)   the way in which a person carries himself or herself

tidal (par. 1)   coming in wave-like motions

continuity (par. 1)   uninterrupted flow of events

slum (par. 1)   a highly congested residential area marked by insanitary buildings, poverty, and social disorder

indignity (par. 1)   humiliating treatment

vitality (par. 2)   lively and animated character

gloaming (par. 2)   a poetic term for *twilight*

ramparts (par. 2)   high broad structures guarding a building

negligently (par. 2)   nonchalantly; neglectfully

loiterer (par. 2)   a person who hangs around aimlessly

spewing (par. 2)   coming in a flood or gush

rover (par. 2)   wanderer; roamer

There are roughly three New Yorks. There is, first, the 1
New York of the man or woman who was born here, who takes the city for granted and accepts its size and its turbu-

lence as natural and inevitable. Second, there is the New York of the commuter—the city that is devoured by locusts each day and spat out each night. Third, there is the New York of the person who was born somewhere else and came to New York in quest of something. Of these three trembling cities the greatest is the last—the city of final destination, the city that is a goal. It is this third city that accounts for New York's high-strung disposition, its poetical deportment, its dedication to the arts, and its incomparable achievements. Commuters give the city its tidal restlessness; natives give it solidity and continuity; but the settlers give it passion. And whether it is a farmer arriving from Italy to set up a small grocery store in a slum, or a young girl arriving from a small town in Mississippi to escape the indignity of being observed by her neighbors, or a boy arriving from the Corn Belt with a manuscript in his suitcase and a pain in his heart, it makes no difference; each embraces New York with the intense excitement of first love, each absorbs New York with the fresh eyes of an adventurer, each generates heat and light to dwarf the Consolidated Edison Company.

The commuter is the queerest bird of all. The suburb he inhabits has no essential vitality of its own and is a mere roost where he comes at day's end to go to sleep. Except in rare cases, the man who lives in Mamaroneck or Little Neck or Teaneck, and works in New York, discovers nothing much about the city except the time of arrival and departure of trains and buses, and the path to a quick lunch. He is deskbound, and has never, idly roaming in the gloaming, stumbled suddenly on Belvedere Tower in the Park, seen the ramparts rise sheer from the water of the pond, and the boys along the shore fishing for minnows, girls stretched out negligently on the shelves of the rocks; he has never come suddenly on anything at all in New York as a loiterer, because he has had no time between trains. He has fished in Manhattan's wallet and dug out coins, but has never listened to Manhattan's breathing, never awakened to its morning, never dropped off to sleep in its night. About 400,000 men and women come charging onto the Island each week-day morning, out of the mouths of tubes and tunnels. Not many among them have ever spent a drowsy afternoon in the great rustling oaken silence of the reading room of the Public Library, with the book elevator (like an old water wheel) spewing out books onto the trays. They tend their furnaces in Westchester and in Jersey, but have never seen the furnaces of the Bowery, the fires that burn in oil drums on zero winter nights. They may work in the financial district downtown and never see the extravagant plantings of Rockefeller Center—the daffodils and grape hyacinths and birches of the flags trimmed to the wind on a fine morning in spring. Or they may work in a midtown office and may let a whole year swing round without sighting Governor's Island from the sea wall. The commuter dies with tremendous mileage to his credit, but he is no rover. His entrances and exits are more devious than those in a prairie-dog village; and he calmly plays bridge while his train is buried in the mud at the bottom of the East River. The Long Island Rail Road alone carried forty million commuters last year; but many of them were the same fellow retracing his steps.

The terrain of New York is such that a resident some-   3
times travels farther, in the end, than a commuter. The journey of the composer Irving Berlin from Cherry Street in the lower East Side to an apartment uptown was through an alley and was only three or four miles in length; but it was like going three times around the world.

BUILDING VOCABULARY

1. One very important aspect of vocabulary development is an ability to understand specific place or name references in whatever you are reading. Underline the numerous references in this essay to buildings, people, and areas in and around New York City and be prepared to identify them. If necessary, consult a guidebook, map, or history of New York City for help.

2. White divides the inhabitants of New York into three categories: commuters, natives, settlers. Write a literal defini-

tion for the word that labels each category; then write at
least one figurative meaning for each (see Glossary).

3. Write a *synonym* (a word that means the same) for each of
these adjectives in the essay:

    a. inevitable (par. 1)
    b. high-strung (par. 1)
    c. essential (par. 2)
    d. drowsy (par. 2)
    e. devious (par. 2)

UNDERSTANDING THE WRITER'S IDEAS

1. What are the three New Yorks?

2. What single-word designation does E. B. White assign to
each of the three types of New Yorkers? Match up each of
the three New Yorks you identified in the first question
with each of the three types of New Yorkers.

3. For what reasons do people born elsewhere come to New
York to live? What three illustrations of such people does
White describe? What is the young girl's indignity? What is
the occupation or hope of the boy from the Corn Belt? Why
might he have "a pain in his heart"?

4. What does each type of New Yorker give to the city?

5. What is White's attitude toward the suburbs? What key
phrases reveal this attitude?

6. What are some of the things commuters miss about New
York by dashing in and out of the city? What does White
ironically suggest will be the commuter's final fate?

7. Are we to take literally White's conclusion that "many of
them are the same fellow retracing his steps"? Why or why
not?

8. Explain the sentence "The terrain of New York is such

that a resident sometimes travels farther, in the end, than a commuter." Be aware that White is using language figuratively.

9. The author tells of composer Irving Berlin's journey through an alley. He is referring to "Tin Pan Alley." Identify this place.

UNDERSTANDING THE WRITER'S TECHNIQUES

1. In this essay what is the thesis? Where is it? Is it developed fully?

2. What is the purpose of classification in this essay? What is the basis of the classification White uses? What key words at the beginning of paragraph 1 direct your attention to each category discussed? How do these key words contrast in tone with the descriptions in the first few sentences? What sort of rhythm is established?

3. White vividly *personifies* (see Glossary) New York City in paragraph 1. List and explain the effects of these personifications. Where else does he personify?

4. Refer to your answer to question 2 in the Building Vocabulary section. Are the literal meanings of those words appropriate to White's three types of New Yorkers? Defend your answer. Figuratively, what does each term make you think of? How do the figurative meanings enhance the essay?

5. How does White use *illustration* in this essay? Where does he use it most effectively?

6. What is the function of *negation* (see page 205) in the first part of paragraph 2? What is the *implied contrast* in this paragraph?

7. How is White's attitude toward New York reflected in the tone of this essay?

8. White makes widespread use of *metaphor* (see Glossary) in this essay. How does his use of metaphor affect the *tone* of the essay? State in your own words the meaning of each of the following metaphors:

   a. ...the city that is devoured by locusts each day and spat out each night. (par. 1)
   b. The commuter is the queerest bird of all. (par. 2)
   c. a mere roost (par. 2)
   d. idly roaming in the gloaming (par. 2)
   e. He has fished in Manhattan's wallet and dug out coins, but he has never listened to Manhattan's breathing. (par. 2)
   f. the great rustling oaken silence (par. 2)

9. Among all the metaphors, White uses just one *simile* (see Glossary). What is it? What is the effect of placing it where he did?

EXPLORING THE WRITER'S IDEAS

1. At the beginning of the essay, E. B. White states that New York's "turbulence" is considered "natural and inevitable" by its native residents. But such a condition is true for any large city. If you live in a large city, or if you have ever visited one, what are some examples of its turbulence? Do you think it is always a good idea to accept the disorder of the place where you live? How can such acceptance be a positive attitude? How can it be negative? How do you deal with disruptions in your environment?

2. White writes of "a young girl arriving from a small town in Mississippi to escape the indignity of being observed by her neighbors." Tell in your own words what might cause her indignity. How can neighbors bring about such a condition?

3. Some people feel the anonymity of a big city like New York makes it easier just to "be yourself" without having to worry about what others might say. Others feel such an-

onymity creates a terrible feeling of impersonality. Discuss the advantages and disadvantages of each attitude.

4. Do you agree that the suburbs have "no essential vitality"? Explain your response by referring to suburbs you have visited, have read about, or have inhabited.

5. White claims that those who choose to leave their homes and who come to live in New York give the place a special vitality. Do you know any people who chose to leave their places of birth to live in a large city like New York? Why did they move? How have things gone for them since they began living in the city? Have you noticed any changes? For what reasons do people leave one place to live in another? When have you moved from place to place? Why?

IDEAS FOR WRITING

Guided Writing

Organize a classification essay around the city or town in which you live.

1. Begin with a simple direct thesis statement that tells the reader how many categories of classification you will consider.

2. Briefly outline the different categories. Indicate each with a key organizational word or phrase.

3. Indicate which category is the most important. Tell why.

4. Develop this category with at least three vivid illustrations.

5. Define one of the categories through both negation and an implied contrast to another category.

6. Use figurative language (metaphors, similes, personification) throughout your essay.

7. Use specific name or place references.

8. End your essay with a brief factual narrative that gives the reader a feel for your town or city.

More Writing Projects

1. Write an essay that classifies three main categories of jobs and the people who work at each.

2. Write a classification essay on the suburbs, or the country.

3. Select a cultural group and classify various characteristics common to that group. Be careful to avoid stereotyping.

How Do We Find the Student in a World of Academic Gymnasts and Worker Ants?

James T. Baker

As you look around your classrooms, school cafeteria, lecture halls, or gymnasium, perhaps you will recognize representatives of the types of students that James Baker classifies in this witty, wry essay. The author's unique categories are enhanced by his use of description, definition, and colloquial language, which help make his deliberate stereotypes "come alive."

Words to Watch

musings (par. 3)   dreamy, abstract thoughts

sabbatical (par. 3)   a paid leave from a job earned after a certain period of time

malaise (par. 3)   uneasiness; feelings of restlessness

impaired (par. 3)   made less effective

clones (par. 4)   exact biological replicas, asexually produced

recuperate (par. 5)   to undergo recovery from an illness

esoteric (par. 7)   understood by a limited group with special knowledge

primeval (par. 7)   primitive; relating to the earliest ages

mundane (par. 8)   ordinary

jaded (par. 20)   exhausted; bored by something from overexposure to it

Anatole France once wrote that "the whole art of teaching 1 is only the art of awakening the natural curiosity of young minds." I fully agree, except I have to wonder if, by using the word "only," he thought that the art of awakening such natural curiosity was an easy job. For me, it never has been—sometimes exciting, always challenging, but definitely not easy.

Robert M. Hutchins used to say that a good education 2 prepares students to go on educating themselves throughout their lives. A fine definition, to be sure, but it has at times made me doubt that my own students, who seem only too eager to graduate so they can lay down their books forever, are receiving a good education.

But then maybe these are merely the pessimistic musings 3 of someone suffering from battle fatigue. I have almost qualified for my second sabbatical leave, and I am scratching a severe case of the seven-year itch. About the only power my malaise has not impaired is my eye for spotting certain "types" of students. In fact, as the rest of me declines, my eye seems to grow more acute.

Has anyone else noticed that the very same students peo- 4 ple college classrooms year after year? Has anyone else found the same bodies, faces, personalities returning semester after semester? Forgive me for violating my students' individual "personhoods," but reality makes it so tempting to see them as types. Doubtless you will recognize at least some of them. They have twins, or perhaps clones, on your campus, too.

There is the eternal Good Time Charlie (or Charlene), 5 who makes every party on and off the campus, who by November of his freshman year has worked his face into a case of terminal acne, who misses every set of examinations because of "mono," who finally burns himself out physically and mentally by the age of 19 and drops out to go home and recuperate, and who returns at 20 after a long talk with Dad to major in accounting.

There is the Young General Patton, the one who comes 6 to college on an R.O.T.C. scholarship and for a year twirls his rifle at basketball games while loudly sniffing out pinko professors, who at midpoint takes a sudden but predictable, radical swing from far right to far left, who grows a beard and moves in with a girl who refuses to shave her legs, who then makes the just as predictable, radical swing back to the right and ends up preaching fundamentalist sermons on the steps of the student union while the Good Time Charlies and Charlenes jeer.

There is the Egghead, the campus intellectual who 7 shakes up his fellow students—and even a professor or two—with references to esoteric formulas and obscure Bulgarian poets, who is recognized by friend and foe alike as a promising young academic, someday to be a professional scholar, who disappears every summer for six weeks ostensibly to search for primeval human remains in Colorado caves, and who at 37 is shot dead by Arab terrorists while on a mission for the C.I.A.

There is the Performer—the music or theater major, the rock or folk singer—who spends all of his or her time working up an act, who gives barely a nod to mundane subjects like history, sociology, or physics, who dreams only of the day he or she will be on stage full time, praised by critics, cheered by audiences, who ends up either pregnant or responsible for a pregnancy and at 30 is either an insurance salesman or a housewife with a very lush garden. **8**

There is the Jock, of course—the every-afternoon intramural champ, smelling of liniment and Brut, with bulging calves and a blue-eyed twinkle, the subject of untold numbers of female fantasies, the walking personification of he-man-ism—who upon graduation is granted managerial rank by a California bank because of his golden tan and low golf score, who is seen five years later buying the drinks at a San Francisco gay bar. **9**

There is the Academic Gymnast—the guy or gal who sees college as an obstacle course, as so many stumbling blocks in the way of a great career or a perfect marriage—who strains every moment to finish and be done with "this place" forever, who toward the end of the junior year begins to slow down, to grow quieter and less eager to leave, who attends summer school, but never quite finishes those last six hours, who never leaves "this place," and who at 40 is still working at the campus laundry, still here, still a student. **10**

There is the Medal Hound, the student who comes to college not to learn or expand any intellectual horizons but simply to win honors—medals, cups, plates, ribbons, scrolls—who is here because this is the best place to win the most the fastest, who plasticizes and mounts on his wall every certificate of excellence he wins, who at 39 will be a colonel in the U.S. Army and at 55 Secretary of something or other in a conservative Administration in Washington. **11**

There is the Worker Ant, the student (loosely rendered) **12** who takes 21 hours a semester and works 49 hours a week at the local car wash, who sleeps only on Sundays and during classes, who will somehow graduate on time and be the owner of his own vending-machine company at 30 and be dead of a heart attack at 40, and who will be remembered for the words chiseled on his tombstone:

All This Was Accomplished Without Ever Having So Much as Darkened The Door Of A Library   13

There is the Lost Soul, the sad kid who is in college only because teachers, parents, and society at large said so, who hasn't a career in mind or a dream to follow, who hasn't a clue, who heads home every Friday afternoon to spend the weekend cruising the local Dairee-Freeze, who at 50 will have done all his teachers, parents, and society said to do, still without a career in mind or a dream to follow or a clue.   14

There is also the Saved Soul—the young woman who has received, through the ministry of one Gospel freak or another, a Holy Calling to save the world, or at least some special part of it—who majors in Russian studies so that she can be caught smuggling Bibles into the Soviet Union and be sent to Siberia where she can preach to souls imprisoned by the Agents of Satan in the Gulag Archipelago.   15

Then, finally, there is the Happy Child, who comes to college to find a husband or wife—and finds one—and there is the Determined Child, who comes to get a degree—and gets one.   16

Enough said.   17

All of which, I suppose, should make me throw up my hands in despair and say that education, like youth and love, is wasted on the young. Not quite.   18

For there does come along, on occasion, that one of a hundred or so who is maybe at first a bit lost, certainly puzzled; who may well start out a Good Timer, an Egghead, a Performer, a Jock, a Medal Hound, a Gymnast, a Worker Ant; who may indeed have trouble settling on a major, who will be distressed by what sometimes passes for education, who might even be a temporary dropout; but who has a vital capacity for growth and is able to fall in love with learning, who acquires a taste for intellectual pleasure, who becomes in the finest sense of the word a Student.   19

This is the one who keeps the most jaded of us going [20] back to class after class, and he or she must be oh-so-carefully cultivated. He or she must be artfully awakened, given the tools needed to continue learning for a lifetime, and let grow at whatever pace and in whatever direction nature dictates.

For I try always to remember that this student is me, my [21] continuing self, my immortality. This person is my only hope that my own search for Truth will continue after me, on and on, forever.

BUILDING VOCABULARY

1. Explain these *colloquialisms* (see Glossary) in Baker's essay:

   a. lay down their books forever (par. 2)
   b. I am scratching a severe case of the seven-year itch (par. 3)
   c. some are suffering from battle fatigue (par. 3)
   d. worked his face into a case of terminal acne (par. 5)
   e. burns himself out physically and mentally (par. 5)
   f. loudly sniffing out pinko professors (par. 6)
   g. working up an act (par. 8)
   h. gives barely a nod (par. 8)
   i. the walking personification of he-man-ism (par. 9)
   j. to spend the weekend cruising the local Dairee-Freeze (par. 14)
   k. he or she must be oh-so-carefully cultivated (par. 20)

2. Identify these references:

   a. R.O.T.C. (par. 6)
   b. C.I.A. (par. 7)
   c. Brut (par. 9)
   d. Dairee-Freeze (par. 14)
   e. Gospel freak (par. 15)
   f. Agents of Satan (par. 15)
   g. Gulag Archipelago (par. 15)

UNDERSTANDING THE WRITER'S IDEAS

1. In common language, describe the various categories of college students that Baker names.

2. Who is Anatole France? What process is described in the quotation from him? Why does Baker cite it at the beginning of the essay? What is his attitude towards France's idea?

3. For how long has Baker been teaching? What is his attitude towards his work?

4. About what age do you think Baker is? Why? Explain the meaning of the sentence: "In fact, as the rest of me declines, my eye seems to grow more acute" (par. 3).

5. Choose three of Baker's categories and paraphrase each description and meaning in a serious way.

6. What does Baker feel, overall, is the contemporary college student's attitude towards studying and receiving an education? How does it differ from Baker's own attitude towards these things?

7. Although Baker's classification may seem a bit pessimistic, he refuses to "throw up...[his] hands in despair" (par. 18). Why?

8. Describe the characteristics that are embodied in the category of *Student*. To whom does Baker compare the "true" Student? Why?

UNDERSTANDING THE WRITER'S TECHNIQUES

1. In this essay Baker deliberately creates, rather than avoids, stereotypes (see Introduction to Chapter 8, page 276). He does so to establish exaggerated representatives of types. Why?

For paragraphs 5–16, prepare a paragraph-by-paragraph outline of the main groups of students classified. For each, include the following information:

    a. type represented by the stereotype
    b. motivation of type for being a student
    c. main activity as a student
    d. condition in which the type ends up

2. What is Baker's thesis in this essay? Does he state it directly or not? What, in your own words, is his purpose?

3. This article was published in "The Chronicle of Higher Education," a weekly newspaper for college and university educators and administrators. How do you think this audience influenced Baker's analysis of types of students? His tone and language?

4. What is Baker's tone in the essay? Give specific examples. In general, how would you characterize his attitude toward the contemporary college student? Why? Does his attitude or tone undergo any shifts in the essay? Explain.

5. Why does Baker use the term "personhoods" in paragraph 4? What attitude, about what subject, does he convey in his use of that word?

6. Why does the author capitalize the names he gives to the various categories of students? Why does he capitalize the word *Truth* in the last sentence?

7. How does Baker use *definition* in this essay? What purpose does it serve?

8. How does Baker use *description* to enhance his analysis in this essay?

9. In this essay, what is the role of *process analysis?* (*Process analysis,* discussed in the next chapter, is telling how something is done or proceeds; see pages 316–317.) Look especially at Baker's descriptions of each type of student. How does process analysis figure into the title of the essay?

10. What is the purpose of the one-sentence paragraph 13? Why does Baker set it aside from paragraph 12, since it is a logical conclusion to that paragraph? Why does he use a two-word sentence as the complete paragraph 17? In what ways do these words signal the beginning of the essay's conclusion?

EXPLORING THE WRITER'S IDEAS

1. Do you think Baker's classifications in this essay are fair? Are they representative of the whole spectrum of students? How closely do they mirror the student population at your school? The article was written in 1982; how well have Baker's classifications held up to the present conditions?

2. Into which category (or categories) would you place yourself? Why?

3. Based on your reaction to and understanding of this article, would you like to have Baker as your professor? Why or why not?

IDEAS FOR WRITING

Guided Writing

Write a classification of at least three "types" in a situation with which you are familiar, other than school—a certain job, social event, sport, or some such situation.

1. Begin your essay with a reference, direct or indirect, to what some well-known writer or expert said about this situation.

2. Identify your role in relation to the situation described.

3. Write about your attitude towards the particular situation and why you are less than thrilled about it at present.

4. Make sure you involve the reader as someone who would be familiar with the situation and activities described.

5. Divide your essay into exaggerated or stereotyped categories which you feel represent almost the complete range of types in these situations. In your categorization, be sure to include motivations, activities, and results for each type.

6. Use description to make your categories vivid.

7. Use satire and a bit of gentle cynicism as part of your description.

8. Select a lively title.

9. In the conclusion, identify another type that you consider the "purest" or "most truthful" representative of persons in this situation. Either by comparison with yourself, or by some other means, explain why you like this type best.

More Writing Projects

1. Write your own classification of three college "types." Your essay can be serious or humorous.

2. Look in current magazines for advertisements directed at men or women, or both. Write an essay in which you classify current advertisements according to some logical scheme. Limit your essay to three to five categories.

What to Listen For in Music

Aaron Copland

Aaron Copland, born at the turn of the century, is among America's most renowned composers and commentators on music. His musical compositions include symphonies, chamber music, film scores, and perhaps best known, his scores for the ballets *Rodeo, Billy the Kid,* and *Appalachian Spring.* In this essay, he classifies three "planes" of the process of listening to music, and he develops his concept of each one through a skillful blending of description, comparison, illustration, and direct appeals to the reader. Ultimately, it is Copland's wish that the reader become more actively involved in the listening process.

Words to Watch

engendered (par. 2)   caused to exist

belittle (par. 3)   ridicule

consolation (par. 4)   comfort; relief

apropos (par. 4)   pertinent to

disproportionate (par. 5)   unbalanced

constitute (par. 5)   to make up or contribute to something

commensurate (par. 6)   proportionate; corresponding

fury (par. 10)   rage; anger

pessimistically (par. 12)   without hope

inherent (par. 14)   involved in the essential character of something

engrossed (par. 17)   mentally absorbed in something

layman (par. 17)   nonprofessional; amateur

correlate (par. 20)   relate to; correspond to

We all listen to music according to our separate capacities. But, for the sake of analysis, the whole listening process may become clearer if we break it up into its component parts, so to speak. In a certain sense we all listen to music on three separate planes. For lack of a better terminology, one might name these: (1) the sensuous plane, (2) the expressive plane,

303

(3) the sheerly musical plane. The only advantage to be gained from mechanically splitting up the listening process into these hypothetical planes is the clearer view to be had of the way in which we listen.

The simplest way of listening to music is to listen for the   2 sheer pleasure of the musical sound itself. That is the sensuous plane. It is the plane on which we hear music without thinking, without considering it in any way. One turns on the radio while doing something else and absentmindedly bathes in the sound. A kind of brainless but attractive state of mind is engendered by the mere sound appeal of the music.

You may be sitting in a room reading this book. Imagine   3 one note struck on the piano. Immediately that one note is enough to change the atmosphere of the room—proving that the sound element in music is a powerful and mysterious agent, which it would be foolish to deride or belittle.

The surprising thing is that many people who consider   4 themselves qualified music lovers abuse that plane in listening. They go to concerts in order to lose themselves. They use music as a consolation or an escape. They enter an ideal world where one doesn't have to think of the realities of everyday life. Of course they aren't thinking about the music either. Music allows them to leave it, and they go off to a place to dream, dreaming because of and apropos of the music yet never quite listening to it.

Yes, the sound appeal of music is a potent and primitive   5 force, but you must not allow it to usurp a disproportionate share of your interest. The sensuous plane is an important one in music, a very important one, but it does not constitute the whole story.

There is no need to digress further on the sensuous   6 plane. Its appeal to every normal human being is self-evident. There is, however, such a thing as becoming more sensitive to the different kinds of sound stuff as used by various composers. For all composers do not use that sound stuff in the same way. Don't get the idea that the value of music is commensurate with its sensuous appeal or that the loveliest sounding music is made by the greatest composer. If that were so,

Ravel would be a greater creator than Beethoven. The point is that the sound element varies with each composer, that his usage of sound forms an integral part of his style and must be taken into account when listening. The reader can see, therefore, that a more conscious approach is valuable even on this primary plane of music listening.

The second plane on which music exists is what I have 7 called the expressive one. Here, immediately, we tread on controversial ground. Composers have a way of shying away from any discussion of music's expressive side. Did not Stravinsky himself proclaim that his music was an "object," a "thing," with a life of its own, and with no other meaning than its own purely musical existence? This intransigent attitude of Stravinsky's may be due to the fact that so many people have tried to read different meanings into so many pieces. Heaven knows it is difficult enough to say precisely what it is that a piece of music means, to say it definitely, to say it finally so that everyone is satisfied with your explanation. But that should not lead one to the other extreme of denying to music the right to be "expressive."

My own belief is that all music has an expressive power, 8 some more and some less, but that all music has a certain meaning behind the notes and that that meaning behind the note constitutes, after all, what the piece is saying, what the piece is about. This whole problem can be stated quite simply by asking, "Is there a meaning to music?" My answer to that would be "Yes." And "Can you state in so many words what the meaning is?" My answer to that would be, "No." Therein lies the difficulty.

Simple-minded souls will never be satisfied with the an- 9 swer to the second of these questions. They always want music to have a meaning, and the more concrete it is the better they like it. The more the music reminds them of a train, a storm, a funeral, or any other familiar conception the more expressive it appears to be to them. This popular idea of music's meaning—stimulated and abetted by the usual run of musical commentator—should be discouraged wherever and whenever it is met. One timid lady once confessed to me that she suspected something seriously lacking in her appreciation of music because of her inability to connect it with anything definite. That is getting the whole thing backward, of course.

Still, the question remains, How close should the intelligent music lover wish to come to pinning a definite meaning to any particular work? No closer than a general concept, I should say. Music expresses, at different moments, serenity or exuberance, regret or triumph, fury or delight. It expresses each of these moods, and many others, in a numberless variety of subtle shadings and differences. It may even express a state of meaning for which there exists no adequate word in any language. In that case, musicians often like to say that it has only a purely musical meaning. They sometimes go farther and say that *all* music has only a purely musical meaning. What they really mean is that no appropriate word can be found to express the music's meaning and that, even if it could, they do not feel the need of finding it. 10

But whatever the professional musician may hold, most musical novices still search for specific words with which to pin down their musical reactions. That is why they always find Tchaikovsky easier to "understand" than Beethoven. In the first place, it is easier to pin a meaning-word on a Tchaikovsky piece than on a Beethoven one. Much easier. Moreover, with the Russian composer, every time you come back to a piece of his it almost always says the same thing to you, whereas with Beethoven it is often quite difficult to put your finger right on what he is saying. And any musician will tell you that that is why Beethoven is the greater composer. Because music which always says the same thing to you will necessarily soon become dull music, but music whose meaning is slightly different with each hearing has a greater chance of remaining alive. 11

Listen, if you can, to the forty-eight fugue themes of Bach's *Well Tempered Clavichord*. Listen to each theme, one after another. You will soon realize that each theme mirrors a different world of feeling. You will also soon realize that the more beautiful a theme seems to you the harder it is to find any word that will describe it to your complete satisfaction. Yes, you will certainly know whether it is a gay theme or a sad one. You will be able, in other words, in your own mind, to 12 draw a frame of emotional feeling around your theme. Now study the sad one a little closer. Try to pin down the exact quality of its sadness. Is it pessimistically sad or resignedly sad; is it fatefully sad or smilingly sad?

Let us suppose that you are fortunate and can describe 13 to your own satisfaction in so many words the exact meaning of your chosen theme. There is still no guarantee that anyone else will be satisfied. Nor need they be. The important thing is that each one feel for himself the specific expressive quality of a theme or, similarly, an entire piece of music. And if it is a great work of art, don't expect it to mean exactly the same thing to you each time you return to it.

Themes or pieces need not express only one emotion, of 14 course. Take such a theme as the first main one of the *Ninth Symphony,* for example. It is clearly made up of different elements. It does not say only one thing. Yet anyone hearing it immediately gets a feeling of strength, a feeling of power. It isn't a power that comes simply because the theme is played loudly. It is a power inherent in the theme itself. The extraordinary strength and vigor of the theme results in the listener's receiving an impression that a forceful statement has been made. But one should never try to boil it down to "the fateful hammer of life," etc. That is where the trouble begins. The musician, in his exasperation, says it means nothing but the notes themselves, whereas the nonprofessional is only too anxious to hang on to any explanation that gives him the illusion of getting closer to the music's meaning.

Now, perhaps, the reader will know better what I mean 15 when I say that music does have an expressive meaning but that we cannot say in so many words what that meaning is.

The third plane on which music exists is the sheerly mu- 16 sical plane. Besides the pleasurable sound of music and the expressive feeling that it gives off, music does exist in terms of the notes themselves and of their manipulation. Most listeners are not sufficiently conscious of this third plane....

Professional musicians, on the other hand, are, if any- 17 thing, too conscious of the mere notes themselves. They often fall into the error of becoming so engrossed with their arpeggios and staccatos that they forget the deeper aspects of the music they are performing. But from the layman's standpoint, it is not so much a matter of getting over bad habits on the sheerly musical plane as of increasing one's awareness of what is going on, in so far as the notes are concerned.

When the man in the street listens to the ''notes them- 18 selves'' with any degree of concentration, he is most likely to make some mention of the melody. Either he hears a pretty melody or he does not, and he generally lets it go at that. Rhythm is likely to gain his attention next, particularly if it seems exciting. But harmony and tone color are generally taken for granted, if they are thought of consciously at all. As for music's having a definite form of some kind, that idea seems never to have occurred to him.

It is very important for all of us to become more alive to 19 music on its sheerly musical plane. After all, an actual musical material is being used. The intelligent listener must be prepared to increase his awareness of the musical material and what happens to it. He must hear the melodies, the rhythms, the harmonies, the tone colors in a more conscious fashion. But above all he must, in order to follow the line of the composer's thought, know something of the principles of musical form. Listening to all of these elements is listening on the sheerly musical plane.

Let me repeat that I have split up mechanically the three 20 separate planes on which we listen merely for the sake of greater clarity. Actually, we never listen on one or the other of these planes. What we do is to correlate them—listening in all three ways at the same time. It takes no mental effort, for we do it instinctively.

Perhaps an analogy with what happens to us when we 21 visit the theater will make this instinctive correlation clearer. In the theater, you are aware of the actors and actresses, costumes and sets, sounds and movements. All these give one the sense that the theater is a pleasant place to be in. They constitute the sensuous plane in our theatrical reactions.

The expressive plane in the theater would be derived 22 from the feeling that you get from what is happening on the stage. You are moved to pity, excitement, or gayety. It is this general feeling, generated aside from the particular words being spoken, a certain emotional something which exists on the stage, that is analogous to the expressive quality in music.

The plot and plot development is equivalent to our 23 sheerly musical plane. The playwright creates and develops a character in just the same way that a composer creates and develops a theme. According to the degree of your awareness of the way in which the artist in either field handles his material will you become a more intelligent listener.

It is easy enough to see that the theatergoer never is con- 24 scious of any of these elements separately. He is aware of them all at the same time. The same is true of music listening. We simultaneously and without thinking listen on all three planes.

In a sense, the ideal listener is both inside and outside 25 the music at the same moment, judging it and enjoying it, wishing it would go one way and watching it go another—almost like the composer at the moment he composes it; because in order to write his music, the composer must also be inside and outside his music, carried away by it and yet coldly critical of it. A subjective and objective attitude is implied in both creating and listening to music.

What the reader should strive for, then, is a more *active* 26 kind of listening. Whether you listen to Mozart or Duke Ellington, you can deepen your understanding of music only by being a more conscious and aware listener—not someone who is just listening, but someone who is listening *for* something.

BUILDING VOCABULARY

1. Identify the following composers mentioned in this essay:

Ravel
Beethoven
Stravinsky
Tchaikovsky
Bach
Duke Ellington

2. Match the words in Column A with their *synonyms* in Column B.

Column A	Column B
1 hypothetical	a irritation
2 deride	b essential
3 potent	c strength
4 usurp	d ridicule
5 integral	e strong
6 intransigent	f idea
7 conception	g calm
8 abetted	h assisted
9 serenity	i artful
10 exuberance	j uncompromising
11 subtle	k conjectural
12 novices	l seize
13 exasperation	m enthusiasm
14 vigor	n beginners

3. Use any five of the words in Column A in original sentences.

UNDERSTANDING THE WRITER'S IDEAS

1. According to Copland, what are the three separate "planes" of the process of listening to music? Does Copland feel that these classifications correspond to real divisions? How do you know? What is his purpose in describing and explaining these planes? Which is most important? Least important?

2. Outline in some detail the elements of each plane of listening.

3. Does the author believe that we all listen to music in the same way? Explain your answer.

4. What is Copland's opinion of those who listen to music primarily on the sensuous plane? How does he involve the reader in his discussion of that plane? What are the main uses of the sensuous plane?

5. What is "sound stuff" (par. 6)?

6. What is Copland's opinion of the composer Igor Stravinsky? How do you know?

7. According to the author, what is the difficulty in trying to assign a meaning to music? To which plane does the attempt to assign meaning belong? What does he call those listeners who insist on trying to assign concrete meaning to a piece of music?

8. Copland states that musical novices "always find Tchaikovsky easier to 'understand' than Beethoven" but that "any musician will tell you that...Beethoven is the greater composer." Why?

9. How would you summarize Copland's attitude toward the majority of music listeners? Support your opinion with examples from the essay. Compare Copland's assessment of the layperson and the professional musician in the purely musical plane.

10. What, in the author's opinion, are the characteristics of "the ideal listener?" What is the ideal condition for a composer at the moment of composition?

11. Summarize the main purpose of this essay.

UNDERSTANDING THE WRITER'S TECHNIQUES

1. How would you characterize Copland's *tone* and *style* (see Glossary)? Give at least five examples from the essay to support your answer.

2. *Jargon* is the use of special, technical words associated with a specific activity or profession (see Glossary). Does Copland use much jargon in this essay? Why? What does that say about his intended *audience?*

3. Which paragraphs does the author devote to each of the three planes? Which paragraphs serve as transitions? How does he order his transition paragraphs? Compare

the use of the word "yes" at the beginning of paragraph 5 and "now" at the beginning of paragraph 15 as transition devices.

4. What *extended analogy* (see Glossary) forms the basis of paragraphs 21–24? What is the purpose of this analogy? Do you find it useful in understanding Copland's discussion of how to listen to music? Why?

5. Evaluate the following sentence both as a transitional device and as a means to involve the reader more directly in the discussion: "The reader can see, therefore, that a more conscious approach is valuable even on this primary plane of music listening" (par. 6).

6. In paragraph 8, why does Copland use a series of questions in quotation marks? To whom are those questions addressed?

7. Where does the author use the techniques of *comparison and contrast?* For what purposes?

8. Note uses of *description* and *illustration* in this essay.

9. How does Copland use *summation* in paragraph 16?

10. Why does Copland use the word "must" three times in paragraph 19? What is the topic sentence of that paragraph? How does the repetition help formulate the topic sentence?

11. What purpose is made clear in the final paragraph? Compare the purpose stated there with the purpose stated in the opening paragraph. How are they related?

12. Repetition, return to thesis, and summary of major points are all techniques used in writing conclusions. Where does Copland use each in the conclusion to this essay?

EXPLORING THE WRITER'S IDEAS

1. In his opening sentence, Copland states: "We all listen to

music according to our separate capacities." Do you agree? Why?

2. Toward the end of this essay, Copland writes an extended analogy relating the experience of listening to music to that of seeing a play in the theater; he says he does this in order to "make this instinctive correlation clearer." Why do you suppose he feels it is easier for most readers to understand the theater experience than it is for them to understand the musical experience? Do you personally find this to be true? Why? In what ways?

3. In paragraph 25, the author states that "in order to write his music, the composer must also be inside and outside his music, carried away by it yet coldly critical of it." This sounds like a very difficult creative process. What is Copland's meaning? What other creative processes are similar? What experiences have you had to which similar descriptions could apply?

4. What is your favorite type of music? What is it that you enjoy most about this music? Do you think your enjoyment fits into any of Copland's "hypothetical planes?" Explain.

5. Copland uses a fairly tightly constructed framework on which to develop his discussion of the subject of music appreciation in general. Yet, he seems to focus almost entirely on classical music. Do you feel that his discussion can apply just as well to other musical forms—rock, jazz, rap, blues, soul, heavy metal, pop, folk? Why or why not?

6. Between the widespread use of Walkmans and portable "boxes," it seems as though people listen to music all the time. What do you feel are the positive and negative sides to this trend?

7. Copland delineates three planes in order to classify his ideas concerning music appreciation, but readily admits that they are artificial creations and that the most important thing to strive for is a "more *active* kind of listening."

Some critics of music videos claim that they encourage *passive* responses to music. That is, instead of listeners

feeling their own sensations or creating their own images to
accompany what they listen to, these images and sensations have become fixed and externalized according to
what the video shows. What is your opinion of music videos? Of this criticism of them?

IDEAS FOR WRITING

Guided Writing

Write a classification essay that deals with what to look for in
_____ (films, television, sculpture, paintings).
Choose one of these four, or another visual medium.

1. Begin with a generalization about the common "looking
   experience."

2. Divide the "looking experience" into three categories.

3. Devote at least two paragraphs to each category. Arrange
   your essay in order of ascending importance of the categories.

4. Throughout the essay, express your opinions about the
   "common looker."

5. Use full-paragraph transitions between sections devoted to
   each category.

6. Compare two well-known creators in the medium you've
   chosen. Explain why one is more popular among "novice
   lookers" while the other is more respected among experts.

7. Describe a particular piece of work in the medium as a way
   to illustrate your main point.

8. At the end of your essay, describe the attributes of an
   "ideal looker" and state what your readers should strive
   for in order to better appreciate and observe the medium.

More Writing Projects

1. Write an essay in which you classify the different types of music in a particular musical genre: for example, jazz, soul, pop, rock, etc. For example, for an essay on the blues, you might deal with delta blues, Chicago blues, and piano blues.

2. The next time you go to the movies, pay attention to the different ways in which the audience reacts. Then, write an essay classifying the different types of moviegoers.

CHAPTER 9

Process Analysis

Process analysis concentrates on *how* something is done, how something works, or how something occurs. If writing aims essentially to explain things, you can see why writers need to use process analysis. Often, the major point that will impress a reader depends on his or her ability to understand the logical steps in some plan of procedure. As a method of paragraph or essay development, process analysis traces all important steps, from beginning to end, in an activity or event. The amount of detail provided for each step in the process will depend on how much the audience knows about the subject.

Whether you are dealing with such subjects as how Columbus discovered America, how a carburetor works, how to deliver a good speech, or how to can fruit at home, you must present all essential information to your audience. Frequently, other methods of essay development help reinforce your analysis of process. (For example, writers often use *definition* to explain terms in a technical process that might not be familiar to readers; and to relate in clear order the steps in a process, an essay might require *narrative* techniques.) These methods will serve your main objective of explaining the process from beginning to end.

Although the purpose of process analysis is to provide your audience with a step-by-step explanation of a procedure, process analysis can also inform readers about the *significance* of the process; that is, it will instruct and inform. A typical problem in explanations of process is that a writer often

316

assumes that readers know more than they do. You can avoid this problem by defining your audience carefully. Certainly, you would use one approach to explain how to make a perfect cheese omelet to newlyweds; and you would use a completely different approach to explain it to students in advanced cooking class. Although both groups might have to follow the same sequence of steps, the kind of information you provide and the range of your explanations would be significantly different. No matter what approach you take to process analysis, remember to present material in a clear and lively manner. In reading about how something is done, or how something works, no reader wants to be bored; make an effort to keep your writing interesting.

Loafing Made Easy

Sam Negri

Sam Negri takes a light-hearted look at a topic that seems funny but is serious business to all those who work hard constantly. He tells us how to do nothing. A self-proclaimed expert in the art of loafing, Negri gives a few step-by-step how to's when it comes to goofing off. Notice how his essay blends narration, classification, and contrast into the analysis of process.

Words to Watch

mediocre (par. 3)   of moderate or low quality

damper (par. 5)   fireplace valve to regulate the air flow

lexicon (par. 11)   dictionary; word list

debilitating (par. 12)   impairing the strength of something

coax (par. 15)   to convince by gentle urging or flattery

lush (par. 15)   covered with abundant natural growth

The fabled season of the sun is upon us and it is once 1 again time to hook our thumbs in our suspenders and talk about America's most treasured art form, loafing.

The purest form of loafing is practiced in Arizona, where 2 summertime temperatures will often exceed 110 degrees. If we regard the Arizona loafer as a natural resource, as I've been doing for the last eight years, we will see that the art form has applications that go far beyond the business of surviving in hot weather.

When I came to Arizona, I was a mediocre loafer, display- 3 ing a definite need for a degree of mental reconditioning. I'd moved here from Connecticut, where people relax by putting aside their copy of Gray's "Anatomy" and picking up a novel by Dostoevsky. In Arizona, this is referred to as insanity.

Here is a better method: 4

To begin with, shut the damper on your fireplace, if you 5 have one, and turn on your air-conditioner, if you have one.

Otherwise, hang a wet sheet in the window and pray for a breeze.

Now you are ready to memorize a handful of important 6 and useful phrases. Try these: "I don't know"; "I don't care"; "no"; and the old standby, "well..."

These phrases are extremely valuable when your jaws 7 are sagging like deflated bicycle tubes and your mind has turned to wax.

For example, it is 106 degrees in the shade and your son 8 comes racing in the house, shouting, "Hey, you seen those long-handled pliers anywhere?" With a minimum of effort you are free to say, "no."

His anger may mount and he'll insist: "But you were us- 9 ing them yesterday! Where'd you leave 'em?"

If you haven't passed out from the strain of this conver- 10 sation, you can then reply, "I don't know."

"But I need those pliers to fix my skateboard," he will 11 cry. Then you break out the ultimate weapon in the loafer's lexicon. Without any inflection whatsoever, you declare, "Well..."

You can now get back to some serious loafing, which 12 means that you will try to prove that Benjamin Franklin was correct when he observed: "It is hard for an empty sack to stand upright." In short, empty your mind. Learn to ask questions like these: "Mail come yet?" and "Anything doin'?" The responses to these questions usually involve one word, and often they aren't debilitating.

There are a few additional rules to keep in mind for suc- 13 cessful loafing.

First, never loaf near a pool or a lake because you might 14 be tempted to go for a swim. Swimming frequently leaves a body feeling refreshed and may lead to a desire to do something.

Second, under no circumstances should you allow any- 15 one to coax you into a camping trip in the mountains. Mountains tend to be lush, green and cool, and next thing you know you'll be wanting to split logs for a fire, go for a hike, or pump up your Coleman stove. Resist. "Patience is a necessary ingredient of genius,'' said Disraeli. If you want to be a fine loafer you have to make enemies.

Of course, it is impossible to get by in life if you don't do 16 something, even in the summer. Household jobs are the easiest for a loafer to contend with, if he is selective and deliberate.

One satisfying and undemanding job involves a ball of 17 twine. Find a ball of twine that a cat has unraveled so badly that you can't find the end. Get scissors and slowly cut it into small pieces, scrunch it into a smaller ball, and throw it away. Now look at all the extra space you have in your junk drawer.

Another relatively simple and useful job for summertime 18 loafing centers on light bulbs. Limp through your house or apartment, removing the light bulbs from every lamp. Coat the very bottom of each bulb with petroleum jelly and put it back in the lampsocket. This will clean some of the crud off the contact point and solve the problems with flickering light-bulbs. For variety you can take the bulb that was in a living-room lamp and put it in a bedroom lamp. It helps to sigh and gaze wistfully at the base of the lightbulb as you are perform-ing this function.

Last, if you have a dog, sit in your most comfortable 19 chair and stare at your dog's eyes for five or 10 minutes. Ev-ery so often, mutter something incomprehensible. Your dog is certain to understand, and your family will not come near you for the rest of the afternoon.

BUILDING VOCABULARY

1. Though some synonyms can be used intercheably within a given piece of writing, often substituting one word for another will change the *tone* or *shades of meaning* of a sentence or phrase. Rewrite the following phrases substi-tuting your own word(s) for those in italics. Then discuss how your substitution changes the meaning or tone.

    a. America's *most treasured* art form (par. 1)
    b. the *business* of surviving in hot weather (par. 2)

c. a definite need for *mental reconditioning* (par. 3)
d. your jaws are sagging like *deflated* bicycle tires (par. 7)
e. If you haven't *passed out* from the *strain* of this conversation (par. 10)
f. the *ultimate* weapon (par. 11)
g. *gaze wistfully* (par. 18)
h. *mutter* something *incomprehensible* (par. 19)

2. Identify:

   a. Gray's "Anatomy"
   b. Dostoevsky
   c. Benjamin Franklin
   d. Benjamin Disraeli

UNDERSTANDING THE WRITER'S IDEAS

1. Why is loafing such an important activity in Arizona?

2. What is the purpose of this essay? Where does the author announce it?

3. According to the author, how do people in Connecticut relax? Why do people in Arizona consider this method insanity?

4. What alternative to air conditioning does Negri offer for relaxing in 110° weather?

5. What is the author's attitude toward making conversation while relaxing? What ways does he suggest to avoid undue strain?

6. When loafing seriously, why should you never be near a place to swim? Why should you never let anyone convince you to go camping?

7. Why are household jobs good activities for loafers? What three relatively painless household jobs does Negri describe? Trace the suggested process for performing each.

UNDERSTANDING THE WRITER'S TECHNIQUES

1. Which paragraphs make up the introduction for this essay? How do they serve as an effective beginning?

2. What is the connection between narration and process analysis in paragraphs 6 through 11?

3. Would you say that Negri is ever ironic (see Glossary) in this essay? Is he ever sarcastic? Point to places in the essay that demonstrate irony or sarcasm or both.

4. In any process analysis, it is important to tailor the depth and range of your explanations to your audience. For whom is Negri writing this essay? How does his language and tone reflect his audience?

5. An *aphorism* is a short, often ingenious saying that states a simple truth, usually in one sentence. Negri uses aphorisms by Benjamin Franklin (par. 12) and Benjamin Disraeli (par. 15). What are they? Explain in your own words what you think the original messages of those aphorisms were. Does Negri use them for their original meanings? If not, how does he adapt the aphorisms to the tone of his essay?

6. Explain Negri's use of transitional devices throughout the essay. Compare Negri's use of transitions with E. B. White's use of them in "The Three New Yorks" (pages 286–288).

7. Where does Negri use a one-word sentence? What is your reaction to it? Why does he use it, do you think?

8. How do paragraphs 16 through 19 make use of classification? How do the same paragraphs contribute to the process analysis?

EXPLORING THE WRITER'S IDEAS

1. In paragraph 3, Negri contrasts loafers in Connecticut with loafers in Arizona. What are some of the contrasting ways

that people relax in two places you know about? What are some of your favorite ways of goofing off?

2. At the beginning of paragraph 16, Negri writes: "Of course, it is impossible to get by in life if you don't do something." Although the essay is written in a humorous vein, there are certainly many serious implications to the above statement. Discuss what the statement means to you.

3. Negri's point is that loafing is an art and that loafing is good for us. Do you agree? Why? What dangers exist for loafers?

IDEAS FOR WRITING

Guided Writing

Write an essay in which you analyze the best ways to succeed in the art of _____.
(Fill in the blank with a word or phrase of your own choice.)

1. Begin by letting the reader know why and how you are intimately familiar with the fine points of this art.

2. State the purpose of your essay at the end of the second paragraph.

3. Contrast a bad way of doing this activity with a good way of doing it.

4. In a tone suited to the activity you are analyzing, describe the best way to avoid letting someone get in the way of your goal. Use narration to illustrate this method.

5. Use an aphorism or two—adapting it to the tone and purpose of your process analysis.

6. Point out two special rules for the reader to keep in mind in order to be successful in this art.

7. Use clear, simple transitions throughout the essay (see Glossary).

8. Somewhere in the essay, use a one-word sentence for a special effect.

9. For your concluding section, consider activities that might be necessary to offset the effects of the art described. Through process analysis, develop examples of the best ways to perform those activities.

More Writing Projects

1. Explain the process you use to *avoid* loafing too much.

2. Give a step-by-step account of what you did the last time you had an unexpected day off from work, school, or other responsibilities.

3. Explain how you keep a balance between working, studying, and relaxing.

Eating Alone in Restaurants

Bruce Jay Friedman

In this selection from his book, *The Lonely Guy's Book of Life,*
Bruce Jay Friedman touches a nerve in all of us as he explains the
process of dining out alone. He may not tell us exactly what to order,
but through his use of ironic narration, vivid description, and thorough illustration, he creates a delightful essay that gives us a consum-
mate personal lesson.

Words to Watch

inconspicuous (par. 1)   not easily noticeable

hors d'oeuvre (par. 7)   appetizer

scenario (par. 8)   script or outline of a plot

foreboding (par. 10)   a feeling of something bad to come

suffice (par. 10)   to be adequate for the purpose

promenade (par. 13)   leisurely walk

imperiously (par. 14)   haughtily; arrogantly

conviviality (par. 17)   condition of enjoyment of good food and drink
and good company

pervade (par. 17)   to spread through every part of something

audacious (par. 24)   daring

Hunched over, trying to be as inconspicuous as possible, 1
a solitary diner slips into a midtown Manhattan steakhouse.
No sooner does he check his coat than the voice of the headwaiter comes booming across the restaurant.

"Alone again, eh?" 2

As all eyes are raised, the bartender, with enormous 3
good cheer, chimes in: "That's because they all left him high
and dry."

And then, just in case there is a customer in the restau- 4
rant who isn't yet aware of his situation, a waiter shouts out
from the buffet table: "Well, we'll take care of him anyway,
won't we fellas!"

Haw, haw, haw, and a lot of sly winks and pokes in the   5
ribs.

Eating alone in a restaurant is one of the most terrifying   6
experiences in America.

Sniffed at by headwaiters, an object of scorn and amuse-   7
ment to couples, the solitary diner is the unwanted and un-
loved child of Restaurant Row. No sooner does he make his
appearance than he is whisked out of sight and seated at a thin
sliver of a table with barely enough room on it for an hors
d'oeuvre. Wedged between busboy stations, a hair's breadth
from the men's room, there he sits, feet lodged in a railing as
if he were in Pilgrim stocks, wondering where he went wrong
in life.

Rather than face this grim scenario, most Lonely Guys   8
would prefer to nibble away at a tuna fish sandwich in the relative safety of their high-rise apartments.

What can be done to ease the pain of this not only starv-   9
ing but silent minority—to make dining alone in restaurants a
rewarding experience? Absolutely nothing. But some small
strategies *do* exist for making the experience bearable.

Before You Get There

Once the Lonely Guy has decided to dine alone at a restau-   10
rant, a sense of terror and foreboding will begin to build
throughout the day. All the more reason for him to get there as
quickly as possible so that the experience can soon be forgotten and he can resume his normal life. Clothing should be light
and loose-fitting, especially around the neck—on the off
chance of a fainting attack during the appetizer. It is best to
dress modestly, avoiding both the funeral-director-style suit as
well as the bold, eye-arresting costume of the gaucho. A single
cocktail should suffice; little sympathy will be given to the
Lonely Guy who tumbles in, stewed to the gills. (The fellow
who stoops to putting morphine in his toes for courage does
not belong in this discussion.) En route to the restaurant, it is
best to play down dramatics, such as swinging the arms pluck-

ily and humming the theme from *The Bridge on the River Kwai.*

Once You Arrive

The way your entrance comes off is of critical importance. Do 11
not skulk in, slipping along the walls as if you are carrying
some dirty little secret. There is no need, on the other hand, to
fling your coat arrogantly at the hatcheck girl, slap the headwaiter across the cheeks with your gloves and demand to be
seated immediately. Simply walk in with a brisk rubbing of the
hands and approach the headwaiter. When asked how many
are in your party, avoid cute responses such as "Jes lil ol'
me." Tell him you are a party of one; the Lonely Guy who
does not trust his voice can simply lift a finger. Do not launch
into a story about how tired you are of taking out fashion models, night after night, and what a pleasure it is going to be to
dine alone.

    It is best to arrive with no reservation. Asked to set aside a 12
table for one, the restaurant owner will suspect either a prank on
the part of an ex-waiter, or a terrorist plot, in which case windows will be boarded up and the kitchen bombswept. An advantage of the "no reservation" approach is that you will appear to
have just stepped off the plane from Des Moines, your first night
in years away from Marge and the kids.

    All eyes will be upon you when you make the promenade 13
to your table. Stay as close as possible to the headwaiter, trying to match him step for step. This will reduce your visibility
and fool some diners into thinking you are a member of the
staff. If you hear a generalized snickering throughout the restaurant, do not assume automatically that you are being
laughed at. The other diners may all have just recalled an
amusing moment in a Feydeau farce.

    If your table is unsatisfactory, do not demand imperi- 14
ously that one for eight people be cleared immediately so that
you can dine in solitary grandeur. Glance around discreetly
and see if there are other possibilities. The ideal table will allow you to keep your back to the wall so that you can see if

anyone is laughing at you. Try to get one close to another couple so that if you lean over at a 45-degree angle it will appear
that you are a swinging member of their group. Sitting opposite a mirror can be useful; after a drink or two, you will begin
to feel that there are a few of you.

Once you have been seated, and it becomes clear to the   15
staff that you are alone, there will follow The Single Most
Heartbreaking Moment in Dining Out Alone—when the second setting is whisked away and yours is spread out a bit to
make the table look busier. This will be done with great ceremony by the waiter—angered in advance at being tipped for
only one dinner. At this point, you may be tempted to smack
your forehead against the table and curse the fates that
brought you to this desolate position in life. A wiser course is
to grit your teeth, order a drink and use this opportunity to
make contact with other Lonely Guys sprinkled about the
room. A menu or a leafy stalk of celery can be used as a shield
for peering out at them. Do not expect a hearty greeting or a
cry of "huzzah" from these frightened and browbeaten people. Too much excitement may cause them to slump over, cur-
tains. Smile gently and be content if you receive a pale wave
of the hand in return. It is unfair to imply that you have come
to help them throw off their chains.

When the headwaiter arrives to take your order, do not   16
be bullied into ordering the last of the gazelle haunches unless
you really want them. Thrilled to be offered anything at all,
many Lonely Guys will say "Get them right out here" and
wolf them down. Restaurants take unfair advantage of Lonely
Guys, using them to get rid of anything from withered liver to
old heels of roast beef. Order anything you like, although it is
good to keep to the light and simple in case of a sudden attack
of violent stomach cramps.

Some Proven Strategies

Once the meal is under way, a certain pressure will begin to   17
build as couples snuggle together, the women clucking sympa-
thetically in your direction. Warmth and conviviality will pervade the room, none of it encompassing you. At this point,

many Lonely Guys will keep their eyes riveted to the restaurant paintings of early Milan or bury themselves in a paperback anthology they have no wish to read.

Here are some ploys designed to confuse other diners 18 and make them feel less sorry for you.

• After each bite of food, lift your head, smack your lips 19 thoughtfully, swallow and make a notation in a pad. Diners will assume you are a restaurant critic.

• Between courses, pull out a walkie-talkie and whisper a 20 message into it. This will lead everyone to believe you are part of a police stake-out team, about to bust the salad man as an international dope dealer.

• Pretend you are a foreigner. This is done by pointing to 21 items on the menu with an alert smile and saying to the headwaiter: "Is good, no?"

• When the main course arrives, brush the restaurant silver- 22 ware off the table and pull some of your own out of a breast-pocket. People will think you are a wealthy eccentric.

• Keep glancing at the door, and make occasional trips to look 23 out at the street, as if you are waiting for a beautiful woman. Half-way through the meal, shrug in a world-weary manner and begin to eat with gusto. The world is full of women! Why tolerate bad manners! Life is too short.

The Right Way

One other course is open to the Lonely Guy, an audacious 24 one, full of perils, but all the more satisfying if you can bring it off. That is to take off your dark glasses, sit erectly, smile broadly at anyone who looks in your direction, wave off inferior wines, and begin to eat with heartiness and enormous confidence. As outrageous as the thought may be—enjoy your own company. Suddenly, titters and sly winks will tail off, the headwaiter's disdain will fade, and friction will build among couples who will turn out to be not as tightly cemented as they appear. The heads of other Lonely Guys will lift with hope as you become the attractive center of the room.

If that doesn't work, you still have your fainting option. 25

BUILDING VOCABULARY

1. *Colloquial language* (see Glossary) is the language used in
   most conversation and in some informal writing. Clearly,
   Friedman uses a good deal of such language in this essay.
   Explain in your own words the following colloquialisms,
   then list and explain five others derived from the essay:

   a. chimes in (par. 3)
   b. stewed to the gills (par. 10)
   c. launch into a story (par. 11)
   d. grit your teeth (par. 15)
   e. wolf them down (par. 16)

2. Identify:

   Restaurant Row (par. 7)
   Pilgrim stocks (par. 7)
   The Bridge on the River Kwai (par. 10)
   gaucho (par. 10)
   Feydeau (par. 13)

UNDERSTANDING THE WRITER'S IDEAS

1. In the opening paragraphs, what is the author's main point
   about eating alone in restaurants? What does he say people who work in restaurants think about those eating
   alone? What does paragraph 5 indicate about this attitude?

2. Who are the "Lonely Guys"?

3. According to the author, how should a Lonely Guy prepare himself to eat alone?

4. Make a step-by-step outline of Friedman's instructions for
   what to do once you arrive at a restaurant to eat alone.

5. Why is it best *not* to make an advance reservation?

6. What is the "ideal table" for a diner alone? What makes it
   so?

7. Explain "The Single Most Heartbreaking Moment in Dining Out Alone." What makes it such a terrible moment?

8. In what ways do restaurants attempt to take advantage of solitary diners?

9. According to Friedman, what is the attitude of other diners toward the person eating alone? What are some of the best ways to combat this attitude?

10. Ultimately, what is the "Right Way" to dine alone? What do the author's ideas about the Right Way suggest about the real meaning and purpose of this essay? Explain your answer.

11. If all the author's suggestions fail, what last resort is available to the Lonely Guy? In the context of this essay, would this be an effective tactic?

UNDERSTANDING THE WRITER'S TECHNIQUES

1. What is the *thesis* statement of this essay?

2. An *anecdote* is a brief narration of an incident, often personal. How does Friedman use an anecdote in the introduction to this essay? Is it effective? Why?

3. *Hyperbole* in writing is the use of extreme exaggeration either to make a particular point or to achieve a special effect. Friedman makes liberal use of hyperbole throughout the essay. What is the main point of the author's hyperbole? What effects are achieved by it? List at least ten examples of hyperbolic writing in this essay.

4. How would you characterize the *tone* of this essay? Look up the definitions of *irony, cynicism,* and *sarcasm*. Which term do you think most closely describes Friedman's tone? Does his tone fit the subject matter? Explain.

Go back to your list of hyperboles and note for each whether you think it is intended to be ironic, cynical, or sarcastic.

5. Friedman also makes liberal use of capitalization throughout the essay. Why? List a few examples of the use of capitalization other than at the beginning of sentences or for proper nouns.

6. Evaluate the use of *classification* (see Chapter 8, pages 275–276) in this essay. How does it affect the process analysis? What are the main categories of classification? How are they organized?

7. Indicate those paragraphs that constitute the introduction, body, and conclusion of this essay.

8. Which sentence in the introduction alerts us that this is a process-analysis essay? Write an outline of the process steps discussed.

9. How does Friedman use a list in this essay? Is it effective in terms of suiting the overall tone and fitting the context of this essay? Explain.

10. Writing teachers often tell their students: "Show. Don't tell." In other words, use gestures and actions to characterize someone or make a point rather than just give the reader an explanation. How does Friedman use gestures and actions to express characters' feelings in this essay? Give five examples.

11. Who is the intended audience for this essay? How do you know?

12. How does Friedman use *narration* in this essay? *Description? Definition? Illustration?*

13. Evaluate the conclusion of this essay. How does it relate to the rest of the essay? Do you feel the last sentence enhances or detracts from the conclusion? Why?

EXPLORING THE WRITER'S IDEAS

1. Do you think Friedman has written this essay from personal experience? Explain your answer.

2. Friedman focuses his essay on a species he calls Lonely Guys. Why do you think he doesn't write about women dining out alone—Lonely Gals? What are your reactions when you see a woman dining alone in a restaurant? How do these reactions differ from your responses when you see a man dining alone?

3. How do you feel about eating out alone? For what reasons might you choose to take yourself out to eat? Do you enjoy it, or do you feel uncomfortable as the author suggests? What preparations do you make in order to make the experience more enjoyable? Do they usually work?

4. Friedman writes here of big city experiences—specifically, midtown Manhattan. Do you feel his analysis and suggestions apply just as well to other environments? How so?

IDEAS FOR WRITING

Guided Writing

Write an essay in which you explain how to do something that is generally thought of as an uncomfortable activity. For example, you might write about asking for a first date, interviewing for a job, meeting a boyfriend's or girlfriend's family for the first time.

1. Begin with an anecdote illustrating the most embarrassing "worst case scenario" that might occur during this activity.

2. Invent a name for the type of person most likely to feel uncomfortable in this situation.

3. Include a direct thesis statement.

4. Make the body of your essay instructions for how to make this process less uncomfortable. Arrange your suggestions into three categories following the chronology of the process. Title your categories.

5. Identify the "Most Uncomfortable Moment" that is likely to occur during the activity's process.

6. Make frequent use of colloquialisms throughout the essay.

7. Use irony and occasional sarcasm and cynicism to add humor to the essay.

8. Include a list of hyperbolic strategies for relieving the pressure once one is fully absorbed in the process.

9. Use your conclusion to make a serious point about human nature and the deeper meaning of overcoming the uncomfortableness of this situation.

10. Leave your reader with a humorous statement that undercuts the seriousness of your conclusion.

More Writing Projects

1. Write about the process you recently used to deal with an extremely embarrassing moment. Make sure to tell what led up to the moment and what happened during and after the incident.

2. Write a process analysis telling how to get satisfaction when you've bought a defective product or gotten bad service in a store.

3. Write a brief description of the process you use when you're out with one person and meet someone else whose name you don't remember.

Coors Beer
Grace Lichtenstein

Process analysis often deals with mechanical or technical procedures. In this short selection by Grace Lichtenstein, who is a corre-
spondent for *The New York Times,* the author examines a mechanical
process—the brewing of beer. As you read this piece, look for the
methods that the author uses to make this technical process interesting and understandable to the general reader.

Words to Watch

palate (par. 1)   taste or sense of taste

mystique (par. 2)   special, almost mysterious attitudes and feelings
surrounding a person, place, or thing

Spartan (par. 3)   simple and severe

rancid (par. 3)   not fresh; having a bad smell

permeate (par. 3)   to spread through everything

nondescript (par. 3)   lacking any recognizable character or quality

cellulose (par. 4)   the main substance in woody parts of plants, used
in many manufacturing processes

Coors is a light-bodied beer, meaning it is brewed with   1
less malt, fewer hops and more rice than beers with a tangy
taste. Compared with Heineken's or other more full-bodied
foreign beers, Coors does seem almost flavorless and it is
this quality that could account for its popularity among
young people just starting to get acquainted with the pleasures of beer drinking. A few locals scoff at Coors, calling it
"Colorado Kool-Aid." But the fact is that, according to Ernest Pyler, "if you conducted a blindfold test of the four
leading beers, the chances of picking our Coors would be
minimal." Indeed, one national newspaper conducted an informal test among eight beer drinkers, finding that only
three could correctly identify Coors. My own admittedly
uneducated palate detects no difference between Coors and
Schaefer. In short, the difference between Coors and any

other decent beer could be 1,800 miles. Maybe, if Paul Newman suddenly switched to Schaefer, Denverites would pay $15 a case for it.

There is one aspect to the Coors mystique that does have 2 measurable validity. Company officials make much of the fact that Coors has good mountain water and the most expensive brewing process in the country. Several elements are unusual, though not unique.

Thousands of visitors have learned about the process on 3 guided tours through the antiseptic, Spartan plant. (For out-of-towners, the tour is often a pilgrimage—but for local students of the Colorado School of Mines, it's usually more in the line of a quick belt before classes. The tour lasts 30 minutes, at the end of which visitors are invited to quaff to their heart's content in the hospitality lounge. "I've come here 50 times," boasted one student as he polished off a glass at 11:30 one morning in the lounge.) Situated in the center of town, between two high, flat mesas in the foothills of the Rockies, the plant dominates the community just as the somewhat rancid smell of malt seems to permeate the air; one-fourth of the town's families are said to owe their jobs to the factory's operations. Anyone expecting to see in Golden the foaming white waterfall amid mountain pines that is pictured on every yellow can of Coors will be disappointed. The water used in the brewing comes from nondescript wells hidden in concrete blockhouses. The brewery now puts out about 12 million barrels of beer a year, but construction sites throughout the grounds bear witness to the company's hopes for doubling that capacity by 1984.

Like other beers, Coors is produced from barley. Most 4 of the big Midwestern brewers use barley grown in North Dakota and Minnesota. Coors is the single American brewer to use a Moravian strain, grown under company supervision, on farms in Colorado, Idaho, Wyoming and Montana. At the brewery, the barley is turned into malt by being soaked in water—which must be biologically pure and of a known mineral content—for several days, causing it to sprout and producing a chemical change—breaking down starch into sugar. The

malt is toasted, a process that halts the sprouting and deter-
mines the color and sweetness (the more the roasting, the
darker, more bitter the beer). It is ground into flour and
brewed, with more pure water, in huge copper-domed kettles
until it is the consistency of oatmeal. Rice and refined starch
are added to make mash; solids are strained out, leaving an
amber liquid malt extract, which is boiled with hops—the
dried cones from the hop vine which add to the bitterness, or
tang. The hops are strained, yeast is added, turning the sugar
to alcohol, and the beer is aged in huge red vats at near-
freezing temperatures for almost two months, during which
the second fermentation takes place and the liquid becomes
carbonated, or bubbly. (Many breweries chemically age their
beer to speed up production; Coors people say only naturally
aged brew can be called a true "lager.") Next, the beer is fil-
tered through cellulose filters to remove bacteria, and finally
is pumped into cans, bottles or kegs for shipping.

The most unusual aspect of the Coors process is that the   5
beer is not pasteurized, as all but a half-dozen of the 90 or so
American beers are. In the pasteurization process, bottles or
cans of beer are passed through a heating unit and then
cooled. This destroys the yeast in the brew which could cause
spoilage, if the cans or bottles or barrels are unrefrigerated for
any long period. However, pasteurization also changes the flavor of beer. Coors stopped pasteurizing its product 18 years
ago because it decided that "heat is an enemy of beer," according to a company spokesman.

Unpasteurized beer must be kept under constant refrig-   6
eration. Thus, Coors does not warehouse any of its finished
product, as many other brewers do, but ships everything out
cold, immediately. In effect, my tour guide, a young management trainee wearing a beer-can tie clip, explained as we wandered through the packaging area, watching workers in surgi-
cal masks feed aluminum lids into machines that sealed cans
whirling by on conveyor belts, the six-pack you buy in a store
contains not only a very fresh beer but also a beer that could
be considered draft, since it has been kept cold from vat to
home refrigerator.

BUILDING VOCABULARY

1. For the italicized word in each example in Column A below select a definition from Column B.

Column A

  1 locals *scoff* (par. 1)
  2 *informal* test (par. 1)
  3 measurable *validity* (par. 2)
  4 the *antiseptic* Spartan plant (par. 3)
  5 to *quaff* to their heart's content (par. 3)
  6 flat *mesas* (par. 3)
  7 construction *sites* (par. 3)
  8 a Moravian *strain* (par. 4)
  9 the *consistency* of oatmeal (par. 4)
10 liquid malt *extract* (par. 4)

Column B

  a drink heartily
  b locations
  c thickness
  d not according to fixed rules
  e a line of certain species
  f a concentrated form of something
  g soundness
  h make fun of
  i free from infection
  j hills

2. Use five of the italicized words in the first exercise in sentences of your own.

UNDERSTANDING THE WRITER'S IDEAS

1. What is a "light-bodied" beer?

2. What does the author mean when she states, "In short, the difference between Coors and any other decent beer could be 1,800 miles"?

3. What *is* special about Coors beer?

4. Why do college students like to visit the Coors plant?

5. Describe the setting of the Coors brewery. How does it contrast with the picture on the Coors can?

6. Explain in your own words the process by which Coors is produced.

7. Why is the pasteurization process important to the final flavor of any beer?

8. Why can Coors almost be considered a draft beer?

UNDERSTANDING THE WRITER'S TECHNIQUES

1. How do comparison and contrast operate in the first paragraph? Does the author also use definition in this paragraph? Where? For what purpose?

2. What is the function of paragraph 2? What is the purpose of paragraph 3? How does the author develop paragraph 3?

3. Analyze the author's use of transitional devices (see Glossary) between paragraphs 2 and 3.

4. Which paragraphs analyze the process of brewing Coors? Make a list of the steps on a sheet of paper. Is the process clear and complete? Does the author use process analysis simply to inform? Does she also provide commentary? Where?

5. Where does the author introduce personal or subjective elements into this essay? Why, at these points, does she provide personal rather than technical details?

EXPLORING THE WRITER'S IDEAS

1. Suppose that three unidentified brands of beer, cola, or cigarettes were placed before you. Would you be able to identify them by taste? What is the importance of "mystique" (or image) or "brand loyalty" to a product's success?

2. Can you think of other products that have a mystique associated with them? What are they, and what accounts for the mystique?

3. Would the fact that Paul Newman drinks Coors affect people's attitudes toward the brand? Why do manufacturers attempt to have certain celebrities associated with their products? Why should consumers be influenced by these associations?

4. Based on this essay, what are some ways to make a technical analysis of process interesting to the reader?

IDEAS FOR WRITING

Guided Writing

Explain how to make or to assemble a particular item or product. For example, you might want to explain how to prepare a certain dish; how to assemble a piece of equipment; how to produce something in a factory. You might want to follow Lichtenstein's example: Explain how a popular drink is made.

1. Start by introducing the reader to your "perfect product," indicating how it is possible to achieve high-quality results in its preparation.

2. Use as examples of the quality of the product, positive statements made by other individuals. These may be the ideas of friends, relatives, or experts.

3. Explain the "mystique," if there is one, surrounding the product.

4. After arousing reader interest sufficiently, describe the actual process involved, concentrating on all important details in the sequence.

5. In your last paragraph, try to capture the taste, look, or feel of the final product.

More Writing Projects

1. Consult an encyclopedia or other reference book to learn about the making of some product—steel, automobiles,

plywood, and so forth. Then explain this process in your own words.

2. Set up an actual testing situation in your class. Have various members test three types of a particular item, such as chocolate, diet soda, a kitchen cleanser. Then write a report describing the process involved in the testing, as well as the process by which results were obtained.

Camping Out

Ernest Hemingway

In this essay by Ernest Hemingway (1899–1961), the author uses the pattern of process analysis to order his materials on the art of camping. Hemingway wrote this piece for the *Toronto Star* in the early 1920s, before he gained worldwide recognition as a major American writer. In it, we see his lifelong interest in the outdoors and in his desire to do things well.

Words to Watch

relief map (par. 2)   a map that shows by lines and colors the various heights and forms of the land

Caucasus (par. 2)   a mountain range in southeastern Europe

proprietary (par. 7)   held under patent or trademark

rhapsodize (par. 9)   to speak enthusiastically

browse bed (par. 9)   a portable cot

tyro (par. 11)   an amateur; a beginner in learning something

dyspepsia (par. 13)   indigestion

mulligan (par. 18)   a stew made from odds and ends of meats and vegetables

Thousands of people will go into the bush this summer to 1
cut the high cost of living. A man who gets his two weeks' salary while he is on vacation should be able to put those two weeks in fishing and camping and be able to save one week's salary clear. He ought to be able to sleep comfortably every night, to eat well every day and to return to the city rested and in good condition.

But if he goes into the woods with a frying pan, an igno- 2
rance of black flies and mosquitoes, and a great and abiding lack of knowledge about cookery the chances are that his return will be very different. He will come back with enough mosquito bites to make the back of his neck look like a relief map of the Caucasus. His digestion will be wrecked after a valiant battle to assimilate half-cooked or charred grub. And

342

he won't have had a decent night's sleep while he has been gone.

He will solemnly raise his right hand and inform you that 3 he has joined the grand army of never-agains. The call of the wild may be all right, but it's a dog's life. He's heard the call of the tame with both ears. Waiter, bring him an order of milk toast.

In the first place he overlooked the insects. Black flies, 4 no-see-ums, deer flies, gnats and mosquitoes were instituted by the devil to force people to live in cities where he could get at them better. If it weren't for them everybody would live in the bush and he would be out of work. It was a rather successful invention.

But there are lots of dopes that will counteract the pests. 5 The simplest perhaps is oil of citronella. Two bits' worth of this purchased at any pharmacist's will be enough to last for two weeks in the worst fly and mosquito-ridden country.

Rub a little on the back of your neck, your forehead and 6 your wrists before you start fishing, and the blacks and skeeters will shun you. The odor of citronella is not offensive to people. It smells like gun oil. But the bugs do hate it.

Oil of pennyroyal and eucalyptol are also much hated by 7 mosquitoes, and with citronella they form the basis for many proprietary preparations. But it is cheaper and better to buy the straight citronella. Put a little on the mosquito netting that covers the front of your pup tent or canoe tent at night, and you won't be bothered.

To be really rested and get any benefit out of a vacation 8 a man must get a good night's sleep every night. The first requisite for this is to have plenty of cover. It is twice as cold as you expect it will be in the bush four nights out of five, and a good plan is to take just double the bedding that you think you will need. An old quilt that you can wrap up in is as warm as two blankets.

Nearly all outdoor writers rhapsodize over the browse 9 bed. It is all right for the man who knows how to make one and has plenty of time. But in a succession of one-night camps on a canoe trip all you need is level ground for your tent floor and you will sleep all right if you have plenty of covers under

you. Take twice as much cover as you think that you will
need, and then put two-thirds of it under you. You will sleep
warm and get your rest.

When it is clear weather you don't need to pitch your 10
tent if you are only stopping for the night. Drive four stakes at
the head of your made-up bed and drape your mosquito bar
over that, then you can sleep like a log and laugh at the mosquitoes.

Outside of insects and bum sleeping the rock that wrecks 11
most camping trips is cooking. The average tyro's idea of
cooking is to fry everything and fry it good and plenty. Now,
a frying pan is a most necessary thing to any trip, but you also
need the old stew kettle and the folding reflector baker.

A pan of fried trout can't be bettered and they don't cost 12
any more than ever. But there is a good and bad way of frying
them.

The beginner puts his trout and his bacon in and over a 13
brightly burning fire the bacon curls up and dries into a dry
tasteless cinder and the trout is burned outside while it is still
raw inside. He eats them and it is all right if he is only out for
the day and going home to a good meal at night. But if he is
going to face more trout and bacon the next morning and other
equally well-cooked dishes for the remainder of two weeks he
is on the pathway to nervous dyspepsia.

The proper way is to cook over coals. Have several cans 14
of Crisco or Cotosuet or one of the vegetable shortenings
along that are as good as lard and excellent for all kinds of
shortening. Put the bacon in and when it is about half cooked
lay the trout in the hot grease, dipping them in corn meal first.
Then put the bacon on top of the trout and it will baste them
as it slowly cooks.

The coffee can be boiling at the same time and in a 15
smaller skillet pancakes being made that are satisfying the
other campers while they are waiting for the trout.

With the prepared pancake flours you take a cupful of 16
pancake flour and add a cup of water. Mix the water and flour
and as soon as the lumps are out it is ready for cooking. Have
the skillet hot and keep it well greased. Drop the batter in and

as soon as it is done on one side loosen it in the skillet and flip
it over. Apple butter, syrup or cinnamon and sugar go well
with the cakes.

While the crowd have taken the edge from their appetites   17
with flapjacks the trout have been cooked and they and the
bacon are ready to serve. The trout are crisp outside and firm
and pink inside and the bacon is well done—but not too done.
If there is anything better than that combination the writer has
yet to taste it in a lifetime devoted largely and studiously to
eating.

The stew kettle will cook you dried apricots when they   18
have resumed their predried plumpness after a night of soaking, it will serve to concoct a mulligan in, and it will cook macaroni. When you are not using it, it should be boiling water for
the dishes.

In the baker, mere man comes into his own, for he can   19
make a pie that to his bush appetite will have it all over the
product that mother used to make, like a tent. Men have always believed that there was something mysterious and difficult about making a pie. Here is a great secret. There is nothing to it. We've been kidded for years. Any man of average
office intelligence can make at least as good a pie as his wife.

All there is to a pie is a cup and a half of flour, one-half   20
teaspoonful of salt, one-half cup of lard and cold water. That
will make pie crust that will bring tears of joy into your camping partner's eyes.

Mix the salt with the flour, work the lard into the flour,   21
make it up into a good workmanlike dough with cold water.
Spread some flour on the back of a box or something flat, and
pat the dough around a while. Then roll it out with whatever
kind of round bottle you prefer. Put a little more lard on the
surface of the sheet of dough and then slosh a little flour on
and roll it up and then roll it out again with the bottle.

Cut out a piece of the rolled out dough big enough to line   22
a pie tin. I like the kind with holes in the bottom. Then put in
your dried apples that have soaked all night and been sweet-
ened, or your apricots, or your blueberries, and then take another sheet of the dough and drape it gracefully over the top,

soldering it down at the edges with your fingers. Cut a couple of slits in the top dough sheet and prick it a few times with a fork in an artistic manner.

Put it in the baker with a good slow fire for forty-five 23 minutes and then take it out and if your pals are Frenchmen they will kiss you. The penalty for knowing how to cook is that the others will make you do all the cooking.

It is all right to talk about roughing it in the woods. But 24 the real woodsman is the man who can be really comfortable in the bush.

BUILDING VOCABULARY

1. For each word below write your own definition, based on how the word is used in the selection. Check back to the appropriate paragraph in the essay.

   a. abiding (par. 2)
   b. assimilate (par. 2)
   c. valiant (par. 2)
   d. charred (par. 2)
   e. solemnly (par. 3)
   f. requisite (par. 8)
   g. succession (par. 9)
   h. studiously (par. 17)
   i. concoct (par. 18)
   j. soldering (par. 22)

UNDERSTANDING THE WRITER'S IDEAS

1. What is Hemingway's main purpose in this essay? Does he simply want to explain how to set up camp and how to cook outdoors?

2. What, according to the writer, are the two possible results of camping out on your vacation?

3. Why is oil of citronella the one insecticide that Hemingway recommends over all others?

4. Is it always necessary to pitch a tent when camping out? What are alternatives to it? How can you sleep warmly and comfortably?

5. Explain the author's process for cooking trout. Also explain his process for baking a pie.

6. Is it enough for Hemingway simply to enjoy "roughing it" while camping out?

UNDERSTANDING THE WRITER'S TECHNIQUES

1. Identify those paragraphs in the essay that involve process analysis, and explain how Hemingway develops his subject in each.

2. What is the main writing pattern in paragraphs 1 and 2? How does this method serve as an organizing principle throughout the essay?

3. How would you characterize the author's style of writing? Is it appropriate to a newspaper audience? Is it more apt for professional fishermen?

4. In what way does Hemingway employ classification in this essay?

5. Analyze the tone of Hemingway's essay.

6. The concluding paragraph is short. Is it effective, nevertheless, and why? How does it reinforce the opening paragraph?

EXPLORING THE WRITER'S IDEAS

1. Camping out was popular in the 1920s, as it is in the 1980s. What are some of the reasons that it remains so attractive today?

2. Hemingway's essay describes many basic strategies for successful camping. He does not rely on "gadgets," or modern inventions to make camping easier. Do such gadgets make camping more fun today than it might have been in the 1920s?

3. The author suggests that there is a right way and a wrong way to do things. Does it matter if you perform a recreational activity right as long as you enjoy doing it? Why?

IDEAS FOR WRITING

Guided Writing

Write a composition on how to do something wrong, and how to do it right—going on vacation, looking for a job, fishing, or whatever.

1. Reexamine the author's first three paragraphs and imitate his method of introducing the right and wrong ways about the subject, and the possible results.

2. Adopt a simple, informal, "chatty" style. Feel free to use a few well-placed clichés and other forms of spoken English. Use several similes.

3. Divide your subject into useful categories. Just as Hemingway treated insects, sleeping, and cooking, try to cover the main aspects of your subject.

4. Explain the process involved for each aspect of your subject. Make certain that you compare and contrast the right and wrong ways of your activity.

5. Write a short, crisp conclusion that reinforces your longer introduction.

More Writing Projects

1. Explain how people camp out today.

2. Describe how to get to your favorite vacation spot, and what to do when you get there.

3. If you have ever camped out, write a process paper explaining one important feature of setting up camp.

CHAPTER 10

Cause-and-Effect Analysis

The analysis of cause and effect—often called *causal analysis*—seeks to explain why events occur, or what the outcome or *expected* results of a chain of happenings might be. Basically, cause-and-effect analysis looks for connections between things and reasons behind them. It involves a way of thinking that identifies conditions (the causes) and establishes results or consequences (the effects). In order to discuss an idea intelligently a writer needs to explore causes and effects. The strength of an explanation may lie simply in his or her ability to point out *why* something is so.

Like all the other writing patterns discussed in this text, cause-and-effect analysis reflects a kind of thinking we do every day. If someone were to ask you why you selected the college that you are now attending, you would offer reasons to explain your choice: the cost, the geographic location, the reputation of the institution, and so forth. These would be the *causes* that you have identified. On the other hand, someone might ask you if and why you like the college now that you are there. You could discuss your satisfaction (or lack of it) with the teachers, the course offerings, the opportunity to work part time, the availability of scholarship money and loans, the beauty of the campus, the variety in your social life. Those are the consequences or results—in other words, the *effects*—of your decision. Of course, basic reasoning and common sense are involved in the way that you identify causes and effects.

How do you determine causal relationships? First, you look at the *immediate* causes that gave rise to a situation— that is, you look at the causes most directly related to it, the ones you discover closest at hand. (Here you must be careful not to assume that because one event simply preceded another it also caused it.) But for most events a good analyst looks beyond immediate causes to more fundamental ones. These are the *ultimate* causes of a situation, the basic conditions that stimulated the more obvious ones.

For example, if you looked for causes to explain why your supervisor dismissed you from your job, your first response might be that you and she did not get along well. That could be an *immediate cause*. (Because one of your coworkers left your supervisor's office after a private conference with her just before you were fired, you could *not* assume safely that that coworker necessarily caused your dismissal.) But the immediate cause you uncovered could certainly be influenced by other underlying conditions. Perhaps your attendance record on the job was poor. Perhaps you did not get your work done quickly enough. Or, on the other hand, perhaps you worked so quickly and efficiently that your supervisor saw you as a threat to her own position. One or more of those and others like them might be the *ultimate* causes to explain why you lost the job.

Of course, as in the above example, causes you name for many situations may be thought of only as possibilities. It's often impossible to *prove* causes and effects absolutely. Yet in evaluating the causal relationships you present in an essay, readers expect you to offer evidence. Therefore, you do have to support the causes and effects you present with specific details drawn from personal experiences, from statistics, or from statements by experts, for example. The more details and evidence you offer, the better your paper will be.

When writers use causal analysis as a pattern, they can concentrate either on causes or effects, or they can attempt to balance the two. Moreover, in longer and more complicated papers, a writer can show how one cause produces an effect that, in turn, creates *another* set of causes leading to a second effect. Wherever the pattern takes you, remember to be thorough in presenting all links in your chain of analysis; to consider all possible factors; to avoid oversimplification; and to emphasize all important major and minor causes and effects.

Why Marriages Fail

Anne Roiphe

Anne Roiphe is the author of the well-known novel about relationships, *Up The Sandbox!*, which was later made into a popular film. In this essay, notice how she presents a series of interconnected reasons for the currently high divorce rate.

Words to Watch

obsolete (par. 1)   out-of-date; no longer in use

perils (par. 2)   dangers

infertility (par. 2)   the lack of ability to have children

turbulent (par. 2)   very chaotic or uneasy

stupefying (par. 2)   bewildering

obese (par. 3)   very fat, overweight

entrapment (par. 4)   the act of trapping, sometimes by devious methods

yearning (par. 4)   a strong desire

euphoric (par. 7)   characterized by a feeling of well-being

proverbial (par. 13)   relating to a proverb or accepted truth

infidelity (par. 13)   sexual unfaithfulness

These days so many marriages end in divorce that our 1
most sacred vows no longer ring with truth. "Happily ever
after" and "Till death do us part" are expressions that seem
on the way to becoming obsolete. Why has it become so hard
for couples to stay together? What goes wrong? What has happened to us that close to one-half of all marriages are destined
for the divorce courts? How could we have created a society
in which 42 percent of our children will grow up in single-parent homes? If statistics could only measure loneliness, regret, pain, loss of self-confidence and fear of the future, the
numbers would be beyond quantifying.

Even though each broken marriage is unique, we can still 2
find the common perils, the common causes for marital de-

spair. Each marriage has crisis points and each marriage tests endurance, the capacity for both intimacy and change. Outside pressures such as job loss, illness, infertility, trouble with a child, care of aging parents and all the other plagues of life hit marriage the way hurricanes blast our shores. Some marriages survive these storms and others don't. Marriages fail, however, not simply because of the outside weather but because the inner climate becomes too hot or too cold, too turbulent or too stupefying.

When we look at how we choose our partners and what 3 expectations exist at the tender beginnings of romance, some of the reasons for disaster become quite clear. We all select with unconscious accuracy a mate who will recreate with us the emotional patterns of our first homes. Dr. Carl A. Whitaker, a marital therapist and emeritus professor of psychiatry at the University of Wisconsin explains, "From early childhood on, each of us carried models for marriage, femininity, masculinity, motherhood, fatherhood and all the other family roles." Each of us falls in love with a mate who has qualities of our parents, who will help us rediscover both the psychological happiness and miseries of our past lives. We may think we have found a man unlike Dad, but then he turns to drink or drugs, or loses his job over and over again or sits silently in front of the T.V. just the way Dad did. A man may choose a woman who doesn't like kids just like his mother or who gambles away the family savings just like his mother. Or he may choose a slender wife who seems unlike his obese mother but then turns out to have other addictions that destroy their mutual happiness.

A man and a woman bring to their marriage bed a 4 blended concoction of conscious and unconscious memories of their parents' lives together. The human way is to compulsively repeat and recreate the patterns of the past. Sigmund Freud so well described the unhappy design that many of us get trapped in: the unmet needs of childhood, the angry feelings left over from frustrations of long ago, the limits of trust and the recurrence of old fears. Once an individual senses this entrapment, there may follow a yearning to escape, and the result could be a broken, splintered marriage.

Of course people can overcome the habits and attitudes   5
that developed in childhood. We all have hidden strengths and
amazing capacities for growth and creative change. Change,
however, requires work—observing your part in a rotten pattern, bringing difficulties out into the open—and work runs
counter to the basic myth of marriage: "When I wed this person all my problems will be over. I will have achieved success
and I will become the center of life for this other person and
this person will be my center, and we will mean everything to
each other forever." This myth, which every marriage relies
on, is soon exposed. The coming of children, the pulls and
tugs of their demands on affection and time, place a considerable strain on that basic myth of meaning everything to each
other, of merging together and solving all of life's problems.

Concern and tension about money take each partner   6
away from the other. Obligations to demanding parents or
still-depended-upon parents create further strain. Couples today must also deal with all the cultural changes brought on in
recent years by the women's movement and the sexual revolution. The altering of roles and the shifting of responsibilities
have been extremely trying for many marriages.

These and other realities of life erode the visions of mar-   7
ital bliss the way sandstorms eat at rock and the ocean nibbles
away at the dunes. Those euphoric, grand feelings that accompany romantic love are really self-delusions, self-hypnotic
dreams that enable us to forge a relationship. Real life, failure
at work, disappointments, exhaustion, bad smells, bad colds
and hard times all puncture the dream and leave us stranded
with our mate, with our childhood patterns pushing us this
way and that, with our unfulfilled expectations.

The struggle to survive in marriage requires adaptability,   8
flexibility, genuine love and kindness and an imagination
strong enough to feel what the other is feeling. Many marriages fall apart because either partner cannot imagine what
the other wants or cannot communicate what he or she needs
or feels. Anger builds until it erupts into a volcanic burst that
buries the marriage in ash.

It is not hard to see, therefore, how essential communi-   9
cation is for a good marriage. A man and a woman must be

able to tell each other how they feel and why they feel the way they do; otherwise they will impose on each other roles and actions that lead to further unhappiness. In some cases, the communication patterns of childhood—of not talking, of talking too much, of not listening, of distrust and anger, of withdrawal—spill into the marriage and prevent a healthy exchange of thoughts and feelings. The answer is to set up new patterns of communication and intimacy.

At the same time, however, we must see each other as   10
individuals. "To achieve a balance between separateness and closeness is one of the major psychological tasks of all human beings at every stage of life," says Dr. Stuart Bartle, a psychiatrist at the New York University Medical Center.

If we sense from our mate a need for too much intimacy,   11
we tend to push him or her away, fearing that we may lose our identities in the merging of marriage. One partner may suffocate the other partner in a childlike dependency.

A good marriage means growing as a couple but also   12
growing as individuals. This isn't easy. Richard gives up his interest in carpentry because his wife, Helen, is jealous of the time he spends away from her. Karen quits her choir group because her husband dislikes the friends she makes there. Each pair clings to each other and are angry with each other as life closes in on them. This kind of marital balance is easily thrown as one or the other pulls away and divorce follows.

Sometimes people pretend that a new partner will solve   13
the old problems. Most often extramarital sex destroys a marriage because it allows an artificial split between the good and the bad—the good is projected on the new partner and the bad is dumped on the head of the old. Dishonesty, hiding and cheating create walls between men and women. Infidelity is just a symptom of trouble. It is a symbolic complaint, a weapon of revenge, as well as an unraveler of closeness. Infidelity is often that proverbial last straw that sinks the camel to the ground.

All right—marriage has always been difficult. Why then   14
are we seeing so many divorces at this time? Yes, our modern social fabric is thin, and yes the permissiveness of society has created unrealistic expectations and thrown the family into

chaos. But divorce is so common because people today are unwilling to exercise the self-discipline that marriage requires. They expect easy joy, like the entertainment on TV, the thrill of a good party.

Marriage takes some kind of sacrifice, not dreadful self-   15
sacrifice of the soul, but some level of compromise. Some of one's fantasies, some of one's legitimate desires have to be given up for the value of the marriage itself. "While all marital partners feel shackled at times, it is they who really choose to make the marital ties into confining chains or supporting bonds, says Dr. Whitaker. Marriage requires sexual, financial and emotional discipline. A man and a woman cannot follow every impulse, cannot allow themselves to stop growing or changing.

Divorce is not an evil act. Sometimes it provides salva-   16
tion for people who have grown hopelessly apart or were frozen in patterns of pain or mutual unhappiness. Divorce can be, despite its initial devastation, like the first cut of the surgeon's knife, a step toward new health and a good life. On the other hand, if the partners can stay past the breaking up of the romantic myths into the development of real love and intimacy, they have achieved a work as amazing as the greatest cathedrals of the world. Marriages that do not fail but improve, that persist despite imperfections, are not only rare these days but offer a wondrous shelter in which the face of our mutual humanity can safely show itself.

BUILDING VOCABULARY

1. Roiphe loads her essay with some very common expressions to make the discussion more easily understandable to the reader. Below is a list of ten such expressions. Use each in a sentence of your own.

   a. ring with truth (par. 1)
   b. crisis points (par. 2)
   c. tender beginnings (par. 3)
   d. mutual happiness (par. 3)

   e. marriage bed (par. 4)
   f. hidden strengths (par. 5)
   g. marital bliss (par. 7)
   h. healthy exchange (par. 9)
   i. childlike dependency (par. 11)
   j. social fabric (par. 14)

2. Locate and explain five terms that the author draws from psychology.

UNDERSTANDING THE WRITER'S IDEAS

1. What are the "sacred vows" the author mentions in paragraph 1? Identify the source of the expressions "happily ever after" and "till death do us part." What does she mean when she says that these expressions "seem on the way to becoming obsolete"?

2. What is a "single-parent home"?

3. How does Roiphe define "endurance" in a marriage? What does she mean by "outside pressures" in paragraph 2? What are some of these pressures? Does Roiphe feel they are the primary causes for marriages failing? Why?

4. According to the essay, how do we choose husbands and wives? What is the meaning of "our first home" in paragraph 3? According to Roiphe, for what reasons is the way we choose mates a possible cause for marriages failing?

5. What is the "basic myth" of marriage? How does it create a possibly bad marriage?

6. How have the women's movement and the sexual revolution created strains on modern marriages?

7. Explain what the writer means by "Real life, failure at work, disappointments, exhaustion, bad smells, bad colds, and hard times" in paragraph 7. How do they affect marriages?

8. What is the role of communication between husband and

wife in a marriage? What are the results of poor communication? What solutions to this problem does Roiphe suggest?

9. What two types of "growth" does Roiphe suggest as necessary to a good marriage? Who are Richard, Helen, and Karen, named in paragraph 12?

10. According to Roiphe, what is the common cause for extramarital sexual affairs? What are her projected results of infidelity?

11. What does Roiphe identify as the primary cause of divorce? What does she propose as a solution to this problem?

12. According to the last paragraph, do you think Roiphe is in favor of each divorce? Why? In this paragraph, she presents both the positive and negative effects of divorce. What are the positive effects? the negative effects?

UNDERSTANDING THE WRITER'S TECHNIQUES

1. How does the title almost predict for the reader that the writer's main technique of development will be cause-and-effect analysis?

2. One strategy for developing an introductory paragraph is to ask a question. What is the purpose of the questions that the author asks in the opening paragraph? What is the relationship among the questions? How do the questions themselves dictate a cause-effect pattern of development? How do they immediately involve the reader in the topic?

3. In which paragraph does Roiphe list the immediate or common causes of marital failure? Why is this placement effective?

4. The use of clear *topic sentences* for each paragraph can often be an important technique in writing a clear causal

analysis because they usually identify main causes for the
effect under discussion. Identify the topic sentences for
paragraphs 3, 4, and 6. What causes for marriage failure
does each identify?

5. What causal chain of behavior does Roiphe build in paragraphs 8 to 13?

6. Why does Roiphe begin paragraph 14 with the words "All
   right"? Whom is she addressing? How does this address
   compare with the technique used in her introduction?

7. What two authorities does Roiphe quote in this essay?
   How are their citations useful? How are they identified? In
   what ways do their identifications add to their credibility as
   sources of opinions or information on Roiphe's topic?

8. Where does Roiphe use statistics in this essay? Why is it
   especially important to the development of the article?

9. Roiphe makes use of *definition* (see pages 238–239) in a
   number of places in this essay. What are her definitions of
   the following:

   a. "work" in a marriage (par. 5)
   b. "A good marriage" (par. 12)
   c. "divorce" (par. 16)
   d. "marriages that do not fail but improve" (par. 16)

   Locate other places where she uses definition.

10. In some essays, the introduction and conclusion are each
    simply the first and last paragraphs. In this essay, the
    writer uses more than one paragraph for each. Which
    paragraphs make up her introduction? Which make up the
    conclusion? Why might she have structured her introduc-
    tion and conclusion in this way? How does the structure
    affect the essay?

11. You have learned that two of the most common types of
    comparisons used by writers to enliven their essays are
    similes and *metaphors*. Look up the definition of these
    terms in the Glossary to refresh your memory. In addi-

tion, writers may use *extended metaphors*. This technique relies upon a number of metaphoric comparisons which revolve around a main idea rather than a single comparison. Roiphe uses comparisons in a number of paragraphs in this essay. In each of the following cases identify and explain the comparisons indicated:

- **a.** extended metaphor (par. 2)
- **b.** metaphor (par. 7)
- **c.** metaphor (par. 8)
- **d.** metaphor (par. 9)
- **e.** simile (par. 14)
- **f.** metaphor (par. 15)
- **g.** similes, metaphors (par. 16)

How does Roiphe's frequent use of metaphors and similes affect the tone of the essay?

12. Why does Roiphe end her essay with references to successful marriages? Would you consider that as being off the topic? Why or why not?

EXPLORING THE WRITER'S IDEAS

1. Roiphe discusses quite a few causes for marriages failing. Discuss with the class some additional causes. Why are they also important?

2. Paragraph 6 states that "Couples today must also deal with all the cultural changes brought on in recent years by the women's movement and the sexual revolution." Identify these two social phenomena. Among the people you know, have these cultural changes affected their marriages? How? If you are not married, and plan to marry, do you feel that the changes will present any foreseeable problems? If you are not married, and do not plan to marry, have they influenced your decision in any ways? What other effects have these two movements had in American society? Do you think these influences have been positive or negative? Why?

3. If you are married or in a close relationship, how did you choose your mate? If you are not married or in a relationship, what qualities would you look for in a mate? Why?

4. In paragraphs 6 and 7, Roiphe mentions "realities of life" that destroy romantic notions of "marital bliss." What other realities can you add to her list?

5. Paragraph 15 discusses the idea of self-sacrifice in marriage. Roiphe writes, "Some of one's fantasies, some of one's legitimate desires have to be given up for the value of the marriage itself." However, some people insist that for a marriage to survive, each partner must maintain complete integrity, that is, must not be forced into major sacrifices of values or life-styles. What is your opinion of these two opposing viewpoints?

6. Both Gregg Easterbrook in "Escape Valve" (pages 248–250) and Judy Syfers in "I Want a Wife" (pages 415–417) provide some insights into marriage that complement Roiphe's. How do their positions compare with hers? How, for example, could the principle of "automatic-out" explain to some degree why marriages fail?

IDEAS FOR WRITING

Guided Writing

Using cause-and-effect analysis, write an essay in which you explain *why marriages succeed.*

1. Limit your topic sufficiently so that you can concentrate your discussion on closely interrelated cause-and-effect patterns.

2. In the introduction, involve your reader with a series of pertinent questions.

3. Identify what many people think are common or immediate

causes of successful marriages; then show how other causes are perhaps even more important.

4. In the course of your essay, cite at least one relevant statistic that will add extra importance to your topic.

5. Try to use at least one quotation from a reputable authority. Consult your library for books and articles that deal with marriage. Be sure to include full identification of your source.

6. Use clear topic sentences in each paragraph as you present analysis of the various causes for successful marriages.

7. Make use of metaphors, similes, and extended metaphors.

8. In your essay, offer necessary definitions of terms that are especially important to your topic. Try for at least one definition by negation.

9. Write a conclusion in which you make some commentary upon divorce. Make your comment as an outgrowth of your discussion of a successful marriage.

More Writing Projects

1. In an essay of approximately 750 to 1000 words, explain the reasons why you ever ended a relationship (a marriage, a close friendship, a relationship with a girlfriend or boyfriend). Also discuss how you knew when you had reached the "breaking point." Did you feel you had hung on too long or had given up too soon?

2. Write a long letter to a friend explaining why you think he or she should end or not end a marriage, relationship, or friendship. Be sure to include clear reasons.

3. Write an essay in which you explain the effects of divorce in the lives of the couple involved. Here, do not concern yourself with causes; look only at the results of the failed marriage.

Rite of Spring

Arthur Miller

The renowned author of such modern dramatic classics as *Death of a Salesman*, *The Crucible*, and *A View from the Bridge* reveals the causes behind his thirty-six-year mixed relationship with his vegetable gardens. Miller's facility with descriptions and transitions allows him to move deftly between the realities of dirt between his fingers and the abstractions of God's purposes for the universe.

Words to Watch

atavism (par. 1)   a throwback to past patterns

wafts (par. 3)   drifts dreamily

bountiful (par. 6)   plentiful; in great supply

paternal (par. 7)   relating to fatherhood

maternal (par. 7)   relating to motherhood

proliferating (par. 7)   growing by rapid reproduction of new parts

botanist (par. 9)   a scientist concerned with plant life

toddles (par. 9)   walks with short, tottering steps

compensations (par. 10)   rewards; payments for services

metamorphose (par. 10)   to change significantly from one form to another

mason (par. 12)   a skilled worker in stone

perpetual (par. 12)   everlasting

unregenerate (par. 12)   not reformed from past ways

I have never understood why we keep a garden and why, 1 over 36 years ago when I bought my first house in the country, I started digging up a patch for vegetables before doing anything else. When you think how easy and cheap, relatively, it is to buy a bunch of carrots or beets, why raise them? And root crops especially are hard to tell apart, when store-bought, from our own. There is an atavism at work here, a kind of back-breaking make-believe that has no reality. Besides, I don't particularly like eating vegetables. I'd much rather eat something juicy and fat. Like hot dogs.

Now, hot dogs and mustard with some warm ₂ sauerkraut—if you could raise *them* outside your window, you'd really have something you could justify without a second's hesitation. Or a hot pastrami vine.

As it is, though, I can't deny that come April I find my- ₃ self going out to lean on the fence and look at that cursed rectangle, resolving with all my rational powers not to plant it again. But inevitably a morning arrives when, just as I am awakening, a scent wafts through the window, something like earth-as-air, a scent that seems to come up from the very center of this planet. And the sun means business, suddenly, and has a different, deeper yellow in its beams on the carpet. The birds begin screaming hysterically, thinking what I am thinking—the worms are deliciously worming their way through the melting soil.

It is not only pleasure sending me back to stare at that ₄ plot of soil, it is really conflict. The question is the same each year—what method should we use? The last few years we unrolled 36-inch-wide black plastic between the rows, and it worked perfectly, keeping the soil moist in dry times and weed-free.

But black plastic looks so industrial, so unromantic, that ₅ I have gradually moved over to hay mulch. We cut a lot of hay and, as it rots, it does improve the soil's composition. Besides, it looks lovely, and comes to us free.

Keeping a garden makes you aware of how delicate, ₆ bountiful, and easily ruined the surface of this little planet is. In that 50-by-70-foot patch there must be a dozen different types of soil. Parsley won't grow in one part but loves another, and the same goes for the other crops. I suppose if you loaded the soil with chemical fertilizer these differences would be less noticeable, but I use it sparingly and only in rows right where seeds are planted rather than broadcast over the whole area. I'm not sure why I do this beyond the saving in fertilizer and my unwillingness to aid the weeds.

The attractions of gardening, I think, at least for a cer- ₇ tain number of gardeners, are neurotic and moral. Whenever life seems pointless and difficult to grasp, you can always get out in the garden and *get something done*. Also, your paternal or maternal instincts come into play because helpless living things are depending on you, require training and encouragement and protection from enemies. In some cases, as with squash and cucumbers, your offspring—as it were—begin to turn upon you in massive numbers, proliferating more and more each morning and threatening to follow you into the house to strangle you in their vines.

Gardening is a moral occupation, as well, because you **8** always start in spring resolved to keep it looking neat this year, just like the pictures in the catalogues. But by July, you once again face the chaos of unthinned carrots, lettuce and beets. This is when my wife becomes—openly now—mistress of the garden. A consumer of vast quantities of vegetables, she does the thinning and hand-cultivating of the tiny plants. Squatting, she patiently moves down each row selecting which plants shall live and which she will cast aside.

At about this time, my wife's 86-year-old mother, a bot- **9** anist, makes her first visit to the garden. She looks about skeptically. Her favorite task is binding the tomato plants to stakes. She is an outspoken, truthful woman, or she was until she learned better. Now, instead of saying, "You have planted the tomatoes in the damp part of the garden," she waits until October when she makes her annual trip to her home in Europe; then she gives me my good-by kiss and says offhandedly, "Tomatoes in damp soil tend more to get fungi," and toddles away to her plane. But by October nothing in the garden matters, so sure am I that I will never plant it again.

I garden, I suppose, because I must. It would be intoler- **10** able to have to pass an unplanted fenced garden a few times a day. There are also certain compensations, and these must be what annually tilt my mind toward all that work. There are few sights quite as gratifyingly beautiful as a vegetable garden glistening in the sun, all dewy and glittering with a dozen shades of green at seven in the morning. Far lovelier, in fact, than rows of hot dogs. In some pocket of the mind there may even be a tendency to metamorphose this vision into a personal reassurance that all this healthy growth, this orderliness

and thrusting life must somehow reflect similar movements in
one's own spirit. Without a garden to till and plant I would not
know what April was for.

As it is, April is for getting irritated all over again at this   11
pointless, time-consuming hobby. I do not understand people
who claim to "love" gardening. A garden is an extension of
oneself—or selves—and so it has to be an arena where striving
does not cease, but continues by other means. As an example:
you simply have to face the moment when you must admit
that the lettuce was planted too deep or was not watered
enough, cease hoping it will show itself tomorrow, and dig up
the row again. But you will feel better for not standing on your
dignity. And that's what gardening is all about—character
building. Which is why Adam was a gardener. (And we all
know where it got him, too.)

But is it conceivable that the father of us all should have   12
been a mason, weaver, shoemaker, or anything but a gardener? Of course not. Only the gardener is capable of end-
lessly reviving so much hope that this year, regardless of
drought, flood, typhoon, or his own stupidity, this year he is
going to do it *right!* Leave it to God to have picked the proper
occupation for his only creature capable of such perpetual and
unregenerate self-delusion.

I suppose it should be added, for honesty's sake, that the   13
above was written on one of the coldest days in December.

BUILDING VOCABULARY

1. Explain the meaning of the following figurative expressions:

   a. I started *digging up a patch* (par. 1)
   b. without *a second's hesitation* (par. 2)
   c. the sun *means business* (par. 3)
   d. my unwillingness *to aid the weeds* (par. 6)
   e. *tilt my mind* (par. 10)
   f. in some *pocket of my mind* (par. 10)
   g. an *arena* where striving does not cease (par. 11)

2. Use any five of the Words to Watch in original sentences that show you understand their meanings.

UNDERSTANDING THE WRITER'S IDEAS

1. Who is the "we" of paragraph 1? The "you"? Why does Miller use these pronouns in the very beginning?

2. What are "root crops" (par. 1)?

3. What is a "rite"? Explain the meaning of the title.

4. What is "that cursed rectangle" (par. 3)? Why is it "cursed"?

5. Why do they cover the garden with black plastic? What is *mulch*? Why do they switch to it from using the plastic?

6. Name the main reasons why Miller *does* garden. Name the reasons why he would consider *not* gardening. How does he relate the two in the essay?

7. What are the "helpless living things" mentioned in paragraph 7?

8. How does Miller's mother-in-law figure in his gardening rites? Does he appreciate her role or not?

9. Why does Miller "not understand people who claim to 'love' gardening"?

10. What is the meaning of the sentence, "Which is why Adam was a gardener" (par. 11)? What attitude or tone is expressed in the parenthetical sentence that follows?

UNDERSTANDING THE WRITER'S TECHNIQUES

1. How does the repetition of the word "why" in paragraph 1 give us clues to the rhetorical nature of this essay?

2. In paragraph 1, Miller seems to make contradictory statements. He calls gardening "back-breaking," yet he also says it is "make-believe" and "has no reality." How can something unreal be back-breaking? Why does he link these elements?

3. Among his categories of reasons for gardening, Miller includes pleasure, conflict, neurosis, and morality. Summarize in your own words Miller's development of each of those categories of causes. How does he organize these categories within the essay? Which does he consider most important? Explain your answer with references to Miller's technique: placement in essay, key words, rhetorical strategies, and so on.

4. Paragraph 3 is particularly descriptive (see Chapter 3). How does Miller use various sensory imagery—olfactory, aural, visual—in this paragraph? How does he use *simile, metaphor,* and *personification* (see Glossary)?

5. Analyze the cause-and-effect development of paragraphs 4 and 5, and of paragraph 6.

6. Miller's use of transitions between paragraphs is highly effective, but not too obvious on first reading. Comment on the various transitions that connect the paragraphs in this piece.

7. How and where does Miller use *personification* (see Glossary) in this essay? Is it effective? Why?

8. Although Miller focuses quite well on specifics, he also makes some broad generalizations, some of them even spiritual in nature. Identify a few such generalizations and explain their meanings.

9. In this essay, does Miller concentrate more on causes or effects? Explain.

10. What would you say is Miller's overall attitude toward vegetable gardening? Does he maintain one attitude throughout the essay? If not, why does he change?

11. Does this essay have a thesis? If so, where is it placed? Why?

12. What is the meaning of Miller's last-paragraph "confession"? What is its purpose?

EXPLORING THE WRITER'S IDEAS

1. Arthur Miller is a world-famous, Pulitzer Prize–winning playwright whose plays have become an integral part of social and political thought from Providence to Peking. How does he qualify to write about vegetable gardening? Do you feel his essay is accurate? Do you feel that Miller is a "city boy" writing about "country things"? How well do you trust Miller's information in this essay? Explain.

2. Miller writes about both the satisfaction and hardship of growing things. What have been your experiences with planting or growing things—from houseplants to farm crops? How does it make you feel?

3. Generally, when you create things, do you get the most satisfaction from the process or the product? From tangible results or from spiritual and emotional uplifts? Explain with examples.

IDEAS FOR WRITING

Guided Writing

Write an essay in which you explain why for years you have pursued a certain hobby or activity about which you have mixed feelings.

1. Begin your essay with a series of questions about your motives for pursuing this activity.

2. State how long you've been involved in it.

3. Use contradictory statements to describe your mixed feelings.

4. Offer some absurd alternative to doing this activity.

5. Organize your essay into broad categories of reasons why you continue.

6. To explain the categories of reasons, use combinations of rhetorical modes that help you make your point.

7. Use some sensory imagery and figurative language.

8. Use clear, yet subtle, transitions between paragraphs.

9. Try to connect your activity—and your reasons for pursuing it—with some result that goes beyond the immediate or obvious ones.

10. Near the end of your essay, identify the main reason why you and others pursue this hobby or activity.

11. Relate your reasoning to more abstract or spiritual reasons.

12. End with a tongue-in-cheek confession about how or why you wrote this essay.

More Writing Projects

1. Write an essay in which you explain why you recently did something you didn't want to.

2. Explain how and why you recently became interested in some new activity or philosophy.

3. Write an essay in which you explain the effects of a certain requirement at your school.

The Ambivalence of Abortion

Linda Bird Francke

In this autobiographical narrative, author Linda Bird Francke tells about her mixed feelings toward the issue of abortion. Although she has strong political convictions on the subject, her ambivalence surfaces when she must confront abortion personally. Notice how she blends descriptive details with personal insights to explain the reasons for her uncertainty.

Words to Watch

dwell (par. 1)   keep attention directed on something

heralded (par. 1)   announced in a joyous manner

rationalize (par. 2)   to justify one's behavior (especially to oneself)

freelance (par. 3)   working without long-range contractual agreements

cycled (par. 5)   moved through a complete series of operations or steps

common denominator (par. 10)   similar traits or themes

rhetoric (par. 13)   ways of speaking or writing effectively

fetus (par. 13)   an unborn child still in the mother's womb

neurotic (par. 14)   emotionally unstable

vaccinated (par. 14)   injected with a harmless virus to produce immunity to a disease

inoculated (par. 14)   treated with a serum or antibody to prevent disease

uterus (par. 16)   the womb; the place within the mother where the fetus develops

sensation (par. 18)   feeling

Novocain (par. 18)   a drug used to numb the feeling of pain

quivered (par. 18)   shook

We were sitting in a bar on Lexington Avenue when I 1
told my husband I was pregnant. It is not a memory I like to
dwell on. Instead of the champagne and hope which had her-

alded the impending births of the first, second and third child, the news of this one was greeted with shocked silence and Scotch. "Jesus," my husband kept saying to himself, stirring the ice cubes around and around. "Oh, Jesus."

Oh, how we tried to rationalize it that night as the start- 2 ing time for the movie came and went. My husband talked about his plans for a career change in the next year, to stem the staleness that fourteen years with the same investment-banking firm had brought him. A new baby would preclude that option.

The timing wasn't right for me either. Having juggled 3 pregnancies and child care with what freelance jobs I could fit in between feedings, I had just taken on a full-time job. A new baby would put me right back in the nursery just when our youngest child was finally school age. It was time for *us,* we tried to rationalize. There just wasn't room in our lives now for another baby. We both agreed. And agreed. And agreed.

How very considerate they are at the Women's Ser- 4 vices, known formally as the Center for Reproductive and Sexual Health. Yes, indeed, I could have an abortion that very Saturday morning and be out in time to drive to the country that afternoon. Bring a first morning urine specimen, a sanitary belt and napkins, a money order or $125 cash—and a friend.

My friend turned out to be my husband, standing awk- 5 wardly and ill at ease as men always do in places that are exclusively for women, as I checked in at nine A.M. Other men hovered around just as anxiously, knowing they had to be there, wishing they weren't. No one spoke to each other. When I would be cycled out of there four hours later, the same men would be slumped in their same seats, locked downcast in their cells of embarrassment.

The Saturday morning women's group was more dispir- 6 ited than the men in the waiting room. There were around fifteen of us, a mixture of races, ages and backgrounds. Three didn't speak English at all and a fourth, a pregnant Puerto Rican girl around eighteen, translated for them.

There were six black women and a hodgepodge of 7

whites, among them a T-shirted teenager who kept leaving the
room to throw up and a puzzled middle-aged woman from
Queens with three grown children.

"What form of birth control were you using?" the vol- 8
unteer asked each one of us. The answer was inevitably
"none." She then went on to describe the various forms of
birth control available at the clinic, and offered them to each
of us.

The youngest Puerto Rican girl was asked through the in- 9
terpreter which she'd like to use: the loop, diaphragm, or pill.
She shook her head "no" three times. "You don't want to
come back here again, do you?" the volunteer pressed. The
girl's head was so low her chin rested on her breastbone. "*Sí,*"
she whispered.

We had been there two hours by that time, filling out 10
endless forms, giving blood and urine, receiving lectures. But
unlike any other group of women I've been in, we didn't talk.
Our common denominator, the one which usually floods
across language and economic barriers into familiarity, today
was one of shame. We were losing life that day, not giving it.

The group kept getting cut back to smaller, more work- 11
able units, and finally I was put in a small waiting room with
just two other women. We changed into paper bathrobes and
paper slippers, and we rustled whenever we moved. One of
the women in my room was shivering and an aide brought her
a blanket.

"What's the matter?" the aide asked her. "I'm scared," 12
the woman said. "How much will it hurt?" The aide smiled.
"Oh, nothing worse than a couple of bad cramps," she said.
"This afternoon you'll be dancing a jig."

I began to panic. Suddenly the rhetoric, the abortion 13
marches I'd walked in, the telegrams sent to Albany to counteract the Friends of the Fetus, the Zero Population Growth
buttons I'd worn, peeled away, and I was all alone with my
microscopic baby. There were just the two of us there, and
soon, because it was more convenient for me and my husband, there would be one again.

How could it be that I, who am so neurotic about life 14
that I step over bugs rather than on them, who spend hours

planting flowers and vegetables in the spring even though we rent out the house and never see them, who make sure the children are vaccinated and inoculated and filled with vitamin C, could so arbitrarily decide that this life shouldn't be?

"It's not a life," my husband had argued, more to convince himself than me. "It's a bunch of cells smaller than my fingernail." 15

But any woman who has had children knows that certain feeling in her taut, swollen breasts, and the slight but constant ache in her uterus that signals the arrival of a life. Though I would march myself into blisters for a woman's right to exercise the option of motherhood, I discovered there in the waiting room that I was not the modern woman I thought I was. 16

When my name was called, my body felt so heavy the nurse had to help me into the examining room. I waited for my husband to burst through the door and yell "stop," but of course he didn't. I concentrated on three black spots in the acoustic ceiling until they grew in size to the shape of saucers, while the doctor swabbed my insides with antiseptic. 17

"You're going to feel a burning sensation now," he said, injecting Novocain into the neck of the womb. The pain was swift and severe, and I twisted to get away from him. He was hurting my baby, I reasoned, and the black saucers quivered in the air. "Stop," I cried. "Please stop." He shook his head, busy with his equipment. "It's too late to stop now," he said. "It'll just take a few more seconds." 18

What good sports we women are. And how obedient. Physically the pain passed even before the hum of the machine signaled that the vacuuming of my uterus was completed, my baby sucked up like ashes after a cocktail party. Ten minutes start to finish. And I was back on the arm of the nurse. 19

There were twelve beds in the recovery room. Each one had a gaily flowered draw sheet and a soft green or blue thermal blanket. It was all very feminine. Lying on these beds for an hour or more were the shocked victims of their sex, their full wombs now stripped clean, their futures less encumbered. 20

It was very quiet in that room. The only voice was that of the nurse, locating the new women who had just come in so 21 she could monitor their blood pressure, and checking out the recovered women who were free to leave.

Juice was being passed about, and I found myself sipping   22 a Dixie cup of Hawaiian Punch. An older woman with tightly curled bleached hair was just getting up from the next bed. "That was no goddamn snap," she said, resting before putting on her miniskirt and high white boots. Other women came and went, some walking out as dazed as they had entered, others with a bounce that signaled they were going right back to Bloomingdale's.

Finally then, it was time for me to leave. I checked out,   23 making an appointment to return in two weeks for an IUD insertion. My husband was slumped in the waiting room, clutching a single yellow rose wrapped in a wet paper towel and stuffed into a Baggie.

We didn't talk the whole way home, but just held hands   24 very tightly. At home there were more yellow roses and a tray in bed for me and the children's curiosity to divert.

It had certainly been a successful operation. I didn't   25 bleed at all for two days just as they had predicted, and then I bled only moderately for another four days. Within a week my breasts had subsided and the tenderness vanished, and my body felt mine again instead of the eggshell it becomes when it's protecting someone else.

My husband and I are back to planning our summer va-   26 cation and his career switch.

And it certainly does make more sense not to be having   27 a baby right now—we say that to each other all the time. But I have this ghost now. A very little ghost that only appears when I'm seeing something beautiful, like the full moon on the ocean last weekend. And the baby waves at me. And I wave at the baby. "Of course, we have room," I cry to the ghost. "Of course, we do."

BUILDING VOCABULARY

1. Develop definitions of your own for the italicized words by relying on context clues, that is, clues from surrounding

words and sentences. Then check your definition against a dictionary definition.

a. "My husband talked about his plans for a career change in the next year, *to stem* the staleness that fourteen years with the same investment-banking firm had brought him. A new baby would *preclude* that *option*." (par. 2)

b. "Though I would march myself into blisters for a woman's right to *exercise* the *option* of motherhood, I discovered there in the waiting room that I was not the modern woman I thought I was." (par. 16)

c. "The pain was *swift* and *severe,* and I twisted to get away from him." (par. 18)

d. "Lying on these beds for an hour or more were the shocked victims of their sex, their full wombs now stripped clean, their futures less *encumbered*." (par. 20)

e. "It had certainly been a successful operation. I didn't bleed at all for two days just as they had predicted, and then I bled only *moderately* for another four days." (par. 25)

2. For each italicized word in Column A, write the correct *synonym* (a word of similar meaning) from Column B. Look up unfamiliar words in a dictionary.

Column A

1 *impending* birth (par. 1)
2 *hovered* around (par. 5)
3 looked *downcast* (par. 5)
4 more *dispirited* (par. 6)
5 *puzzled* middle-aged woman (par. 7)
6 *inevitably* "none" (par. 8)
7 *taut* swollen breasts (par. 16)
8 how *obedient* (par. 19)
9 curiosity to *divert* (par. 24)
10 had *subsided* (par. 25)

Column B

a decreased
b complying
c confused
d lingered
e about to happen
f tight
g distract
h dejected
i unavoidable
j discouraged

UNDERSTANDING THE WRITER'S IDEAS

1. What is the setting in which Francke breaks the news to her husband that she is pregnant? How does he receive the news?

2. What reasons does the husband give for not wanting another child? Why does Francke feel it is a bad time for herself as well?

3. What is the attitude of the men waiting at the abortion clinic? Explain.

4. Why is there a women's group meeting before Francke actually gets her abortion? Are all the women pretty much alike at this meeting? How so? What is Francke's attitude toward these other women? Give specific examples to support your answer.

5. What common reason do all the women in the group share for being pregnant?

6. In the past, what was the author's viewpoint concerning women's rights to have abortions? What specific examples does she give to illustrate this point of view? Do you assume that she still holds this opinion? Why?

7. What examples does Francke give to illustrate that she supports life? Are they convincing?

8. Explain what the author means by the statement "Though I would march myself into blisters for a woman's right to exercise the option of motherhood, I discovered there in the waiting room that I was not the modern woman I thought I was" (par. 16).

9. When she is in the examining room, what does the author do to deal with her anxieties about the abortion?

10. Explain what the woman means when she says to Francke, " 'That was no goddamn snap.' "

11. How does Francke know the operation has been successful?

UNDERSTANDING THE WRITER'S TECHNIQUES

1. What rhetorical strategy does the word "ambivalence" in the title suggest? How does Francke use that strategy in the very first paragraph? Where does she use it elsewhere in the essay?

2. Does Francke successfully explain the ambivalence named in the title? Why or why not?

3. Which does this analysis concentrate on more—causes, effects, or a combination of the two? What evidence can you offer to support your answer? What specifically is the relationship between cause and effect in paragraphs 6 to 10? Analyze the pattern of cause and effect in paragraphs 19 to 22.

4. What is the use of narration in this essay? What is the narrative *point of view* (see Glossary) in this selection? How is it used to enhance the essay?

5. What would you say is the overall tone of the selection? The author uses repetition in this essay to help set that tone. How does the repetition in "We both agreed. And agreed. And agreed." (par. 3) contribute to it?

6. *Paradox* is a special variety of irony (see Glossary) in which there is a clear contradiction in a situation. A paradox is a statement or attitude which, on the surface, seems unlikely, and yet, on analysis, can indeed be true. For example, it is paradoxical that the author should have such ambivalent feelings about abortion while she is sitting in an abortion clinic. Why is that situation considered paradoxical? What other paradoxes do you find in this essay?

7. What is the function of description in this essay? Select passages in which you feel the descriptions are especially vivid. How is description used by the author to characterize the women mentioned in paragraph 22? Are the women stereotyped in this description? Explain.

8. Only toward the last part of the essay does Francke use any metaphors or similes—some of them quite startling. Identify the metaphors or similes in paragraph 19, paragraph 25, and paragraph 27. Why do you think she saved this figurative language for the end?

9. Analyze the last paragraph. What causes and effects discussed throughout the essay are echoed here? What new ones are suggested? Compare the effect of the statement " 'Of course, we have room' " to the statement in paragraph 3, "There just wasn't room...." How does this repetition affect the conclusion?

10. Writers who write about highly charged emotional issues must take special care to avoid *sentimentality*—the excessive display of emotion (see Glossary). Has Francke been successful in avoiding it everywhere in the essay? How has she used concrete descriptions to avoid being sentimental? Does the conclusion strike you as being excessively emotional or does it strike you simply as a dramatic but effective closing? Explain your responses.

EXPLORING THE WRITER'S IDEAS

1. When this article was originally published in 1976, it appeared under the *pseudonym* (a fictitious name) "Jane Doe." What reason might Linda Francke have had for not using her real name? Why do you think that a few years later she admitted to the authorship of the article? In general, what do you think about a writer publishing his or her work under an assumed name? Explain. What historical examples can you offer for the use of pseudonyms?

2. Francke describes some very intimate personal emotions and experiences in her attempt to explain what causes her ambivalence toward abortion. On the basis of the material presented, do you think she is justified in feeling ambivalent? Do you feel she should have been more definite one way or the other? Why?

3. In her description of the Saturday morning women's group (pars. 6 to 10), Francke shows that the women present were of all types—"a mixture of races, ages, and backgrounds." This suggests, of course, that abortion is a subject affecting all women. Does it, in fact, affect all women equally? Explain your answer.

4. In paragraph 5, the author describes her husband as "standing awkwardly and ill at ease as men always do in places that are exclusively for women." What sorts of places are exclusively for persons of one sex? Discuss how you felt and acted if you were ever in a place which was really more for persons of the opposite sex.

5. Much controversy about abortion revolves around modern definitions of life and death. Some people argue that life begins at conception; others argue that life begins at birth. With which group do you agree? Why? How has modern science complicated our concepts of life and death?

6. Abortion and antiabortion forces have increased their attacks against each other dramatically in recent years. How does Francke's essay crystallize both sides of the complex, emotionally charged issue?

IDEAS FOR WRITING

Guided Writing

Select an important issue facing society, an issue with which you have had personal experience and about which you have mixed feelings. After you fill in the blank, write an essay titled "Two Sides of _____ ." In your essay explore the reasons for your ambivalence. You can select from a wide range of social, moral, health, or education topics. For example, you might want to consider ambivalence toward interracial dating or marriages, a compulsory draft, legalization of drugs, cigarette smoking, a liberal arts education—but feel free to select any issue that is especially important to you.

1. Write the essay as a first-person narrative. Begin with an incident when you first clearly realized the ambivalent nature of the issue, and explain why or how this particular incident focused your attention on the subject.

2. Tell about how and for what reasons you came to a decision to take a certain action despite your mixed feelings. What rationalizations did you or others use to help you feel you were doing the right thing?

3. Narrate in detail the sequence of events that followed your decision. Make the narrative come to life with concrete sensory detail. As you tell your story, analyze the various causes and effects of your decision and actions.

4. Discuss how the same event you experienced affects others. Explain how the causes and effects of the action are different or similar for you and for others.

5. Explain how you felt immediately before, during, and after the crucial experience.

6. In your conclusion, express your deepest feelings about the consequences of your decision and experiences. Use similes, metaphors, and an echo of your original attempts to rationalize your ambivalence.

More Writing Projects

1. Write an essay in which you analyze the reasons for your own attitudes toward abortion.

2. Write an essay in which you explain the causes and/or effects of a political standpoint you feel very strongly about.

3. In an essay of analysis, propose the effects on children if elementary schools throughout the country offered compulsory sex education programs.

4. In 1968, Black Panther party leader Eldridge Cleaver ended a speech with the statement, "If you're not part of the solution, you're part of the problem." Analyze what you think Cleaver meant by that statement.

When Bright Girls Decide That Math Is "a Waste of Time"

Susan Jacoby

In this article, Susan Jacoby explains how cultural expectations and societal stereotyping are overshadowed by women's own decisions to keep themselves away from scientific and technological studies. Notice how she uses narrative and process analysis to reinforce the causes and effects she is exploring here.

Words to Watch

sanguine (par. 3) cheerful, hopeful

vulnerable (par. 6) open to attack or suggestion

syndrome (par. 7) a group of symptoms that characterize a condition

akin to (par. 7) similar to

phobia (par. 7) an excessive fear of something

constitute (par. 7) to make up; compose

epitomize (par. 8) to be a prime example of

prone (par. 15) disposed to; susceptible

accede to (par. 16) give in to

Susannah, a 16-year-old who has always been an A 1 student in every subject from algebra to English, recently informed her parents that she intended to drop physics and calculus in her senior year of high school and replace them with a drama seminar and a work-study program. She expects a major in art or history in college, she explained, and "any more science or math will just be a waste of my time."

Her parents were neither concerned by nor opposed to 2 her decision. "Fine, dear," they said. Their daughter is, after all, an outstanding student. What does it matter if, at age 16, she has taken a step that may limit her understanding of both machines and the natural world for the rest of her life?

383

This kind of decision, in which girls turn away from stud- 3
ies that would given them a sure footing in the world of science and technology, is a self-inflicted female disability that
is, regrettably, almost as common today as it was when I was
in high school. If Susannah had announced that she had decided to stop taking English in her senior year, her mother and
father would have been horrified. I also think they would have
been a good deal less sanguine about her decision if she were
a boy.

In saying that scientific and mathematical ignorance is 4
a self-inflicted female wound, I do not, obviously, mean
that cultural expectations play no role in the process. But
the world does not conspire to deprive modern women of
access to science as it did in the 1930's, when Rosalyn S.
Yalow, the Nobel Prize-winning physicist, graduated from
Hunter College and was advised to go to work as a secretary because no graduate school would admit her to its
physics department. The current generation of adolescent
girls—and their parents, bred on old expectations about women's interests—are active conspirators in limiting their
own intellectual development.

It is true that the proportion of young women in science- 5
related graduate and professional schools, most notably medical schools, has increased significantly in the past decade. It
is also true that so few women were studying advanced science and mathematics before the early 1970's that the percentage increase in female enrollment does not yet translate into
large numbers of women actually working in science.

The real problem is that so many girls eliminate them- 6
selves from any serious possibility of studying science as a result of decisions made during the vulnerable period of midad-
olescence, when they are most likely to be influenced—on
both conscious and subconscious levels—by the traditional
belief that math and science are "masculine" subjects.

During the teen-age years the well-documented phenom- 7
enon of "math anxiety" strikes girls who never had any problem handling numbers during earlier schooling. Some men,
too, experience this syndrome—a form of panic, akin to a
phobia, at any task involving numbers—but women constitute

the overwhelming majority of sufferers. The onset of acute math anxiety during the teen-age years is, as Stalin was fond of saying, "not by accident."

In adolescence girls begin to fear that they will be unat- 8 tractive to boys if they are typed as "brains." Science and math epitomize unfeminine braininess in a way that, say, foreign languages do not. High-school girls who pursue an advanced interest in science and math (unless they are students at special institutions like the Bronx High School of Science where everyone is a brain) usually find that they are greatly outnumbered by boys in their classes. They are, therefore, intruding on male turf at a time when their sexual confidence, as well as that of the boys, is most fragile.

A 1981 assessment of female achievement in mathemat- 9 ics, based on research conducted under a National Institute for Education grant, found significant differences in the mathematical achievements of 9th and 12th graders. At age 13 girls were equal to or slightly better than boys in tests involving algebra, problem solving and spatial ability; four years later the boys had outstripped the girls.

It is not mysterious that some very bright high-school 10 girls suddenly decide that math is "too hard" and "a waste of time." In my experience, self-sabotage of mathematical and scientific ability is often a conscious process. I remember deliberately pretending to be puzzled by geometry problems in my sophomore year in high school. A male teacher called me in after class and said, in a baffled tone, "I don't see how you can be having so much trouble when you got straight A's last year in my algebra class."

The decision to avoid advanced biology, chemistry, 11 physics and calculus in high school automatically restricts academic and professional choices that ought to be wide open to anyone beginning college. At all coeducational universities women are overwhelmingly concentrated in the fine arts, social sciences and traditionally female departments like education. Courses leading to degrees in science- and technology-related fields are filled mainly by men.

In my generation, the practical consequences of mathe- 12 matical and scientific illiteracy are visible in the large number of special programs to help professional women overcome the anxiety they feel when they are promoted into jobs that require them to handle statistics.

The consequences of this syndrome should not, how- 13 ever, be viewed in narrowly professional terms. Competence in science and math does not mean one is going to become a scientist or mathematician any more than competence in writing English means one is going to become a professional writer. Scientific and mathematical illiteracy—which has been cited in several recent critiques by panels studying American education from kindergarten through college—produces an incalculably impoverished vision of human experience.

Scientific illiteracy is not, of course, the exclusive prov- 14 ince of women. In certain intellectual circles it has become fashionable to proclaim a willed, aggressive ignorance about science and technology. Some female writers specialize in ominous, uninformed diatribes against genetic research as a plot to remove control of childbearing from women, while some well-known men of letters proudly announce that they understand absolutely nothing about computers, or, for that matter, about electricity. This lack of understanding is nothing in which women or men ought to take pride.

Failure to comprehend either computers or chromo- 15 somes leads to a terrible sense of helplessness, because the profound impact of science on everyday life is evident even to those who insist they don't, won't, can't understand why the changes are taking place. At this stage of history women are more prone to such feelings of helplessness than men because the culture judges their ignorance less harshly and because women themselves acquiesce in that indulgence.

Since there is ample evidence of such feelings in ado- 16 lescence, it is up to parents to see that their daughters do not accede to the old stereotypes about "masculine" and "feminine" knowledge. Unless we want our daughters to share our intellectual handicaps, we had better tell them no, they can't stop taking mathematics and science at the ripe old age of 16.

BUILDING VOCABULARY

1. Like Anne Roiphe (pages 353–357), Susan Jacoby uses a number of common expressions, but these are at a higher level of *diction* (the writer's choice of words depending on audience and purpose). Below are some of these expressions, which may contain words that are unfamiliar to you. First, look up any unfamiliar words in your dictionary. Then, write a short explanation of each expression as Jacoby uses it.

   a. sure footing (par. 3)
   b. cultural expectations (par. 4)
   c. overwhelming majority (par. 7)
   d. male turf (par. 8)
   e. spatial ability (par. 9)
   f. the exclusive province (par. 14)
   g. ominous, uninformed diatribes (par. 14)
   h. acquiesce in that indulgence (par. 15)
   i. ample evidence (par. 16)
   j. our intellectual handicaps (par. 16)

2. Explain the connotations (see Glossary) that the following words have for you: "disability" (par. 3), "conspire" (par. 4), adolescent (par. 4), "vulnerable" (par. 6), "acute" (par. 8). Use each of these words correctly in sentences of your own.

UNDERSTANDING THE WRITER'S IDEAS

1. What condition is Jacoby trying to analyze? Is the main *effect* analyzed in this cause-and-effect analysis? On what primary cause does she blame women's "scientific and mathematical ignorance"? What exactly does she mean by that term? How is society to blame? What is the "process" mentioned in paragraph 4? What point does the example of Rosalyn S. Yalow illustrate?

2. Why does Jacoby think that the greater proportion of women students now in science and medical graduate and professional schools does not really mean that there are many women working in these areas?

3. According to Jacoby, when do most girls decide not to study the sciences? Why does this happen?

4. What is "math anxiety"? Who suffers more from it—boys or girls? Why? What does the author mean by "brains" (par. 8)?

5. Who was Joseph Stalin (par. 7)?

6. What subjects does Jacoby identify as "feminine"? Which are "unfeminine"?

7. According to the research evidence discussed in paragraph 9, how do the math abilities of girls and boys change between ninth and tenth grades? What does Jacoby say is the *cause* for this change? What are the *results?*

8. Explain what Jacoby means by the expression "self-inflicted female wound" (par. 4) and "self-sabotage" (par. 10). How are these expressions similar? How are they different?

9. What is the difference between what men and women study at coeducational universities?

10. What does Jacoby mean by "mathematical and scientific illiteracy" (par. 12)? Do only women suffer from this syndrome? According to Jacoby, why does it lead to "an incalculably impoverished vision of human experience"? What does she mean by this phrase? What examples of scientific illiteracy does Jacoby offer?

11. Why does the author think women feel more helpless than men do about scientific changes?

12. What suggestion does Jacoby offer in her conclusion?

UNDERSTANDING THE WRITER'S TECHNIQUES

1. Which paragraphs make up the introductory section of this essay? What cause-and-effect relation does Jacoby establish and how does she present it? How does Jacoby use narration in her introduction? How does she use illustration?

2. What is the thesis statement of this essay? Why is it placed where it is? Find another statement before it that expresses a similar cause-and-effect relation. How are the two different?

3. Both sentences of paragraph 5 begin with the phrase "It is true," yet the sentences contradict each other. How and why does the author set up this contradiction? What is the effect on Jacoby's analysis of beginning paragraph 6 with the words "The real problem is..."?

4. How does she use *process analysis* (see pages 316–317) from paragraph 6 to paragraph 8?

5. Where does the author use definition in this essay?

6. Trace the cause-and-effect developments in paragraphs 7 and 8.

7. In paragraph 9, Jacoby mentions a study conducted under "a National Institute for Education grant." How does the evidence she presents support her position in the essay?

8. What is the effect of the phrase "in my experience" in paragraph 10? What expository technique does she use there?

9. Trace the cause-and-effect patterns in paragraphs 11 through 13. Be sure to show the interrelationship between the causes and the effects (that is, how can the effect of something also be the cause of something else?).

10. How is the first sentence of paragraph 15 ("Failure to

comprehend...."") a good example in itself of cause-and-effect development?

11. Why does Jacoby use quotation marks around the words "masculine" and "feminine" in the phrase "'masculine' and 'feminine' knowledge" (par. 16)?

12. What is the overall tone of this essay? At three points, Jacoby switches tone and uses irony (see Glossary). Explain the irony in the following sentences:

    a. "What does it matter if, at age 16, she has taken a step that may limit her understanding of both machines and the natural world for the rest of her life?" (par. 2)

    b. "The onset of acute math anxiety during the teenage years is, as Stalin was fond of saying, 'not by accident'." (par. 7)

    c. "Unless we want our daughters to share our intellectual handicaps, we had better tell them no, they can't stop taking mathematics and science at the ripe old age of 16." (par. 16)
       Compare the irony in paragraph 16 with that in paragraph 2. How is the impact the same or different?

13. Who do you think is the intended *audience* for this essay? Cite evidence for your answer.

14. Jacoby uses a variety of transitional devices to connect smoothly the ideas expressed in the various paragraphs of this essay. Look especially at paragraphs 1 to 4. How does the writer achieve coherence between paragraphs? What transitional elements do you find in the opening sentences of each of those paragraphs? What other transitions do you find throughout the essay?

EXPLORING THE WRITER'S IDEAS

1. One of the underlying suggestions in this essay is that society has long considered there to be "masculine" and "feminine" subjects to study. What is your opinion on this

issue? Do you feel that any subjects are particularly more suited to men or women? Which? Why? Are there any other school activities that you feel are exclusively masculine or feminine? Why? Are there any jobs that are more suited to men or women?

2. In paragraph 4, Jacoby mentions the "old expectations about women's interests." What do you think these expectations are? What do you consider *new* expectations for women?

3. A *stereotype* is an opinion of a category of people that is unoriginal and often based on strong prejudices. For example, some prejudicial stereotypes include "All immigrants are lazy"; "All Republicans are rich"; "All women are terrible drivers." What other stereotypes do you know? Where do you think they originate?

4. The general implication of paragraph 8 is that people minimize their skills in order to be socially acceptable. In your experience, where have you seen this principle operating? Do people sometimes pretend to be unable to achieve something? What motivates them, do you think?

5. A recent study shows that among major nations in the world America's students—boys and girls—are the worst mathematics students. How do you account for the poor showing of Americans as mathematicians? How would you remedy this situation?

IDEAS FOR WRITING

Guided Writing

Select a job or profession that is usually male-dominated. Write a cause-and-effect analysis explaining how and why women both have been excluded from this profession *and* (or) have self-selected themselves from the job. (Some examples may include firefighters, physicians, marines, bank executives, carpenters, and so on.)

1. Begin with an anecdote to illustrate the condition that you are analyzing.

2. Present and analyze the partial causes of this condition that arise from society's expectations and norms.

3. State your main point clearly in a thesis statement.

4. Clearly identify what you consider "the real problem."

5. If you believe that women have deliberately excluded themselves, explain when and how the process of self-selection begins for women.

6. Analyze the consequences of this process of self-selection and give examples of the results of it.

7. Provide evidence that supports your analysis.

8. Link paragraphs with appropriate transitions.

9. In your conclusion offer a suggestion to change or improve this situation.

More Writing Projects

1. Margaret Mead, the famous anthropologist, once wrote, "Women in our society complain of the lack of stimulation, of the loneliness, of the dullness of staying at home." Write a causal analysis of this situation.

2. Write an analysis of why boys and men exclude themselves from a certain field of profession—nursing, cooking, grammar-school teaching, and so on.

CHAPTER 11

Argumentation
and Persuasion

Argumentation in prose is an attempt to convince the reader to have the opinion *you* have on a subject; frequently, it also involves an effort to persuade the reader to act in a particular manner. In many ways, argumentation is a good end point for a course in writing. In a formal argument, you can use, according to your purpose, all the prose strategies and principles of sound composition practiced until now.

You can see how important it is to state your thesis very clearly in argumentation, and to support your main point with convincing minor points. You have to make these points according to reason, and you need to arrange them so they have the greatest effect on your reader. Moreover, as in any prose, writers of argument must offer the reader particulars of details, whether sensory, quoted, statistical, or based upon historical evidence. Finally, techniques of comparison, process analysis, description, narration, cause and effect, definition, all can help strengthen an argument.

Although argumentation reflects all these earlier prose techniques, it is important for you to understand the special characteristics of this method. To begin with, although argumentation as a written form is often emotional, it differs sharply from those little battles and those major disagreements with friends over coffee or in hallways outside class. Perhaps that last shouting match between you and your friend about who would win the World Series is, no doubt, one that you would call an argument: There is a disagreement there for which each of you tries to make your own point of view stick. Yet often these argumentative conversations deteriorate into loss of temper, angry personal comments about your friend's judgment or character, departures from the argument itself, and inability to reason.

In written arguments, writers always should keep clearly in mind the point they wish to make, and should not lose sight of it. They may try to convince readers that some issue requires action ("Colleges and businesses should follow special admissions procedures for minority applicants"). Or, they may try to convince readers that something is true ("Wives are taken for granted"). Whatever the point, writers always offer their reasons for their beliefs in a logical way, without losing command of their subject and without attacking anyone personally; they may, though, attack someone's ideas or attitudes.

The main point in an argument—often termed the *major proposition*—is an idea which is debatable or can be disputed. As such it differs from theses in ordinary essays, which state main ideas without necessarily taking sides. The major proposition gives an essay its "argumentative edge." Frequently this argumentative edge appears in the very title of the essay, and it should form the basis of a crisp introductory paragraph laying out the terms of the position that you plan to take.

Once you state clearly and carefully your major proposition at the outset of the essay, you must then proceed to *convince* readers about the position that you have taken. There are basic strategies to succeed in this goal, beginning with the ordered presentation of reasons to defend the major proposition. We term these reasons *minor propositions*—in other words, assertions designed to support your main argument. To support each minor proposition, the writer must offer *evidence* in the form of facts, statistics, testimony from authorities, and personal experience. Here, a variety of writing methods, ranging from comparison and contrast to definition to causal analysis, can serve to develop minor propositions effectively.

In addition to presenting your own argument logically and convincingly, you must also recognize and deal with opposing arguments, a technique called *refutation*. Obviously, there has to be more than one side to any debatable issue, and you have to take this fact into account. For one thing, acknowledgment of the opposition indicates fairness on your part—a willingness to recognize that there *are* two sides to the argument. More significantly, your refutation of rival propositions, both major and minor, makes your own case more convincing. Whether at the outset of your argumentative essay or in the body as you are developing your own minor propositions, you should take care to indicate opposing views and to refute them effectively.

An argumentative essay ultimately is only as strong as the logic that a writer brings to it. Such logical errors as hasty generalizations (main ideas unsupported by sufficient evidence), attacks on the opposition's character, faulty conclusions that do not follow from the facts, faulty analogies, and excessive appeals to emotion damage your argument. In short, any convincing argument requires clear, orderly thinking. By learning how to present ideas logically through the preparation of convincing argumentative essays, you will strengthen your overall reasoning ability. You will also learn how to deal with those arguments, many of which are important, that occur in your daily life.

Softening the Stories for Children

Stephen Leacock

In this selection from *The Leacock Roundabout* (1969), the author argues against the revision of children's stories in the name of reducing the horror and violence. In his view, such horror is not real to children in the same way it is to adults; on the contrary, it actually seems to be a valuable and time-tested learning device. Leacock richly illustrates his proposition, and his discussion remains accessible and "nonclinical" throughout.

Words to Watch

tendencies (par. 11)   trends; personal inclinations

fundamental (par. 12)   basic; essential

feebly (par. 17)   with little strength

pathetic (par. 17)   pitiful

conglomeration (par. 18)   collection; mixed coherent mass

inveigled (par. 18)   lured; enticed

iota (par. 19)   an infinitesimal amount

unscathed (par. 20)   physically or emotionally unhurt

vitals (par. 23)   inner organs

scope (par. 24)   range of subject

oscillation (par. 25)   back-and-forth motion

chasm (par. 30)   deep canyon

ogres (par. 31)   monsters

timorous (par. 32)   shy; nervous

What is the story that you are reading, Peggy?" I asked 1
of a wide-eyed child of eight, who sat buried in a story book.

"Little Red Riding Hood," she answered. 2

"Have you come to the part," I asked, "where the 3
grandmother gets eaten?"

"She didn't get eaten!" the child protested in surprise. 4

"Yes—the wolf comes to her cottage and knocks at the 5

door and she thinks that it is Little Red Riding Hood and opens the door and the wolf eats her.''

She shook her head.   6

''That's not it at all in this book,'' she said.   7

So I took a look at the page before her and I read: 8

''Then the wolf pushed open the door of the cottage and   9
rushed in but the grandmother was not there as she happened not to be at home.''

Exactly! The grandmother, being a truly up-to-date   10
grandmother, was probably out on the golf links, or playing bridge with a few other grandmothers like herself.

At any rate she was not there and so she escaped getting   11
eaten by the wolf. In other words, Little Red Riding Hood, like all the good old stories that have come down from the bad old times, is having to give way to the tendencies of a human age. It is supposed to be too horrible for the children to read. The awful fate of the grandmother, chawed up by the wolf— or, no, swallowed *whole* like a Malpecque oyster, is too terrible for them to hear. So the story, like a hundred other stories and pictures, has got to be censored, re-edited, and incidentally—spoiled.

All of which rests on a fundamental error as to literature   12
and as to children. There is no need to soften down a story for them. They like it rough.

''In the real story,'' I said to the little girl, ''the grand-   13
mother was at home, and the wolf rushed in and ate her in one mouthful!''

''Oh! that's *much* better!'' she exclaimed.   14

''And then, afterwards, when the hunters came in, they   15
killed the wolf and cut his stomach open and the grandmother jumped out and was saved!''

''Oh, isn't that splendid!'' cried the child.   16

In other words, all the terror that grown-up people see in   17
this sort of story is there for grown-up people only. The children look clean over it, or past it, or under it. In reality, the vision of the grandmother feebly defending herself against the savage beast, or perhaps leaping round the room to get away from him, and jumping up on top of the grandfather's clock— is either horrible, or weird, or pathetic, or even comic, as we

may happen to see it. But to the children it is just a story—and a good one—that's all.

And all the old stories are the same! Consider Jack the 18 Giant-Killer. What a conglomeration of weeping and wailing, of people shut into low dungeons, of murder, of sudden death, of blood, and of horror! Jack, having inveigled an enormous giant into eating an enormous quantity of porridge, then rips him up the stomach with a huge sword! What a mess!

But it doesn't disturb Jack or his young readers one iota. In 19 fact, Jack is off again at once with his young readers trailing eagerly after him, in order to cut off at one blow the three huge heads of a three-headed giant and make a worse mess still.

From the fairy stories and the giant stories the children 20 presently pass on—quite unscathed as I see it—to the higher range of the blood-and-thunder stories of the pirates and the battles. Here again the reality, for the grown-up mind that can see it, is terrible and gruesome; but never so for the boys and girls who see in it only the pleasant adventure and bright diversity.

Take, for instance, this familiar scene as it appears and 21 reappears in the history of Jack Dare-devil, or Ned Fearnothing, or any of those noble boys who go to sea, in books, at the age of fourteen and retire, as admirals, at twenty-two.

"The fire from both ships was now becoming warm. A 22 round shot tearing across the deck swept off four of our fellows. 'Ha! ha!' said Jack, as he turned towards Ned on the quarterdeck, 'this bids fair to become lively.' "

It certainly did. In fact, it would be lively already if one 23 stopped to think of the literal and anatomical meaning of a round shot—twenty-five pounds of red-hot iron—tearing through the vitals of four men. But the boy reader never gets it this way. What is said is, that four of our fellows were "swept off"—just that; merely "swept off" and that's the way the child reader takes it. And when the pirates "leap on deck," Jack himself "cuts down" four of them and Ned "cuts down" three. That's all they do—"they cut them down," they just "shorten them" so to speak.

Very similar in scope and method was the good old 24

"half-dime novel," written of the days of the "prairie," and the mountain trail, the Feathered Indian and the Leathered Scout. In these, unsuspecting strangers got scalped in what is now the main street of Denver—where they get skinned.

These stories used to open with a rush and kept in rapid 25 oscillation all the time. In fact they began with the concussion of firearms.

"'Bang! Bang! Bang!' Three shots rang out over the 26 prairie and three feathered Indians bit the dust."

It seemed always to be a favourite pastime of the Indi- 27 ans—"biting dust."

In grim reality—to the grown-up mind—these were sto- 28 ries of terror—of midnight attack, of stealthy murder with a knife from without the folds of the tent, of sudden death in dark caverns, of pitiless enemies, and of cruel torture.

But not so to the youthful mind. He followed it all 29 through quite gayly, sharing the high courage of his hero— Dick Danger the Dauntless. "I must say," whispered Dick to Ned (this was when the Indians had them tied to a tree and were piling grass and sticks round it so as to burn them alive), "I must say, old man, things begin to look critical. Unless we can think of some way out of this fix, we are lost."

Notice, please, this word "lost": in reality they would 30 be worse than lost. They'd be *cooked*. But in this class of literature the word "lost" is used to cover up a multitude of things. And, of course, Dick does think of a way out. It occurs to him that by moving his hands he can slip off the thongs that bind him, set Ned free, leap from the tree to the back of a horse, of two horses, and then by jumping over the edge of a chasm into the forest a thousand feet below, they can find themselves in what is called "comparative safety." After which the story goes calmly on, oblivious of the horrible scene that nearly brought it to an end.

But as the modern parent and the modern teacher have 31 grown alarmed, the art of story-telling for children has got to be softened down. There must be no more horror and blood and violent death. Away with the giants and the ogres! Let us have instead the stories of the animal kingdom in which Wee-

Wee the Mouse has tea on a broad leaf with Goo-Goo the Cat-
erpillar, and in which Fuzzy the Skunk gives talks on animal
life that would do for Zoology Class I at Harvard.

But do we—do they—can we escape after all from the   32
cruel environment that makes up the life in which we live? Are
the animals after all so much softer than the ogres, so much
kinder than the pirates? When Slick the Cat crackles up the
bones of Wee-Wee the Mouse, how does that stand! And when
Old Mr. Hawk hovers in the air watching for Cheep-Cheep the
chicken who tries in vain to hide under the grass, and calls for its
lost mother—how is that for terror! To my thinking the timorous
and imaginative child can get more real terror from the pictured
anguish of a hunted animal than from the deaths of all the Welsh
giants that ever lived on Plynlimmon.

The tears of childhood fall fast and easily, and evil be to   33
him who makes them flow.

How easily a child will cry over the story of a little boy   34
lost, how easily at the tale of poverty and want, how incon-
solably at death. Touch but ever so lightly these real springs of
anguish and the ready tears will come. But at Red Riding
Hood's grandmother! Never! She didn't *die!* She was merely
eaten. And the sailors, and the pirates, and the Apache Indians! They don't *die,* not in any real sense to the child. They
are merely "swept off," and "mowed down"—in fact, scattered like the pieces on an upset chessboard.

The moral of all which is, don't worry about the appar-   35
ent terror and bloodshed in the children's books, the real children's books. There is none there. It only represents the way
in which little children, from generation to generation, learn in
ways as painless as can be followed, the stern environment of
life and death.

BUILDING VOCABULARY

1. A *euphemism* is the substitution of an agreeable or inoffen-
   sive expression for one that may offend or suggest something unpleasant. Throughout the essay, Leacock illus-

trates how children's stories often use such expressions. In your own words, explain the following italicized euphemisms, which Leacock claims appear commonly in children's stories.

 a. A round shot tearing across the deck *swept off four of our fellows.* (par. 22)
 b. they *cut him down* (par. 23)
 c. three feathered Indians *bit the dust* (par. 26)
 d. Unless we can think of some way out of *this fix, we are lost.* (par. 29)

2. Leacock uses various adjective-noun combinations where the adjective isn't necessary for meaning, but makes the writing more vivid and interesting. For each of the following combinations, write a synonym or definition for the adjective. Then, write *two* new sets of combinations: In the first, use the same noun, but a different, equally descriptive adjective; in the second, keep the original adjective, but use another noun. For example, "familiar scene" (par. 21) might be recast first as "idyllic scene" and then as "familiar surroundings."

 a. wide-eyed child (par. 1)
 b. up-to-date grandmother (par. 10)
 c. fundamental error (par. 12)
 d. savage beast (par. 17)
 e. bright diversity (par. 20)
 f. noble boys (par. 21)
 g. anatomical meaning (par. 23)
 h. grim reality (par. 28)
 i. midnight attack (par. 28)
 j. stealthy murder (par. 28)
 k. pitiless enemies (par. 28)
 l. cruel torture (par. 28)
 m. comparative safety (par. 30)
 n. ready tears (par. 34)
 o. apparent terror (par. 35)
 p. stern environment (par. 35)

UNDERSTANDING THE WRITER'S IDEAS

1. Who is the little girl reading "Little Red Riding Hood" in the beginning of the essay? How does the version of the story she's reading differ from the traditional tale? Why has it been changed? In what way did the story "give way to the tendencies of a human age"? What is the girl's reaction to hearing the original story? Why?

2. What does Leacock mean by "the bad old times" (par. 11)?

3. Briefly summarize Leacock's attitude toward "softening down" stories for children.

4. In general, how do adults deal with the violence and terror in children's stories? How do children deal with it?

5. Name and describe the different *types* of children's stories that Leacock discusses (*not* the specific stories themselves).

6. Discuss the reality and fairy tale meanings of two of the examples that the author presents.

7. What is a "half-dime novel"? The "days of the 'prairies'"?

8. According to Leacock, what is the attitude of "the modern parent and the modern teacher" toward children's stories? Does he agree or disagree? How do you know?

9. Are the stories referred to in paragraphs 31 and 32 real children's stories? Explain. What is the author trying to say when he writes: "Fuzzy the Skunk gives talks in animal life that would do for Zoology Class I at Harvard"? What is the main meaning of paragraph 32? Why does Leacock refer to "Welsh giants" and "Plynlimmon"?

10. Explain the meaning of the single-sentence paragraph 33.

11. According to the author, what is the ultimate purpose or value of children's stories to which some adults object?

12. For Leacock, what is the use and value of *euphemisms* (see Building Vocabulary, page 400) in children's stories? Illustrate your answer with examples from the essay.

UNDERSTANDING THE WRITER'S TECHNIQUES

1. Describe Leacock's argumentative *purpose* in this essay. Is it primarily to *convince* or to *persuade?*

2. Is there a single-sentence statement of the *main proposition* (see page 400) of this essay? Explain.

3. Leacock uses *refutation* (see page 395) both as a running theme and at a specific point of development in the essay. Analyze his use of refutation as an argumentative strategy. How does he use *hyperbole* (see Glossary) as a means to develop his refutation?

4. How does the author make use of *illustration* and *classification?*

5. Where does Leacock use *anecdotal narration* in the essay? What purpose does it serve?

6. Write the sentences that are the *minor propositions* of this essay. How do they help to organize Leacock's thoughts?

7. The author uses *comparison and contrast* as a means to advance his thesis by pointing out the differences in adults' and children's views on various stories or types of stories. Go through the essay again, and for each story or type discussed, summarize the different views.

8. Excluding the dialogue, Leacock makes use of two 1-sentence paragraphs in this essay. What are they? Why does he use them?

9. Describe the overall *tone* of this essay. By what techniques does the author create that tone?

10. Leacock begins paragraph 32, "But do we—do they—can we escape...." Why does he shift pronouns? Why does he use dashes?

11. At some points, Leacock makes a direct address to the reader. Where does he do this? For what purpose?

12. Evaluate Leacock's use of *transitions*. What transitions does he use between his discussions of the various categories of children's stories? Between the introduction and main body of the essay? Between the main body and the conclusion?

EXPLORING THE WRITER'S IDEAS

1. What is your opinion of Leacock's basic premise that "there is no need to soften down a story" for children? "They like it rough."

2. In recent years, television cartoons for children have come under attack for being excessively violent. Do you agree or disagree with this criticism? Use specific examples to illustrate your opinion.

3. In his essay, "Fairy Tales and Modern Stories" (pages 230–233), psychologist Bruno Bettelheim claims that fairy tales can be very useful in helping children deal with problems. Compare Bettelheim's and Leacock's views concerning the value of children's stories.

4. Censorship or revision of works for moral or political reasons is an age-old, hotly debated, and sensitive issue. In the recent past, Nazi book burnings and Orwell's book *1984* have been but two vivid reminders of this issue. What examples of such censorship or revisionism have you observed in very recent times? Include examples from areas other than writing. Do you feel such actions could ever be justified? Explain and illustrate your answer.

5. Do you think it is a good idea to use *euphemisms* (see page

400) when talking with children? Why? Make a list of some of the most common euphemisms adults use with children and indicate their literal meanings. What euphemisms do adults use with other adults? Illustrate your answer.

6. What are some of your favorite children's stories? Why? Which have you found most frightening or upsetting? Why?

7. What effects do horror films such as *Friday the 13th, Nightmare on Elm Street, Psycho,* or *The Texas Chain Saw Massacre* have on people? At some showings of such films, many in the audience—including kids—laugh and seem to enjoy the horror. Is it possible that people have become desensitized to such horror? Explain. How are you affected by such films?

IDEAS FOR WRITING

Guided Writing

Write an essay in which you argue for or against stricter censorship of violence on television.

1. Begin with an anecdote that illustrates your opinion and invokes a specific TV program.

2. Evaluate how a specific incident of television violence affected someone in a way consistent with your main idea.

3. State your major proposition in a short paragraph.

4. Continue the original anecdote in such a way that it further reinforces your proposition.

5. Organize the body of your essay around specific illustrations of programs or types of programs.

6. Include clear *minor propositions* that help organize your essay.

7. Throughout the essay, compare two points of view concerning your thesis and the types of program that you are using as illustrations.

8. Explain a number of euphemisms used on violent programs in order to make them more or less acceptable. Depending on your thesis, indicate how such euphemisms have a positive or negative affect on viewers.

9. Devote a paragraph or two to *refutation*.

10. Make some direct appeals or addresses to your reader.

11. End with a moral judgment as to the ultimate value of imposing stricter censorship on television violence.

More Writing Projects

1. Write an essay in which you favor the elimination of the ratings system for movies. (Or, write in favor of its being made more strict.)

2. Argue for or against such magazines as *Playboy* or *Penthouse* being sold in supermarkets and convenience stores.

3. Write a letter to a friend in which you attempt to persuade him or her to break a particular habit (smoking, drinking, nail biting, daydreaming, or some other habit).

The Vandal and the Sportsman
Joseph Wood Krutch

Joseph Wood Krutch is a renowned author, scholar, and social commentator. Here he argues forcefully—sometimes even righteously—
against sports hunting. He uses language for its fullest impact, telling
us of "pure evil," "a fathomless abyss," and "wicked ideas." This
essay, from *The Best Nature Writing of Joseph Wood Krutch,* is a
model of both logical and emotional appeal in argumentative writing.

Words to Watch

impediment (par. 3)   obstacle

vitality (par. 3)   the quality distinguishing the living from the dead

wantonly (par. 3)   without moral restraint

unassailable (par. 5)   unquestionable

compassion (par. 6)   deep understanding of others' feelings

quail (par. 7)   a stout-bodied game bird

delinquency (par. 7)   living immorally

cultivate (par. 7)   develop

It would not be quite true to say that "some of my best 1
friends are hunters." Nevertheless, I do number among my
respected acquaintances some who not only kill for the sake
of killing but count it among their keenest pleasures. I can
think of no better illustration of the fact that men may be separated at some point by a fathomless abyss yet share elsewhere much common ground.

To me it is inconceivable how anyone should think an 2
animal more interesting dead than alive. I can also easily
prove to my own satisfaction that killing "for sport" is the
perfect type of that pure evil for which metaphysicians have
sometimes sought.

Most wicked deeds are done because the doer proposes 3
some good to himself. The liar lies to gain some end; the swindler and thief want things which, if honestly got, might be

good in themselves. Even the murderer may be removing an impediment to normal desires or gaining possession of something which his victim keeps from him. None of these usually does evil for evil's sake. They are selfish or unscrupulous, but their deeds are not gratuitously evil. The killer for sport has no such comprehensible motive. He prefers death to life, darkness to light. He gets nothing except the satisfaction of saying, "Something which wanted to live is dead. There is that much less vitality, consciousness, and, perhaps, joy in the universe. I am the Spirit that Denies." When a man wantonly destroys one of the works of man we call him Vandal. When he wantonly destroys one of the works of God we call him Sportsman.

The hunter-for-food may be as wicked and as misguided   4 as vegetarians sometimes say; but he does not kill for the sake of killing. The rancher and the farmer who exterminate all living things not immediately profitable to them may sometimes be working against their own best interests; but whether they are or are not, they hope to achieve some supposed good by their exterminations. If to do evil not in the hope of gain but for evil's sake involves the deepest guilt by which man can be stained, then killing for killing's sake is a terrifying phenomenon and as strong a proof as we could have of that "reality of evil" with which present-day theologians are again concerned.

Despite all this I know that sportsmen are not necessar-   5 ily monsters. Even if the logic of my position is unassailable, the fact still remains that men are not logical creatures; that most if not all are blind to much they might be expected to see and are habitually inconsistent; that both the blind spots and the inconsistencies vary from person to person.

To say as we all do: "Any man who would do A would   6 do B," is to state a proposition mercifully proved false almost as often as it is stated. The murderer is not necessarily a liar any more than the liar is necessarily a murderer, and few men feel that if they break one commandment there is little use in keeping the others. Many have been known to say that they considered adultery worse than homicide but not all adulterers are potential murderers and there are even murderers to whom incontinence would be unthinkable. So the sportsman

may exhibit any of the virtues—including compassion and respect for life—everywhere except in connection with his
"sporting" activities. It may even be often enough true that,
as "antisentimentalists" are fond of pointing out, those ten-
derest toward animals are not necessarily most philanthropic.
They no more than sportsmen are always consistent.

When the Winchester gun company makes a propaganda   7
movie concluding with a scene in which a "typical American
boy" shoots a number of quail and when it then ends with the
slogan "Go hunting with your boy and you'll never have to go
hunting for him," I may suspect that the gun company is
moved by a desire to sell more guns at least as much as by a
determination to do what it can toward reducing the incidence
of delinquency. I will certainly add also my belief that there
are even better ways of diminishing the likelihood that a boy
will grow up to do even worse things. Though it seems to me
that he is being taught a pure evil I know that he will not necessarily cultivate a taste for all or, for that matter, any one of
the innumerable other forms under which evil may be loved.

BUILDING VOCABULARY

1. Match each word or phrase in Column A with the word or
   phrase in Column B which most closely matches its meaning.

Column A

   1 keenest (par. 1)
   2 fathomless abyss (par. 1)
   3 pure evil (par. 2)
   4 gratuitously evil (par. 3)
   5 unscrupulous (par. 3)
   6 comprehensible motive
      (par. 3)
   7 habitually inconsistent
      (par. 5)
   8 incontinence (par. 6)
   9 philanthropic (par. 6)
   10 propaganda (par. 7)

Column B

   a immeasurable depths
   b ideas used to damage
      an opposing cause
   c understandable reason
   d dishonest
   e absolute immorality
   f lack of self-restraint
   g most special
   h with great generosity
   i usually changeable
   j vicious without cause

2. Both "metaphysicians" (par. 2) and "theologians" (par. 4) deal with questions of virtues (par. 6). Look up each word and write a definition.

3. What are the crimes of "adultery" and "homicide" (par. 6)?

UNDERSTANDING THE WRITER'S IDEAS

1. Does Krutch have many close friends who are hunters? How do you know? What does he think of his acquaintances that do enjoy hunting? Explain the sentence that tells you this information.

2. What is Krutch's opinion of hunting as a sport?

3. According to Krutch, what is the major motivation for which people do bad things? What examples does he offer to support his opinion? What does Krutch say is the primary motivation for sports hunters? How does this motivation differ from that of other "evil doers"?

4. For what does the author substitute the phrase "killer for sport" (par. 3)? Why?

5. Explain the difference between a Vandal and a Sportsman in your own words.

6. How are the hunters-for-food different from sports hunters? How are the ranchers and farmers different?

7. Try to explain the meaning of the sentence at the end of paragraph 4 which begins, "If to do evil...."

8. Explain the statement "men are not logical creatures" (par. 5) as it is used by Krutch in this essay.

9. What excuses does the author offer for sports hunters? Do you feel he believes these excuses? Why? In paragraph 6 what does he say about the ethics of sports hunting?

10. What does the phrase "if they break one commandment" refer to?

11. What is the Winchester gun company? What is Krutch's opinion of the film made by that company?

UNDERSTANDING THE WRITER'S TECHNIQUES

1. In your own words, what is Krutch's *major proposition* in this essay? Does he ever state it as a single-thesis statement? Why?

2. How does Krutch use logical explanation and appeals to intelligence in this essay? What is he trying to "prove"?

3. A special type of argumentative strategy is *ethical* appeal, in which the writer addresses the moral standards of his or her audience. What is the nature of Krutch's ethical appeal? How is it presented?

4. Throughout this essay Krutch uses very emotionally charged language to describe or explain things. One of the techniques of argumentation is to use such language subtly to influence your readers' opinions. For example, in paragraph 3, Krutch helps the reader to make unconscious connections between a sports hunter and "wicked deeds," a "liar," a "swindler," a "thief," and a "murderer." How and why does he do this?

   Read through the essay once again and find as many other examples of emotionally charged language as you can. How do these emotional or nonlogical appeals affect Krutch's intended audience?

5. One of the techniques the author uses is to put quotation marks (" ") around words or groups of words other than for the purpose of quotation or citation. What does the quotation mark indicate about the enclosed words? Find all the places Krutch uses this technique and explain the meaning of each word or phrase.

6. Krutch also uses exaggeration to influence his readers. *Hyperbole* is a type of very extravagant exaggeration—

heightened exaggeration, so to speak. Explain the hyperbole of the last part of paragraph 3, from "The Killer for
sport had...." to the end. How does this section influence your opinion? Why?

7. A good argumentative essay will in some way deal with
the opposition's argument to show that the writer has at
least recognized that differing opinions exist. Usually,
however, a writer will rebut (disprove) the opposition argument to enhance the correctness of his or her own opinions. Where in this essay does Krutch present the opposition argument? How does he deal with it? How does he
feel about the correctness of his own opinions? What one
sentence tells us so?

8. What is the tone of this essay? Give at least three examples to support your answer, at least one of which should
come from the introductory paragraph.

9. What is the purpose of the discussion of the film made by
the Winchester gun company? How does it connect to the
rest of the essay? How does Krutch use extended example in this discussion?

10. Explain the significance of the title.

EXPLORING THE WRITER'S IDEAS

1. In paragraph 3, Krutch compares sports hunters to liars,
thieves, even murderers. Do you think they are compara-
ble? Why?
    Krutch also says sports hunters enjoy killing and death.
Do you agree or disagree? Why?

2. Krutch makes a distinction between hunters-for-food and
sports hunters. What do you think are the differences between the two? Do you feel either is more or less justified
in his or her activity? Why?

3. The expression in quotations in the first paragraph ("some
of my best friends are hunters") is a parody of an expres-

sion often used by people attempting to hide or defend their prejudices. For example, a person might say, "But some of my best friends are Jewish (or black, or Irish, or Chinese, or...)" after making an ethnic slur or offensive remark. What is the purpose of Krutch's parody here? What does it tell us about the author?

4. Are there degrees of humaneness in sports hunting? For example, is it more humane to use a rifle, a shotgun, or a bow and arrow? Why?

If you have ever gone sports hunting, describe how you felt when you pulled the trigger or let the arrow fly. Explain what made you feel this way.

5. Research the sports hunting laws in your state. What are they? Do you think they are fair? If possible, find out on what basis some of the laws, quotas, and restrictions were made.

6. Krutch is very forceful and dogmatic in this essay, perhaps even a bit self-righteous at times. For instance, in paragraph 5 he says, "...the logic of my position is unassailable." How did the tone of this essay affect you? Were you ever put off by it or did it draw you nearer to the writer's position?

IDEAS FOR WRITING

Guided Writing

Write an argumentative essay in which you support or oppose hunting.

1. Acknowledge your opposition in the first paragraph of the essay. Explain your possible closeness to such individuals, but take a critical attitude toward their position regarding hunting.

2. Tell why it is "inconceivable" to you that anyone would support or oppose hunting.

3. Logically refute the propositions of those who oppose your position. After explaining your opposition's viewpoint, you can *deny* that their point is right or true; or you can *admit* that what they say seems reasonable, but that they have left out important ideas; or you can try to find a *shortcoming* in the way they reason about the topic.

4. Make your essay strong in *emotional* appeals. Lace your essay generously with emotionally charged terms and comparisons.

5. Introduce *ethical* appeals in support of your argument.

6. Carefully draw distinctions between different types of opponents.

7. End your essay with an extended example from an outside source that substantiates your proposition, that is, that puts your opponents in an unfavorable position.

More Writing Projects

1. Write a letter to the editor in which you argue for or against handgun controls.

2. Write an argumentative essay that responds to the following quotation from the American novelist and screenplay writer Nathaniel West: "In America violence is daily."

I Want a Wife

Judy Syfers

Judy Syfers, a wife and mother of two children, argues in this essay for a wife of her own. Although her argument might seem strange, her position will become apparent once you move into the essay. She presents many points to support her position, so you want to keep in mind those you think are the strongest.

Words to Watch

nurturant (par. 3)   giving affectionate care and attention

hors d'oeuvres (par. 6)   food served before the regular courses of the meal

monogamy (par. 8)   the habit of having only one mate; the practice of marrying only once during life

I belong to that classification of people known as wives. 1 I am A Wife. And, not altogether incidentally, I am a mother.

Not too long ago a male friend of mine appeared on the 2 scene fresh from a recent divorce. He had one child, who is, of course, with his ex-wife. He is obviously looking for another wife. As I thought about him while I was ironing one evening, it suddenly occurred to me that I, too, would like to have a wife. Why do I want a wife?

I would like to go back to school so that I can become 3 economically independent, support myself, and, if need be, support those dependent upon me. I want a wife who will work and send me to school. And while I am going to school I want a wife to keep track of the children's doctor and dentist appointments. And to keep track of mine, too. I want a wife to make sure my children eat properly and are kept clean. I want a wife who will wash the children's clothes and keep them mended. I want a wife who is a good nurturant attendant to my children, who arranges for their schooling, makes sure that they have an adequate social life with their peers, takes them to the park, the zoo, etc. I want a wife who takes care of the children when they are sick, a wife who arranges to be around when the children need special care, because, of course, I cannot miss classes at school. My wife must arrange to lose time at work and not lose the job. It may mean a small cut in my wife's income from time to time, but I guess I can tolerate that. Needless to say, my wife will arrange and pay for the care of the children while my wife is working.

I want a wife who will take care of *my* physical needs. I 4
want a wife who will keep my house clean. A wife who will pick up after me. I want a wife who will keep my clothes clean, ironed, mended, replaced when need be, and who will see to it that my personal things are kept in their proper place so that I can find what I need the minute I need it. I want a wife who cooks the meals, a wife who is a *good* cook. I want a wife who will plan the menus, do the necessary grocery shopping, prepare the meals, serve them pleasantly, and then do the cleaning up while I do my studying. I want a wife who will care for me when I am sick and sympathize with my pain and loss of time from school. I want a wife to go along when our family takes a vacation so that someone can continue to care for me and my children when I need a rest and change of scene.

I want a wife who will not bother me with rambling com- 5
plaints about a wife's duties. But I want a wife who will listen to me when I feel the need to explain a rather difficult point I have come across in my course of studies. And I want a wife who will type my papers for me when I have written them.

I want a wife who will take care of the details of my so- 6
cial life. When my wife and I are invited out by my friends, I want a wife who will take care of the babysitting arrangements. When I meet people at school that I like and want to entertain, I want a wife who will have the house clean, will prepare a special meal, serve it to me and my friends, and not interrupt when I talk about the things that interest me and my friends. I want a wife who will have arranged that the children are fed and ready for bed before my guests arrive so that the children do not bother us. I want a wife who takes care of the needs of my guests so that they feel comfortable, who makes sure that they have an ashtray, that they are passed the hors d'oeuvres, that they are offered a second helping of the food,

that their wine glasses are replenished when necessary, that their coffee is served to them as they like it.

And I want a wife who knows that sometimes I need a 7 night out by myself.

I want a wife who is sensitive to my sexual needs, a wife 8 who makes love passionately and eagerly when I feel like it, a wife who makes sure that I am satisfied. And, of course, I want a wife who will not demand sexual attention when I am not in the mood for it. I want a wife who assumes the complete responsibility for birth control, because I do not want more children. I want a wife who will remain sexually faithful to me so that I do not have to clutter up my intellectual life with jealousies. And I want a wife who understands that *my* sexual needs may entail more than strict adherence to monogamy. I must, after all, be able to relate to people as fully as possible.

If, by chance, I find another person more suitable as a 9 wife than the wife I already have, I want the liberty to replace my present wife with another one. Naturally, I will expect a fresh, new life; my wife will take the children and be solely-responsible for them so that I am left free.

When I am through with school and have a job, I want 10 my wife to quit working and remain at home so that my wife can more fully and completely take care of a wife's duties.

My God, who *wouldn't* want a wife?   11

BUILDING VOCABULARY

1. After checking a dictionary write definitions of each of these words:

   a. attendant (par. 3)
   b. adequate (par. 3)
   c. peers (par. 3)
   d. tolerate (par. 3)
   e. rambling (par. 5)
   f. replenished (par. 6)
   g. adherence (par. 8)

2. Write an original sentence for each word above.

UNDERSTANDING THE WRITER'S IDEAS

1. What incident made Syfers think about wanting a wife?

2. How would a wife help the writer achieve economic independence?

3. In what ways would a wife take care of the writer's children? Why would the writer like someone to assume those responsibilities?

4. What physical needs would Syfers's "wife" take care of?

5. How would a wife deal with the writer's social life? Her sex life?

UNDERSTANDING THE WRITER'S TECHNIQUES

1. In formal argumentation, we often call the writer's main point the *major, or main, proposition*. What is Syfers's major proposition? Is it simply what she says in paragraph 2, or is the proposition more complex than that? State it in your own words.

2. What is the value of the question Syfers asks in paragraph 2? Where else does she ask a question? What value does this other question have in its place in the essay? What impact does it have on the reader?

3. The points a writer offers to support the major proposition are called *minor propositions*. What minor propositions does Syfers present to show why she wants a wife? In which instance do they serve as topic sentences within paragraphs? What details does she offer to illustrate those minor propositions?

4. What order has the writer chosen to arrange the minor propositions? Why has she chosen such an order? Do you think she builds from the least to the most important reasons for having a wife? What changes would you urge in the order of the minor propositions?

5. Most of the paragraphs here develop through illustration. Where has Syfers used a *simple listing* of details? Why has she chosen that format?

6. Syfers's style is obviously straightforward, her sentences for the most part simple and often brief. Why has she chosen such a style? What is the effect of the repetition of "I want" at the start of so many sentences? Why has Syfers used several short paragraphs (5, 7, 9, 10, 11) in addition to longer ones?

7. What is the author's *tone* (see Glossary)? Point out the uses of *irony* (see Glossary) in the essay. How does irony contribute to Syfers's main intent in this essay? How does the fact that Syfers is a woman contribute to this sense of irony?

EXPLORING THE WRITER'S IDEAS

1. By claiming she wants a wife, Syfers is showing us all the duties and responsibilities of the woman in a contemporary household. Has Syfers represented these duties fairly? Do husbands generally expect their wives to do all these things?

2. To what degree do wives today fit Syfers's description? How could a wife avoid many of the responsibilities spelled out in the essay? How does the "modern husband" figure in the way many couples meet household responsibilities now?

3. Syfers has characterized all the traditional and stereotyped roles usually assigned to wives. What "wifely responsibilities" has she left out?

4. Has Syfers presented a balanced picture of the issues or is her argument one-sided? Support your opinion with specific references to the essay. Could the author have dealt effectively with opposing arguments? Why or why not? What might these opposing arguments be?

5. Answer the question in the last line of the essay.

IDEAS FOR WRITING

Guided Writing

Write an essay of 750 to 1,000 words, which you call, "I Want a Husband."

1. Write the essay from the point of view of a *man*. As Syfers wrote as a woman who wanted a wife, you write this essay as a man who wants a *husband*.

2. Start your essay with a brief personal story as in paragraph 2 in "I Want a Wife."

3. Support your main point with a number of minor points. Expand each minor point with details that explain your premises.

4. Arrange your minor premises carefully so that you build to the most convincing point at the end.

5. Use a simple and straightforward style. Connect your points with transitions; use repetition as one transitional device.

6. Balance your longer paragraphs with occasional shorter ones.

7. End your essay with a crisp, one-sentence question of your own.

More Writing Projects

1. Write an essay in which you argue *for* or *against* this issue: "A married woman belongs at home."

2. Write an essay in which you argue about whose role you think harder to play effectively in today's society: the role of the mother or the role of the father.

If Black English Isn't a Language, Then Tell Me, What Is?

James Baldwin

James Baldwin (1924–1988) was one of America's foremost fiction
writers and essayists, despite the fact that he spent much of his time
and did most of his writing in southern France. His first two novels,
Go Tell It on the Mountain (1953) and *Giovanni's Room* (1956), were
early successes, and his essay collections such as *Notes of a Native
Son* (1955) and *The Fire Next Time* (1963) were astonishing records
of racism in America. In this essay, Baldwin takes an aggressive look
at Black English, making clear his ideas about the political and sociological implications of the issue. He develops his opinions through
a blend of causal analysis, historical illustration, and strong emotional appeal.

Words to Watch

status (par. 1)   condition; situation

dubiously (par. 1)   doubtfully

articulate (par. 2)   express in words

temporal (par. 3)   of time

antecedents (par. 4)   precursors; things that came before

qualms (par. 5)   misgivings; sudden fears

chattel (par. 7)   property

tabernacle (par. 7)   house of worship

alchemy (par. 7)   power or process of transforming something common into something precious

unassailable (par. 9)   not open to question or attack

patronizingly (par. 10)   in a manner looking down on someone else

repudiate (par. 11)   turn down; decline

sustenance (par. 11)   nourishment

limbo (par. 11)   place or state of neglect or oblivion

The argument concerning the use, or the status, or the   1
reality, of black English is rooted in American history and has

421

absolutely nothing to do with the question the argument sup-
poses itself to be posing. The argument has nothing to do with
language itself but with the *role* of language. Language, incon-
testably, reveals the speaker. Language, also, far more dubiously, is meant to define the other—and, in this case, the
other is refusing to be defined by a language that has never
been able to recognize him.

People evolve a language in order to describe and thus   2
control their circumstances, or in order not to be submerged
by a reality that they cannot articulate. (And, if they cannot
articulate it, they *are* submerged.) A Frenchman living in Paris
speaks a subtly and crucially different language from that of
the man living in Marseilles; neither sounds very much like a
man living in Quebec; and they would all have great difficulty
in apprehending what the man from Guadeloupe, or Martinique, is saying, to say nothing of the man from Senegal—although the "common" language of all these areas is French.
But each has paid, and is paying, a different price for this
"common" language, in which, as it turns out, they are not
saying, and cannot be saying, the same things: They each
have very different realities to articulate or control.

What joins all languages, and all men, is the necessity to   3
confront life, in order, not inconceivably, to outwit death: The
price for this is the acceptance, and achievement, of one's
temporal identity. So that, for example, though it is not taught
in the schools (and this has the potential of becoming a political issue) the south of France still clings to its ancient and
musical Provençal, which resists being described as a "dialect." And much of the tension in the Basque countries, and
in Wales, is due to the Basque and Welsh determination not to
allow their languages to be destroyed. This determination also
feeds the flames in Ireland for among the many indignities the
Irish have been forced to undergo at English hands is the English contempt for their language.

It goes without saying, then, that language is also a po-   4
litical instrument, means, and proof of power. It is the most
vivid and crucial key to identity: It reveals the private identity, and connects one with, or divorces one from, the larger
public, or communal identity. There have been, and are,

times, and places, when to speak a certain language could be dangerous, even fatal. Or, one may speak the same language, but in such a way that one's antecedents are revealed, or (one hopes) hidden. This is true in France, and is absolutely true in England: The range (and reign) of accents on that damp little island make England coherent for the English and totally incomprehensible for everyone else. To open your mouth in England is (if I may use black English) to "put your business in the street": You have confessed your parents, your youth, your school, your salary, your self-esteem, and, alas, your future.

Now, I do not know what white American would sound   5
like if there had never been any black people in the United States, but they would not sound the way they sound. *Jazz,* for example, is a very specific sexual term, as in *jazz me, baby,* but white people purified it into the Jazz Age. *Sock it to me,* which means, roughly, the same thing, has been adopted by Nathaniel Hawthorne's descendants with no qualms or hesitations at all, along with *let it all hang out* and *right on! Beat to his socks,* which was once the black's most total and despairing image of poverty, was transformed into a thing called the Beat Generation, which phenomenon was, largely, composed of *uptight,* middle-class white people, imitating poverty, trying to *get down,* to get *with it,* doing their *thing,* doing their despairing best to be *funky,* which we, the blacks, never dreamed of doing—we *were* funky, baby, like *funk* was going out of style.

Now, no one can eat his cake, and have it, too, and it is   6
late in the day to attempt to penalize black people for having created a language that permits the nation its only glimpse of reality, a language without which the nation would be even more *whipped* than it is.

I say that this present skirmish is rooted in American his-   7
tory, and it is. Black English is the creation of the black diaspora. Blacks came to the United States chained to each other, but from different tribes: Neither could speak the other's language. If two black people, at that bitter hour of the world's history, had been able to speak to each other, the institution of chattel slavery could never have lasted as long as it did. Sub-

sequently, the slave was given, under the eye, and the gun, of his master, Congo Square, and the Bible—or, in other words, and under these conditions, the slave began the formation of the black church, and it is within this unprecedented tabernacle that black English began to be formed. This was not, merely, as in the European example, the adoption of a foreign tongue, but an alchemy that transformed ancient elements into new language: *A language comes into existence by means of brutal necessity, and the rules of the language are dictated by what the language must convey.*

There was a moment, in time, and in this place, when my brother, or my mother, or my father, or my sister, had to convey to me, for example, the danger in which I was standing from the white man standing just behind me, and to convey this with a speed, and in a language, that the white man could not possibly understand, and that, indeed, he cannot understand, until today. He cannot afford to understand it. This understanding would reveal to him too much about himself, and smash that mirror before which he has been frozen for so long. **8**

Now, if this passion, this skill, this (to quote Toni Morrison) "sheer intelligence," this incredible music, the mighty achievement of having brought a people utterly unknown to, or despised by "history"—to have brought this people to their present, troubled, troubling, and unassailable and unanswerable place—if this absolutely unprecedented journey does not indicate that black English is a language, I am curious to know what definition of language is to be trusted. **9**

A people at the center of the Western world, and in the midst of so hostile a population, has not endured and transcended by means of what is patronizingly called a "dialect." We, the blacks, are in trouble, certainly, but we are not doomed, and we are not inarticulate because we are not compelled to defend a morality that we know to be a lie. **10**

The brutal truth is that the bulk of the white people in America never had any interest in educating black people, except as this could serve white purposes. It is not the black child's language that is in question, it is not his language that is despised: It is his experience. A child cannot be taught by anyone who despises him, and a child cannot afford to be **11** fooled. A child cannot be taught by anyone whose demand, essentially, is that the child repudiate his experience, and all that gives him sustenance, and enter a limbo in which he will no longer be black, and in which he knows that he can never become white. Black people have lost too many black children that way.

And, after all, finally, in a country with standards so un- 12 trustworthy, a country that makes heroes of so many criminal mediocrities, a country unable to face why so many of the non-white are in prison, or on the needle, or standing, future-less, in the streets—it may very well be that both the child, and his elder, have concluded that they have nothing whatever to learn from the people of a country that has managed to learn so little.

BUILDING VOCABULARY

1. In paragraph 5, Baldwin uses several examples of Black English. He defines some; others he simply uses in a de-scriptive sentence. List all the black English terminology included in this essay, then write standard English equiva-lents (*not* definitions) that are also figurative expressions or slang.

2. Explain the following figurative expressions from the essay and use each one in a sentence of your own. Then, rewrite the sentences using language that isn't figurative.

   a. paying a...price for (par. 2)
   b. feeding the flames (par. 3)
   c. can eat his cake, and have it, too (par. 6)
   d. it is late in the day (par. 6)
   e. smash that mirror (par. 8)

3. Identify the following *allusions* in this essay:

   Paris
   Marseilles
   Quebec
   Guadeloupe

Martinique
Provençal
the Basque
Wales
the Jazz Age
the Beat Generation

UNDERSTANDING THE WRITER'S IDEAS

1. According to Baldwin, what is the difference between dialect and language. What examples does he offer of this distinction? How have some groups used this distinction for purposes other than communication? What does Baldwin think about those who consider black English a dialect rather than a language?

2. Why would it be difficult for native French speakers from different parts of the world to understand each other?

3. In your own words, write a one-sentence summary of paragraph 5. According to Baldwin, how and why have white Americans "purified" black English? Give three examples of such purification. What does he mean by "Nathaniel Hawthorne's descendants"? Is there an unsaid contrast implied in this description?

4. What, according to the author, is the relationship between language and experience? What is the "black diaspora"? Summarize how the experiences of the black diaspora led to the rise of black English.

5. Briefly outline what Baldwin feels are the main uses of language. How is language "a political instrument"?

6. What is the main purpose of Baldwin's argument? What would he like the reader to be convinced about in relation to black English? About language in general? How does he challenge various preconceived or prevailing notions about black English? About language in general?

7. What is the author's attitude toward England? How do

you know? What does he feel is a primary role of language in England?

8. Define "the present skirmish" referred to in paragraph 7.

9. What was the role of the black church in shaping Black English?

10. In paragraph 8, to whom is the author referring when he writes: "my brother, or my mother, or my father, or my sister"? Is he referring to his actual family? Explain.

11. Baldwin makes the point that whites "cannot afford to understand" black English. Why? Historically, what has been the attitude of the majority of whites toward black English? Toward black education?

12. Who is Toni Morrison? Why does he quote her? (par. 9)

13. What is the meaning of the concluding paragraph? What does Baldwin mean by "criminal mediocrities"? What does he mean by "on the needle"? Is the last paragraph concerned only with gaining recognition of black English as a language? Explain.

UNDERSTANDING THE WRITER'S TECHNIQUES

1. What does Baldwin tell us about his position on black English by offering, in the opening sentence, three points of view? How does he use *negation* in that first paragraph to clarify his position and limit his argument?

2. Is there a directly stated *major proposition* in this essay? If so, what is it? Where is it placed in the essay? Why?

3. Outline the *minor propositions* of this essay.

4. Describe Baldwin's *tone* throughout the essay. How does he invoke this tone in the very first paragraph? Who is "the other" mentioned in paragraph 1? How does that word choice help set the tone? In paragraph 4, how does

his use of the parenthetical expression "(if I may use black English)" contribute to the tone? List five other examples of phrases or statements that influence the essay's tone.

5. The introduction to this chapter discusses the importance of *refutation* (see page 395)—recognizing and dealing with opposing arguments—to the development of a successful argument. Does Baldwin use refutation? Explain.

6. Parenthetical expressions are used throughout this essay. Generally, for what purpose are they used? Is the purpose mainly informational or attitudinal? Explain.

7. Why is the final sentence of paragraph 7 italicized?

8. How does Baldwin use *cause-and-effect analysis* (see pages 350–352) to advance his argument?

9. What is the purpose of *illustration* in this essay? With so many examples, how does Baldwin maintain *coherence* (see Glossary)?

10. To whom would you say this argument is addressed? Is it directed more toward whites or blacks? Would the meaning be the same for both? Explain with specific references to the essay.

11. An argument will often include highly emotional language and appeals to the reader, especially if the topic is personally important to the writer. Would you characterize Baldwin's essay as especially emotional? Why? Does the emotion ever detract from the argument? Compare the level of emotionalism in this essay with that in the other three selections in this chapter.

12. Do you feel Baldwin has written an effective conclusion? Why?

EXPLORING THE WRITER'S IDEAS

1. In paragraph 3, Baldwin states: "What joins all languages, and all men, is the necessity to confront life, in order, not

inconceivably, to outwit death.'' William Saroyan, in his essay ''Why I Write'' (pages 5–8), states: ''I felt impelled from the time I had memory to do something about the past, about endings, about human death.... Thus, death would not be death.''

Compare Baldwin's and Saroyan's connections between death on the one hand and language and the writing process on the other. Why would death figure so strongly as a concept among writers?

2. Baldwin feels that ''language is also a political instrument, means, and proof of power. It is the most vivid and crucial key to identity.'' How does this view compare with Malcolm X's view of the individual political implications of language (see ''Prison Studies,'' pages 62–65)?

   Other writers in this book also deal with various political and sociological implications of language and writing. Compare Baldwin's opinions with Rita Mae Brown's (pages 266–268), Elizabeth Janeway's (pages 256–259), or Elizabeth Wong's (pages 129–131).

3. Throughout the essay, Baldwin uses ''man'' or ''men'' as a generic reference to people in general. Do you find this odd for a writer who is so acutely aware of the political nature of language? Explain.

4. Baldwin writes that ''There have been, and are, times, and places, where to speak a certain language could be dangerous, even fatal.'' In what cases might this be true? What is the double meaning of the phrase ''a certain language''? Can you point to historical or current events that support this statement?

5. Recently, there have been legislative efforts to make English (presumably Standard English, not Black) the *official* language of certain states or the United States as a whole. What are your opinions about such efforts?

6. Whether it is tagged a language or a dialect, black English is certainly a real entity in the United States. Additionally, some also talk of ''Spanglish,'' a mixture of Spanish and English, as a kind of dialect. With the ever-growing diver

sity of cultural and ethnic groups in the United States, can you foresee such hybrids as Asian English, Haitian English, and so forth?

7. Paragraph 5 illustrates how certain expressions from black English have become common in all Americans' daily speech. Make a list of words or expressions from other cultural or ethnic groups that have also entered the common language.

IDEAS FOR WRITING

Guided Writing

Write an argumentative essay in which you defend a position as to whether or not black English *is* a language in its own right.

1. Limit the scope of your argument in the very first paragraph by categorizing various aspects of language usage.

2. Use *illustration* and *cause-and-effect analysis* to illustrate how and why languages get to be defined as separate entities.

3. Limit your argument by taking a nonlinguistic approach— political, cultural, sociological, or practical, for example.

4. Use examples of Black English expressions to illustrate your point of view.

5. Develop a historical basis for your argument.

6. If possible, make a personal connection to black English and show how that connection has influenced your opinion.

7. Use an emotional, somewhat aggressive tone.

8. Use minor propositions as a means of organizing your essay.

9. End your essay by generalizing your opinion to larger societal issues.

More Writing Projects

1. Write an essay in which you support an opinion for or against bilingual education in areas where most residents are not native English speakers.

2. Do you believe there is such a thing as Standard English, or is it just an academic concept? Write an essay expressing your opinion. Be sure to include a refutation as part of your argument.

CHAPTER 12

Prose for
Further Reading

In Deep
Maxine Kumin

Early winter. Foliage gone, the woods reveal their inner architecture. In a strong wind, oak and maple branches creak and rub against each other, cranky as old door hinges. I can see in deep now, deep into this second-growth forest where pastures once were, and farms prospered. I can spot the occasional apple tree and lilac sprawl, the tumbled stone walls and caved-in foundations at a considerable distance.

The deerflies, those scourges of midsummer shaped like tiny deltoid planes, have vanished. Ground wasps that lurked in rotten logs waiting to pounce on the unwary traveler are now in hibernation. Only the deer hunters are left for us to contend with.

Weekends we ride out in threes and fours, horses and people bedecked in extremely orange pinnies—Ten Mile Cloth, the manufacturer calls it, claiming it can be seen at that remove. Each of us has a cowbell tied to one stirrup. I carry a folding saw across the cantle of my saddle. Aurally and visually we make a fearsome procession. Of course the hunters hate us, but these are *our* woods too, and this is our only season for bushwhacking.

Midweek, theorizing that the Sunday shooters have gone home, I risk my neck alone. Riding along old rangeways between vanished settlements I peer down every track. All those roads not taken! Bending low under overhanging branches, sometimes stopping to saw my way clear, I take them one by one. And one by one they peter out like rambling thoughts, glimmering ideas unrealized.

Somehow I am never cured of my fantasy; surely one will carry me through? One day, riding in deep, the perfect trail will materialize, a leafy carpet underfoot, and overhead just room enough—a tunnel for my chestnut horse and me. We will trot for miles this way, admiring the crackle we make in late November, admiring the configurations of hummocks and rivulets underfoot with glistens of ice between, and bits of bright blue sky visible over the next rise. Eventually we will come out on the other side.

What is waiting on the other side? Maybe nothing special, maybe only more of the same, dear enough for this watcher. But the quest is real. To get there you have to go in deep.

Babyhood

Akira Kurosawa

I was in the washtub naked. The place was dimly lit, and I was soaking in hot water and rocking myself by holding on to the rims of the tub. At the lowest point the tub teetered between two sloping boards, the water making little splashing noises as it rocked. This must have been very interesting for me. I rocked the tub with all my strength. Suddenly it overturned. I have a very vivid memory of the strange feeling of shock and uncertainty at that moment, of the sensation of that wet and slippery space between the boards against my bare skin, and of looking up at something painfully bright overhead.

After reaching an age of awareness, I would occasionally recall this incident. But it seemed a trivial thing, so I said nothing about it until I became an adult. It must have been after I had passed twenty years of age that for some reason I mentioned to my mother that I remembered these sensations. For a moment she just stared at me in surprise; then she informed me that this could only have been something that occurred when we went to my father's birthplace up north in Akita Prefecture to attend a memorial service for my grandfather. I had been one year old at the time.

The dimly lit place where I sat in a tub lodged between two boards was the room that served as both kitchen and bath in the house where my father was born. My mother had been about to give me a bath, but first she put me in the tub of hot water and went into the next room to take off her kimono. Suddenly she heard me start wailing at the top of my lungs. She rushed back and found me spilled out of the tub on the floor crying. The painfully bright, shiny thing over head, my mother explained, was probably a hanging oil lamp of the type still used when I was a baby.

This incident with the washtub is my very first memory of myself. Naturally, I do not recall being born. However, my oldest sister, now deceased, used to say, "You were a strange baby." Apparently I emerged from my mother's womb without uttering a sound, but with my hands firmly clasped together. When at last they were able to pry my hands apart, I had bruises on both palms.

I think this story may be a lie. It was probably made up to tease me because I was the youngest child. After all, if I really had been born such a grasping person, by now I would be a millionaire and surely would be riding around in nothing less than a Rolls-Royce.

After the washtub incident of my first year, I can now recall only a few other events from my babyhood, in a form resembling out-of-focus bits of film footage. All of them are things seen from my infant's vantage point on my nurse's shoulders.

One of them is something seen through a wire net. People dressed in white flail at a ball with a stick, run after it as it dances and flies through the air, and pick it up and throw it around. Later I understood that this was the view from behind the net of the baseball field at the gymnastics school where my father was a teacher. So I must say that my liking for baseball today is deep-rooted; apparently I've been watching it since babyhood.

Another memory from babyhood, also a sight viewed from my nurse's back, comes to mind: a fire seen from a great distance. Between us and the fire stretches an expanse of dark water. My home was in the Ōmori district of Tokyo, so this was probably the Ōmori shore of Tokyo Bay, and since the fire appeared very far away, it must have taken place somewhere near Haneda (now the site of one of Tokyo's international airports). I was frightened by this distant fire and cried. Even now I have a strong dislike of fires, and especially when I see the night sky reddened with flames I am overcome by fear.

One last memory of babyhood remains. In this case, too, I am on my nurse's back, and from time to time we enter a small dark room. Years later I would occasionally recall this frequent occurrence and wonder what it was. Then one day all at once, like Sherlock Holmes solving a mystery, I understood: my nurse, with me still on her back, was going to the toilet. What an insult!

Many years later my nurse came to see me. She looked up at this person who had reached nearly six feet and more than 150 pounds and just said, "My dear, how you've grown," as she clasped me around the knees and broke into tears. I had been ready to reproach her for the indignities she had caused me to suffer in the past, but suddenly I was moved by this figure of an old woman I no longer recognized, and all I could do was stare vacantly down at her.

The Grey Seas Under

Farley Mowat

The North Atlantic is a hungry ocean, hungry for men and ships, and it knows how to satisfy its appetites. From September through to June a sequence of almost perpetual gales march eastward down the great ditch of the St Lawrence valley and out to the waiting sea. They are abetted by the hurricanes which spawn in the Caribbean and which drive northeastward up the coasts as far as Labrador. Only in summer are there periods of relative calm on the eastern approaches to the continent, and even in summer, fierce storms are common.

Gales, and the high seas that accompany them are, of course, the weapons of all oceans; but this unquiet seaboard has two special weapons of its own.

First of all it has the ice—continental masses of it that come sweeping down with the Greenland current to form a great, amoeba-like bulge extending from the coasts of Nova Scotia eastward as much as a thousand miles, and southward five hundred miles from Flemish Cap. The bulge swells and shrinks and throws out new pseudopods from mouth to mouth, but there is no season of the year when it or its accompanying icebergs withdrew completely from the shipping lanes.

The second weapon is in many ways the most formidable of all. It is the fog. There is no fog anywhere to compare with the palpable grey shroud which lies almost perpetually across the northern sea approaches, and which often flows far over the land itself. There are not a score of days during any given year when between Labrador and the Gulf of Maine the fog vanishes completely. Even in the rare fine days of summer it remains in wait, a dozen or so miles offshore, ready at any moment to roll in and obliterate the world. It has presence, continuity, and a vitality that verges on the animate. In conjunction with its ready ally, the rock-girt coasts, it is a great killer of men and ships.

The coasts themselves are brutally hard. Newfoundland, Labrador, Nova Scotia, and the Gulf shores appear to have been created for the special purpose of destroying vessels.

They are of malignant grey rock that has flung its fragments into the sea with an insane abandon until, in many places, these form an impenetrable *chevaux-de-frise* to which the Newfoundland seamen, out of a perilous familiarity, have given the prophetic name of 'sunkers.'

The coasts are of tremendous length. Newfoundland alone exposes nearly six thousand miles of rock to the breaking seas. Everywhere the shores are indented with false harbors that offer hope to storm-driven ships and which then repulse them with a multitude of reefs. The names upon those coasts betray their nature. Cape aux Morts, Cape Diable, Rocks of Massacre, Dead Sailor's Rock, Bay of Despair, Malignant Cove, Baie Mauvais, Misery Point, Mistaken Point, False Hope, Confusion Bay, Salvage Point, and a plethora of Wreck Bays, Points and Islands.

Yet by the very nature of their animosity towards seafaring men these coasts have brought out of themselves the matter of their own defeat. Men in these parts have always had to take their living from the sea, or starve; and those who survived the merciless winnowing became a race apart. There are no finer seamen in the world. The best of them come from the outports of Newfoundland and Nova Scotia, and from the islands of Cape Breton and the Magdalens. The best of them are men to ponder over, for they can hold their own no matter how the seas and the fog and ice and rocks may strive against them.

And yet it is also true that these men do not properly belong in our times, for they follow an outmoded creed with undeviating certainty. They believe that man must not attempt to overmaster the primordial and elemental forces and break them to his hand. They believe that he who would survive must learn to be a part of wind and water, rock and soil, nor ever stand in braggarts' opposition to these things.

'Ah, me son,' as one old Newfoundland skipper phrases it, 'we don't be *takin'* nothing from the sea. We has to sneak up on what we wants, and wiggle it away.'

"The Fight"

Maya Angelou

The last inch of space was filled, yet people continued to wedge themselves along the walls of the Store. Uncle Willie had turned the radio up to its last notch so that youngsters on the porch wouldn't miss a word. Women sat on kitchen chairs, dining-room chairs, stools and upturned wooden boxes. Small children and babies perched on every lap available and men leaned on the shelves or on each other.

The apprehensive mood was shot through with shafts of gaiety, as a black sky is streaked with lightning.

"I ain't worried 'bout this fight. Joe's gonna whip that cracker like it's open season."

"He gone whip him till that white boy call him Momma."

At last the talking was finished and the string-along songs about razor blades were over and the fight began.

"A quick jab to the head." In the Store the crowd grunted. "A left to the head and a right and another left." One of the listeners cackled like a hen and was quieted.

"They're in a clench, Louis is trying to fight his way out."

Some bitter comedian on the porch said, "That white man don't mind hugging that niggah now, I betcha."

"The referee is moving in to break them up, but Louis finally pushed the contender away and it's an uppercut to the chin. The contender is hanging on, now he's backing away. Louis catches him with a short left to the jaw."

A tide of murmuring assent poured out the doors and into the yard.

"Another left and another left. Louis is saving that mighty right..." The mutter in the Store had grown into a baby roar and it was pierced by the clang of a bell and the announcer's "That's the bell for round three, ladies and gentlemen."

As I pushed my way into the Store I wondered if the announcer gave any thought to the fact that he was addressing as

440

"ladies and gentlemen" all the Negroes around the world who sat sweating and praying, glued to their "master's voice."

There were only a few calls for R. C. Colas, Dr. Peppers, and Hire's root beer. The real festivities would begin after the fight. Then even the old Christian ladies who taught their children and tried themselves to practice turning the other cheek would buy soft drinks, and if the Brown Bomber's victory was a particularly bloody one they would order peanut patties and Baby Ruths also.

Bailey and I lay the coins on top of the cash register. Uncle Willie didn't allow us to ring up sales during a fight. It was too noisy and might shake up the atmosphere. When the gong rang for the next round we pushed through the near-sacred quiet to the herd of children outside.

"He's got Louis against the ropes and now it's a left to the body and a right to the ribs. Another right to the body, it looks like it was low... Yes, ladies and gentlemen, the referee is signaling but the contender keeps raining the blows on Louis. It's another to the body, and it looks like Louis is going down."

My race groaned. It was our people falling. It was another lynching, yet another Black man hanging on a tree. One more woman ambushed and raped. A Black boy whipped and maimed. It was hounds on the trail of a man running through slimy swamps. It was a white woman slapping her maid for being forgetful.

The men in the Store stood away from the walls and at attention. Women greedily clutched the babes on their laps while on the porch the shufflings and smiles, flirtings and pinching of a few minutes before were gone. This might be the end of the world. If Joe lost we were back in slavery and beyond help. It would all be true, the accusations that we were lower types of human beings. Only a little higher than the apes. True that we were stupid and ugly and lazy and dirty and, unlucky and worst of all, that God Himself hated us and ordained us to be hewers of wood and drawers of water, forever and ever, world without end.

We didn't breathe. We didn't hope. We waited.

"He's off the ropes, ladies and gentlemen. He's moving

towards the center of the ring." There was no time to be relieved. The worst might still happen.

"And now it looks like Joe is mad. He's caught Carnera with a left hook to the head and a right to the head. It's a left jab to the body and another left to the head. There's a left cross and a right to the head. The contender's right eye is bleeding and he can't seem to keep his block up. Louis is penetrating every block. The referee is moving in, but Louis sends a left to the body and it's the uppercut to the chin and the contender is dropping. He's on the canvas, ladies and gentlemen."

Babies slid to the floor as women stood up and men leaned toward the radio.

"Here's the referee. He's counting. One, two, three, four, five, six, seven...Is the contender trying to get up again?"

All the men in the store shouted, "NO."

"—eight, nine, ten." There were a few sounds from the audience, but they seemed to be holding themselves in against tremendous pressure.

"The fight is all over, ladies and gentlemen. Let's get the microphone over to the referee...Here he is. He's got the Brown Bomber's hand, he's holding it up...Here he is..."

Then the voice, husky and familiar, came to wash over us—"The winnah, and still heavyweight champeen of the world...Joe Louis."

Champion of the world. A Black boy. Some Black mother's son. He was the strongest man in the world. People drank Coca-Colas like ambrosia and ate candy bars like Christmas. Some of the men went behind the Store and poured white lightning in their soft-drink bottles, and a few of the bigger boys followed them. Those who were not chased away came back blowing their breath in front of themselves like proud smokers.

It would take an hour or more before the people would leave the Store and head for home. Those who lived too far had made arrangements to stay in town. It wouldn't do for a Black man and his family to be caught on a lonely country road on a night when Joe Louis had proved that we were the strongest people in the world.

A Return to Basics: Mealtime Without Guilt

Garrison Keillor

Eating is a perfectly natural activity, we all have natural urges to eat, and we should be able to satisfy those urges simply and naturally without shame and anxiety and numbing self-consciousness either alone or with one other person or two or (if we prefer, and it's strictly a matter of personal preference) with larger groups. It should be a joyous life-affirming experience, not (as I'm afraid it is to so many) *A Problem*.

When I was a boy way out on the open prairie of the American heartland, we were happy eaters and weren't ashamed to have big appetites. Out there in Breughel, N.D., surrounded by an ocean of durum wheat, we got three squares a day, piled our plates and cried "Yes!" to seconds. Tables groaned at picnics, church suppers, Sunday dinners, holiday feasts. Food was a relief against our flat landscape: steamy mountains of fried chicken and pork among foothills of creamed onions, spinach, mashed potatoes with lakes of gravy and great promontories of pie. At least once a week we sat down to table and scaled the Sierras. And what we called "a little lunch" would knock the socks off Pavarotti.

All that has changed in Breughel and everywhere else, thanks to a tiny flock of puritanical food writers who have nagged and bullied and made us a picky people who take small bites and mull the food over in our mouths: Is it excellent? Are we having a truly unique dining experience? No, probably not, for once you pick food apart and hold it up to the light and examine it, you don't feel like eating the stuff. For one thing, it's probably cold.

So church suppers at Breughel Lutheran now are dismal affairs to which people bring elegant casseroles and sip dry wines and talk dry talk and exchange nervous glances. In the fall, the threshing crews sit down at plank tables under the cottonwood trees and eat stir-fried shrimp and pea pods, and each man talks about another meal he had at this absolutely marvelous little out-of-the-way farm that nobody ever heard of before. And Mom's Cafe has changed hands and is now a nouvelle Bulgarian restaurant but nobody goes there, they all know a better one in Bismarck.

Where are the great meals of my youth when we were loose and happy and loved the chow? Gone! Scared off by food authorities, ridiculed, made to seem cheap and coarse and not in good taste. Julia Child, James Beard—both meant to raise our sights, but their effect has been to make eaters nervous that what is set before us may not be good enough and, worse, that we may not realize it and may actually enjoy it. They have also permanently eliminated macaroni and cheese or hamburger-noodle hot dish as anything you'd dare serve to guests or eat in public. A person who truly enjoys macaroni and cheese is forced to eat alone in the dark. A person would rather confess to being from Breughel than admit to any dealings with macaroni and cheese.

I happen to love it, the kind that Kraft makes with the noodles and a packet of powdered cheese in one box. You boil water, cook noodles, drain and dump cheese powder on it. It's no trouble to make, tastes good and reminds me of how simple eating used to be in our home when I was a boy. (My mother, who has studied northern Italian cooking in the Breughel adult education program, now claims to have made Kraft macaroni and cheese "once or twice when I wasn't feeling well," but in fact we had it every Monday night.)

There were no menus at that kitchen table, and when Dad poured milk, he didn't pour a little bit in your glass and wait for you to swish it around in your mouth and say if it was O.K. My mother taught us to be grateful for the meal, to think of Asian children and to make mealtime a pleasant occasion, not a meeting of critics saying "Yuccchh" and "Ish, beet greens" or "The tuna casserole, while plentiful, is sadly underseasoned."

Maybe it's time all of us got back to basics in the food line, especially those whose appetites have been dulled by too much reading about food, who have been intimidated by cuisine. Here are some helpful guidelines:

1. Eat when you're hungry. Food tastes much better then. Past the age of 30, you don't need much to keep going so you'll need to pass up some meals before you arrive at one

you're really up for. You say, "I'm so hungry I could eat bark off trees," and if you are, that meat loaf will have an aura about it and those string beans will be the best you ever ate.

2. Don't ever explain food to your guests, as you bring it to the table: "The soup is burnt" or "The fish fell on the floor so most of the cream sauce got washed off" or "I just saw this recipe for curried chicken in Parade, this is the first time I made it, and then I discovered I was all out of robin's eggs so I had to substitute partridge instead." Don't do that. Simply put the hay down where the goats can get it, say grace and tell a couple of jokes.

3. When you go to a restaurant, don't read the menu. Ask the waiter what's good or look around the room until you see something you like and ask for that. Or if you have a definite meal in mind—say, a cup of soup, a peanut butter sandwich, a dill pickle and lemon gelatin with mayonnaise—say so, and let the restaurant worry about it.

Menu study is a useless exercise; it tells you nothing about the food, and yet people sit and pore over it as if it were the racing form and only one dish can be a winner. Nobody wants to be wrong, nobody wants to order first. "You go ahead," they say. "I'm still thinking." Don't think so hard. Point. Say "Bring me some of that—what those people over there got, the ones with the big smiles and the grease stains." Be happy, say grace, tell a couple of jokes.

4. Don't discuss food while you're eating it. Don't frame judicious compliments for the hosts. Don't compare the food to other foods of its sort, don't inquire about ingredients, don't be reminded of a wonderful meal you had with other people a long time ago—just plain don't talk about it. A sound here and there ("Hooooo-ah!" or "Hah!" or growls and barks) will do for compliments, and any other discussion can wait. Food is a blessing to us, the stuff that sustains our little flame, and we should eat it with gratitude and gusto and talk of many things but not this. Tell jokes.

5. Insofar as possible, given the tangled thread of fate, the requirements of business and the difficulty of worming out of some invitations, avoid eating with people you don't like. If you're with people in front of whom you're afraid to spill food

on yourself, you're probably with the wrong bunch. The steam shovel operator can't enjoy food if he is worried about spilling beans from his bucket. Eat with your friends. They're the ones who, if you do spill, won't whip their heads the other way and start up a conversation about tax-increment financing. They'll look right at you and get a good laugh out of it.

In fact, your *true* friends are ones you could toss a little bit of food at—if the situation seemed to call for it. Not as a regular thing, and not a big hunk of something, but a pea or crouton or pinch of tofu thrown at the right moment can be a profound expression of brotherhood and sisterhood. Don't get me wrong: I'm not advocating food fights. I only feel that, at the very happiest meals, the *possibility* has to be there.

Throwing food is a perfectly natural thing. We all have an urge now and then to let fly with a little glistening morsel and plant it on someone's forehead, and I see no reason why mature adults shouldn't feel free to do it—among friends, of course. In Breughel before good taste clamped down on us, we'd often look up and see a pat of butter coming our way, or a single cheesy macaroni, and it lent an intimacy to dining I haven't experienced since.

He Rocked, I Reeled

Tama Janowitz

In high school, I took a remedial English class—maybe it wasn't remedial, exactly, but without my knowing it, I had signed up for some kind of English class for juvenile delinquents.

Well, it wasn't supposed to be a class for juvenile delinquents, but somehow everybody but me knew that that was who it was for; maybe it was listed in the course catalog as being for those students in the commercial program, the general program, whatever it was called to distinguish it from the academic precollege preparation program.

But anyway, on the first day I figured out who this course was directed at: The students were surly and wore leather jackets, and the girls all had shag hair-dos as opposed to straight and ironed, which was how the "nice" girls wore their hair.

Knowing me, I must have signed up for that class because it indicated that no work would be involved. And I was prepared for the worst, because somehow, having moved and switched schools so many times, I had been stuck in juvenile delinquent classes before.

The juvenile delinquent classes generally meant angry teachers and angry students who never read the books assigned and never spoke in class, which was no wonder because the teacher was generally contemptuous and sneering.

But this class ended up being different; the main thing was that the teacher, Mr. Paul Steele, didn't seem to know he was teaching students who weren't supposed to be able to learn. He assigned the books—by Sherwood Anderson, by Hemingway, by Melville—and somehow by the due date everyone had read them and was willing to talk about them.

Mr. Steele was a little distracted, a little dreamy, and most excellent. It was one of the few times up until that age I had a teacher who spoke to me—and the rest of the class—with the honesty of one adult talking to others, without pretense or condescension; there was no wrong or right, just discussion.

447

In college, I had another great course—in geology, a subject for which I had no interest. Once again, I had signed up for something that looked easy, a "gut" course to fulfill the science requirement.

But this guy—I believe his name was Professor Sand, an apt name for a geology teacher—was so excited and in love with rocks, with everything pertaining to the formation of the earth, that to this day rocks and everything pertaining to the formation of the earth still get me excited.

Oolitic limestone, feldspar, gypsum, iron pyrite, Manhattan schist—the names were like descriptions of food, almost edible, and as around that time I was starting to become interested in writing, the enthusiasm that the teacher had for the subject was transferred to me into an enthusiasm for language.

And the names of the different periods—the Jurassic, the Pre-Cambrian—even though I can't remember much about them, the words still hold mystery and richness.

At the end of the semester, there was a field trip up to the Catskills, to put into practice some of the techniques discussed in class. We were taken to a fossil bed of trilobites where, due to the particular condition of the sedimentary bed, only the trilobite bodies had been preserved over the millenia.

After a few minutes of listening to the professor's explanation, I bent over and picked up a piece of rock with a small lump sticking out of it and took it over to him.

To me, all I had found was a rock with a lump; but Professor Sand was totally amazed—I was the only one ever to find a fossilized trilobite complete with head.

Really, at that point there was little to stop me from becoming a geologist except for the fact that I knew I could never do anything involving numbers, weights or measurements, which I suspected would at some point have some bearing on the subject.

I remember another teacher, in graduate school, Francine du Plessix Gray, who taught a course called Religion and Literature—another subject in which I had no interest. But the way she spoke was so beautiful, in an accent slightly French-tinged. And because she was so interested in her topic, the students became interested, and her seminars were alive and full of argument.

Of course, I had many other fine teachers along the way, but the ones who stand out in my mind were those who were most enthusiastic about what they were teaching.

Many subjects in which I initially thought I was interested were totally destroyed for me by the teacher's dry, aloof, pompous, disengaged way of speaking.

But when the teacher was as excited about the topic—as if he or she was still a little kid, rushing in from the yard to tell a story—that was when the subject became alive for me.

"Ever Et Raw Meat?" and Other Weird Questions

Stephen King

It seems to me that, in the minds of readers, writers actually exist to serve two purposes, and the more important may not be the writing of books and stories. The primary function of writers, it seems, is to answer readers' questions. These fall into three categories. The third is the one that fascinates me most, but I'll identify the other two first.

The One-of-a-Kind Questions: Each day's mail brings a few of these. Often they reflect the writer's field of interest—history, horror, romance, the American West, outer space, big business. The only thing they have in common is their uniqueness. Novelists are frequently asked where they get their ideas (see category No. 2), but writers must wonder where this relentless curiosity, these really strange questions, come from.

There was, for instance, the young woman who wrote to me from a penal institution in Minnesota. She informed me she was a kleptomaniac. She further informed me that I was her favorite writer, and she had stolen every one of my books she could get her hands on. "But after I stole 'Different Seasons' from the library and read it, I felt moved to send it back," she wrote. "Do you think this means you wrote this one the best?" After due consideration, I decided that reform on the part of the reader has nothing to do with artistic merit. I came close to writing back to find out if she had stolen "Misery" yet but decided I ought to just keep my mouth shut.

From Bill V. in North Carolina: "I see you have a beard. Are you morbid of razors?"

From Carol K. in Hawaii: "Will you soon write of pimples or some other facial blemish?"

From Don G., no address (and a blurry postmark): "Why do you keep up this disgusting mother worship when anyone with any sense knows a MAN has no use to his mother once he is weened?"

From Raymond R. in Mississippi: "Ever et raw meat?" (It's the laconic ones like this that really get me.)

450

I have been asked if I beat my children and/or my wife. I have been asked to parties in places I have never been and hope never to go. I was once asked to give away the bride at a wedding, and one young woman sent me an ounce of pot, with the attached question: "This is where I get my inspiration—where do you get yours?" Actually, mine usually comes in envelopes—the kind through which you can view your name and address printed by a computer—that arrive at the end of every month.

My favorite question of this type, from Anchorage, asked simply: "How could you write such a why?" Unsigned. If E. E. Cummings were still alive, I'd try to find out if he'd moved to the Big North.

The Old Standards: These are the questions writers dream of answering when they are collecting rejection *slips, and the ones they tire of quickest once they start* to publish. In other words, they are the questions that come up without fail in every dull interview the writer has ever given or will ever give. I'll enumerate a few of them:

Where do you get your ideas? (I get mine in Utica.)

How do you get an agent? (Sell your soul to the Devil.)

Do you have to know somebody to get published? (Yes; in fact, it helps to grovel, toady and be willing to perform twisted acts of sexual depravity at a moment's notice, and in public if necessary.)

How do you start a novel? (I usually start by writing the number 1 in the upper right-hand corner of a clean sheet of paper.)

How do you write best sellers? (Same way you get an agent.)

How do you sell your book to the movies? (Tell them they don't want it.)

What time of day do you write? (It doesn't matter; if I don't keep busy enough, the time inevitably comes.)

Do you ever run out of ideas? (Does a bear defecate in the woods?)

Who is your favorite writer? (Anyone who writes stories I would have written had I thought of them first.)

There are others, but they're pretty boring, so let us march on.

The Real Weirdies: Here I am, bopping down the street, on my morning walk, when some guy pulls over in his pickup truck or just happens to walk by and says, "Hi, Steve! Writing any good books lately?" I have an answer for this; I've developed it over the years out of pure necessity. I say, "I'm taking some time off." I say that even if I'm working like mad, thundering down homestretch on a book. The reason *why* I say this is because no other answer seems to fit. Believe me, I know. In the course of the trial and error that has finally resulted in "I'm taking some time off," I have discarded about 500 other answers.

Having an answer for "You writing any good books lately?" is a good thing, but I'd be lying if I said it solves the problem of *what the question means.* It is this inability on my part to make sense of this odd query, which reminds me of that Zen riddle—"Why is a mouse when it runs?"—that leaves me feeling mentally shaken and impotent. You see, it isn't just *one* question; it is a *bundle* of questions, cunningly wrapped up in one package. It's like that old favorite, "Are you still beating your wife?"

If I answer in the affirmative, it means I may have written—how many books? two? four?—(all of them good) in the last—how long? Well, how long is "lately"? It could mean I wrote maybe three good books just last week, or maybe two *on this very walk up to Bangor International Airport and back!* On the other hand, if I say no, what does *that* mean? I wrote three or four *bad* books in the last "lately" (surely "lately" can be no longer than a month, six weeks at the outside)?

Or here I am, signing books at the Betts' Bookstore or B. Dalton's in the local consumer factory (nicknamed "the mall"). This is something I do twice a year, and it serves much the same purpose as those little bundles of twigs religious people in the Middle Ages used to braid into whips and flagellate themselves with. During the course of this exercise in madness and self-abnegation, at least a dozen people will approach the little coffee table where I sit behind a barrier of books and ask brightly, "Don't you wish you had a rubber stamp?"

I have an answer to this one, too, an answer that has been developed over the years in a trial-and-error method similar to "I'm taking some time off." The answer to the rubber-stamp question is: "No, I don't mind."

Never mind if I really do or don't (this time it's my own motivations I want to skip over, you'll notice); the question is, Why does such an illogical query occur to so many people? My signature is actually stamped on the covers of several of my books, but people seem just as eager to get these signed as those that aren't so stamped. Would these questioners stand in line for the privilege of watching me slam a rubber stamp down on the title page of "The Shining" or "Pet Sematary"? I don't think they would.

If you still don't sense something peculiar in these questions, this one might help convince you. I'm sitting in the cafe around the corner from my house, grabbing a little lunch by myself and reading a book (reading at the table is one of the few bad habits acquired in my youth that I have nobly resisted giving up) until a customer or maybe even a waitress sidles up and asks, "How come you're not reading one of your own books?"

This hasn't happened just once, or even occasionally; it happens *a lot*. The computer-generated answer to this question usually gains a chuckle, although it is nothing but the pure, logical and apparent truth. "I know how they all come out," I say. End of exchange. Back to lunch, with only a pause to wonder why people assume you want to read what you wrote, rewrote, read again following the obligatory editorial conference and yet again during the process of correcting the mistakes that a good copy editor always prods, screaming, from their hiding places (I once heard a crime writer suggest that God could have used a copy editor, and while I find the notion slightly blasphemous, I tend to agree).

And then people sometimes ask in that chatty, let's-strike-up-a-conversation way people have, "How long does it take you to write a book?" Perfectly reasonable question—at least until you try to answer it and discover there *is* no answer. This time the computer-generated answer is a total falsehood, but it at least serves the purpose of advancing the conversation to some more discussable topic. "Usually about nine months," I say, "the same length of time it takes to make a baby." This satisfies everyone but me. I know that nine months is just an average, and probably a completely fictional one at thæt. It ignores "The Running Man" (published under the name Richard Bachman), which was written in four days during a snowy February vacation when I was teaching high school. It also ignores "It" and my latest, "The Tommyknockers." "It" is over 1,000 pages long and took four years to write. "The Tommyknockers" is 400 pages shorter but took five years to write.

Do I mind these questions? Yes...and no. Anyone minds questions that have no real answers and thus expose the fellow being questioned to be not a real doctor but a sort of witch doctor. But no one—at least no one with a modicum of simple human kindness—resents questions from people who honestly want answers. And now and then someone will ask a really interesting question, like, Do you write in the nude? The answer—not generated by computer—is: I don't think I ever have, but if it works, I'm willing to try it.

Living with My VCR
Nora Ephron

When all this started, two Christmases ago, I did not have a video-cassette recorder. What I had was a position on video-cassette recorders. I was against them. It seemed to me that the fundamental idea of the VCR—which is that if you go out and miss what's on television, you can always watch it later—flew in the face of almost the only thing I truly believed—which is that the whole point of going out is to miss what's on television. Let's face it: Part of being a grown-up is that every day you have to choose between going out at night or staying home, and it is one of life's unhappy truths that there is not enough time to do both.

Finally, though, I broke down, but not entirely. I did not buy a video-cassette recorder. I rented one. And I didn't rent one for myself—I myself intended to stand firm and hold to my only principle. I rented one for my children. For $29 a month, I would tape "The Wizard of Oz" and "Mary Poppins" and "Born Free," and my children would be able to watch them from time to time. In six months, when my rental contract expired, I would re-evaluate.

For quite a while, I taped for my children. Of course I had to subscribe to Home Box Office and Cinemax in addition to my normal cable service, for $19 more a month—but for the children. I taped "Oliver" and "Annie" and "My Fair Lady" for the children. And then I stopped taping for the children— who don't watch much television, in any case—and started to tape for myself.

I now tape for myself all the time. I tape when I am out, I tape when I am at home and doing other things, and I tape when I am asleep. At this very moment, as I am typing, I am taping. The entire length of my bedroom bookshelf has been turned over to video cassettes, mostly of movies; they are numbered and indexed and stacked in order in a household where absolutely nothing else is. Occasionally I find myself browsing through publications like Video Review and worrying whether I shouldn't switch to chrome-based videotape or have my heads cleaned or upgrade to a machine that does six or seven things at once and can be set to tape six or seven months in advance. No doubt I will soon find myself shopping at some Video Village for racks and storage systems especially made for what is known as "the serious collector."

How this happened, how I became a compulsive videotaper, is a mystery to me, because my position on videocassette recorders is very much the same as the one I started with. I am still against them. Now, though, I am against them for different reasons: Now I hate them out of knowledge rather than ignorance. The other technological breakthroughs that have made their way into my life after my initial pigheaded opposition to them—like the electric typewriter and the Cuisinart—have all settled peacefully into my home. I never think about them except when I'm using them, and when I'm using them I take them for granted. They do exactly what I want them to do. I put the slicing disk into the Cuisinart, and damned if the thing doesn't slice things up just the way it's supposed to. But there's no taking a VCR for granted. It squats there, next to the television, ready to rebuke any fool who expects something of it.

A child can operate a VCR, of course. Only a few maneuvers are required to tape something, and only a few more are required to tape something while you are out. You must set the time to the correct time you wish the recording to begin and end. You must punch the channel selector. You must insert a videotape. And, on my set, you must switch the "on" button to "time record." Theoretically, you can then go out and have a high old time, knowing that even if you waste the evening, your video-cassette recorder will not.

Sometimes things work out. Sometimes I return home, rewind the tape, and discover that the machine has recorded exactly what I'd hoped it would. But more often than not, what is on the tape is not at all what I'd intended; in fact, the moments leading up to the revelation of what is actually on my video cassettes are without doubt the most suspenseful of my humdrum existence. As I rewind the tape, I have no idea of what, if anything, will be on it; as I press the "play" button, I have not a clue as to what in particular has gone wrong. All I ever know for certain is that something has.

Usually it's my fault. I admit it. I have mis-set the timer

or channel selector or misread the newspaper listing. I have knelt at the foot of my machine and methodically, carefully, painstakingly set it—and set it wrong. This is extremely upsetting to me—I am normally quite competent when it comes to machines—but I can live with it. What is far more disturbing are the times when what has gone wrong is not my fault at all but the fault of outside forces over which I have no control whatsoever. The program listing in the newspaper lists the channel incorrectly. The cable guide inaccurately lists the length of the movie, lopping off the last 10 minutes. The evening's schedule of television programming is thrown off by an athletic event. The educational station is having a fund-raiser.

You would be amazed at how often outside forces affect a video-cassette recorder, and I think I am safe in saying that video-cassette recorders are the only household appliances that outside forces are even relevant to. As a result, my video-cassette library is a raggedy collection of near misses: "The Thin Man" without the opening; "King Kong" without the ending; a football game instead of "Murder, She Wrote"; dozens of PBS auctions and fundraisers instead of dozens of episodes of "Masterpiece Theater." All told, my success rate at videotaping is even lower than my success rate at buying clothes I turn out to like as much as I did in the store; the machine provides more opportunities per week to make mistakes than anything else in my life.

Every summer and at Christmastime, I re-evaluate my six-month rental contract. I have three options: I can buy the video-cassette recorder, which I would never do because I hate it so much; I can cancel the contract and turn in the machine, which I would never do because I am so addicted to videotaping; or I can go on renting. I go on renting. In two years I have spent enough money renting to buy two video-cassette recorders at the discount electronics place in the neighborhood, but I don't care. Renting is my way of deluding myself that I have some power over my VCR; it's my way of believing that I can still some day reject the machine in an ultimate way (by sending it back)—or else forgive it (by buying it)—for all the times it has rejected me.

In the meantime, I have my pathetic but ever-expanding

collection of cassettes. "Why don't you just rent the movies?" a friend said to me recently, after I finished complaining about the fact that my tape of "The Maltese Falcon" now has a segment of "Little House on the Prairie" in the middle of it. Rent them? What a bizarre suggestion. Then I would have to watch them. And I don't watch my videotapes. I don't have time. I would virtually have to watch my videotapes for the next two years just to catch up with what my VCR has recorded so far; and in any event, even if I did have time, the VCR would be taping and would therefore be unavailable for use in viewing.

So I merely accumulate video cassettes. I haven't accumulated anything this mindlessly since my days in college, when I was obsessed with filling my bookshelf, it didn't matter with what; what mattered was that I believed that if I had a lot of books, it would say something about my intelligence and taste. On some level, I suppose I believe that if I have a lot of video cassettes, it will say something—not about my intelligence or taste, but about my intentions. I intend to live long enough to have time to watch my videotapes. Any way you look at it, that means forever.

My Grandmother's Illness
Mordecai Richler

The seventh summer of my grandmother's illness she was supposed to die and we did not know from day to day when it would happen. I was often sent out to eat at an aunt's or at my other grandmother's house. I was hardly ever at home. In those days they let boys into the left-field bleachers of Delormier Downs free during the week and Duddy, Gas sometimes, Hershey, Stan, Arty and me spent many an afternoon at the ball park. The Montreal Royals, kingpin of the Dodger farm system, had a marvellous club at the time. There was Jackie Robinson, Roy Campanella, Lou Ortiz, Red Durrett, Honest John Gabbard, and Kermit Kitman. Kitman was our hero. It used to give us a charge to watch that crafty little Jew, one of ours, running around out there with all those tall dumb southern crackers. "Hey, Kitman," we would yell, "Hey, shmo-head, if your father knew you played ball on *shabus*—" Kitman, alas, was all field and no hit. He never made the majors. "There goes Kermit Kitman," we would holler, after he had gone down swinging again, "the first Jewish strike-out king of the International League." This we promptly followed up by bellowing choice imprecations in Yiddish.

It was after one of these games, on a Friday afternoon, that I came home to find a crowd gathered in front of our house.

"That's the grandson," somebody said.

A knot of old people stood staring at our front door from across the street. A taxi pulled up and my aunt hurried out, hiding her face in her hands.

"After so many years," a woman said.

"And probably next year they'll discover a cure. Isn't that always the case?"

The flat was clotted. Uncles and aunts from my father's side of the family, strangers, Dr. Katzman, neighbours, were all milling around and talking in hushed voices. My father was in the kitchen, getting out the apricot brandy. "Your grandmother's dead," he said.

459

"Where's Maw?"

"In the bedroom with...You'd better not go in."

"I want to see her."

My mother wore a black shawl and glared down at a knot of handkerchief clutched in a fist that had been cracked by washing soda. "Don't come in here," she said.

Several bearded round-shouldered men in shiny black coats surrounded the bed. I couldn't see my grandmother.

"Your grandmother's dead."

"Daddy told me."

"Go wash your face and comb your hair."

"Yes."

"You'll have to get your own supper."

"Sure."

"One minute. The *baba* left some jewellery. The necklace is for Rifka and the ring is for your wife."

"Who's getting married?"

"Better go and wash your face. Remember behind the ears, please."

Telegrams were sent, the obligatory long distance calls were made, and all through the evening relatives and neighbours and old followers of the Zaddik poured into the house. Finally, the man from the funeral parlour arrived.

"There goes the only Jewish businessman in town," Segal said, "who wishes all his customers were German."

"This is no time for jokes."

"Listen, life goes on."

My Cousin Jerry had begun to affect a cigarette holder. "Soon the religious mumbo-jumbo starts," he said to me.

"Wha'?"

"Everybody is going to be sickeningly sentimental."

The next day was the sabbath and so, according to law, my grandmother couldn't be buried until Sunday. She would have to lie on the floor all night. Two grizzly women in white came to move and wash the body and a professional mourner arrived to sit up and pray for her. "I don't trust his face," my mother said. "He'll fall asleep."

"He won't fall asleep."

"You watch him, Sam."

"A fat lot of good prayers will do her now. Alright!
Okay! I'll watch him."

My father was in a fury with Segal.

"The way he goes after the apricot brandy you'd think
he never saw a bottle in his life before."

Rifka and I were sent to bed, but we couldn't sleep. My
aunt was sobbing over the body in the living room; there was
the old man praying, coughing and spitting into his handkerchief whenever he woke; and the hushed voices and whimpering from the kitchen, where my father and mother sat. Rifka
allowed me a few drags off her cigarette.

"Well, *pisherke,* this is our last night together. Tomorrow you can take over the back room."

"Are you crazy?"

"You always wanted it for yourself, didn't you?"

"She died in there, but."

"So?"

"I couldn't sleep in there now."

"Good night and happy dreams."

"Hey, let's talk some more."

"Did you know," Rifka said, "that when they hang a
man the last thing that happens is that he has an orgasm?"

"A wha'?"

"Skip it. I forgot you were still in kindergarten."

"Kiss my Royal Canadian—"

"At the funeral, they're going to open the coffin and
throw dirt in her face. It's supposed to be earth from Eretz.
They open it and you're going to have to look."

"Says you."

A little while after the lights had been turned out Rifka
approached my bed, her head covered with a sheet and her
arms raised high. "Bouyo-bouyo. Who's that sleeping in my
bed? Woo-woo."

My uncle who was in the theatre and my aunt from
Toronto came to the funeral. My uncle, the rabbi, was there
too.

"As long as she was alive," my mother said, "he
couldn't even send her five dollars a month. I don't want him
in the house, Sam. I can't bear the sight of him."

"You're upset," Dr. Katzman said, "and you don't know what you're saying."

"Maybe you'd better give her a sedative," the rabbi said.

"Sam will you speak up for once, please."

Flushed, eyes heated, my father stepped up to the rabbi. "I'll tell you this straight to your face, Israel," he said. "You've gone down in my estimation."

The rabbi smiled a little.

"Year by year," my father continued, his face burning a brighter red, "your stock has gone down with me."

My mother began to weep and she was led unwillingly to a bed. While my father tried his utmost to comfort her, as he muttered consoling things, Dr. Katzman plunged a needle into her arm. "There we are," he said.

I want to sit on the stoop outside with Duddy. My uncle, the rabbi, and Dr. Katzman stepped into the sun to light cigarettes.

"I know exactly how you feel," Dr. Katzman said. "There's been a death in the family and the world seems indifferent to your loss. Your heart is broken and yet it's a splendid summer day...a day made for love and laughter... and that must seem very cruel to you."

The rabbi nodded; he sighed.

"Actually," Dr. Katzman said, "it's remarkable that she held out for so long."

"Remarkable?" the rabbi said. "It's written that if a man has been married twice he will spend as much time with his first wife in heaven as he did on earth. My father, may he rest in peace, was married to his first wife for seven years and my mother, may she rest in peace, has managed to keep alive for seven years. Today in heaven she will be able to join my father, may he rest in peace."

Dr. Katzman shook his head. "It's amazing," he said. He told my uncle that he was writing a book based on his experiences as a healer. "The mysteries of the human heart."

"Yes."

"Astonishing."

My father hurried outside. "Dr. Katzman, please. It's

my wife. Maybe the injection wasn't strong enough. She just doesn't stop crying. It's like a tap. Can you come in, please?"

"Excuse me," Dr. Katzman said to my uncle.

"Of course." My uncle turned to Duddy and me. "Well, boys," he said, "what would you like to be when you grow up?"

Complexion

Richard Rodriguez

Complexion. My first conscious experience of sexual excitement concerns my complexion. One summer weekend, when I was around seven years old, I was at a public swimming pool with the whole family. I remember sitting on the damp pavement next to the pool and seeing my mother, in the spectators' bleachers, holding my younger sister on her lap. My mother, I noticed, was watching my father as he stood on a diving board, waving to her. I watched her wave back. Then saw her radiant, bashful, astonishing smile. In that second I sensed that my mother and father had a relationship I knew nothing about. A nervous excitement encircled my stomach as I saw my mother's eyes follow my father's figure curving into the water. A second or two later, he emerged. I heard him call out. Smiling, his voice sounded, buoyant, calling me to swim to him. But turning to see him, I caught my mother's eye. I heard her shout over to me. In Spanish she called through the crowd: 'Put a towel on over your shoulders.' In public, she didn't want to say why. I knew.

That incident anticipates the shame and sexual inferiority I was to feel in later years because of my dark complexion. I was to grow up an ugly child. Or one who thought himself ugly. *(Feo.)* One night when I was eleven or twelve years old, I locked myself in the bathroom and carefully regarded my reflection in the mirror over the sink. Without any pleasure I studied my skin. I turned on the faucet. (In my mind I heard the swirling voices of aunts, and even my mother's voice, whispering, whispering incessantly about lemon juice solutions and dark, *feo* children.) With a bar of soap, I fashioned a thick ball of lather. I began soaping my arms. I took my father's straight razor out of the medicine cabinet. Slowly, with steady deliberateness, I put the blade against my flesh, pressed it as close as I could without cutting, and moved it up and down across my skin to see if I could get out, somehow lessen, the dark. All I succeeded in doing, however, was in shaving my arms bare of their hair. For as I noted with disappointment, the dark would not come out. It remained. Trapped. Deep in the cells of my skin.

Throughout adolescence, I felt myself mysteriously marked. Nothing else about my appearance would concern me so much as the fact that my complexion was dark. My mother would say how sorry she was that there was not money enough to get braces to straighten my teeth. But I never bothered about my teeth. In three-way mirrors at department stores, I'd see my profile dramatically defined by a long nose, but it was really only the color of my skin that caught my attention.

I wasn't afraid that I would become a menial laborer because of my skin. Nor did my complexion make me feel especially vulnerable to racial abuse. (I didn't really consider my dark skin to be a racial characteristic. I would have been only too happy to look as Mexican as my light-skinned older brother.) Simply, I judged myself ugly. And, since the women in my family had been the ones who discussed it in such worried tones, I felt my dark skin made me unattractive to women.

Thirteen years old. Fourteen. In a grammar school art class, when the assignment was to draw a self-portrait, I tried and I tried but could not bring myself to shade in the face on the paper to anything like my actual tone. With disgust then I would come face to face with myself in mirrors. With disappointment I located myself in class photographs—my dark face undefined by the camera which had clearly described the white faces of classmates. Or I'd see my dark wrist against my long-sleeved white shirt.

I grew divorced from my body. Insecure, overweight, listless. On hot summer days when my rubber-soled shoes soaked up the heat from the sidewalk, I kept my head down. Or walked in the shade. My mother didn't need anymore to tell me to watch out for the sun. I denied myself a sensational life. The normal, extraordinary, animal excitement of feeling my body alive—riding shirtless on a bicycle in the warm wind created by furious self-propelled motion—the sensations that first had excited in me a sense of my maleness, I denied. I was too ashamed of my body. I wanted to forget that I had a body because I had a brown body. I was grateful that none of my classmates ever mentioned the fact.

I continued to see the *braceros,* those men I resembled in one way and, in another way, didn't resemble at all. On the watery horizon of a Valley afternoon, I'd see them. And though I feared looking like them, it was with silent envy that I regarded them still. I envied them their physical lives, their freedom to violate the taboo of the sun. Closer to home I would notice the shirtless construction workers, the roofers, the sweating men tarring the street in front of the house. And I'd see the Mexican gardeners. I was unwilling to admit the attraction of their lives. I tried to deny it by looking away. But what was denied became strongly desired.

In high school physical education classes, I withdrew, in the regular company of five or six classmates, to a distant corner of a football field where we smoked and talked. Our company was composed of bodies too short or too tall, all graceless and all—except mine—pale. Our conversation was usually witty. (In fact we were intelligent.) If we referred to the athletic contests around us, it was with sarcasm. With savage scorn I'd refer to the 'animals' playing football or baseball. It would have been important for me to have joined them. Or for me to have taken off my shirt, to have let the sun burn dark on my skin, and to have run barefoot on the warm wet grass. It would have been very important. Too important. It would have been too telling a gesture—to admit the desire for sensation, the body, my body.

Fifteen, sixteen. I was a teenager shy in the presence of girls. Never dated. Barely could talk to a girl without stammering. In high school I went to several dances, but I never managed to ask a girl to dance. So I stopped going. I cannot remember high school years now with the parade of typical images: bright drive-ins or gliding blue shadows of a Junior Prom. At home most weekend nights, I would pass evenings reading. Like those hidden, precocious adolescents who have no real-life sexual experiences, I read a great deal of romantic fiction. 'You won't find it in your books,' my brother would playfully taunt me as he prepared to go to a party by freezing the crest of the wave in his hair with sticky pomade. Through my reading, however, I developed a fabulous and sophisticated sexual imagination. At seventeen, I may not have known how to engage a girl in small talk, but I had read *Lady Chatterley's Lover*.

It annoyed me to hear my father's teasing: that I would never know what 'real work' is; that my hands were so soft. I think I knew it was his way of admitting pleasure and pride in my academic success. But I didn't smile. My mother said she was glad her children were getting their educations and would not be pushed around like *los pobres*. I heard the remark ironically as a reminder of my separation from *los braceros*. At such times I suspected that education was making me effeminate. The odd thing, however, was that I did not judge my classmates so harshly. Nor did I consider my male teachers in high school effeminate. It was only myself I judged against some shadowy, mythical Mexican laborer—dark like me, yet very different.

GLOSSARY

Abstract and concrete are ways of describing important qualities of language. Abstract words are not associated with real, material objects that are related directly to the five senses. Such words as "love," "wisdom," "patriotism," and "power" are abstract because they refer to ideas rather than to things. Concrete language, on the other hand, names things that can be perceived by the five senses. Words like "table," "smoke," "lemon," and "halfback" are concrete. Generally you should not be too abstract in writing. It is best to employ concrete words naming things that can be seen, touched, smelled, heard, or tasted in order to support your more abstract ideas.

Allusion is a reference to some literary, biographical, or historical event. It is a "figure of speech" (a fresh, useful comparison) used to illuminate an idea. For instance, if you want to state that a certain national ruler is insane, you might refer to him as a "Nero"—an allusion to the Emperor who burned Rome.

Alternating method in comparison and contrast involves a point-by-point treatment of the two subjects that you have selected to discuss. Assume that you have chosen five points to examine in a comparison of the Volkswagen "Golf" (subject A) and the Honda "Accord" (subject B): cost, comfort, gas mileage, road handling, and frequency of repair. In applying the alternating method, you would begin by discussing cost in relation to A & B; then comfort in relation to A & B, and so on. The alternating method permits you to isolate points for a balanced discussion.

Ambiguity means uncertainty. A writer is ambiguous when using a word, phrase, or sentence that is not clear. Ambiguity usually results in misunderstanding, and should be avoided in essay writing. Always strive for clarity in your compositions.

Analogy is a form of figurative comparison that uses a clear illustration to explain a difficult idea or function. It is unlike a formal comparison in that its subjects of comparison are from different

468

categories or areas. For example, an analogy likening "division of labor" to the activity of bees in a hive makes the first concept more concrete by showing it to the reader through the figurative comparison with the bees.

Antonym is a word that is opposite in meaning to that of another word: "hot" is an antonym of "cold"; "fat" is an antonym of "thin"; "large" is an antonym of "small."

Argumentation is a form of writing in which you offer reasons in favor of or against something. (See Chapter 11, pp. 393–395.)

Block method in comparison and contrast involves the presentation of all information about your first subject (A), followed by all information about the second subject (B). Thus, using the objects of comparison explained in the discussion of the "alternating method" (see entry, p. 217), you would for the block method first present all five points about the Volkswagen. Then you would present all five points about the Honda. When using the block method, remember to present the same points for each subject, and to provide an effective transition in moving from subject A to subject B.

Causal analysis is a form of writing that examines causes and effects of events or conditions as they relate to a specific subject (see Chapter 10, pp. 350–352).

Characterization is the description of people. As a particular type of description in an essay, characterization attempts to capture as vividly as possible the features, qualities, traits, speech, and actions of individuals.

Chronological order is the arrangement of events in the order that they happened. You might use chronological order to trace the history of the Vietnam War, to explain a scientific process, or to present the biography of a close relative or friend. When you order an essay by chronology, you are moving from one step to the next in time.

Classification is a pattern of writing where the author divides a subject into categories and then groups elements in each of those categories according to their relationships to each other (see Chapter 8, pp. 275–276).

Clichés are expressions that were once fresh and vivid, but have become tired and worn from overuse. "I'm so hungry that I could eat a horse" is a typical cliché. People use clichés in conversation, but writers should generally avoid them.

Closings or "conclusions" are endings for your essay. Without a closing, your essay is incomplete, leaving the reader with the feeling that something important has been left out. There are numerous closing possibilities available to writers: summarizing main points in the essay; restating the main idea; using an effective quotation to bring the essay to an end; offering the reader the climax to a series of events; returning to the conclusion and echoing it; offering a solution to a problem; emphasizing the topic's significance; or setting a new frame of reference by generalizing from the main thesis. Whatever type of closing you use, make certain that it ends the essay in a firm and emphatic way.

Coherence is a quality in effective writing that results from the careful ordering of each sentence in a paragraph, and each paragraph in the essay. If an essay is coherent, each part will grow naturally and logically from those parts that come before it. Coherence depends on the writer's ability to organize materials in a logical way, and to order segments so that the reader is carried along easily from start to finish. The main devices used in achieving coherence are *transitions,* which help to connect one thought with another.

Colloquial language is language used in conversation and in certain types of informal writing, but rarely in essays, business writing, or research papers. There is nothing wrong with colloquialisms like "gross," "later," or "rap" when used in conversational settings. However, they are often unacceptable in essay writing—except when used sparingly for special effects.

Comparison/contrast is a pattern of essay writing treating similarities and differences between two subjects. (See Chapter 6, pp. 204–205).

Composition is a term used for an essay or for any piece of writing that reveals a careful plan.

Concrete (See Abstract/Concrete)

Connotation/denotation are terms specifying the way a word has meaning. Connotation refers to the "shades of meaning" that a word might have because of various emotional associations it calls up for writers and readers alike. Words like "American," "physician," "mother," "pig," and "San Francisco" have strong connotative overtones to them. With denotation, however, we are concerned not with the suggestive meaning of a word but with its exact, literal meaning. Denotation refers to the "dictionary definition" of a word—its exact meaning. Writers must understand the connotative and denotative value of words, and must control the shades of meaning that many words possess.

Context clues are hints provided about the meaning of a word by another word or words, or by the sentence or sentences coming before or after it. Thus in the sentence, "Mr. Rome, a true *raconteur,* told a story that thrilled the guests," we should be able to guess at the meaning of the italicized word by the context clues coming both before and after it. (A "raconteur" is a person who tells good stories.)

Definition is a method of explaining a word so that the reader knows what you mean by it. (See Chapter 7, pp. 238–239.)

Derivation is how a word originated and where it came from. Knowing the origin of a word can make you more aware of its meaning, and more able to use it effectively in writing. Your dictionary normally lists abbreviations (for example, O.E. for Old English, G. for Greek) for word origins and sometimes explains fully how they came about.

Description is a type of writing that uses details of sight, color, sound, smell, and touch to create a word picture and to explain or illustrate an idea. (See Chapter 3, pp. 92–93.)

Dialogue is the exact duplication in writing of something people say to each other. Dialogue is the reproduction of speech or conversation; it can add concreteness and vividness to an essay, and can also help to reveal character. When using dialogue, writers must be careful to use correct punctuation. Moreover, to use dialogue effectively in essay writing, you must develop an ear for the way other people talk, and an ability to create it accurately.

Diction refers to the writer's choice or use of words. Good diction reflects the topic of the writing. Steiner's diction, for example, is rather formal, despite his purpose of expressing deeply felt emotions. Malcolm X's diction is more varied, including subtle descriptions in standard diction and conversational sarcasms. Levels of diction refer both to the purpose of the essay and to the writer's audience. Skillful choice of the level of diction keeps the reader intimately involved with the topic.

Division is that aspect of classification (see Chapter 8, pp. 275–276) where the writer divides some large subject into categories. For example, you might divide "fish" into salt water and fresh water fish; or "sports" into team and individual sports. Division helps writers to split large and potentially complicated subjects into parts for orderly presentation and discussion.

Effect is a term used in causal analysis (see Chapter 10, pp. 350–352) to describe the outcome or expected result of a chain of happenings. When dealing with the analysis of effects, writers should determine whether they want to work with immediate or final effects, or both. Thus, a writer analyzing the effects of an accidental nuclear explosion that happened in 1956 might choose to analyze effects immediately after the blast, as well as effects that still linger.

Emphasis suggests the placement of the most important ideas in key positions in the essay. Writers can emphasize ideas simply by placing important ones at the beginning or at the end of the paragraph or essay. But several other techniques help writers to emphasize important ideas: (1) key words and ideas can be stressed by repetition; (2) ideas can be presented in climactic order, by building from lesser ideas at the beginning to the main idea at the end; (3) figurative language (for instance, a vivid simile) can call attention to a main idea; (4) the relative proportion of detail offered to support an idea can emphasize its importance; (5) comparison and contrast of an idea with other ideas can emphasize its importance; and (6) mechanical devices like underlining, capitalizing, or using exclamation points (all of which should be used sparingly) can stress significance.

Essay is the name given to a short prose work on a limited topic. Essays take many forms, ranging from a familiar narrative account of an event in your life, to explanatory, argumentative, or critical investigations of a subject. Normally, in one way or the other, an essay will convey the writer's personal ideas about the subject.

Euphemism is the use of a word or phrase simply because it seems less distasteful or less offensive than another word. For instance, "mortician" is a euphemism for "undertaker"; "sanitation worker" for "garbage collector."

Fable is a narrative with a moral (see Chapter 4, pp. 127–128). The story from which the writer draws the moral can be either true or imaginary. When writing a fable, it is important that a writer clearly presents the moral to be derived from the narrative, as Rachel Carson does in "A Fable for Tomorrow."

Figurative language, as opposed to *literal,* is a special approach to writing that departs from what is typically a concrete, straightforward style. It involves a vivid, imaginative comparison that goes beyond plain or ordinary statements. For instance, instead of saying that "Joan is wonderful," you could write that "Joan is like a summer's rose" (a *simile*); "Joan's hair is wheat, pale and soft and yellow" (a *metaphor*); "Joan is my Helen of Troy" (an *allusion*); or a number of other comparative approaches. Note that Joan is not a rose, her hair is not wheat, nor is she some other person named Helen. Figurative language is not logical; instead, it requires an ability on the part of the writer to create an imaginative comparison in order to make an idea more striking.

Flashback is a narrative technique in which the writer begins at some point in the action and then moves into the past in order to provide necessary background information. Flashback adds variety to the narrative method, enabling writers to approach a story not only in terms of straight chronology, but in terms of a back-and-forth movement. However, it is at best a very difficult technique and should be used with great care.

General/specific words are necessary in writing, although it is wise to keep your vocabulary as specific as possible. General words refer to broad categories and groups, while specific words capture with more force and clarity the nature of a term. The distinction between general and specific language is always a matter of degree. "A woman walked down the street" is more general than "Mrs. Walker walked down Fifth Avenue," while "Mrs. Webster, elegantly dressed in a muslin suit, strolled down Fifth Avenue" is more specific than the first two examples. Our ability to use specific language depends on the extent of our vocabulary. The more words we know, the more specific we can be in choosing words.

Hyperbole is obvious and intentional exaggeration.

Illustration is the use of several examples to support our idea (see Chapter 5, pp. 164–165).

Imagery is clear, vivid description that appeals to our sense of sight, smell, touch, sound, or taste. Much imagery exists for its own sake, adding descriptive flavor to an essay, as when Richard Selzer in "The Discus Thrower" writes, "I unwrap the bandages from the stumps, and begin to cut away the black scabs and the dead, glazed fat with scissors and forceps. A shard of white bone comes loose." However, imagery can also add meaning to an essay. For example, in Francke's essay, the pattern of imagery connected with the setting and procedure of her abortion alerts the reader to the importance of that event in the author's life. Again, when Orwell writes at the start of "A Hanging," "It was in Burma, a sodden morning of the rains. A sickly light, like yellow tinfoil, was slanting over the high walls into the jail yard," we see that the author uses imagery to prepare us for the sombre and terrifying event to follow. Writers can use imagery to contribute to any type of wording, or they can rely on it to structure an entire essay. It is always difficult to invent fresh, vivid description, but it is an effort that writers should make if they wish to improve the quality of their prose.

Introductions are the beginning or openings of essays. Introductions should perform a number of functions. They should alert the reader to the subject, set the limits of the essay, and indicate what the thesis (or main idea) will be. Moreover, they should arouse the reader's interest in the subject, so that the reader will want to continue reading into the essay. There are several devices available to writers that will aid in the development of sound introductions.

1. Simply state the subject and establish the thesis. See the Rita Mae Brown essay (p. 266), and "The Three New Yorks" (p. 286), by E. B. White.
2. Open with a clear, vivid description of a setting that will become important as your essay advances. Save your thesis for a later stage, but indicate what your subject is. See the essay by Laurence (p. 94).
3. Ask a question or a series of questions, which you might answer in the introduction or in another part of the essay. See the Jordan essay (p. 240) and the Didion essay (p. 34).
4. Tell an anecdote (a short, self-contained story of an entertaining nature) that serves to illuminate your subject. See the Williams essay (p. 166).
5. Use comparison or contrast to frame your subject and to present the thesis. See the Goodman essay (p. 221).

6. Begin by stating your personal attitude toward a controversial issue. See the Steiner essay (p. 82).

These are only some of the devices that appear in the introductions to essays in this text. Writers can also ask questions, give definitions, or provide personal accounts—there are many techniques that can be used to develop introductions. The important thing to remember is that you *need* an introduction to an essay. It can be a single sentence or a much longer paragraph, but it must accomplish its purpose—to introduce readers to the subject, and to engage them so that they want to explore the essay further.

Irony is the use of language to suggest the opposite of what is stated. Writers use irony to reveal unpleasant or troublesome realities that exist in life, or to poke fun at human weaknesses and foolish attitudes. For instance, in ''A Hanging,'' the men who are in charge of the execution engage in laughter and lighthearted conversation after the event. There is irony in the situation and in their speech because we sense that they are actually very tense—almost unnerved—by the hanging; their laughter is the opposite of what their true emotional state actually is. Many situations and conditions lend themselves to ironic treatment.

Jargon is the use of special words associated with a specific area of knowledge or a specific profession. It is similar to ''shop talk'' that members of a certain trade might know, but not necessarily people outside it. For example, in Bettelheim's essay there are several terms or applications of jargon relating to psychology. Use jargon sparingly in your writing, and be certain to define all specialized terms that you think your readers might not know.

Journalese is a level of writing associated with prose types normally found in newspapers and popular magazines. A typical newspaper article tends to present information factually or objectively; to use simple language and simple sentence structure; and to rely on relatively short paragraphs. It also stays close to the level of conversational English without becoming chatty or colloquial.

Metaphor is a type of figurative language in which an item from one category is compared briefly and imaginatively with an item from another area. Writers create metaphors to assign meaning to a word in an original way.

Narration is telling a story in order to illustrate an important idea (see Chapter 4, pp. 127–128).

Objective/subjective writing refers to the attitude that writers take toward their subject. When writers are objective, they try not to report their own personal feelings about their subject. They attempt to control, if not eliminate, their own attitude toward the topic. Thus in the essay by L'Amour (see pp. 186–189), we learn about how "wild" the Old West really was, but we don't learn about the writer's opinions about the rightness or wrongness of such wildness. Many essays, on the other hand, reveal the authors' personal attitudes and emotions. In George Steiner's essay (see pp. 82–85), the author's personal fears about the decline of reading seem clear. He takes a highly subjective approach to the topic. For some kinds of college writing, such as business or laboratory reports, research papers, or literary analyses, it is best to be as objective as possible. But for many of the essays in composition courses, the subjective touch is fine.

Order is the manner in which you arrange information or materials in an essay. The most common ordering techniques are *chronological order* (involving time sequence); *spatial order* (involving the arrangement of descriptive details); *process order* (involving a step-by-step approach to an activity); *deductive order* (in which you offer a thesis and then the evidence to support it); and *inductive order* (in which you present evidence first and build toward the thesis). Some rhetorical patterns such as comparison and contrast, classification, and argumentation require other ordering techniques. Writers should select those ordering principles that permit them to present materials clearly.

Paradox is a statement that *seems* to be contradictory but actually contains an element of truth. Writers use it in order to call attention to their subject.

Parallelism is a variety of sentence structure in which there is "balance" or coordination in the presentation of elements. "I came, I saw, I conquered" is a good example of parallelism, presenting both pronouns and verbs in a coordinated manner. Parallelism can also be applied to several sentences and to entire paragraphs (see the Syfers's essay, pages 415–417). It can be an effective way to emphasize ideas.

Personification is giving an object, thing, or idea lifelike or human qualities. For instance, Ray Bradbury personifies Halloween when he writes that it "didn't just stroll into our yards" (see p. 177). Like all forms of figurative writing, personification adds freshness to description, and makes ideas vivid by setting up striking comparisons.

Point of view is the angle from which a writer tells a story. Many personal or informal essays take the *first-person* (or "I") point of view, as the essays by Malcolm X, Saroyan, Moon, Hughes, Orwell, Didion, Miller, and others reveal. The first-person "I" point of view is natural and fitting for essays when the writer wants to speak in a familiar and intimate way to the reader. On the other hand, the *third-person* point of view ("he," "she," "it," "they") distances the reader somewhat from the writer. The third-person point of view is useful in essays where writers are not talking exclusively about themselves, but about other people, things, and events as in the essays by L'Amour, Carson, and White. Occasionally, the second-person ("you") point of view will appear in essays, notably in essays involving process analysis where the writer directs the reader to do something; part of Ernest Hemingway's essay (which also utilizes third-person point of view) uses this strategy. The position that you take as a writer depends largely on the type of essay you write.

Prefix is one or more syllables attached to the front of another word in order to influence its meaning or to create a new word. A knowledge of prefixes and their meanings aids in establishing the meanings of words and in increasing the vocabulary that we use in writing. Common prefixes and their meanings include *bi-* (two), *ex-*(out, out of), *per-*(through), *pre-*(before), *re-*(back), *tele-*(distant), and *trans-*(across, beyond).

Process analysis is a pattern of writing that explains in a step-by-step way the methods for doing something or reaching a desired end (see Chapter 9, pp. 316–317).

Proposition is the main point in an argumentative essay. It is like a *thesis* except that it usually presents an idea that is debatable or can be disputed.

Refutation is a technique in argumentative writing where you recognize and deal effectively with the arguments of your opponents. Your own argument will be stronger if you can refute— prove false or wrong—all opposing arguments.

Root is the basic part of a word. It sometimes aids us in knowing what the larger word means. Thus if we know that the root *doc-* means "teach" we might be able to figure out a word like "doctrine." *Prefixes* and *suffixes* are attached to roots to create words.

Sarcasm is a sneering or taunting attitude in writing. It is designed to hurt by ridiculing or criticizing. Basically, sarcasm is a heavy-handed form of irony, as when an individual says, "Well, you're exactly on time, aren't you" to someone who is an hour late, and says it with a sharpness in the voice, a sharpness designed to hurt. Writers should try to avoid sarcastic writing and to use more acceptable varieties of irony and satire to criticize their subject.

Satire is the humorous or critical treatment of a subject in order to expose the subject's vices, follies, stupidities, and so forth. Syfers, for instance, satirizes stereotyped notions of wives, hoping to change these attitudes by revealing them as foolish. Satire is a better weapon than sarcasm in the hands of the writer because satire is used to correct, whereas sarcasm merely hurts.

Sentimentality is the excessive display of emotion in writing, whether it is intended or unintended. Because sentimentality can distort the true nature of a situation, writers should use it cautiously, or not at all. They should be especially careful when dealing with certain subjects, for example the death of a loved one, remembrance of a mother or father, a ruined romance, the loss of something valued, that lend themselves to sentimental treatment. Only the best writers—Thomas, Francke, Hughes, and others in this text—can avoid the sentimental traps rooted in their subjects.

Simile is an imaginative comparison using "like" or "as." When Orwell writes, "A sickly light, like yellow tinfoil, was slanting over the high walls into the jail yard," he uses a vivid simile in order to reinforce the dull description of the scene.

Slang is a level of language that uses racy and colorful expressions associated more often with speech than with writing. Slang expressions like "Gerald's my boss man" or "She's totally max" should not be used in essay writing, except when the writer is reproducing dialogue or striving for a special effect. Hughes is one writer in this collection who uses slang effectively to convey his message to the reader.

Suffix is a syllable or syllables appearing at the end of a word and influencing its meaning. As with prefixes and roots, you can build vocabulary and establish meanings by knowing about suffixes. Some typical suffixes are -*able* (capable of), -*al* (relating to), *-ic* (characteristic of), *-ion* (state of), *-er* (one who) appear often in standard writing.

Symbol is something that exists in itself but also stands for something else. Thus the "stumps" in paragraph 20 of Selzer's essay "The Discus Thrower" are not just the patient's amputated legs, but they serve as symbols of the man's helplessness and immobility. As a type of figurative language, the symbol can be a strong feature in an essay, operating to add depth of meaning, and even to unify entire essays.

Synonym is a word that means roughly the same as another word. In practice, few words are exactly alike in meaning. Careful writers use synonyms to vary word choice, without ever moving too far from the shade of meaning intended.

Theme is the central idea in an essay; it is also often termed the *thesis*. Everything in an essay should support the theme in one way or another.

Thesis is the main idea in an essay. The *thesis sentence,* appearing early in the essay, and normally somewhere in the first paragraph, serves to convey the main idea to the reader in a clear way. It is always useful to state your central idea as soon as possible, and before you introduce other supporting ideas.

Title for an essay should be a short, simple indication of the contents of your essay. Titles like "On Keeping a Notebook," "What to Listen for in Music," "The Ambivalence of Abortion," and "The Future of Reading" are the sorts of titles that convey the central subjects of these essays in brief, effective ways. Others, such as "Survival," "Catfish," and "I Became Her Target" also convey the central idea, but more abstractly. Always provide titles for your essays.

Tone is the writer's attitude toward his or her subject or material. An essay writer's tone may be objective ("Arizona 87"), ironic ("I Want A Wife"), comic ("Eating Alone in Restaurants"), nostalgic ("Moon on a Silver Spoon"), or a reflection of numerous other attitudes. Tone is the "voice" that you give to an essay; every writer should strive to create a "personal voice" or tone that will be distinctive throughout any type of essay under development.

Transition is the linking of one idea to the next in order to achieve essay coherence (See *Coherence*). Transitions are words that connect these ideas. Among the most common techniques to achieve smooth transition are: (1) repeating a key word or phrase; (2) using a pronoun to refer back to a key word or phrase; (3) relying on traditional connectives like "thus," "for example," "moreover," "therefore," "however," "finally," "likewise," "afterwards," and "in conclusion"; (4) using parallel structure (see *Parallelism*); and (5) creating a sentence or an entire paragraph that serves as a bridge from one part of your essay to the next. Transition is best achieved when the writer presents ideas and details carefully and in logical order. Try not to lose the reader by failing to provide for adequate transition from idea to idea.

Unity is that feature in an essay where all material relates to a central concept and contributes to the meaning of the whole. To achieve a unified effect in an essay, the writer must design an introduction and conclusion, maintain a consistent tone and point of view, develop middle paragraphs in a coherent manner, and always stick to the subject, never permitting unimportant elements to enter. Thus, unity involves a successful blending of all elements that go into the creation of a sound essay.

Vulgarisms are words that exist below conventional vocabulary, and which are not accepted in polite conversation. Always avoid vulgarisms in your own writing, unless they serve an illustrative purpose.

Acknowledgments

May Angelou, "The Flight," from *I Know Why the Caged Bird Sings*, by Maya Angelou. Copyright © 1969 by Maya Angelou. Reprinted by permission of Random House, Inc.

Margaret Atwood, "Survival," excerpt from *Survival: A Thematic Guide to Canadian Literature*, (Toronto: House of Anasi Press, 1972). Reprinted by permission.

James T. Baker, "How Do We Find the Students in a World of Academic Gymnasts and Worker Ants?" from *The Chronicle of Higher Education*. Copyright 1982, The Chronicle of Higher Education. Reprinted with permission.

Russell Baker, "The Two Ismo's" from *The New York Times*, 1982. Copyright © 1982 by The New York Times Company. Reprinted with permission.

James Baldwin, "If Black English Isn't A Language, Then Tell Me What Is?" from *The New York Times*, 1979. Copyright © 1979 by The New York Times Company. Reprinted with permission.

Bruno Bettelheim, "Fairy Tales and Modern Stories" from *The Uses of Enchantment*, by Bruno Bettelheim. Copyright © 1975, 1976 by Bruno Bettelheim. Portions of this book originally appeared in *The New Yorker*. Reprinted with permission of Alfred A. Knopf, Inc.

Ray Bradbury, "Tricks! Treats! Gangway!" from *Reader's Digest*, October, 1975. Copyright © 1975 by Ray Bradbury. Reprinted by permission of Don Congdon Associates, Inc.

Rita Mae Brown, "You Say Begin, I Say Commence—To the Victor Belongs the Language" from *Starting from Scratch: A Different Kind of Writer's Manual* by Rita Mae Brown. Copyright © 1988 by Speakeasy Productions, Inc. Reprinted by permission of Bantam Books. All rights reserved.

Rachel Carson. "A Fable for Tomorrow" from *Silent Spring* by

Ms., January 1985. Copyright © 1985 by Elizabeth Janeway. Reprinted by permission of Elizabeth Janeway.

Suzanne Britt Jordan, "Fun, Oh Boy. Fun. You Could Die from It," from *The New York Times,* December 23, 1979. Copyright © 1979 by The New York Times Company. Reprinted by permission.

Garrison Keillor, "A Return to Basics: Mealtime without Guilt," from by *The New York Times,* February 2, 1983. Copyright © 1983 by The New York Times Company. Reprinted by permission.

Maxine Hong Kingston, "Catfish," from *The Woman Warrior: Memoirs of a Girlhood among Ghosts* by Maxine Hong Kingston. Copyright © 1975, 1976 by Maxine Hong Kingston. Reprinted by permission of Alfred A. Knopf, Inc.

Joseph Wood Krutch, "Reverence for Life: The Vandal and the Sportsman," from *The Great Chain of Life* by Joseph Wood Krutch. Copyright © 1956 by Joseph Wood Krutch. Copyright © renewed 1984 by Marcelle L. Krutch. Reprinted by permission of Houghton Mifflin Company.

Akira Kurosawa, "Babyhood," from *Something Like an Autobiography* by Akira Kurosawa, translated by Audie E. Bock. Copyright © 1982 by Akira Kurosawa. Reprinted by permission of Alfred A. Knopf, Inc.

Louis L'Amour, "How Wild *Was* the West?"Copyright © 1987 by Louis L'Amour. Published originally in the Febrary 28, 1987, issue of *T V Guide.* Reprinted by permission of Bantam Books, Inc.

Margaret Laurence, "The Shack," from *Heart of a Stranger* by Margaret Laurence. Used by permission of the Canadian Publishers, McClelland & Stewart, Toronto and JCA Literary Agency. Copyright © 1976 by Margaret Laurence.

Stephen Leacock, "Softening the Stories for Children," reprinted by permission of Dodd, Mead & Company, Inc. from *Short Circuits* by Stephen Leacock. Copyright © 1928 by Dodd, Mead and Company, Inc. Copyright renewed 1955 by George Leacock.

Grace Lichtenstein, "Coors Beer," portion of article from "Rocky Mountain High," from *The New York Times Magazine,* December 28, 1975. Copyright © 1975 by The New York Times Company. Reprinted by permission.

Arthur Miller, "Rite of Spring," reprinted by permission of House & Garden. Copyright © 1983 by The Condé Nast Publications, Inc.

William Least Heat Moon, "Arizona 87," from *Blue Highways: A*

Jouney into America by William Least Heat Moon. Copyright © 1982 by William Least Heat Moon. By permission of Little, Brown and Company.

Sam Negri, "Loafing Made Easy," from *The New York Times,* July 12, 1980. Copyright © 1980 by The New York Times Company. Reprinted by permission.

George Orwell, "A Hanging," from *Shooting an Elephant and Other Essays* by George Orwell, copyright 1950 by Sonia Brownell Orwell, renewed 1978 by Sonia Pitt-Rivers, reprinted by permission of Harcourt Brace Jovanovich, Inc., the estate of the late Sonia Brownell Orwell and Martin Secker & Warburg.

Richard Rodriguez, "Complexion," from *Hunger of Memory* by Richard Rodriguez. Copyright © 1981 by Richard Rodriguez. Reprinted by permission of David R. Godine, Publisher.

Anne Roiphe, "Why Marriages Fail," from *Family Weekly,* February 27, 1983. Copyright © 1983 by Anne Roiphe. Reprinted by permission of Anne Roiphe.

William Saroyan, "Why I Write," from *The William Saroyan Reader.* Copyright © 1988, by the William Saroyan Foundation. Reprinted by permission.

Richard Selzer, "The Discus Thrower," from *Confessions of a Knife* by Richard Selzer. Copyright © 1979 by David Goldman and Janet Selzer, Trustees. By permission of William Morrow and Company, Inc.

George Steiner, "The Future of Reading," excerpt from "Books in An Age of Post-Literacy," by George Steiner. Published in *Publishers Weekly* on May 24, 1985. Copyright © 1985 by George Steiner. Reprinted by permission of Georges Borchardt, Inc. and the author.

Judy Syfers, "I Want a Wife," from *The First Ms. Reader.* Copyright © 1970 by Judy Syfers. Reprinted by permission of Judy Syfers.

Lewis Thomas, "Death in the Open," from *The Lives of a Cell* by Lewis Thomas. Copyright © 1973 by the Massachusetts Medical Society. Originally published in the *New England Journal of Medicine.* Reprinted by permission of Viking Penguin, Inc.

Judith Viorst, "Friends, Good Friends—and Such Good Friends." Copyright © 1977 by Judith Viorst. Orginially appeared in *Redbook.* Reprinted with permission of Lescher & Lescher, Ltd.

Eudora Welty, "Moon on a Sliver Spoon," excerpted by permission of the publishers from *One Writer's Beginnings* by Eudora

Welty. Cambridge: Harvard University Press, copyright ©
1983, 1984 by Eudora Welty.

E. B. White, "The Three New Yorks," in "Here Is New York,"
from the book *Essays of E. B. White,* copyright © 1949. Reprinted by permission of Harper & Row, Publishers.

Roger Wilkins, "I Became Her Target," from *Newsday,* September
6, 1987. Reprinted by permission of the author.

Randall Williams, "Daddy Tucked the Blanket," from *The New York
Times,* July 10, 1975. Copyright © 1975 by The New York
Times Company. Reprinted by permission.

Elizabeth Wong, "The Struggle to Be an All-American Girl." Originally appeared in the *Los Angeles Times.* Reprinted by permission of Elizabeth Wong.

Malcolm X, "Prison Studies" from *The Autobiography of Malcolm
X* by Malcolm X with the assistance of Alex Haley. Copyright
© 1964 by Alex Haley and Malcolm X. Copyright © 1965 by
Alex Haley and Betty Shabazz. Reprinted by permission of
Random House, Inc.

William Zinsser, "Simplicity," from *On Writing Well.* Copyright ©
1976 by William K. Zinsser. Reprinted by permission of the
author.